Decolonizing Psychoa

Daniel José Gaztambide

Decolonizing Psychoanalytic Technique

Putting Freud on Fanon's Couch

Daniel José Gaztambide
Department of Psychology
Queens College, CUNY
New York, NY, USA

ISBN 978-3-031-48475-9   ISBN 978-3-031-48476-6   (eBook)
https://doi.org/10.1007/978-3-031-48476-6

Cover credit: © MaryValery/iStock

This Palgrave Macmillan imprint is published by the registered company Springer Nature Switzerland AG
The registered company address is: Gewerbestrasse 11, 6330 Cham, Switzerland

Paper in this product is recyclable.

Preface: Looking for Home

I am sitting in the balcony of *The Mezzanine* in San Juan, Puerto Rico, a bar housed in the home of Afro-Puerto Rican revolutionary Pedro Albizu Campos, enjoying a drink and the afternoon breeze while writing this book, one among many open tabs on my laptop. One of these tabs is open on Google Maps—which lets you view an address in 3D—set to my childhood home, canopied in the shade of a great *palo de mango*—a mighty mango tree. Will I finally reconnect with the home I lost? With what many of us lost? A car drives by outside, playing Bad Bunny's "*El Apagón*" for all to hear.

I take a sip from my drink and turn to a book I'm citing, Quintero Rivera's (1976) *Workers' Struggle in Puerto Rico*. I flip to an 1874 letter from an artisan concerned about a disease infecting their guild. "The colonial system which ruins nations," they write, "has left latent among us the germ of its demoralizing habits… that system of privilege which recognizes one race's supremacy over another" (pp. 185–186). They sound the alarm on how racism divides the working class, calling on Puerto Ricans—white, Black, and Brown—to "grasp hands and recognize each other for what they are, brothers" (p. 186). I think about Don Pedro (1972), in whose home I enjoy this drink, who called on Puerto Ricans to realize "it is idiocy to lift up the division of human beings based on skin" (p. 193, my translation), connecting how racism and sexism turn us against each other. I am moved by the insights of my countrymen. Insights that, from the perspective of this book, are profoundly psychoanalytic.

Books about psychotherapy often start by waxing philosophical about the "human condition," the yearning for "self-actualization," or the banality of suffering, grasping for some abstract universal as if the therapist writing them does not come from a place, a people, a pain. I start with home because for me, Puerto Rico is that place, people, and pain to which I yearned to return after my doctoral studies. But after college, my parents sold our home to escape the soaring costs of living on the island. A piece of my childhood was gone.

Puerto Rican revolutionaries may also seem an odd topic for the preface to a psychotherapy book. I start here because how racism, sexism, and queerphobia maintain division is *central* to understanding suffering in social context, and for imagining a politics of suffering beyond the couch. This book is an account of these insights from theory to *praxis*. While I am told clinical practice is separate from politics and communal service, that is not the psychoanalysis I grew up with.

I learned about psychoanalysis in the shade of that mango tree, the scent of *café* adorned by my youth pastor's laugh and my mother's smile. My youth pastor and I talked about Sigmund Freud, Carl Rogers, and Albert Ellis while my mother, a church secretary with an eighth-grade education, was a voracious reader who taught me about psychology. "*Un ministerio sanador,*" "A healing ministry," was the name of my church, where psychology was synonymous with service to the community. But my interest in psychoanalysis was also the result of subtle tensions I noticed in my world around color, class, gender, and sexuality. My mother was a white Cuban woman while my father was an ambiguously "Brown" Puerto Rican man. My brother and I had white skin and straight hair, alongside a "certain something" that marked us as "non-white." Some called it my *mancha de planato*—a "plantain stain" making my Puerto Ricanness legible.

Though I can be read as non-white, my skin and hair allowed access to a world not granted to other Puerto Ricans. I witnessed colorism, rigid norms around gender and sexuality, and the economic exploitation that stole our daily bread, each a silent haunting of the colony. Psychoanalysis for me is a tool for breaching this silence and understanding the unconscious roots of our suffering, how a language that is not ours leaves us tongue-tied, and how to sever that knot to reclaim our voice. This book is about reclaiming a way of working with patients "in the room," and a call to action beyond it—a psychoanalysis for all, from Puerto Rico to the moon.

I take another sip from my drink, take a deep breath, and start writing about the questions that birthed this book.

New York, USA

Daniel José Gaztambide

References

Albizu Campos, P. (1972). *La conciencia nacional puertorriqueña*. Siglo XXI.
Quintero Rivera, A. G. (1976). *Workers' struggle in Puerto Rico: A documentary history*. C. Belfrage (trans.). Monthly Review Press.

Acknowledgments

I am grateful to all the people who have helped me survive, my family foremost among them. This includes the *Titere Poets*—thank you for showing me *familia* in my home away from home.

My deepest gratitude to Anthony Smith and Kerri Ann Norton for putting up with my impostor syndrome the past two decades—thank you for believing in me when I did not.

Thanks to Beth Farrow and the Palgrave team for their invaluable work on this book, as well as the reviewers who contributed feedback to strengthen its voice. I am incredibly thankful to the colleagues who supported me in this work: Usha Tummala-Narra, Derek Hook, Patricia Gherovici, Dionne Powell, Elizabeth Danto, Francisco Gonzales, Lillian Comas-Diaz, Hector Adames, Rossana Echegoyen, Annie Lee Jones, Steven Knoblauch, Katie Gentile, Steven Boticcelli, and many others—the list is endless.

A healtfelt thanks to the Mellon Fellowship and my Mellon brothers and sisters, both during seminar and after-seminar drinks—where the real scholarship happened.

A special thanks to Tara Menon and Indira Murillo for helping me with translations from French and German, respectively. To the faculty and fellow candidates of the NYU post-doctoral program in psychotherapy and psychoanalysis: I have learned so much from you and learn from you still. You may yet make me a psychoanalyst.

To the Miranda Family Fellowship: Thank you for supporting my analytic training—this book is both a critique of that learning and my most full-throated expression of it.

To my students—this book is written *for* you, and the result of learning *from* you.

To my ancestors: Thank you for your sacrifices, your blessings, and your joy.

To those who come after us: May you be our heirs, and not our descendants.

Praise for *Decolonizing Psychoanalytic Technique*

"*Decolonizing Psychoanalytic Technique* is compelling and practical. Leveraging psychological theory, scientific insights, and practical experience, Gaztambide skillfully demonstrates how sociopolitical forces are intricately intertwined with the process of healing. This book is a gift to psychotherapists and an open call to embrace political action."

—Hector Y. Adames, *PsyD, Professor, The Chicago School of Professional Psychology; Co-Director, IC-RACE Lab (Immigration, Critical Race, And Cultural Equity)*

"Gaztambide has produced an authorial, eminently readable, and fascinating account of the relationships between the contemporary psychoanalytic clinic and anti-coloniality. His book is a remarkable achievement which deserves to be read, enjoyed, and cited for years to come."

—Sinan Richards, *British Academy Research Fellow, King's College London*

"What would psychoanalysis look like if it assumed intrapsychic realities derive not only from our relationships but also the conditions in which we exist? Drawing out the clinical implications of this vision, Gaztambide imagines such a psychoanalysis in this bold and passionate book, a decolonial psychoanalysis construed as a preferential option for the marginalized."

—Celia Brickman, *Faculty, Chicago Center for Psychoanalysis and Psychoanalytic Therapy, author of* Race in Psychoanalysis

"'The couch is *ours*,' asserts Gaztambide, a New York-based Puerto Rican psychoanalytic psychologist and poet who brings his imaginatively curated research to the ways in which anti-colonial struggle informed (consciously or not) the thinking of Freud, Ferenczi, Lacan and Fanon. The foundations of psychoanalysis 'from below' have been laid out, and we can now take on the vital task of building the decolonial practice of the future."
—Elizabeth Danto, *Professor of Social Welfare Emeritus, Hunter College-CUNY, author of* Freud's Free Clinics: Psychoanalysis and Social Justice, 1918–1938

"Gaztambide subjects Freud, Ferenczi, and Lacan to a decolonizing analysis guided by Fanon, narrating a personal trip demonstrating how white supremacy, anti-Blackness, and CISheteropatriarchy exercised violent control over psychoanalysis. This is done gracefully, resulting in a easy-to-read account welcoming readers with varying levels of knowledge, helping us untangle the complex weave of psyche-culture that undergird the work of psychotherapy."
—Katie Gentile, *Professor and Chair, Department of Interdisciplinary Studies, John Jay College of Criminal Justice, author and editor of* The Business of Being Made: The temporalities of reproductive technologies, in psychoanalysis and culture

"Gaztambide's goal of decolonizing psychoanalytic technique, and I add theory, is a formidable undertaking for which he does a commendable job, laying out the groundwork drawn out by the Holmes Commission Final Report. This text is superbly written for graduate students, candidates and senior analysts to benefit from and I highly recommend it to all in our field."
—Kirkland C. Vaughans, *Ph.D., Adjunct Professor at the Derner School of Psychology, Member, Holmes Commission on Racial Equality in American Psychoanalysis, featured in* Black Psychoanalysts Speak

"What is unique and brilliant about this book is that it connects the future of psychoanalysis to a psychoanalytic reading of its history. There is much to be learned from this book. In highlighting Fanon but linking his theory and practice to relational psychoanalysis, Lacan, and research, Gaztambide makes a major contribution to the emergent radical spirit of psychoanalysis."
—Elliot Jurist, *Professor of Psychology and Philosophy at the Graduate Center and The City College of New York, author of* Minding Emotions: Cultivating Mentalization in Psychotherapy

"Many of us feel torn between psychotherapy and social action as responses to human suffering. With this book, Gaztambide has broken through an impasse that has kept many psychotherapists feeling that we've left out half the job we would like to take on: to address the larger social world's role in generating personal suffering."

—Neil Altman, *Faculty, Massachusetts Institute for Psychoanalysis, author of* The Analyst in the Inner City: Race, Class and Culture through a Psychoanalytic Lens, *and* White Privilege: Psychoanalytic Perspectives

"This is an extraordinary treatise. Gaztambide transforms what we knew of our forefathers by revealing, with bristling depth, the broken circuits where race, class and culture were lost. He not only develops a rich decolonial theory, but with brilliance guides us through its clinical application, navigating his own feelings and dilemmas with aplomb and sensitivity, a complex explication of intersectionality in action. It is as if we are witnessing an embodiment of Fanon in today's world."

—Melanie Suchet, *Faculty, New York University's post-doctoral program in psychotherapy and psychoanalysis, co-editor of* Relational Psychoanalysis: Volume 3—New Voices

"Gaztambide is one of our field's foremost scholars of Fanon. In this impressive volume he sketches a 'decolonial psychoanalysis,' developing a clinical approach that attends to difference no matter the identities of patient and therapist. What comes through most strongly is Gaztambide's deep appreciation of Fanon as activist, theorist and budding clinical practitioner."

—Steve Botticelli, *Clinical Assistant Professor of Psychology, NYU, co-editor of* First Do No Harm: The Paradoxical Encounters of Psychoanalysis, Warmaking, and Resistance

"Gaztambide traces contemporary research pointing to Fanon's sociogenic vision beyond internal or interpersonal dynamics, unfolding weblike networks of unconscious and social forces, continually interacting with embodiment and language. Here is a psychoanalysis that integrates the intersection of interpersonal affiliation and social hierarchies, but centers the role of race, class, culture, ethnicity and sexual orientation in human experience. A must read!"

—Steven Knoblauch, *Adjunct Associate Professor at The New York University post-doctoral program in psychotherapy and psychoanalysis, author of* Bodies and Social Rhythms: Navigating Unconscious Vulnerability and Emotional Fluidity

"In a powerful foundational text, Gaztambide takes up the 'broken circuits' left by our founding fathers by analyzing them from a Fanonian perspective. A response to his first book, *A People's History of Psychoanalysis*, this volume is rich with accounts of what got lost along the way of developing technique when it comes to race, class, gender, and sexuality. A broad sociogenic assessment is necessary, not so much for our patients, but for ourselves collectively."

—Rossanna Echegoyen, *LCSW, Faculty, Manhattan Institute for Psychoanalysis*

"I highly recommend Gaztambide's *Decolonizing Psychoanalytic Technique* to scholars, activists, and practitioners interested in decolonial psychoanalysis. His revolutionary intervention focuses on technique through carefully unpacked case studies from his practice and beyond, stretching psychoanalytic praxis through Fanon by highlighting the interconnections between psychoanalysis and the Black Radical Tradition as critiques of racial capitalism, and how it employs anti-Semitism and anti-Black racism to divide and conquer the oppressed, whose distress manifests in a variety of symptoms."

—Robert K. Beshara, *Assistant Professor of Psychology & Humanities, Northern New Mexico College, author of* Decolonial Psychoanalysis: Towards Critical Islamophobia Studies and Freud and Said: Contrapuntal Psychoanalysis as Liberation Praxis

Contents

1

Introduction: Decolonizing the Psychoanalytic Canon

I remember the moment everything "clicked," of how to seamlessly integrate the interpersonal and sociopolitical in psychotherapy. I stumbled into it through my work with "Berto" (pseudonym), a young adult, a Spanish-speaking Afro-Latinx[1] working class cisgender queer man who struggled with anxiety and depression, substance use, work instability, and self-harm. In our work, I practiced from a relational psychoanalytic perspective grounded in cultural humility (Tummala-Narra, 2016, 2022). Relational psychoanalysis is a psychoanalytic approach that focuses on the therapeutic relationship between patient and therapist. "Cultural humility" refers to a stance that is open to the patient's culture and identities as defined by them, even as the therapist maintains a responsibility to "broach" or initiate conversations around these themes. The tension I experienced with Berto between a focus on the therapeutic relationship, and the question of how to address the sociocultural within it, are central to this book.

Berto sought me as a Spanish-speaking therapist, and although he was comfortable with me as a Puerto Rican man I was also aware that my being a *white* Puerto Rican—the ambiguity of my "white but not quite" phenotype—could be salient for him. Race and colorism textured my experience across Puerto Rico and the US mainland, but I did not want to assume Berto's experience, only broach the subject to convey that culture and identity were welcome in our work. During that first session, Berto alluded to his mother

---

[1] In this text, I use "Latinx," "Latino," and "Latina," sometimes interchangeably depending on the person.

disparaging his hair as *pelo malo*, "bad hair." In exploring this with him I shared that while I appreciated his comfort with me, I wondered how he experienced race in his life and how that might come up in our work. He appreciated my question, but stressed that race is not something he thinks would be relevant, as it is not something he really thinks about.

I took Berto at his word, though a part of me was aware that *he* had brought up the subject of race while at the same time denying that it played any role in his life. Over the course of our work, a subtle "dance" ensued in which he periodically, without prompting, raised the subject of race only to quickly disavow it, with my attempts to explore this not really "working." I began to consider that Berto might feel *conflicted* about race. Psychoanalysis, founded by Sigmund Freud, invites us to consider how we are often torn, ambivalent, and of more than one mind. It was in the process of working with Berto that I stumbled across a series of techniques that did not contradict the importance of attending to culture or the therapeutic relationship but radically recontextualized them, shifting how I work in a way that allowed the relational and sociopolitical to be evoked as a matter of course. And not just with patients from marginalized communities—with *all* patients.

At the time I lacked a framework for understanding what I was doing and why. This book attempts to articulate such a framework to facilitate a nuanced, theoretically rich, and pragmatic way of attending to *both* the relational and sociocultural in the consulting room, and of thinking holistically about human suffering—we not only need to find meaning, relatedness, and purpose in our lives, we also need social, political, and economic conditions that make flourishing possible. My primary goal is to equip beginning and seasoned clinicians with theoretical and pragmatic tools for helping the patient in front of us, while imagining how to intervene in the world *outside* the clinical encounter. This framework is not original to me, though it has been hiding in plain sight since the beginnings of our field—the very underside of psychoanalysis. This missing link, this "broken circuit," is a *decolonial* psychoanalysis.

What does "decolonial" mean? Decolonial approaches critique structures of inequality and the values that support them even after the end of formal slavery and colonialism (Quijano, 2000). It understands the legacy of colonialism in its modern form as "racial capitalism," the ways in which racism is integral to the development of capitalist society (Robinson, 1983/2020, p. 2). The decolonial perspective draws on a diversity of critical theories, including critical race theory (Delgado & Stefancic, 2023), the Black Radical and Black Radical feminist traditions (Robinson, 1983/2020; Taylor, 2017), post-colonial theorists of the global south (e.g., Mbembe, 2019; Mignolo &

Walsh, 2018; Quijano, 2000), queer and feminist theories (e.g., Anzaldúa, 2009; Lugones, 2010), and Marxist thinking (e.g., Chibber, 2014; Žižek, 2019), among others. Decolonial approaches have two interconnected goals: (a) to "delink" our knowledge, values, and practices from oppressive ways of being (Maldonado-Torres, 2017), and (b) to dismantle the political and material structures that maintain inequality through the redistribution of wealth, land, and resources (Fernández et al., 2021; cf. Rodney, 2022).

Decolonizing Psychoanalytic Technique: Putting Freud on Fanon's Couch provides an introduction—perhaps, a *reintroduction*—to psychotherapy theory and practice from a decolonial perspective that is clinically actionable, pragmatic, and effective. Over the course of this introduction, I unpack some conundrums practitioners often struggle with at the intersection of the clinical and the political, provide a history of decolonial psychoanalysis that sets the stage for my method and assumptions in approaching these dilemmas, and end with an overview of this book.

Decolonial Psychoanalysis: From Theory to Practice

In my first book, *A People's History of Psychoanalysis: From Freud to Liberation Psychology* (Gaztambide, 2019), I outlined how the first psychoanalysts developed a prescient theory of how racism and other "isms" function as tools of class warfare, and how this theory was adapted by scholars, clinicians, and activists of the global south committed to liberation, from Martiniquan revolutionary psychiatrist Frantz Fanon to Brazilian educator Paulo Freire to the founder of liberation psychology Ignacio Martín-Baró. Since the publication of that book, students and seasoned clinicians have often asked how this history translates into clinical practice, while raising questions on whether psychoanalytic treatment is "dated" and lacks empirical support.

The latter is in some ways easier to answer. Since Shedler's (2010) landmark review, more and more research has validated the effectiveness of psychodynamic therapy, with a recent up-to-date review establishing that psychodynamic therapy meets criteria as an evidence-based treatment with a classification of "strong" research support (Leichsenring et al., 2023). Research also supports psychoanalytic mechanisms of change such as insight, transference work, emotional processing, the therapeutic alliance, addressing defenses, and repairing ruptures—moments of tension or misunderstanding between patient and therapist (Leichsenring et al., 2023; Crits-Christoph & Gibbons, 2021). Psychological science similarly attests to the existence of unconscious processes that are associative, embodied, and organized around relationships (see Weinberger & Stoycheva, 2019). No treatment is a panacea, however, with evidence suggesting psychoanalytic approaches can be made more effective by integrating tools from other schools such as cognitive-behavioral therapy (CBT), and vice versa (Katz et al., 2021).

But the question of how *decolonial* psychoanalysis is clinically applicable remained elusive. Introductory texts on psychoanalytic technique—whose authors may be sympathetic to issues of culture and identity—often assume an abstract universality of human suffering (e.g., Maroda, 2009; McWilliams, 2004; Summers & Barber, 2010), leaving issues of power, culture, and identity to be elaborated predominantly by scholar-practitioners of color to "fill in the gaps." This has resulted in two separate literatures—one focused on "the basics" of theory and technique, the other on extending psychoanalysis to "the social" (Holmes et al., 2023). Almost as if one must first read Nancy McWilliams' (2004) *Psychoanalytic Therapy: A Practitioners' Guide*, and then complement it with Usha Tummala-Narra's (2016) *Psychoanalytic theory and cultural competence in psychotherapy*. My aim is not to replace these texts but offer a different starting point that bridges this gap, offering a decolonial psychoanalytic theory *and* clinical technique.

Similarly, I observed across conferences and case consultations how colleagues often have rich *theoretical* discussions on the intersectionality of identity, race and culture, social oppression as trauma, etc., but in discussing actual cases there was often a struggle to articulate what we were doing *practically* outside of a general call to "address culture," "broach identity," or "talk politics." While we all had an intuitive sense that both interpersonal relationships and sociocultural issues are important in mental health and its treatment, the theoretical *why* and the technical *how* of bringing these together was surprisingly unclear, something I noticed in what Hollander (2023) dubbed the recent "decolonial turn" in contemporary psychoanalysis.

The Decolonial Turn: Promises and Challenges

Beginning in the 1990s with the pioneering work of African American psychoanalysts Dorothy Holmes (1992) and Kimberlyn Leary (1995), a diverse group of scholar-clinicians from relational, Lacanian, and contemporary Freudian traditions emerged to expand the contours of psychoanalysis to issues of race, class, gender, and sexuality. This growing choir includes Black psychoanalysts exploring anti-Blackness and class (e.g., Jones & Obourn, 2014; Stoute, 2017; Vaughan, 2015); Latinx clinicians adapting psychoanalytic work to Latin American peoples (see Gherovici & Christian, 2019);

Asian and South Asian clinicians working on decoloniality and non-white/non-Black subjectivities (e.g., Eng & Dadlani, 2020; Han, 2019; Merchant, 2020); white therapists reflecting on race, class, and coloniality (e.g., Altman, 2011; Layton, 2018; Hook, 2012; Ryan, 2017; Suchet, 2007); scholars theorizing intersectionality in psychotherapy (see Belkin & White, 2020); clinicians developing a community psychoanalysis (e.g., González, 2020; Tubert-Oklander, 2006); Arab scholars and clinicians re-engaging Frantz Fanon's relevance for decoloniality today (e.g., Sheehi & Sheehi, 2021); and clinicians "returning" to Fanon as a practicing therapist (e.g., Knoblauch, 2020; Turner & Neville, 2020).

Those comprising this tradition have called for the inclusion of social context as *central* to psychoanalytic training, research and practice in graduate programs and institutes (Holmes et al., 2023; Tummala-Narra, 2022; Woods, 2020). Tummala-Narra (2022) outlines the heart of the matter: "Can we decolonize psychoanalytic theory and practice?" She notes the theoretical confusion that maintains a "false split between the psychic and the social" (p. 218), inviting us to imagine how patient and therapist can "confront through direct, conscious communication and through enactments dissociated and unformulated traumatic experiences related to race, culture, religion, and other aspects of context and self" (p. 228). Cultural humility is central for therapists to "understand their own cultural values and remain curious about the patients' cultural values and experiences without assuming the superiority of their own values" (p. 229), listening closely to the patient's experience while addressing relational and cultural ruptures.

Several pragmatic questions remain, however. What *is* decolonial technique? What are its theoretical foundations and treatment principles? Relatedly, we have yet to overcome conundrums that come up routinely in supervision, training, and practice: *Who* brings up culture, identity and power, the patient or the therapist? *Why* and *when*? *What* clinical purpose does this serve? If clinically relevant (and often is), *how* do we do this? To answer such questions, we need to overcome the divide between first learning the clinical "basics," and later learning about "diversity" as an "advanced topic" in our training.

Behind this bifurcation lies the assumption that "psychotherapy" and its theories of attachment, family systems, etc., are applicable to "everyone," i.e., white/middle-upper class/cisheterosexual people, whereas one acquires "cultural competence" to learn about those "others" whose suffering is due to social, cultural, and political context, i.e., people of color/women/the poor/LGBTQ folks, etc. (Brown, 2009). Such binaries obfuscate clinical practice, as if we can clearly delineate what pain is due to "attachment difficulties" or due to "social context." One of my goals is to develop an integrated account of human suffering that facilitates exploring its relational and social contexts organically.

I should note that what I am referring to as the "decolonial turn" here is distinct from the application of psychoanalytic theory in the humanities. I recommend Beshara's (2021a) excellent review covering core figures of that tradition such as Albert Memmi, Gayatri Spivak, Edward Said, and Homi Bhabha, among others (pp. 34–71). For this book, I will be focusing on clarifying our theoretical and clinical foundations in ways that facilitate integrating these thinkers.

To set the stage for how I plan to rethink our foundations, I want to tell you a story about the origins of decolonial psychoanalysis. The scholar-clinicians reviewed above are really the *resurgence* of a very old tradition that has been with us since the inception of the field, born between chance and possibility, the "missed encounter" of a series of ships and letters between Vienna and the world. Some of its practitioners focused on delinking psychoanalytic thought from Freud's culturally specific assumptions. Some were also committed to anti-racist, anti-colonial, and anti-capitalist struggle. Some did both. By no means a unified tradition, it is from this negative space, this series of "broken circuits," that one derives its existence.

Origins: Recovering Our Historical Memory

On August 27, 1909, the ocean liner *George Washington* pulled into New York City carrying Freud and his colleagues Carl Jung and Sandor Ferenczi. Freud and Jung were the founders of schools bearing their names, while Ferenczi was the originator of an interpersonal and relational perspective in psychoanalysis. The three traveled to the United States for Freud to deliver the Clark University lectures at the invitation of G. Stanley Hall, the first president of the American Psychological Association. Freud faced rejection and marginality in Europe, his work deemed the product of a diseased, criminal Jewish mind (Aron & Starr, 2013). But the conference at Clark promised to introduce him to an international audience, receiving a warm welcome that provided him what he hungered for—recognition (Evans & Koelsch, 1985).

What Freud was not aware of was that he had already achieved an international reach. Just ten years earlier, in 1899, Juliano Moreira, the first Afro-Brazilian psychiatrist, was the first outside of Freud's Vienna to teach and practice psychoanalysis (Plotkin & Honorato, 2017, pp. 28–29). Born in 1872 in the shadow of Brazilian slavery, Moreira pursued medical school after its abolition in 1888, discovering Freud's work during a trip to Germany (Castro & Facchinetti, 2015). His turn to psychoanalysis was part of his goal to modernize Brazilian psychiatry and combat its reductionistic biologism that asserted the inferiority of Black peoples. His commitment to psychoanalysis was such that the first Brazilian dissertation on the subject in 1914 referred to Moreira as a *psychoanalyst* who stressed free association in his clinical technique (p. 34), and whose patients remember fondly as a tender clinician (Moretzsohn, 2018, p. 169). Moreira was among the first in a tradition Freud could not have conceived of, existing in the very underside of psychoanalysis.

Unaware of Moreira's contributions, Freud set foot on that American stage, experiencing the audience's reception "like the realization of some incredible day-dream: psychoanalysis was no longer a product of delusion, it had become a valuable part of reality" (cited in Evans & Koelsch, 1985, p. 945). Here he was a scientist of repute, his Jewishness no longer haunting him in the background, his whiteness taking center stage. After Freud had received an honorary doctorate, Freud, Jung and Ferenczi were treated to a "private conference" in Hall's New England home, an academic's grotto filled to the brim with books and cigars—which Freud likely enjoyed. Jung gives us a glimpse into this evening, relating how they discussed the latest topics in psychology amidst good food and drink. But something else stood out to Jung. He and his Jewish colleagues witnessed the United States' racial hierarchy firsthand, as Black men who themselves or their parents would have been enslaved just decades earlier served them in "grotesque solemnity" (see Rosenzweig, 1992, p. 79). That evening had an impact on the Europeans, who on their return from America wrote a series of letters comparing anti-Blackness and anti-Semitism, developing a nascent analysis of the psychological function of racism.

Witnessing "[the] persecution of blacks in America," Ferenczi remarked on Jung's insight that Black people were made the recipients of whites' unconscious projections. As a Hungarian Jew surviving anti-Semitism, Ferenczi was struck by the similarity between their oppression in Europe and that of African Americans in the States. "Thus, the hate, the reaction formation against one's own vices," he wrote to Freud, "could also be the basis for *anti-Semitism*" (Brabant et al., 1993, pp. 186–187, emphasis original). Whites and gentiles project their disavowed wishes onto a racial other upon whom violence is enjoyed as compensation for their own suffering, leading Ferenczi to echo the Hungarian saying, "I hate him like my sins" (p. 187).

Ferenczi cites the poet Anatole French to compare white Americans and gentiles to "sheep… nourished by lies" (cited in Brabant et al., 1993, p. 187).

Instead of "[destroying] its inherited prejudices through reason, [sheep] carefully preserves the inheritance… from its ancestors" (p. 187). The lies embedded in racism both "protect [the sheep] from errors that could harm it" yet "is deceived by everything and it feels miserable" (p. 187). Ferenczi underscores how racism provides a psychological compensation in exchange for economic exploitation, yielding a psychic "benefit" even as it maintains the "costs" of rising misery for all.

The (Repressed) History of Social Democratic Psychoanalysis

Freud's world was one in which medical and political discourses positioned Jews as "white Negroes," framing "the male Jew and the male African as equivalent dangers to the 'white' races" (Gilman, 1993, p. 19; cf. Brickman, 2017). In reality, Jews are a racially diverse people—whether from Europe, the Middle East, Africa, the Caribbean, Latin America, or Asia. But in Freud's time, he was repeatedly exposed to the idea that Jewishness was not-white and somehow associated with Blackness (Ginsburg, 1999). In his treatment of the American Smiley Blanton, for example, Freud asked "if Jews were not put in the same category as Negroes." When Blanton replied he had not heard this comparison, Freud exclaimed "I often have!" (cited in Ginsburg, 1999, p. 245). Born in Moravia in 1856—eight years after Jewish emancipation— Freud grew up with recurrent right-wing backlash, giving rise to Karl Lueger after the 1873 economic crash. Lueger, the fascist mayor of Vienna, inspired white nationalists across Europe—including Adolf Hitler (Weber, 2020)— through his use of anti-Semitism as a strategy for exploiting working-class resentment, with racism "an excellent means of propaganda and of getting ahead in politics… the sport of the rabble" (cited in Kangas, 2015, p. 384).

The critique of racism as a psychological compensation serving elite interests was further developed by the early psychoanalytic movement, whose members were also socialists or social democrats who saw the political potential of the new theory (Danto, 2005). Marie Bonaparte (1947) wrote that "The anti-Semite projects on to the Jew… [his] unconscious bad instincts… and sees himself in shining purity… The Negro in the United States assumes the same function" (p. 141). Otto Fenichel (1940) intuited that the "general misery" produced by capitalism generates a "rebellious tendency directed against the ruling powers" (p. 26). Elites, in turn, draw on racism as "A weapon in the class-warfare dominating the present civilized world" (p. 39), to divide and rule by scapegoating Jews and Black people as the source of one's pain. Magnus Hirschfeld (1938) put it succinctly—fascists wage "Race war instead of class war" (p. 35).

This analysis of race and class went hand in hand with a progressive politics inspired by the socialist and social democratic movements of the post-WWI period. Danto's (2005) research shows how the first psychoanalysts pushed for policies to develop a "psychotherapy for the people," including the decriminalization of homosexuality, provision of birth control, abortion rights, and maternity leave for women, laws preventing child labor, and advocating for socialized medicine and a strong social safety net (Danto, 2016). Among these initiatives were "free clinics" treating patients regardless of income (Danto, 2005). The historical record reveals a different psychoanalysis from what we are typically taught, "grounded in social rights and infused with the energy of interwar social democracy, psychoanalytic practice was, at least until 1938, significantly more public than conventional narratives would have us believe" (Danto, 2022, p. 18).

This history presents a contradiction this book will wrestle with—how psychoanalysis provides important tools for thinking about psyche and society *and* was also used to uphold injustice. For example, Freud critiqued patriarchal norms *and* reproduced sexist scripts (Mitchell, 2000). He provided a fascinating account of race and class *and* reproduced racist, colonial beliefs (Brickman, 2017). His desire for status led him to often reverse his more revolutionary insights when these chaffed with the ideologies of his day (Aron & Starr, 2013), keeping his leftist politics separate from his clinical thinking at the behest of his more conservative Anglo-American disciples. Ernest Jones, for example, cautioned Freud, "In your private political opinions you might be a Bolshevist [a far-left political party], but you would not help the spread of [psychoanalysis] to announce it" (Freud & Jones, 1926/1993, p. 592). Although Freud bifurcated the clinical and the political to "protect" psychoanalysis from being derided as socialist and Jewish, this book undoes this repression to reconnect the political history of psychoanalysis with its clinical technique.

However, neither Freud's blind spots nor his aspirations protected him in the wake of the Second World War. The Nazis learned from Karl Lueger's anti-Semitism alongside their study of *American* racism for inspiration (see Wilkerson, 2020, p. 81), sweeping across Europe, "Aryanising" the free clinics by displacing or killing Jewish analysts, with Freud losing friends and family to the concentration camps (Danto, 2005). It was not until his daughter Anna was interrogated by the Gestapo that he escaped with his family to England in 1938. Once in London, Freud received a letter from D. L. Datta (1938), an Indian psychoanalyst who was glad to hear of his safe arrival.

Datta posed him a question, "Has [sic] the psychoanalysts ever thought—why throughout the civilized world *dark* has been considered to be the inferior colour?" (pp. 1–2).

Between anti-Semitism and Anti-Blackness: The Missed Encounter Between Psychoanalysis and the Black Radical Tradition

Psychoanalysis' answer to this question was preceded by another tradition wrestling with the aftermath of slavery and colonialism—the Black Radical Tradition. The European revolutions culminating in Jewish emancipation in 1848 were followed by another brutal conflict in the 1860s. The American Civil War, fought over the institution of slavery, was closely followed by an intrepid reporter from the British press, one Karl Marx—like Freud, a secular Jew. Marx observed how ethnic animus was used by elites to divide the working class in Britain, and felt he was witnessing something similar in America. After the Civil War, Marx (1867/1967) wrote that "Labor in white skin cannot emancipate itself where the black skin is branded" (p. 301), recognizing that racism was "the true secret of the preservation of [capitalist] power" (cited in Anderson, 2017, p. 29). Five years after the 1863 Emancipation Proclamation, the Black Marxist and pioneer of the Black Radical Tradition, W. E. B. Du Bois, was born.

As a Black man growing up in the afterlife of slavery, Du Bois came to conclusions similar to his Jewish counterparts. In 1892 he traveled to Berlin on a fellowship, coinciding with an economic recession and a rise in anti-Semitic politics, making him witness the conditions of Jews in Europe (Thomas, 2020). Du Bois (1998) realized "the basis of the neo-antisemitism is economic and its end socialism," meaning that anti-Semitism was a displacement of class conflict, and could only be fought by dismantling capitalism (pp. 174–175). In hearing his German colleagues speak passionately about their nationalism and hatred of Jews, Du Bois (1968) realized white Americans and gentile Germans felt something that Black and Jewish people were barred from, "I began to feel the dichotomy which all my life has characterized my thought: how far can love for my oppressed race accord with love for the oppressing country?" (p. 127).

Nine years later, Du Bois (1903/2015) expressed these feelings in *The Souls of Black Folk*: "this double-consciousness, this sense of always looking at one's self through the eyes of others, of measuring one's soul by the tape of a world that looks on in amused contempt and pity" (p. 8). His observations of anti-Blackness and anti-Semitism informed his understanding of how racism is internalized, and how racial fearmongering overthrew multiracial labor coalitions through a cross-class alliance between white elites and poor whites. In *Black Reconstruction*, Du Bois (1935) wrote that white workers, "while they received a low wage, were *compensated* in part by a sort of *public and psychological* wage" (p. 700, emphasis added). Although this "higher status" did not change their economic conditions, "it had great effect upon their personal treatment and the deference shown them" (p. 701). By contrast, Black people were subjected to "badges of inferiority" through social, economic, and physical violence (p. 701).

As a result, "the wages of both classes could be kept low" (Du Bois, 1935, p. 701) inequality for all scaffolded by a compensation providing whites with real and illusory pleasures, such that "every problem of labor advance in the South was skillfully turned by demagogues into a matter of inter-racial jealousy" (p. 701). Years later in a piece on capitalism, colonialism, and racism, Du Bois (1944/1990) lamented that he "was not at the time sufficiently Freudian to understand how little human action is based on reason" (p. 41). Du Bois's thinking reflects an almost psychoanalytic reflection on racism and capitalism, something that may not have been coincidental. Indeed, from Juliano Moreira onwards, Freud has been engaged by thinkers and clinicians of color and the global south more than is often known.

Decolonial Psychoanalysis Across the Global South

To understand this history we return to Freud's 1909 trip. A famous group photo of that visit which can be found online showcases Freud in the front row (type in "Freud Clark University" on Google). At first glance, this photo illustrates a view of psychiatry, psychology, and social work as predominantly "white" disciplines, tacitly communicating who does and does not belong in the "frame." Although I have seen this photo multiple times throughout my training, I later realized that with many of these black-and-white pictures you can struggle to "see color." But if you look at the third row to the far right of this picture, you will find Sakyo Kanda and Hikozo Kakise, two students from Japan interested in the application of psychoanalysis to Japanese myths (Takasuna, 2016). They were among the first in the Asian and South Asian world interested in psychoanalysis from the 1910s onward (Varvin & Gerlach, 2011), with one of the first global south clinicians to critically engage Freud being the Indian psychologist Girindrasekhar Bose, who corresponded with him from 1921 to 1937. Bose had treated patients in psychoanalysis since 1909, teaching it at Calcutta University while running a study group modeled on Freud's "Wednesday Society," and founding—with Freud's blessing—the Indian Psychoanalytic Society in 1922 (Hartnack, 1990).

While Freud praised his scholarship, Bose challenged him on the universality of the Oedipus complex and resisted his invitations to publish in the *International Journal of Psychoanalysis*: "if my works are of any worth… they will be translated by the foreigners in their languages. No Englishman will write his work in Bengali for the benefit of the Bengalee" (cited in Hartnack, 1990, p. 926). Bose fused psychoanalysis and Hindu thought, stressing the role of early maternal caregiving, relationality, and the interconnectedness of human beings. His contributions include a theory of splitting predating British object-relations theory, the use of homework (see Bose, 1935), and the centering of free association to note grammatical changes in patients' speech, their use of "double negatives," and their switching back and forth between conflicted self-states (Bose, 1926; cf. Akhtar & Tummala-Narra, 2005; Hiltebeitel, 2018).

Bose's work represents an early attempt at decolonizing Freud, an "ab-Original psychoanalysis" embedding it in his own cultural world while creating something new (Dhar, 2018). We find another example of this "ab-Originalizing" when Japanese psychiatrist Heisaku Kosawa contacted Freud in 1925, a correspondence culminating in a trip to Vienna in 1932 to train as a psychoanalyst (Harding, 2020). Over the course of their interview, Kosawa demonstrated his knowledge of technique by noting Freud's "slips," including his switching off the light when he meant to press a bell to call his next appointment—something Kosawa interpreted as Freud's desire for him to stay longer (p. 7).

Kosawa entered analysis with Richard Sterba while seeing patients under Paul Federn's supervision, returning to Japan in 1933 where he opened a private practice and founded the Japan Psychoanalytic Society. In adapting analysis to his cultural context, he emphasized the "maternal," relational dimension of the therapeutic encounter as an experience to be "lived through" (Harding, 2022, p. 50). Although he never discussed Buddhism overtly, he once told a patient that he practiced psychoanalysis "with the heart of [a] Buddhist" (cited in p. 50).

Like Bose, Kosawa (1931) challenged the centrality of the Oedipus complex, writing a paper he shared with Freud on what he called the "Ajase complex." Drawing on Shinshu Buddhism, the Ajase complex stresses the role of early attachment conflict, guilt, and reparation between parent and child. Kosawa's view of psychoanalysis as "seeing" in the "route of Freud" also reflected connotations from his cultural surround. Harding (2022) explains, "In the Jōdo Shinshū tradition seeing one's own weakness in particular is crucially important, because this awareness helps give rise to *shinjin*, or 'true entrusting'" (p. 49). Humility has transformative potential for the patient as much as the analyst, a vulnerability that allows trust to form.

Around the same time in 1932, the Chinese sociologist Bingham Dai entered analysis with Harry Stack Sullivan, and later trained at the Chicago Institute with Karen Horney—both descendants of Ferenczi's relational-interpersonal thinking. Dai (1944) wrote one of the first papers on psychoanalytic treatment under colonial occupation—specifically, imperial Japan's occupation of Beijing in 1937—and presciently named a fundamental tension in psychoanalysis:

> there are two ways of looking at the neurotic and his problems. One is to regard… his difficulties as complexes centering around instinctual drives… The other is to think of the neurotic principally as a social and cultural being and his difficulties as problems of struggling for a place in society or for the sense of security and belonging in his relations with other people as well as with the ways of his group. (p. 337)

Dai predated Greenberg and Mitchell's (1983) distinction between a "classical-drive" model and a "relational" model in psychoanalysis, except he included both the interpersonal *and* sociocultural context in describing the therapeutic relationship as a space where both are enacted. Dai (1944) also drew attention to how symbols in language become a medium through which our sociocultural world "speaks."

On the other side of the globe in Latin America, Juliano Moreira's disciples Arthur Ramos and Julio Pires Porto Carrero corresponded with Freud, describing their development of psychoanalysis in Brazil (Plotkin & Honorato, 2017, pp. 78–81). Freud also received visits from other Latin American analysts such as Nerio Rojas from Argentina and Gregorio Bermann from Colombia (pp. 201–203). The founder of the Argentina Psychoanalytic Association Maria Langer was herself originally from Vienna, a member of the communist party who trained under Anna Freud and Richard Sterba in the 1930s. After fighting fascism in Spain, she fled to Latin America where she continued her activism while training future psychoanalysts (Hollander, 1997).

I would be remiss if I did not mention the first Puerto Rican psychoanalyst, Ramon Fernandez Marina, who trained in Washington, DC in 1941 and was an adherent of Sullivan's interpersonal psychoanalysis (Bernal & Delrio, 1981). He and German social scientist Ursula von Eckardt at the University of Puerto Rico wrote an erudite text integrating interpersonal psychoanalysis and cultural studies (Fernandez Marina & Von Eckardt, 1964), stressing that psychoanalysts must attend to "the etiology of a specific belief, both for an individual and for a culture, and with the psychological significance of symbols and rituals in religion as in politics or in any other aspect of human life" (p. 39). Fernandez and von Eckardt also participated in Senate hearings in Puerto Rico on civil rights for women (ELA de Puerto Rico, 1970, p. 779), and wrote about the psychological impact of Puerto Rico's socioeconomic conditions.

Notably, in a 1972 presentation at the American Academy of Psychoanalysis conference in New York, von Eckardt (1974) discussed the socioeconomic factors implicated in heroin addiction from Puerto Rico to Appalachia to Harlem, highlighting the impact of colonialism, capitalism, and racism. "What does this mean at a Psychoanalytical Convention?" she posed to the audience. "Well, perhaps it serves as a plea for more social and cultural understanding and less psychiatric doctrine, at least in dealing with drug abuse which may not really be a psychoanalytical or even—in the classical sense—a psychiatric problem at all" (p. 137).

The Decolonial Cohort in Jacques Lacan's Circle

We have named some global south analysts who expanded the scope of Freudian (Moreira, Bose, Kosawa) and relational-interpersonal (Dai, Fernandez Marina, von Eckardt) perspectives. Another cohort from the global south gathered in the 1950s onward around the enigmatic French psychoanalyst Jacques Lacan. In the decade after Freud's death, psychoanalysis in England and the United States took a "conservative turn" which the *avant-garde* Lacan critiqued as "adapting" patients to oppressive conditions, articulating a theory of language as a vehicle for the social, cultural, and political that left an impact on psychoanalysis, political theory, and cultural studies worldwide (see Malone, 2012).

These Lacanian analysts included Moustapha Safouan (Egypt), Willy Apollon (Haiti), Adnan Houbballah (Lebanon), Solange Faladé (Benin), Betty Milan (Brazil), and Alice Cherki (Algeria), among others. Safouan was the first North African to enter analysis with Lacan in 1949 and promote psychoanalysis in Egypt and beyond (Safouan, 2007). Apollon developed novel approaches to the treatment of psychosis while writing about decolonization in Haiti (Apollon, 1996). Houbballah returned to Lebanon to build one of the first psychoanalytic societies in the Arab world while writing about political violence, trauma, and exile (see Ayouch, 2002). Betty

Milan, a Brazilian-Lebanese analyst, wrote a moving memoir of her analysis with Lacan touching on immigration, colonialism, colorism, and racism (see Chapter 4). Alice Cherki (2006), an Algerian Jew, attended Lacan's seminars, yet prior to her analytic training she was also a student of the revolutionary Martiniquan psychiatrist Frantz Fanon.

Faladé was Lacan's right-hand woman and protégée, the treasurer and later vice president of their training institute (Roudinesco, 1990). She was the first Black African woman to enter analysis with Lacan in 1952, later returning to West Africa to develop, with Lacan and Jean Laplanche's support, a psychoanalytic treatment and research program focused on the training of African clinicians (Faladé, 1963, 1964). Although she aimed to increase mental health infrastructure in African countries, her vision went beyond the clinical domain to address racism across all sectors of society (1964, p. 604). Faladé and her peers informed Lacan's politics, including his condemnation of imperialism in Africa (Obiwu, 2015, p. 79). How this may have played a role in Lacan's theory and clinical work will be considered in this book.

The Black Radical Psychoanalytic Tradition in North America

Remember again that photograph of Freud's trip to Clark. Remember how it can be hard to "see color" in these black-and-white pictures? I am indebted to Dionne Powell (2018) for bringing this to my attention—look at the fourth row to the far right, and you will find Solomon Carter Fuller, the first African American psychiatrist and psychoanalyst (born the same year as Juliano Moreira), and a pioneer in Alzheimer's research. Fuller was an eager audience member in Freud's lectures, sharing with Charles Pinderhughes his desire to talk to him (Sharpley, 1978). Fuller was one of the first proponents of psychoanalysis in the United States, teaching it while keeping abreast of the psychoanalytic literature, a practitioner widely regarded as having "mastered psychoanalysis" (Sharpley, 1978; pp. 193–194; cf. Kaplan, 2005, p. 51).

Fuller kept company with other noted Black psychiatrists as well as artists and activists through his wife, the Harlem Renaissance poet Meta Warrick—including Du Bois, a regular at their household (Kaplan, 2005, p. 45; Sharpley, 1978, p. 193). Fuller was not, however, the only psychoanalyst in Du Bois' circle. Margaret Morgan Lawrence, the first Black woman psycho-analyst who graduated from Columbia Psychoanalytic in 1951, was the wife of radical sociologist Charles Lawrence II, a student of Du Bois (Lightfoot, 1995, pp. 153; 241). Lawrence developed community-oriented programs in Harlem Hospital in New York, writing avidly about child and family work while pioneering the role of the "therapist's use of self." In a powerful paper at the 1980 meeting of the American Academy of Psychoanalysis in San Juan, Puerto Rico (!), she (1982) advocated for a view of treatment as a form of play, in which "history and culture… take part," with therapeutic action going beyond the clinical encounter: "Necessary social change must reflect acts of caring among human beings" (p. 242).

In discussing her work with poor Black and Brown families, Lawrence (1982) described her "use of self" to build a human relationship, conceiving of the analytic encounter as "a sharing of inner worlds." "Even sharing food," she writes, "represents a basic need known to all" (p. 248). During house visits to families, she would allow space for sharing food and drink as a way of building relationship (p. 249). She also addressed the race and class anxieties white therapists *and* therapists of color might feel when working with poor people of color, stressing the importance of recognizing patient strengths and a "loving use of ourselves" in our work (p. 253). This again goes beyond psychotherapy, insofar as mental health workers

> must recognize the limitations of their collaborative efforts, given society's failures. Families of the poor and those who share their concerns require access to the halls of decision and power on all levels of the social scene. This too is a part of our commitment to the common good. (p. 254)

As the "mother" of community psychoanalysis and practicing therapy "in the real world" (cf. Boyd-Franklin et al., 2013), she also made contributions beyond psychoanalytic practice. For example, critical race theorist Charles Lawrence III (1987)—her son—consulted with her on a seminal paper introducing the notion of unconscious racism into the legal field, an important link between psychoanalysis and critical race theory (fn. 181, pp. 356–357).

Other contributors to this generation of Black psychoanalysts include Jeanne Spurlock, June Dobbs Butts, Hugh F. Butts, and Fuller's mentee Charles Pinderhughes. Pinderhughes (1979) drew attention to the "pathogenic social structures" underlying mental illness, writing a fascinating paper on attachment and hierarchy which his son, the anti-colonial Marxist Charles Pinderhughes Jr., noted was compatible with dialectical materialist Marxist thinking (July 26, personal communication). Predating contemporary social psychology by three decades, he identified two interlocking social cognitive systems, an "approach-affiliative-affectionate" system based on attachment and closeness, and a "avoidance-differentiative-aggressive" system organized around verticality and hierarchy, functioning according to Freud's "pleasure principle"—to pursue pleasure and avoid pain—based on the body's position in space. Writing presciently with respect to beliefs around how society should be organized, he argued these "are organically linked to the body in the body image: to change them would thus introduce an instability in physiology that must be resisted" (p. 36).

Hugh Butts (1979a), writing around the same time, drew attention to the connection between capitalism, racism, and mental well-being, advocating for "a national health insurance program based on tax-levy monies that will cover all aspects of health and mental health care," alongside a training program for clinicians from working-class and ethnic-minority backgrounds (p. 375). Calling for a "politics of mental health," Butts cites Du Bois' call for a package of anti-racist and universal policies including free education, a housing program, a higher living wage, and public ownership of resources to preserve "freedom for dreams of beauty, creative art, and joy of living. Call this socialism, communism, reformed capitalism, or holy rolling. Call it anything—but get it done!" (cited in p. 379).

Du Bois was not only connected to Black analysts who may have introduced him to psychoanalytic thinking—hence the psychoanalytic flavor of the "psychological wages of whiteness"—but also inspired them. Alongside Du Bois was another revolutionary thinker, also a clinician, who has influenced many Black analysts since. This was an idealistic young man who, five years after Freud's death in London, would fight the Nazis across the English Channel in France. Originally from the Caribbean, this young man saw himself as part of a global struggle against fascism and oppression, recognized by post-colonial scholar Edward Said (2003) as "Freud's most disputatious heir" (p. 18), a cornerstone of the Black Radical Tradition after Du Bois himself, and a foundation to decolonial and liberation psychology worldwide (Bulhan, 1985).

That young man was Frantz Fanon.

Frantz Fanon: Decolonial Psychoanalysis' Most Disputatious Ancestor

Frantz Omar Fanon was born in 1925 to a middle-class Black Martiniquan family, growing up a proud Frenchman committed to the revolutionary values of *liberté*, *égalité*, *fraternité* (liberty, equality, fraternity). He felt it his duty to fight the Nazis as a fight against all forms of oppression, declaring "Where freedom is denied to one person, it's denied to everyone" (cited in Finn, 2021). But after the war he was not received as a hero but derided as an "other," becoming painfully aware of France's racism and Martinique's colonial status. After the war, Fanon moved to France to study psychiatry, completing his residence in 1951 under the Marxist Catalan psychiatrist Francois de Tosquelles, a pioneer of community psychiatry. After residency he practiced as head of service at the Blida-Joinville hospital in Algeria in 1953, experimenting with cultural adaptations of Tosquelles' "socio-therapy." When the Algerian revolution broke out in 1954, Fanon joined the Front de Libération Nationale (FLN) while keeping an active clinical practice, treating both war victims and the French soldiers and police who tortured them. Unable to abide this contradiction, Fanon resigned in 1957.

Fanon and his family moved to Tunis, where he continued in the FLN alongside his routine clinical practice—including psychoanalytic treatment. Although his early death from leukemia at the age of 36 tragically cut short his generativity as a clinician and scholar before he could systematize his clinical thinking, it was out of that synergy between activism and clinical care that he developed a decolonial practice that reinvented psychoanalysis itself.

Fanon as Revolutionary Psychoanalytic Therapist

Although Fanon is remembered as a revolutionary, those closest to him remember an empathic psychotherapist. His friend and confidante Marie-Jeanne Manuellan (2017) notes how scholars often separate Fanon the revolutionary from Fanon the psychiatrist, remarking "I don't have a Fanon cut into slices in my head" (p. 13, my translation). Butts (1979b) also noted Fanon "never abandoned his psychoanalytic posture, but merely refined it and translated theory into practice" (p. 1018). Fanon was a voracious reader of psychoanalytic literature, drawing on Freud, Ferenczi, and Lacan even as he reinvented them, expanding the Blida hospital library's collection of psychoanalytic texts, and assigning his residents hefty reading lists including Freud, Ferenczi, Adler, Wilhelm Stekel, and Helene Deutsch (Cherki, 2006, pp. 79–80). Cherki recalls Fanon's interest in Ferenczi's theories on trauma, always on the lookout for translations of his works (p. 118).

We also know Fanon appreciated Lacan's theory of language and stance before the "otherness" of the other, someone he was likely exposed to through Tosquelles, an avid reader of both Lacan and Ferenczi (Gaztambide, 2019, p. 98). Remembering his trainee, Tosquelles (1975/2017) wrote that "Fanon embodied above all respect and freedom of the other… to be able to speak" (p. 224, my translation). He recalled Fanon's question, "What were the limits of the psychiatrist's field of professional action?" (p. 225, my translation). Could the clinician intervene beyond the session, in the social structures that lead to mental illness? Butts (1979b) reminds us of the continued relevance of Fanon's question today:

There are still colonies, exploitation, and racism… One such 'colony' consists of 1.4 million citizens, two thirds of whom are third-world individuals. They are vulnerable to mental illness, and among the most impoverished, health impaired group in New York City… The 'colony' is called The Bronx…. (p. 1018)

The "colony" includes everywhere and anywhere systemic exploitation and violence are felt, from the Bronx to Puerto Rico, from the streets of Harlem to the favelas of Sao Paolo, from the global north to the global south. Fanon's questions urge us to reflect not only on how to help the patient in front of us, but on what policies and politics heal the world around us. To move from inside to outside, like a mobius strip.

A Methodological Mobius Strip: From Freud to Fanon, and Fanon to Freud

My method for reimagining the foundations of psychoanalysis is to read Freud, Ferenczi, and Lacan through Fanon. The fact that Fanon read and reinvented three of the major schools in psychoanalysis globally—Freudian, relational-interpersonal, and Lacanian—presents a unique opportunity for a decolonial "comparative psychoanalysis" (cf. Greenberg & Mitchell, 1983). Fanon also presents a unique distillation of trends found throughout the decolonial tradition reviewed above. He draws on psychoanalysis to critique racism and capitalism, decenters the Oedipus complex in favor of relationality in cultural context, and sees treatment as a human encounter between patient and therapist. Like others—especially those in Lacan's circle—he drew on a theory of language that saw free association as a vehicle for both relational and sociopolitical experience, and offers a radical delinking of psychoanalysis from its oppressive tendencies. He also issued a passionate demand for transformative material and political change. Just as important, Fanon understood that although our suffering is different depending on our positionality it is fundamentally interconnected, just as we are interconnected with one another.

Why not jettison these white men and build on Fanon? My approach is pragmatic. While one cannot derive a developed framework of theory and technique from Fanon's texts alone, it is possible to reconstruct what his clinical approach might have looked like by cross-referencing his writings, first-person accounts of his clinical work, and the psychoanalytic theorists he cited. A decolonial approach does not simply replace white authors with authors of color—a facile tokenism—but systematically deconstructs them to make room for something else. Hence, my plan is to re-read our field's foundations *through* Fanon, uncovering dimensions of Freud's, Ferenczi's, and Lacan's thinking that reintegrate the relational and political. I plan to read Freud in ways he could not have imagined and (probably) make him turn in his grave.

I am treating this canon like a "mobius strip," a concept I borrow from Lacan—see here for an illustration: https://www.youtube.com/shorts/YYJ5l5Vuz4U (OnlineKyne, 2021). If you trace the "outside" of a mobius strip with your finger, you move from the "outside" to its "inside" and back. By tracing the influence of Freud, Ferenczi, and Lacan ("inside" the canon) on Fanon ("outside" the canon), we retrace how Fanon reinvented them, turning the canon *inside out*. In this way, we work toward integrating what I call "broken circuits" of psychoanalysis.

The Broken Circuits of Psychoanalysis: Theory of Mind, Clinical Technique, and Social Critique

As Stoute (2017) observed, Freud had an "awareness of the cultural and socioeconomic status of his patient population, though he chose not to emphasize those factors in his clinical work or theory" (p. 15). This leaves us with what I call a series of "broken circuits." Freud developed a theory of mind (psychoanalytic *theory*), and from that articulated an approach to clinical work (psychoanalytic *technique*). But Freud also applied his theory to sociocultural phenomena such as race, class, culture, and religion (a psycho-analytic *critical theory*). While Freud never connected his technique and his critical theory in his writing, his cases hint at ways he addressed race, class, and culture that "flow" from his theory of mind and clinical technique.

I apply the same method to Ferenczi and Lacan, reviewing their theory of subjectivity, clinical practice, and theorizing of culture and context, drawing on cases that illustrate how they addressed power and identity—or not. In this way, I "connect the circuits" between each author's (a) theory of mind, (b) clinical technique, and (c) theories of race, class, context, and identity. The same applies to Fanon, whose clinical papers and accounts of his therapeutic work help "connect the circuits" between his decolonial theory and his clinical practice. I connect these circuits *within* Freud, Ferenczi, Lacan, and Fanon, as well as *between* them, revealing how decolonial psychoanalysis emerges from the "gap" between these circuits.

What of psychoanalysis in relation to decolonial psychoanalysis? If you remember the mobius strip metaphor, and keep in mind the history reviewed above, you will find some options to choose from. You might be happy with tracing the "canon" of decolonial psychoanalysis inside and out—Freud, Ferenczi, and Lacan to Fanon and vice versa. Or, as the presenter in the video suggests, you can "cut [the strip] *off center*," resulting in *two* strips interlocking with each other. This exercise symbolizes that while decolonial psychoanalysis may "break" from "traditional" psychoanalysis, they will always be interlinked. With this perspective as a backdrop, I unpack my assumptions about the world in relation to this project and conclude by reviewing the structure of this book.

A Decolonial Approach to Understanding Our World

As stated earlier, the decolonial tradition defines racial capitalism as a "colonial materiality" (Beshara, 2021a) which, following the Black socialist feminist Combahee River Collective (Taylor, 2017), "interlocks" with other systems of oppression around gender and sexuality. Just as these systems interlock, so too at an individual level we have identities that "intersect," meaning we inhabit different group memberships, experiences, and levels of privilege and marginalization related to race, class, gender, and sexuality, among others (Crenshaw, 2017). These interactions are not merely additive, nor do they interact in linear fashion, but transform one another in dynamic, contingent ways (Adames et al., 2018).

Complementing the intersectionality of identities and systems is what Angela Davis (2016) calls the "intersectionality of struggles" (p. 154). Struggles intersect in that struggles against racism, capitalism, and cisheteropatriarchy are interrelated though not necessarily the same. As Beshara (2021b) puts it, "we must struggle together not because we are of the same identity but because we have common desires as comrades" (p. 8). This is foundational to what I call the "intersectionality of suffering." The intersectionality of suffering underscores how despite having different identities, experiences, and privileges we are all *interconnected*. Although the suffering of the privileged and the marginalized is *not* the same, they are interrelated through complex, systemic forces. Critical to the intersectionality of suffering is what Frantz Fanon calls "sociogeny," the political, economic, and sociocultural determinants of human suffering. We begin, then, with a sociogenic assessment of our world.

Patriarchy, Slavery, and War: Common Origins

Although there is no clear "origin" to inequality, scholars suggest a link between patriarchy, slavery, and war (Christ, 2016; Ferguson, 2021; Martin, 2021). Patriarchal arrangements are intimately related to wars of expansion, raids, and the subjection of the conquered to enslavement—a form of "social death" that deprives one of rights and humanity (Patterson, 1982/2018). Enslaved women were coerced to provide emotional care in the domestic sphere, while enslaved men who were not killed were symbolically (often literally) castrated, with sexualized violence a common experience of both (Curry, 2017). The rise of slavery and patriarchy was not a linear process, as our species frequently resisted and rejected systems of domination over the course of history (Graeber & Wengrow, 2021). Communities often oscillated and *split* between favoring egalitarian structures or hierarchical ones. By defining ourselves by who we *are not*, such choices and identities become "structures of refusal" (p. 176).

"Each society performs a mirror image of the other," Graeber and Wengrow (2021) write, "an indispensable alter ego, the necessary and ever-present example of what one should never wish to be" (p. 180). Slavery also provided such an alter ego, a "non-human" category defining who is "human" and "free." However, Patterson (1982/2018) identifies a conundrum at the heart of slavery. While a "free" citizen might be exploited through their labor, slavery provided an "ideological camouflage" to this exploitation (p. 34). The enslaved's degraded status offered a kind of *pleasure* elevating the position of even the most exploited in a society (Flesberg, 2016; Myers, 2022). For example, in the ancient world the poorest "free" citizen would go into debt—and risk their children being enslaved—rather than sell their slave and lose status (Patterson, 1982/2018). Hence, the distinction between the "free" and the elite—whether priests, kings, or aristocracy—often depended on the existence of the enslaved. The problem from the point of view of elites, whether Roman senators or colonial Europeans, "was a perennial shortage, not of labour as such but of controllable labour… the problem to which slavery addressed itself" (Graeber & Wengrow, 2021, p. 200).

Colonialism, Anti-Blackness, and Whiteness: The Dawn of Racial Capitalism

In the long period prior to European colonialism, the Welsh was no less likely to be enslaved than the Greek, the Arab, or the African (Patterson, 1982/2018). This begins to change in the seventh to tenth centuries CE as

Arab kingdoms invade deeper into Africa, leading to a rise in the enslavement of African peoples and racial justifications for it, leading to the first reference to people from Africa as "Black," and equating "Blackness" with slavery (Ochonu, 2021). As Said (1978) argued in his post-colonial classic *Orientalism*, Europe drew on conflict with the Arab world as a form of self-definition, even as it drew inspiration from its philosophies and ideologies—including anti-Blackness. After the expulsion of the Moors and Jews, Spain began its colonial adventures in earnest through one Christopher Columbus, who by accident happened upon a "new world," resulting in the enslavement of the indigenous Tainos of the Caribbean.

By the sixteenth century the "meme" that Africans were "born to be slaves" rationalized an increase in the enslavement of Africans to replace brutalized indigenous peoples, jump-starting the earliest embers of globalization (Horne, 2020, p. 18). Ultimately, resistance by indigenous and African peoples and conflict with other European powers led Spain to flounder, and as Spain fell, Britain rose through the development of a "pan-European" identity, paving the way for what Horne (2020) calls a "whiteness project," "the diabolical 'genius' of settler colonialism, notably as it matured in North America, was that those who had once been victimized by enslavers instead were invited to become enslavers themselves… in the new guise of 'whiteness'" (p. 24). Through whiteness, previously oppressed peoples could be reborn.

Anti-Blackness and whiteness did not emerge overnight, nor were they monolithic or omnipotent. In the history of the Caribbean and the Americas, indigenous, white and Black people have seen common cause fighting against elites for economic and civil rights (Battalora, 2021; Dabiri, 2021; Reed, 2020). However, the "psychological wages of whiteness" eviscerated these movements time and again, such that concessions in labor and civil rights were often followed by a "white backlash" orchestrated by elites to roll back their gains. This history suggests that racism is not a naturally occurring force but a political and economic strategy of divide and conquer that needs to be *repeated* to be maintained (Dabiri, 2021; Lopez, 2019). The Black novelist James Baldwin intuited this when he said that in the United States, "there was one thing of which one could be certain. One knew *where* one was, by knowing where the Negro was… you were not on the bottom because the Negro was there" (IRL Server, 2019, emphasis added). At the same time, it must be reiterated this was not a linear process. Although, to borrow from Reverend Dr. Martin Luther King, while I am not confident that the arc of history always bends toward justice, the historical record shows that we have fought and bled to bend it.

Across our history, it seems hierarchical societies maintained their coherence by creating a "bottom" that could be perennially brutalized, exploited, and abused, providing a form of collective release or catharsis for one's pain while maintaining the power structure of an elite, ruling class. In many Euro-American countries, this takes the form of a white identity framed against a racial other haunting its contours—the feared "underclass," immigrant horde, and so on—in ways implicated by gender, sexuality, and class. The argument that whiteness and anti-Blackness are tools of division is not an attempt to let individual white people "off the hook." Rather, it is an analysis about exactly *which* white people comprise the root of the problem—the politically connected, often though not exclusively male, and wealthy. The godfather of critical race theory and Fanon reader Derrick Bell (1993) argued that racism is a

> stabilizing force that enables whites to bind across a wide socio-economic chasm. Without the deflecting power of racism, masses of whites would likely wake up to and revolt against the severe disadvantage they suffer in income and opportunity when compared with those whites at the top of our socio-economic heap. (p. 571)

What maintains racism is not some mythical essence hidden deep within the white psyche, but a series of political, economic, and social arrangements organized to benefit the powerful. Bell argues this not to foment pessimism, but to call on us into a "lifetime commitment to fight against the racism that diminishes the lives of its supporters as well as its victims" (p. 572).

The Intersectionality of Suffering as Key Concept in Decolonial Psychoanalysis

To understand racism, cisheteropatriarchy, and capitalism as structures "that diminish the lives of its supporters as well as its victims" is one of the organizing principles of the intersectionality of suffering. In exploring the theoretical, clinical, and critical dimensions of Freud, Ferenczi, Lacan, and Fanon, I theorize how these forces confer a set of benefits upon while simultaneously exerting a series of *costs* (cf. McIntosh, 2021). It is by understanding how privileges and their costs intersect across privileged and marginalized groups that we can develop a model for addressing identity and power alongside attachment and relatedness that is embedded into psychotherapeutic technique and mechanisms of change.

I am aware this is a strong claim. Most understandings of privilege frame inequality as a zero-sum game of advantages and disadvantages—white people/cis-het men/the rich are privileged, people of color/women/LGBTQ+ people/the poor are underprivileged. Although there is truth to this formulation, it is analytically incomplete. Our collective history suggests that although the costs of inequality are not equally distributed, they impact everyone, albeit in different ways (cf. McGhee, 2021). The fundamental issue is how *the relationship of inequality* between rich and poor, white and non-white, men and women, queer and straight, itself makes us sick. As Marmot (2005) put it, "Wherever we are in the hierarchy, our health is likely to be better than those below us and worse than those above us… it is the social gradient in health, the status syndrome, that is the challenge" (p. 15).

Research shows that as income inequality increases, a diverse array of outcomes worsen, including life expectancy, infant and adult mortality, medical health, childhood outcomes, trauma exposure, upward mobility, homicide, substance use, and mental health, among others—disproportionately impacting the most vulnerable *and* leading to worse outcomes for the middle class and the wealthy (Wilkinson & Pickett, 2020). This relationship is mediated by communal trust, with lower trust leading to hypervigilance around one's position in a hierarchy, alongside the anxiety to achieve or maintain status through extreme interpersonal dominance or submission (Cheng et al., 2021; Lipps & Schraff, 2021). These negative outcomes—the result of our collective history—"trickle down" not in the form of wealth, but of misery.

Eichner (2019) reviews the differential impacts of runaway capitalism on low-, middle-, and high-income US families, noting that while their struggles are different, they are all the symptom of neoliberal policies. Across the hierarchy we become entrapped in a "king of the hill" mentality, sacrificing our well-being to "get ahead," clawing our way out of the bottom and anxiously reaching for the top, even if this leaves us drained and overwhelmed,

> We often talk about this competition in zero-sum terms, as if the more families at the bottom lose, the more families at the top win. But this isn't at all correct: Market competition among families is better thought of as what might be called a 'negative-sum game'… It's just that some families lose more than others. (p. xxi)

Indeed, one often hears about poverty as an isolated phenomenon ("*they*" are poor) as opposed to the symptom of a *relationship* of exploitation which obviously harms the poor, but also leads to pathology among the wealthy and the middle class—again, we are interconnected.

Mechanic (2021) provides a synthesis of research alongside interviews documenting the substance use, suicide, and mental illness that come with living in a world where extreme wealth pollutes everything—revealing a pecking order *among the 1% as well*. He writes,

> In some ways, being very rich and very poor are strangely similar. Just as having not enough money creates fear and anxiety, so can having more than you know what to do with. At both ends of the spectrum, money tinkers with our notions of self-worth, our egos, our social lives, the stability of our marriages, our relationships with children, parents, and siblings—even our mental health. (p. 75)

These hierarchies do not exist in a vacuum. In the United States, they reflect retreats from the New Deal and the rise of Reaganomics and "third-way" neoliberalism (Reed, 2020). What empowers the politicians who enact these policies is racism as a strategy of divide and conquer. Racism as an individual prejudice is a symptom of racism in its essence—a system whose purpose is to foment division while empowering the wealthy (Lopez, 2019).

Here is where the intersectionality of suffering is clarifying. If, as Wilderson (2020) puts it, racism is "a healing balm for the Human mind" (p. 200), then what is it trying to "heal?" What is the relationship between the pleasures and privileges afforded by racism, sexism, classism, and its costs? "Where racial inequality increases," economist Michael Reich (2021) writes, "low- and middle-income Whites lose financially. Simultaneously, the earnings of the upper 1% of Whites increase" (p. 21). Conversely, reducing economic and racial inequality is correlated with lower corporate profits, higher wages, and greater unionization for white workers and workers of color (p. 21). When the wealth and power of the richest is constrained, everybody wins.

However, where racial fear is stoked, this triggers status anxiety among whites and some people of color, reducing support for redistributive programs framed as benefiting "the undeserving" (Newman et al., 2022), while supporting politicians who enact tax cuts for the wealthy while feeding moral panic toward "the other" (Lopez, 2019; McGhee, 2021). "Law and order" policies and the rolling back of civil rights lead to specific harms to women, people of color and LGBTQ+ folks (Freeman, 2021), quality of life worsens for all, while white privilege provides the "salve" that maintains the system: "White identity politics… become more important than economic interest" (Reich, 2021, p. 28).

Metzl's (2019) research examining the impact of right-wing gun, health-care, and educational policy illustrates how as white people vote their fears, this has a disproportionate impact on people of color *and* impacts the medical and mental health of white people. Making guns more accessible and restricting healthcare and education for "the undeserving" worsens gun-related suicide and outcomes for whites, even as these policies disproportionately harm people of color. Draconian criminal justice policies exert similar effects—leading to the disproportionate murder and incarceration of Black and Brown people, in turn increasing police murder and incarceration of white men in racially segregated areas, on which Bowser and Austin (2021) comment "Police and gun reforms might reduce the disproportion… of Black men killed, but it would benefit numerically more White men" (p. 239).

Gender is implicated as well. Dunham (2021) found that for white women, schemas of Black and Brown women as "dangerous welfare queens" and white women as fragile and needing white male protection increases support of racial and gender hierarchies. These same images of Black women as "gaming" the welfare system facilitated gutting public assistance programs that disproportionately impact Black and Latinx women while impacting working-class white women who are the majority of welfare recipients. Similar policies on child welfare and drug use designed to punish Black women have spill-over effects for white and non-Black women as well. As Khiara Bridges (2020) put it, white women are "reaping the bitter seeds of the racism that the government directed toward—and designed—for people of color" (p. 80).

Spanierman and Clark (2021) add an important caveat—while recognizing how racism affects everyone is important, "the costs of racism to Whites are in no way comparable to the costs of racism that people of color face" (p. 118). While the experience of the privileged and marginalized are not the same, we *must* think about patriarchy when working with men, whiteness when working with white people, and class when working with wealthier patients. Just because the patient in front of you is not a person of color, female-presenting, LGBTQ+, or poor *does not mean* race, gender, sexuality, and class are not "in the room."

One final point before leaving this section. While I write from a United States context the politics of division, racial or otherwise, are hardly unique to it. I often hear that discussions of race are only applicable to the United States as opposed to Europe—despite the increasingly militant and fascistic surge in racism on the far right of the continent (Georgi, 2019). While I want to be mindful of the limitations of my theorizing, *none* of the four theorists centered in this book are American thinkers. In addition, discussions of inequality and status—including race and colonialism—are likely applicable to the European world if not worldwide (cf. Andrews, 2021).

Definition and Clinical Illustrations

Before illustrating some clinical insights of the intersectionality of suffering, let me reiterate what it is *not*. It is emphatically *not* "rich/male/white/all lives matter," nor does it put all suffering on an equal plane. What the intersectionality of suffering underscores is our interconnectedness—while the suffering of marginalized and privileged people is *different and distinct*, it is nonetheless *related* through systems of hierarchy. This definition comprises several principles. First, how we construct our identities in social context involves benefits and costs. Second, those benefits often function as a *compensation* for those costs. Third, these benefits fluctuate, requiring behaviors that maintain those benefits and the structures they emerge from. Fourth, change is possible when we recognize our privileges have costs. Fifth, to borrow from a speech Du Bois (1909) gave the same year as Freud's visit to America, we need to recognize that "The cost of liberty is less than the price of repression" (p. 25).

Let us take the example of patriarchy. Patriarchy privileges (in the US, predominantly white) cisgender men and marginalizes cisheterosexual women, queer men and women, and non-binary people. At the same time, patriarchy *wounds* cisgender men and weaponizes this wound to maintain itself. Vulnerability, for example, is deemed "not-man," with cisgender men who do not perform "correct" masculinity finding their gender identity in question. Patriarchy introduces both wound and "cure"—to engage in the "correct," often toxic forms of "masculinity" against those who are "not-man," including cisgender men who fall short of this standard. By redirecting cisgender men's suffering toward "others," the cause of their suffering is masked—patriarchy itself. For a cisgender man to recognize that male privilege comes with costs that are related to the suffering of others begins the process of working through the "wages of patriarchy," reclaim their humanity, and explore alternate models of masculinity. This does not mean the suffering of cisgender men is "the same" as queer women, only that they intersect through patriarchy.

This leads to the sixth, overtly political principle. To work through the "wages" of privilege means engaging in social justice not out of charity but *solidarity* in recognition that our destinies are linked (Beshara, 2021b; Dabiri, 2021; Lopez, 2019; McGhee, 2021). We return to this political implication in this book's conclusion. For now, we explore the clinical implication of these principles. Imagine two very different patients—"Robert," (pseudonym) a middle-aged white cisheterosexual businessman with panic disorder, and

"Yesenia" (pseudonym) a young adult, queer, working-class Latinx woman college student struggling with depression.

Over the course of treatment, Robert became aware of how his anxiety was connected to his identity as a businessman who must "succeed at all costs," climbing the social ladder even if this created distance from his family. In our work we became aware of how he internalized scripts around being a "tough man" who "pushes through" any limitations while putting up a wall with his loved ones. As he became more aware of how the drive to "man up" and "make more money" led him to experience these panic attacks, he made more time for family and reimagined his identity not as a rugged individual trying to "win" the market, but as a caretaker.

Yesenia worked multiple jobs, caring for her ailing parents and siblings while attending college. Our work explored messages she internalized from her family, culture, and broader society on how she must be a "strong Latina" who takes care of everyone and does not need care in turn. This identity was for a long time a source of strength, but recently led to emotional wear and tear as she explored how her queerness chafed with her parents' traditional beliefs. She started to access how lonely she felt despite being surrounded by family. By hiding behind the image of a "strong Latina," she secured her position in her family at the cost of living her truth. As Yesenia reimagined her identity, she negotiated caretaking responsibilities with her cousins, expressed herself more openly, and broached the subject of her sexuality with her parents.

Although these patients were very different, both treatments explored how their identities served them and accrued a cost. The more tightly they bound themselves to those ways of being, the more they wrestled with anxiety and depression. To borrow from Du Bois, change involved the recognition that the "cost of liberty is less than the price of repression." Further, while they inhabited distinct positionalities, their struggles were *linked* by interlocking systems—white supremacy, capitalism, and patriarchy. The more Robert pushed to "fit" himself to the image of the successful white business-*man* the more he suffered, while the more Yesenia made herself "fit" the image of the (cisheterosexually coded) "strong Latina," the more she struggled. The goal is not to pathologize patients' identities, but examine how they help and hinder to reimagine them in a more freeing way. All the while, remembering these symptoms take place in a social context that impacts us differently but in a related fashion.

The intersectionality of suffering accounts for the social determinants of mental health for the oppressed and relatively privileged alike. Rather than think about social context *only* with marginalized patients, we think about how to address it clinically with *all* our patients, while imagining politics and policies that support thriving and well-being. A decolonial approach underscores the sociogenic foundations of suffering so we can intervene with the patient in front of us without losing sight of the inequality around us, conjoining therapeutic and political action.

The Structure of this Book

In Chapter 2, "To cure through love: Recovering the Clinical and Critical Freud," we begin working through our "mobius strip" by examining Freud's theory of mind, clinical approach, and critical theory, showing how his understanding of the unconscious as associative, embodied, and mediated through language is central to a decolonial approach. Key to this is his formulation of symptoms as compensations that helps us avoid pain (the symptom's benefit), even if it results in suffering (its cost)—what Lacan later termed *jouissance*, or "pleasure in pain." I show how his clinical stance is surprisingly "relational" and was attuned to language, culture, and identity in the consulting room. Although he did not integrate his tacit theory of race, class, and culture in his clinical writings, I draw on Freud's cases to repair this "broken circuit," and reconstruct what a "decolonial Freud" might look like through a Fanonian lens.

In Chapter 3, "The Promises and Limitations of Relational-Interpersonal Psychoanalysis: Returning to Ferenczi's Legacy," I review how Ferenczi expanded psychoanalysis into an active treatment that combined in-session work in the therapeutic relationship with behavioral experiments outside of sessions, inaugurating the foundations of relational and interpersonal psychoanalysis culminating in his posthumous *Clinical Diary*. Through this text, I explore two cases surprisingly preoccupied with race—an element of his work that has received little commentary in the literature. I draw attention to Ferenczi's thinking on how perpetrators "cannibalize" their victims to relieve their own suffering, and how he extended this theory to understand racism as a form of cannibalistic enjoyment. At the same time, I critique how he struggled to think beyond a "two-person," dyadic model of the therapeutic relationship, hobbling his ability to address the social in his clinical work—a difficulty that persists in relational and interpersonal approaches today (see Layton, 2018). Foregrounding Lacan and Fanon, I argue a third term is needed beyond the two-person relation—the social as it "slips through" speech.

In Chapter 4, "Lacan atop a Mango Tree: Retrieving the Decolonial Lacan," I provide a "plain English" (or close to it) description of Lacan's theory and technique. Given how Fanon engaged Lacan, I show how Lacan's "return to Freud" repositions the unconscious within a wider social, cultural, and linguistic surround, critiquing Ferenczi's emphasis on the two-person dyad by centering a "third term"—speech as a field upon which the social "speaks through" us. I also show how he made explicit commentary on racism and capitalism based on his theory, revealing a decolonial influence on his work. Case examples will illustrate how attending to the patient's speech facilitates exploring relational and social realities.

In Chapter 5, "A Caregiving Psychiatrist: Reconstructing the Clinical Fanon" we dive into Fanon's recently translated clinical papers and first-person accounts of his clinical work, providing an account of his clinical theory, practice, and attention to culture and context as a practicing psychoanalytic therapist. I note how Fanon cites and uses Freud, Ferenczi, and Lacan to develop a *reconstruction* of his therapeutic approach, emphasizing Fanon's attention to psyche in the context of culture and language, the therapeutic relationship in a broader systemic and institutional surround, and his conceptualization of the therapeutic process as providing the patient with a new experience that helps them "relearn the meaning of freedom." I review how Fanon stressed the importance of adapting psychoanalytic ideas and interventions to the sociocultural context, and conclude by summarizing his legacy in the history of psychoanalysis.

In Chapter 6, "Sociogenic Foundations of Theory and Practice: Revolutionizing Psychoanalysis," I review Fanon's oeuvre, *Black Skin, White Masks* and demonstrate how it is *the* foundation of decolonial psychoanalysis. I unpack Fanon's psychoanalytic theory of colonialism, capitalism, and race while underscoring emergent critiques of Freud and Ferenczi I draw from his work. I show how Fanon drew on the psychoanalytic theory of race and class developed by the first psychoanalysts to critique how different kinds of exploited people, despite being victims of oppression, can turn to racism as a "healing balm" to compensate for their pain and "ascend" within racial capitalism. Further, like Lacan, Fanon offers a critique of relational logic emphasizing the role of a "third term"—the social context as it is expressed through (verbal and body) language. I draw on some of Fanon's case studies in *The Wretched of the Earth* to show how we all take a position in relation to social hierarchy, a particular arrangement of pleasure and pain that binds us to the social order—the pivotal question being whether we *renounce* the benefits that privilege affords us and become cognizant of its costs.

Chapter 7, "Integrating Decolonial Psychoanalytic Theory and Research: Clinical Implications and Case Illustrations," bridges psychoanalysis' theory of mind, clinical theory, and critical theory by interpreting it through contemporary research to articulate the foundations of a decolonial, comparative psychoanalysis. I articulate a theory of the unconscious as associative, linguistic, embodied, and *political*, organized around two complementary goals: (a) pursuing relationships and preventing their loss and (b) pursuing and preventing the loss of power and position—resulting in strategies and compromises that provide a benefit while extracting a cost. Psychoanalytic treatment proceeds by building a relationship with the patient that encourages working through the anxieties that maintain their symptoms, building insight as to their costs, and renouncing the benefits of the symptom to make room for freedom and liberation.

Across these chapters we encounter the clinical role of a *contrast* with the patient's experience of the world that is spontaneous and *surprising*, disrupting their habitual ways of existing to pave the way for something new, with clinical and political ramifications. Following this review, I provide case examples that illustrate how to work with relational themes in the context of culture, society, and politics simultaneously. While some may find this chapter's focus on research jarring, it is important for both beginning and advanced clinicians to know the evidence base that supports my assertions.

In the Conclusion, "A Psychotherapy for All: Building a World Worth Living In," I transition from the clinic to politics. Following Fanon, I argue clinicians must look beyond the walls of the consulting room and pursue not just therapeutic action but political action in the community, shifting from the symptoms of a system to the underlying disease. I end by reviewing public policies and strategies practitioners can advocate for in the interest of social change that will contribute to our patients, our communities, and our own well-being. To borrow a mantra from dialectical behavior therapy, it is not enough to help our clients "build a life worth living"—we must also build a world worth living in.

Coda

"Love," Margaret Morgan Lawrence (2001) teaches us, "is universal, generational, and exists only in relationship" (p. 62). Love is related to drive as an "activity affect," something that frees us *to move into* the world in line with our commitments to those we love, and/or to a cause we care for. As a clinician and advocate, Lawrence teaches us that love is the recognition of our common humanity, "a concern for justice and peace for all people. It is a commitment which we may share with those with whom we work" (p. 70). Although identity, power, and politics is central to this book, at its heart this is a book about love. "People need love, affection and poetry in order to live," Fanon (2018) presciently wrote, "Patients show this privation in their illnesses by closing up inside themselves" (p. 333). If being deprived of care gives birth to our symptoms—our closing up to protect ourselves—then perhaps this is why Freud intuited that "the secret of therapy is to cure through love" (cited in Falzeder, 2019, p. 30). To love and recognize another requires, as Ferenczi (1926/1994) observed, "a sacrifice of our narcissism" (p. 377), de-centering the self to make room for the other. The ever enigmatic Lacan (1972–1973) himself quipped that "Love is the sign... that one is changing discourse" (p. 78), going beyond the language of dominant and dominated. But love also carries profoundly political implications. Facing the colonizer who claims that Algeria "belongs" to him, Fanon (2018) retorts "We agree, *Algeria belongs to all of us*, let us build it on democratic bases and together build an Algeria that is commensurate with our *ambition* and our *love*" (p. 656, emphasis added). Fanon imagined a revolutionary love in which the world belongs to all of us, a post-colonial futurity beyond the manichean vision of a dog-eat-dog, doer done-to world. Reflecting on these psychoanalytic ancestors, I am reminded of Jaime "*El Maestro*" Emeric, an elder in the Puerto Rican poetry scene who recently transitioned. Jaime repeated the following like he was born to say nothing but these words, "Love *is* the answer!" To my sisters and brothers and I, Jaime's words were a mantra, an inheritance, a *bendición*, a call provoking a response. This book is one such response from a poet who happens to be a psychoanalyst in training, a poem born from the streets of San Juan draped in scholarly drag.

Reflection Questions

- What have I heard or been taught about the history of psychoanalysis? What are my reactions to the historical account of this book?
- For mental health professionals: How do I notice clinicians discuss identity and culture in case conferences, trainings, and courses? What is helpful (or not) about talking about it in this way? Do they offer actionable tools for addressing identity and culture in your own practice?

- We often think of privilege, marginalization, and suffering in all or nothing terms. What would it mean to consider how the struggles of different groups—although different—are nonetheless connected? What reactions do you have to this idea?
- We live in a world of tremendous inequality. What would it mean to think about our patients both in terms of their intimate relationships and in terms of their culture and social position? What would this add to your practice? What reactions do you notice having to this idea? What challenges do you experience to thinking in this way?

Further Reading

Introductory Readings on Psychoanalytic Therapy

McWilliams, N. (2004). *Psychoanalytic psychotherapy: A practitioner's guide*. Guilford Press.
Shedler, J. (2022). That was then, this is now: Psychoanalytic psychotherapy for the rest of us. *Contemporary Psychoanalysis, 58*, 405–437.
Tummala-Narra, P. (2016). *Psychoanalytic theory and cultural competence in psychotherapy*. American Psychological Association.

Introductory Readings on Decolonial Thought

Lugones, M. (2010). Toward a decolonial feminism. *Hypatia, 25*, 742–759.
Mignolo, W. D. (2007). Introduction: Coloniality of power and de-colonial thinking. Globalization and the decolonial option. *Cultural Studies, 21*, 155–167.
Rodney, W. (2022). *Decolonial Marxism: Essays from the Pan-African revolution*. Verso Books.

References

Adames, H. Y., Chavez-Dueñas, N. Y., Sharma, S., & La Roche, M. J. (2018). Intersectionality in psychotherapy: The experiences of an AfroLatinx queer immigrant. *Psychotherapy, 55*, 73–79.
Akhtar, S., & Tummala-Narra, P. (2005). *Psychoanalysis in India*. Other Press.
Altman, N. (2011). *The analyst in the inner city: Race, class, and culture through a psychoanalytic lens*. Routledge.
Anderson, K. B. (2017). Marx's intertwining of race and class during the Civil War in the United States. *Journal of Classical Sociology, 17*, 28–40.

Andrews, K. (2021). *The new age of empire: How racism and colonialism still rule the world*. Penguin UK.

Anzaldúa, G. (2009). *The Gloria Anzaldúa reader*. Duke University Press.

Apollon, W. (1996). Postcolonialism and psychoanalysis: The example of Haiti. *Journal for the Psychoanalysis of Culture and Society, 1*(1), 43–51.

Aron, L., & Starr, K. (2013). *A psychotherapy for the people: Toward a progressive psychoanalysis*. Routledge.

Ayouch, T. (2002). Adnan Houbballah: de l'exil d'un psychanalyste à une psychanalyse de l'exil. *Topique, 3*, 81–88.

Battalora, J. (2021). *Birth of a white nation: The invention of white people and its relevance today*. Routledge.

Belkin, M., & White, C. (Eds.). (2020). *Intersectionality and relational psychoanalysis: New perspectives on race, gender, and sexuality*. Routledge.

Bell, D. A., Jr. (1993). The racism is permanent thesis: Courageous revelation or unconscious denial of racial genocide. *Capital University Law Review, 22*, 571–584.

Bernal, V., & Delrio, Y. (1981). Ramon Fernandez Marina (1909–1981). *International Review of Psycho-Analysis, 8*, 341–341.

Beshara, R. K. (2021a). *Freud and Said: Contrapuntal psychoanalysis as liberation praxis*. Palgrave Macmillan.

Beshara, R. K. (2021b). Ten concepts for critical psychology praxis. In *Critical psychology praxis* (pp. 1–12). Routledge.

Bonaparte, M. (1947). *Myths of war*. Imago.

Bose, D. (1926). The free association method in psychoanalysis. *Indian Journal of Psychology, 191*, 32–36.

Bose, D. (1935). Opposite fantasies in the release of repression. *Indian Journal of Psychology, 10*, 36–31.

Bowser, B. P., & Austin, D. W. (2021). Summary: Racism's impact on White Americans in the age of Trump. In D. W. Austin & B. P. Bowser (Eds.), *The impact of racism on White Americans in the age of Trump* (pp. 235–252). Palgrave Macmillan.

Boyd-Franklin, N., Cleek, E. N., Wofsy, M., & Mundy, B. (2013). *Therapy in the real world: Effective treatments for challenging problems*. Guilford Press.

Brabant, E., Falzeder, E., & Giampieri-Deutsch, P. (1993). *The correspondence of Sigmund Freud and Sándor Ferenczi, volume 1: 1908–1914*. Belknap Press.

Brickman, C. (2017). *Race in psychoanalysis: Aboriginal populations in the mind*. Routledge.

Bridges, K. M. (2020). Race, pregnancy, and the opioid epidemic: White privilege and the criminalization of opioid use during pregnancy. *Harvard Law Review, 133*, 770–851.

Brown, L. S. (2009). Cultural competence: A new way of thinking about integration in therapy. *Journal of Psychotherapy Integration, 19*(4), 340–353.

Bulhan, H. A. (1985). *Frantz Fanon and the psychology of oppression*. Plenum Press.

Butts, H. F. (1979a). Economic stress and mental health. *Journal of the National Medical Association, 71*(4), 375–379.

Butts, H. F. (1979b). Frantz Fanon's contribution to psychiatry: The psychology of racism and colonialism. *Journal of the National Medical Association, 71*(10), 1015–1018.

Castro, R., & Facchinetti, C. (2015). A psicanálise como saber auxiliar da psiquiatria no início do século XX: o papel de Juliano Moreira. *Revista Culturas Psi, 4*, 24–52.

Cheng, L., Hao, M., & Wang, F. (2021). Beware of the 'bad guys': Economic inequality, perceived competition, and social vigilance. *International Review of Social Psychology, 34*, 1–12.

Cherki, A. (2006). *Frantz Fanon: A portrait*. Cornell University Press.

Chibber, V. (2014). *Postcolonial theory and the specter of capital*. Verso Books.

Crenshaw, K. W. (2017). *On intersectionality: Essential writings*. The New Press.

Christ, C. P. (2016). A new definition of patriarchy: Control of women's sexuality, private property, and war. *Feminist Theology, 24*, 214–225.

Crits-Christoph, P., & Gibbons, M. B. C. (2021). Psychotherapy process—Outcome research: Advances in understanding causal connections. In *Bergin and Garfield's handbook of psychotherapy and behavior change* (pp. 263–296). Wiley.

Curry, T. J. (2017). *The man-not: Race, class, genre, and the dilemmas of black manhood*. Temple University Press.

Dabiri, E. (2021). *What white people can do next: From allyship to coalition*. Penguin UK.

Dadlani, M. B. (2020). Queer use of psychoanalytic theory as a path to decolonization: A narrative analysis of Kleinian object relations. *Studies in Gender and Sexuality, 21*(2), 119–126.

Dai, B. (1944). Divided loyalty in war: A study of cooperation with the enemy. *Psychiatry, 7*(4), 327–340.

Danto, E. A. (2005). *Freud's free clinics: Psychoanalysis and social justice, 1918–1938*. Columbia University Press.

Danto, E. A. (2016). Trauma and the state with Sigmund Freud as witness. *International Journal of Law and Psychiatry, 48*, 50–56.

Danto, E. A. (2022). Our psychotherapy for the people. *Division Review, 28*, 16–18.

Datta, D. L. (1938). *Letter to Sigmund Freud*, 19 June 1938a. Sigmund Freud Archive. Library of Congress.

Davis, A. Y. (2016). *Freedom is a constant struggle: Ferguson, Palestine, and the foundations of a movement*. Haymarket Books.

Delgado, R., & Stefancic, J. (2023). *Critical race theory: An introduction*. NYU Press.

de Puerto Rico, E. L. A. (1970). Comision de Derechos Civiles. *La igualdad de derechos y oportunidades de la mujer puertorriquena, San Juan, PR, 9*.

Dhar, A. (2018). Girindrasekhar Bose and the history of psychoanalysis in India. *Indian Journal of History of Science, 53*(4), T198–T204.

Du Bois, W. E. B. (1903/2015). *Souls of black folk*. Routledge.

Du Bois, W. E. B. (1909, March). Evolution of the race problem. In *Proceedings of the national Negro conference* (pp. 142–158). National Negro Conference.

Du Bois, W. E. B. (1935). *Black reconstruction in America*. Harcourt, Brace and Company.

Du Bois, W. E. B. (1944/1990). My evolving program for Negro freedom. *Clinical Sociology Review, 8*, 27–57.

Du Bois, W. E. B. (1968). *The autobiography of W. E. B. Du Bois: A soliloquy on viewing my life from the last decade of its first century*. International Publishers.

Du Bois, W. E. B. (1998). The present condition of German politics. *Central European History, 31*, 170–187.

Dunham, C. C. (2021). Gender: White women in the age of Trump. In D. W. Austin & B. P. Bowser (Eds.), *The impact of racism on White Americans in the age of Trump* (pp. 91–114). Palgrave MacMillan.

Eichner, M. (2019). *The free-market family*. Oxford University Press.

Eng, D. L., & Han, S. (2019). *Racial melancholia, racial dissociation: On the social and psychic lives of Asian Americans*. Duke University Press.

Evans, R. B., & Koelsch, W. A. (1985). Psychoanalysis arrives in America: The 1909 psychology conference at Clark University. *American Psychologist, 40*(8), 942–948.

Faladé, S. (1963). Women of Dakar and the surrounding urban area. In *Women of tropical Africa* (pp. 217–229). Routledge.

Faladé, S. (1964). Rapport sur le fonctionnement de l'Institut d'ethno-psychopathologie africaine. *Cahiers D'Etudes Africaines, 4*(16), 603–620.

Fanon, F. (2018). *Alienation and freedom*. Bloomsbury Publishing.

Fenichel, O. (1940). Psychoanalysis of antisemitism. *American Imago, 1*, 24–39.

Ferenczi, S. (1994). *Further Contributions to the Theory and Technique of Psycho-Analysis*. Karnac Books.

Ferguson, R. B. (2021). Masculinity and war. *Current Anthropology, 62*(S23), S108–S120.

Fernández, J. S., Sonn, C. C., Carolissen, R., & Stevens, G. (2021). Roots and routes toward decoloniality within and outside psychology praxis. *Review of General Psychology, 25*(4), 354–368.

Fernandez Marina, R., & Von Eckardt, U. M. (1964). *The horizons of the mind: A new odyssey*. Philosophical Library.

Finn, D. (2021, September 7). Frantz Fanon and the revolution against racism: An interview with Peter Hudis. *Jacobin*.

Flesberg, E. O. (2016). *On the Pleasures of Owning Persons: The Hidden Face of American Slavery*. Taylor & Francis.

Freeman, J. (2021). *Rich thanks to racism: How the ultra-wealthy profit from racial injustice*. Cornell University Press.

Freud, S., & Jones, E. (1993). *The complete correspondence of Sigmund Freud and Ernest Jones, 1908–1939* (Vol. 1). Harvard University Press.

Gaztambide, D. (2019). *A people's history of psychoanalysis: From Freud to liberation psychology*. Lexington Books.

Gherovici, P., & Christian, C. (2019). *Psychoanalysis in the barrios: Race, class, and the unconscious*. Routledge.

Gilman, S. L. (1993). *Freud, race, and gender*. Princeton University Press.

Ginsburg, L. M. (1999). Sigmund Freud's racial vocabulary and related fragments from the analyses of Clarence P. Oberndorf and Smiley Blanton. *International Forum of Psychoanalysis, 8*, 243–248.

Georgi, F. (2019). The role of racism in the European 'migration crisis': A historical materialist perspective. In *Racism after apartheid: Challenges for Marxism and anti-racism* (pp. 96–117). Wits University Press.

González, F. (2020). Trump cards and Klein bottles: On the collective life of the individual. *Psychoanalytic Dialogues, 30*, 383–398.

Graeber, D., & Wengrow, D. (2021). *The dawn of everything: A new history of humanity*. Farrar, Straus and Giroux. Kindle Edition.

Greenberg, J., & Mitchell, S. A. (1983). *Object relations in psychoanalytic theory*. Harvard University Press.

Harding, C. (2020). Sigmund's Asian fan-club? The Freud franchise and independence. In R. Clarke (Ed.), *Celebrity colonialism: Fame, power and representation in colonial and postcolonial cultures* (pp. 73–90). Cambridge Scholars Publishing.

Harding, C. (2022). The therapeutic method of Kosawa Heisaku: "Religion" and "the Psy disciplines." *The Journal of the Japanese Psychoanalytic Society, 4*, 42–58.

Hartnack, C. (1990). Vishnu on Freud's desk: Psychoanalysis in colonial India. *Social Research, 57*(4), 921–949.

Hiltebeitel, A. (2018). *Freud's India: Sigmund Freud and India's first psychoanalyst Girindrasekhar Bose*. Oxford University Press.

Hirschfeld, M. (1938). *Racism*. Victor Gollancz Ltd.

Hollander, N. C. (1997). *Love in a time of hate: Liberation psychology in Latin America*. Rutgers University Press.

Hollander, N. C. (2023). *Uprooted minds: A social psychoanalysis for precarious times* (2nd ed.). Routledge.

Holmes, D. E. (1992). Race and transference in psychoanalysis and psychotherapy. *The International Journal of Psycho-Analysis, 73*(1), 1–11.

Holmes, D. R., Hart, A., Powell, D. R., & Stoute, B. J. (2023, June 19). *The Holmes Commission report on racial equality in American psycho-analysis*. American Psychoanalytic Association. Retrieved August 30, 2023, from https://apsa.org/wp-content/uploads/2023/06/Holmes-Commission-Final-Report-2023-Report-rv6-19-23.pdf?ver

Hook, D. (2012). *A critical psychology of the postcolonial: The mind of apartheid*. Taylor & Francis Group.

Horne, G. (2020). *The dawning of the apocalypse: The roots of slavery, white supremacy, settler colonialism, and capitalism in the long sixteenth century*. Monthly Review Press.

IRL Server. (2019, April 2). *James Baldwin on the Black experience in America* [Video]. YouTube. https://www.youtube.com/watch?v=YPaBXcEVpOE

Jones, A. L., & Obourn, M. (2014). Object fear: The national dissociation of race and racism in the era of Obama. *Psychoanalysis, Culture, & Society, 19*, 392–412.

Kangas, R. R. (2015). Mahler's early summer journeys through Vienna, or what anthropomorphized nature tells us. *Journal of the American Musicological Society, 68*(2), 375–428.

Kaplan, M. (2005). *Solomon Carter Fuller: Where my caravan has rested*. University Press of America.

Katz, M., Hilsenroth, M., Moore, M., & Gold, J. R. (2021). Profiles of adherence and flexibility in psychodynamic psychotherapy: A cluster analysis. *Journal of Psychotherapy Integration, 31*(4), 348–362.

Knoblauch, S. H. (2020). Fanon's vision of embodied racism for psychoanalytic theory and practice. *Psychoanalytic Dialogues, 30*, 299–316.

Kosawa, H. (1931/2022). Two kinds of guilt feelings: The Ajase complex. *Journal of the Japan Psychoanalytic Society, 4*, 18–25.

Lacan, J. (1972–1973). *The Seminar of Jacques Lacan: Book XX*, Encore. Transl. C. Gallagher. Retrieved from http://www.lacaninireland.com/web/translations/seminars/ on October 10th, 2022.

Lawrence, C. R. (1987). The id, the ego, and equal protection: Reckoning with unconscious racism. *Stanford Law Review, 39*(2), 317–388.

Lawrence, M. M. (1982). Psychoanalytic psychotherapy among poverty populations and the therapist's use of the self. *Journal of the American Academy of Psychoanalysis, 10*(2), 241–255.

Lawrence, M. M. (2001). The roots of love and commitment in childhood. *Journal of Religion and Health, 40*(1), 61–70.

Layton, L. (2018). Relational theory in socio-historical context: Implications for technique. In *De-idealizing relational theory* (pp. 209–234). Routledge.

Leary, K. (1995). "Interpreting in the dark": Race and ethnicity in psychoanalytic psychotherapy. *Psychoanalytic Psychology, 12*(1), 127–140.

Leichsenring, F., Abbass, A., Heim, N., Keefe, J. R., Kisely, S., Luyten, P., Rabung, S., & Steinert, C. (2023). The status of psychodynamic psychotherapy as an empirically supported treatment for common mental disorders—An umbrella review based on updated criteria. *World Psychiatry, 22*(2), 286–304.

Lightfoot, S. L. (1995). *Balm in Gilead: Journey of a healer*. Penguin Books.

Lipps, J., & Schraff, D. (2021). Regional inequality and institutional trust in Europe. *European Journal of Political Research, 60*(4), 892–913.

Lopez, I. H. (2019). *Merge left*. The New Press.

Lugones, M. (2010). Toward a decolonial feminism. *Hypatia, 25*(4), 742–759.

Malone, K. R. (2012). Lacan, Freud, the humanities, and science. *The Humanistic Psychologist, 40*(3), 246–257.

Manuellan, M. J. (2017). *Sous la dictée de Fanon*. l'Amourier.

Marmot, M. (2005). *Status syndrome: How your social standing directly affects your health*. A&C Black.

Maroda, K. J. (2009). *Psychodynamic techniques: Working with emotion in the therapeutic relationship*. Guilford Press.

Martin, D. L. (2021). Violence and masculinity in small-scale societies. *Current Anthropology, 62*(S23), S169–S181.

Marx, K. (1867/1967). *Capital: A critique of political economy.* International Publishers.

Mbembe, F. (2019). *Necropolitics.* Duke University Press.

McGhee, H. (2021). *The sum of us: What racism costs everyone and how we can prosper together.* One World/Ballantine.

McIntosh, P. (2021). Foreword. In D. W. Austin & B. P. Bowser (Eds.), *Impacts of racism on White Americans in the age of Trump* (pp. vii–xi). Palgrave Macmillan.

McWilliams, N. (2004). *Psychoanalytic psychotherapy: A practitioner's guide.* Guilford Press.

Mechanic, M. (2021). *Jackpot: How the super-rich really live—And how their wealth harms us all.* Simon and Schuster.

Merchant, A. (2020). Don't be put off by my name. *Studies in Gender and Sexuality, 21,* 104–112.

Metzl, J. M. (2019). *Dying of whiteness: How the politics of racial resentment is killing America's heartland.* Hachette UK.

Mignolo, W. D., & Walsh, C. E. (2018). *On decoloniality: Concepts.* Duke University Press.

Mitchell, J. (2000). *Psychoanalysis and feminism: A radical reassessment of Freudian psychoanalysis.* Basic Books.

Moretzsohn, M. A. G. (2018). From the alienist to modernists and psychoanalysts. *Revista Brasileira de Psicanálise , 52*(1), 160–177.

Myers, E. (2022). *The gratifications of whiteness: W.E.B. Du Bois and the enduring rewards of anti-blackness.* Oxford University Press.

Newman, B. J., Reny, T. T., & Ooi, B. S. (2022). The color of Disparity: racialized income inequality and support for liberal economic policies. *The Journal of Politics, 84*(3), 1818–1822.

Obiwu. (2015). Jacques Lacan in Africa: Travel, Moroccan cemetery, Egyptian Hieroglyphics, and other passions of theory. In M. Nwosu & Obiwu (Eds.), *The Critical imagination in African literature: Essays in honor of Michael J. C. Echeruo* (pp. 75–93). Syracuse University Press.

Ochonu, M. E. (2021). Slavery, theology, and anti-blackness in the Arab world. *Research Africa Reviews, 5,* 10–19.

Onlinekyne. (2021, December 11). *The magic of the Mobius Strip!* [Video]. YouTube. https://www.youtube.com/shorts/YYJ5l5Vuz4U

Patterson, O. (1982/2018). *Slavery and social death: A comparative study, with a new preface.* Harvard University Press.

Pinderhughes, C. A. (1979). Differential bonding: Toward a psychophysiological theory of stereotyping. *American Journal of Psychiatry, 136,* 33–37.

Pinderhughes Jr., C. C. (2023, July 26). *Personal communication.*

Plotkin, M. B., & Honorato, M. R. (2017). *Estimado doctor Freud: una historia cultural del psicoanálisis en América Latina.* Edhasa.

Powell, D. R. (2018). Race, African Americans, and psychoanalysis: Collective silence in the therapeutic situation. *Journal of the American Psychoanalytic Association, 66*(6), 1021–1049.

Quijano, A. (2000). Coloniality of power and Eurocentrism in Latin America. *International Sociology, 15*(2), 215–232.

Reed, T. (2020). *Toward freedom: The case against race reductionism*. Verso Books.

Reich, M. (2021). Economy: Racism's continuing economic cost to Whites—A second look. In D. W. Austin & B. P. Bowser (Eds.), *The impact of racism on White Americans in the age of Trump* (pp. 21–30). Palgrave Macmillan.

Robinson, C. J. (1983/2020). *Black Marxism, revised and updated third edition: The making of the black radical tradition*. UNC Press Books.

Rodney, W. (2022). *Decolonial Marxism: Essays from the Pan-African revolution*. Verso Books.

Rosenzweig, S. (1992). *Freud, Jung, and Hall the King maker: The historic expedition to America (1909) with G. Stanley Hall as Host and William James as guest*. Rana House Press.

Roudinesco, E. (1990). *Jacques Lacan & co: A history of psychoanalysis in France, 1925–1985*. University of Chicago Press.

Ryan, J. (2017). *Class and psychoanalysis: Landscapes of inequality*. Routledge.

Safouan, M. (2007). *Why are the Arabs not free?: The politics of writing*. Blackwell.

Said, E. (1978). *Orientalism: Western concepts of the orient*. Pantheon.

Said, E. (2003). *Freud and the non-European*. Verso Books.

Sharpley, R. H. (1978). Solomon Carter Fuller. In G. E. Gifford (Ed.), *Psychoanalysis, psychotherapy and the New England medical scene, 1894–1944* (pp. 181–195). Science History Publications.

Shedler, J. (2010). The efficacy of psychodynamic psychotherapy. *American Psychologist, 65*(2), 98–109.

Sheehi, S., & Sheehi, L. (2021). *Psychoanalysis under occupation*. Routledge.

Spanierman, L. B., & Clark, D. A. (2021). Psychological science: Taking white racial emotions seriously—Revisiting the costs of racism to White Americans. In D. W. Austin & B. P. Bowser (Eds.), *The impact of racism on White Americans in the age of Trump* (pp. 115–136). Palgrave Macmillan.

Stoute, B. (2017). Race and racism in psychoanalytic thought: The ghosts in our nursery. In *The Trauma of Racism* (pp. 13–41). Routledge.

Suchet, M. (2007). Unraveling whiteness. *Psychoanalytic Dialogues, 17*, 867–886.

Summers, R. F., & Barber, J. P. (2010). *Psychodynamic therapy: A guide to evidence-based practice*. Guilford Press.

Takasuna, M. (2016). *Japanese at Clark 1909*. Retrieved online on July 31, 2023, from http://commons.trincoll.edu/macecourses/japanese-at-clark-1909/

Taylor, K. Y. (Ed.). (2017). *How we get free: Black feminism and the Combahee River Collective*. Haymarket Books.

Thomas, J. M. (2020). Du Bois, double consciousness, and the "Jewish question." *Ethnic and Racial Studies, 43*(8), 1333–1356.

Torres, N. M. (2017). Fanon and decolonial thought. In M. A. Peters (Ed.), *Encyclopedia of educational philosophy and theory* [Ebook]. Springer. https://doi.org/10.1007/978-981-287-588-4_506

Tosquelles, F. (1975/2017). Frantz Fanon en Saint-Alban (1975). *Teoría y Crítica de la Psicologia, 9,* 223–229.

Tubert-Oklander, J. (2006). The individual, the group and society: Their psychoanalytic inquiry. *International Forum of Psychoanalysis, 15,* 146–150.

Tummala-Narra, P. (2016). *Psychoanalytic theory and cultural competence in psychotherapy.* American Psychological Association.

Tummala-Narra, P. (2022). Can we decolonize psychoanalytic theory and practice? *Psychoanalytic Dialogues, 32*(3), 217–234.

Turner, L., & Neville, H. (Eds.). (2020). *Frantz Fanon's psychotherapeutic approaches to clinical work: Practicing internationally with marginalized communities.* Routledge.

Varvin, S., & Gerlach, A. (2011). The development of psychodynamic psychotherapy and psychoanalysis in China. *International Journal of Applied Psychoanalytic Studies, 8*(3), 261–267.

Vaughan, K. (2015). To unchain haunting blood memories: Intergenerational trauma among African-Americans. In L. O'Loughlin & M. Charles (Eds.), *Fragments of trauma and the social production of suffering—Trauma, history and memory.* Bowman and Littlefield.

Von Eckardt, U. (1974). Cultural factors in heroin addiction in Puerto Rico. *Journal of the American Academy of Psychoanalysis and Dynamic Psychiatry, 2,* 129–137.

Weber, T. (2020). The pre-1914 origins of Hitler's antisemitism revisited. *The Journal of Holocaust Research, 34*(1), 70–86.

Weinberger, J., & Stoycheva, V. (2019). *The unconscious: Theory, research, and clinical implications.* Guilford Publications.

Wilderson III, F. B. (2020). *Afropessimism.* Liveright Publishing.

Wilkerson, I. (2020). *Caste: The origins of our discontents.* Random House.

Wilkinson, R. G., & Pickett, K. (2020). *The inner level: How more equal societies reduce stress, restore sanity and improve everyone's well-being.* Penguin Books.

Woods, A. (2020). The work before us: Whiteness and the psychoanalytic institute. *Psychoanalysis, Culture & Society, 25*(2), 230–249.

Žižek, S. (2019). *The sublime object of ideology.* Verso Books.

2

"To Cure Through Love": Recovering the Clinical and Critical Freud

Fanon (1952/2008) had a fundamental belief in "the possibility of love," which is why he endeavored "to trace its imperfections, its perversions" (p. 28). This is the task of analysis—to explore and disrupt how love becomes distorted in the interest of survival. If, as Freud asserted, "the secret of therapy is to cure through love" (cited in Falzeder, 2019, p. 30), then this requires wrestling with love's conundrums. Love is unexpected, surprising, untimely, a chance encounter. Yet because of its unpredictability love is chronically late yet always on time. It is in its irruption, out of time and out of sync, that love cures. Psychoanalysis intervenes—as my college professor Carlton James would say—in the tension between love and the loss of love. And, I would add, where love is confused with power and control.

I want to clarify some things about Freud's language, as he was not interested in using obtuse jargon in his original context. The German words we translate as "ego," "id," and "super-ego" were part of everyday language to his original readers, and Freud *intended* to make his theories accessible to a lay audience (Bettelheim, 1984). The German *ich* (ego) refers to our sense of self or "I," whereas *es* (id) means "it," what is experienced as "other" to ourselves. Put differently, the "ego" refers to what is allowed to be a part of "me," and the "id" is what must be pushed away as *not* a part of me—an *it*. Regulating the relationship between "I" and "it" is the *über ich* (super-ego), literally the "over-I" looking over our shoulder. It is the voice of other people, values, and institutions whispering in our ear and judging our thoughts, feelings, and desires. Freud's use of the German word *Seele*, which we often translate as "psyche" or "the mind" also had a more immediate, even spiritual meaning— "soul." Psychoanalysis—or more appropriately, *soul* analysis—is a method for

D. J. Gaztambide, *Decolonizing Psychoanalytic Technique*, https://doi.org/10.1007/978-3-031-48476-6_2

understanding the conflict between those parts of ourselves deemed "unacceptable" by our families, cultures, and society. Ultimately, for understanding what it is that tears at our soul, and what can bring peace to our spirit.

The Unconscious as an Associative System for Regulating Arousal

Psychoanalysis starts from the premise of an unconscious, those "gaps" in awareness that come up when we "mean one thing but say another," and those processes that influence our behavior but are not accessible to conscious reflection. The unconscious is made up of *associations*—the relationships we form between thoughts, feelings, wishes, and experiences. If you read the phrase "magic kingdom," for example, this may cue the word "Disney" or "Mickey Mouse," associations formed through lived experience. The unconscious also includes associations experienced as dangerous in some way. In his topographical model (a "hierarchy" of states of mind), Freud (1915) theorized (1) a conscious mind, (2) a preconscious layer of what can become conscious, and (3) the repressed unconscious proper. Between the preconscious and unconscious exists a "censorship" (which he later called the "over-I" or superego), which subjects associations to "a kind of testing" (p. 173). If "on testing," a feeling, thought, or wish "is rejected … it is then said to be 'repressed' and must remain unconscious. If, however, it passes this testing, it [becomes conscious]" (p. 173). Like a red or green light of the mind, marking what it is we are and are not allowed to think, feel, and do.

The "repression" or turning away from feelings, thoughts or desires is related to what Freud (1920) called "the pleasure principle," our need to seek pleasure and avoid pain. Feelings are psychological and embodied, an energy that courses through the body and can become "bound" or "unbound," organized and disorganized (Freud, 1895/1950). Put differently, we seek to regulate our emotions within our "window of tolerance" (see Siegel, 2012), the amount of bodily excitation we can tolerate before it becomes overwhelming—we become *unbound*. To manage the level of arousal in the body, the psyche depends on two interconnected processes, what Freud (1911) called the primary and secondary process.

The primary process is fast, automatic, emotional, intuitive, associative and seeks discharge through action. At its best, the primary process is behind those "Aha!" moments that help us solve a problem, the "gut" feeling that lets us know something is wrong, or the improvization that comes with music and poetry. At its worst, we become overwhelmed and "unbound" by an excess of energy, such as a panic attack where we "feel we are going to die." The secondary process by contrast is slow, logical, methodical, and serves to modulate, organize, and "bind" excitations in the body. At its best it helps us problem solve, keeps us regulated and able to function, and "checks" our gut to see if what we feel matches the situation. At its worst, we become "overly bound" and rigid, unable to stay flexible in the face of life's challenges.

Per Freud (1925), the psyche seeks to keep as low as possible the amount of disruptive excitation in the body. When our capacity to regulate collapses due to an excess of affect, say, when we "run into danger without being prepared for it; *[the psyche] emphasizes the factor of surprise*" (Freud, 1920, p. 11, emphasis added). Trauma can be thought of as a sudden, unexpected excess that catches us off guard. This excess is associated with pain, and the defense mechanisms that help us survive become associated with a form of pleasure. When we turn away from our experience, we insert a "cut" in the link between an idea and a painful feeling. The repressed affect, however, may become associated—through the primary process—to an entirely separate thought even if it is not completely "rational."

Imagine someone who learned early on that anger is dangerous, as it might "make loved ones leave." If we imagine that association as a code, a binding of meaning, it might look like "*If* I am angry toward a loved one, *then* they will abandon me," or simply the association "anger = abandonment." To avoid this, they learn to repress their anger. Yet the repressed anger might seek expression by connecting itself (*cathects*, as Freud would say) to another object, such as our co-workers. Although angry outbursts may lead us to lose our job, it becomes a *comparatively* preferable and safer expression of anger than directing it toward our loved ones.

Drives, Wishes, Object Relations, and Symptoms as Compensatory Substitutes

Psychoanalysis is based on the premise that symptoms serve a purpose, compensating for wishes, needs, and feelings that have been disavowed. These all gesture toward a linguistic feature of the word emotion—e-*motion* gets us *in motion*. Emotions are related to the "drives," the somatic sources of affect that make a "demand" on the mind to engage in some form of work. Drives have four components: (1) a bodily impulse with a somatic source (2) that *drives* us to search for an object, (3) to fulfill an aim that (4) satisfies the drive through motoric activity. For example, a rumble in my stomach (the source), *drives* me to my fridge for a cheesecake (the object), with the goal of eating it (the aim), to satisfy the drive by stuffing it in my mouth (the motoric action).

By object or "object relation," Freud means a real or imagined relationship with another person, but it can also be a thing—like cheesecake—or a broader concept such as a religious figure (e.g., God), culture, or society. Wishes, feelings, and drives move our bodies toward action in specific object-relational contexts to achieve a specific aim. For example, anger *drives* us to set boundaries with others and assert ourselves. Love *moves* us closer together. Sadness contracts our bodies, signaling others to come close and comfort us. When we associate these feelings with danger we learn to avoid, turn away from, or "push" them away as an *it* separate from our sense of "I." Imagine someone who says "I *don't really* get angry"—anger is framed as outside themselves. Should they ever get angry, they might say "I was *not* myself (anger = not-I = *it*)."

Repression prevents "the setting-off of muscular activity" (Freud, 1915, p. 179). It is, again, a "severance" between a thought, memory, or experience and an affect with its bodily, behavioral tendencies (come closer, fight, run away, etc.). You cannot, for example, get angry at your partner and set boundaries if you suppress the feeling to begin with. In the process, this "solution" to the problem creates an even bigger problem, like telling yourself "*Don't* think about pink elephants." Eventually you cannot help it, as the proposition carries the linguistic injunction "*think about pink elephants.*" As the two statements are associated to one another, repression no longer works—a "return of the repressed" where you think about pink elephants even *more*. In pursuing pleasure and avoiding pain, we sometimes pick a cure worse than the disease—this becomes our *symptom*. Our avoidance works short term at long-term cost: "anxiety can to some extent be dammed up, *but only at a heavy sacrifice of personal freedom*" (p. 184, emphasis added).

Compromise Formation and the Dialectics of Pleasure and Pain

How can a symptom be "pleasurable?" Substance misuse provides an example. Someone might drink alcohol to cope with social anxiety, and at first this helps. Over time, however, they need to drink more to achieve the desired effect. They start missing work or family events and experience medical problems. These consequences produce anxiety, turning them back to the very thing used to "treat" their pain. The behavior becomes so automatic they find themselves in unbearable suffering. They *want* to stop drinking but cannot. Facing their fears is experienced as *more* unbearable in fantasy than the loss of freedom taking place in reality, their drinking now a form of pleasure in pain—what Lacan called *jouissance* (see Chapter 4). Pleasure can also be understood as a relief, an *absence* of pain produced by a behavior—when we are in physical or social danger, escaping that danger becomes physiologically reinforcing. The psyche starts to misfire, rewarding us for things that hurt us—substances, toxic relationships and so on.

Avoiding pain and pursuing pleasure organizes, regulates, and "binds" our somatic state to maintain homeostasis, protecting us from becoming dysregulated and "unbound." The primary process—fast, intuitive, given to wit and fancy—interacts with our wishes in counterintuitive ways. In the unconscious, our wishes "co-ordinate with one another, exist side by side without being influenced by one another, and are exempt from mutual contradiction" (Freud, 1915, p. 186). When wishes that are incompatible are activated, they do not "cancel" each other, "but combine to form an intermediate aim, a compromise. There are in this system no negation, no doubt, no degrees of certainty… there are only contents, cathected [i.e., associated] with greater or lesser strength" (p. 186). The primary process is at times an *anti-logic* out of time and out of synch, "timeless; i.e. they are not ordered temporally, are not altered by the passage of time; they have no reference to time at all. Reference to time is bound up [with consciousness]" (p. 187). We will review research in Chapter 7 that very much supports Freud's claims.

Unconscious Processes, the Body, and Language Between Neurosis and Psychosis

One way to understand unconscious processes is through Freud's (1915) comparison between psychosis and neurosis. In psychosis, speech is often tangential (not "logically" related) or circumstantial (e.g., roundabout), to the point of being incomprehensible, with a prominence of references to the body (p. 197). Further, in psychotic speech, "words are subjected to… the primary psychical process" (p. 199). A person who is psychotic says aloud what for neurotics are *unconscious* associations between words, ideas, and feelings, with a "predominance of what has to do with words over what has to do with things" (p. 201).

Freud cites the case of a young woman with psychosis who accused her boyfriend of replacing her eyes with his, and in another instance she said her body was contorting itself as if someone put her in a "lower position." She then accused her boyfriend of having placed her in a "false position" below him—even though she was of higher class status than him "she thought she would be better if she were like him" (p. 198). Although this was not literally true, as metaphors they captured her experience of being "gaslit" by her partner (his "eyes" were now hers, he made her believe she needed to be like him). A non-psychotic patient might experience somatic sensations such as an eye twitch or body pain, but without any *conscious* connection to their partner's gaslighting behavior.

To further illustrate how the primary process functions in the unconscious, I borrow a different case from Chapter 7. In this case, a college student struggling with obsessive–compulsive disorder avoided showering due to a fear of being contaminated by bacteria in water, which led to him missing school. The student and his therapist discovered that he avoided going to class because when he read the chemical formula for water in his chemistry textbook or heard it spoken—"H_2O"—he experienced the same anxiety fueling his avoidance. Although he was not in danger of getting "wet" or physically "contaminated" by reading the word H_2O, the linguistic association "bacteria = water = H_2O" evoked a powerful reaction. As Freud (1915) writes, "What has dictated the substitution is not the resemblance between the things denoted but the sameness of the words used to express them" (p. 201). For this patient, "dirty water"—filled with bacteria—"water from the shower," "water to drink," and "H_2O is the formula for water," were all linked by the word "water." The patient's obsessions around "dirty water" metaphorically "polluted" his associations, making even words on a page a trigger for fears of contamination.

Here Freud (1915, p. 201) distinguished between words and what they point to, what Lacan called the signifier and the signified, respectively (see Chapter 4). For example, the word "dog" evokes the image of a four-legged animal that is "man's best friend," and we know that "a dog is not a cat." But in the unconscious the word "dog" and its being "four-legged" is related not only to another four-legged animal such as "cat," but can also render the non-logical association "dog is chair"—all three have "four legs." Similarly, the unconscious can invert the word "dog" into "god," forming the association "dog is god." Suddenly, we dream of a bearded dog on a heavenly throne (another "chair") who loves us unconditionally ("a dog is man's best friend"). These associations are non-logical, connected through superficial traits mediated by the words that point to them, the sound of these words, etc. In this way, the unconscious "treats concrete things as though they were abstract" (p. 204). The secondary process prunes associations so only what is "logical" enters consciousness, but in psychosis this breaks down dramatically, proliferating primary process in speech. For a neurotic (i.e., non-psychotic) person the secondary process periodically breaks down during times of heightened arousal or stress. Think of "Freudian slips" or "slips of the tongue," such as when someone calls their partner by an ex's name during a heated argument, or during love making. In this example their previous partner and their new partner are both mediated by (associated to) the category "partner," with the distinction between the two breaking down during conflict or stress.

Two Core Drives: The Human Soul Between "Life" and "Death"

Let us review what we have established. The mind operates according to two mental processes: the primary ("fast," associative, intuitive, automatic, emotional) and the secondary process ("slow," logical, deliberative, planned, rational). These processes organize themselves according to the pleasure principle: we seek pleasure (or what helps us survive) and avoid pain. We avoid pain to keep the level of bodily excitation low and reduce the possibility of being overwhelmed—caught off guard by the "surprise" a trauma or loss present to the psyche. In pursuing pleasure and avoiding pain, the primary and secondary process help us arrive at strategies for addressing life's problems—a compromise formation. This compromise balances benefit and cost, risk and reward in ways that help us survive in the short term, even if in the long term it creates problems in living. All of this takes place within a psychic system whose basic "building blocks" are associations between feelings, thoughts, behavior, and experiences.

Around what concerns do associations form? What motivations "drive" us, and what threats do we try to avoid? Freud posits two core drives motivating our behavior. One is the "eros" or "life" drive whose aim is to "bind together" parts into a greater whole. This desire to "come together" emerges both in the sense of pursuing internal wholeness as well as in seeking connection with others—within our family, culture, communities, even nations. The other is the destructive or "death" drive, which seeks to undo connections, pull apart, and destroy. We see this drive, for example, in thrill-seeking behavior. We might say a person bungie jumping has a "death wish" not because they want to die, but because they want their body to be "shaken up," to experience the thrill of *not* maintaining homeostasis and feel the rush of a "brush" with death.

But there is another way in which the death drive expresses itself—as an "instinct for mastery, or the will to power" (Freud, 1924, p. 163). We desire not only to achieve wholeness or relationships with other people (the "life" drive), we also desire to feel valued in the community, seen as compentent, and achieve some kind of power in our lives. We not only fear the loss of bodily integrity (e.g., being overwhelmed, physically hurt or killed, dying, etc.) or fear the loss of love and relationship (e.g., someone close to us dies, rejects, abandons, hurts us, etc.), we also fear losing our "place," being devalued, and "put down." These two "drives" or motivations underlie the associations we form in the interest of survival. While I nuance Freud's account with contemporary research (see Chapter 7), the broad strokes of his model form an important foundation for this book, even as later theorists reimagined those foundations.

Psychoanalytic Treatment: Free Association, Resistance, Repetition, and Transference

Given this model of the mind, how does psychoanalytic treatment work? First, the patient is invited to "pledge himself to overcome the objections of the censorship" (Freud, 1915, p. 193) according to the fundamental rule of free association—to say whatever comes to mind, without judging it as silly, bad, or shameful. The purpose of this simple invitation is not to point out to the patient how they avoid or harbor a repressed feeling, as this will just provoke a renewed rejection of it. "To have heard something," Freud writes, "and to have experienced something are in their psychological nature two quite different things, even though the content of both is the same" (p. 176). Psychoanalysis is an experience that *moves* the patient, with insight not as a set of new "thoughts," but a *surprise* that dislodges their habitual ways of being.

In a classic paper, "Remembering, repeating, and working-through," Freud (1914) described a division of labor in which the patient says what comes to mind to the best of their abilities, and the therapist brings attention to those moments where they turn away from the fundamental rule—what is called "resistance" or "defenses." The goal of treatment "is to fill in gaps in memory… to overcome resistances due to repression" (p. 148). This is not about restoring "repressed memories" but repairing broken circuits—*gaps* in memory. Freud comments that when patients become aware of feelings, memories, and thoughts they had otherwise "forgotten," they often add "I've always known it; only I've never thought of it" (p. 148). His concept of repression is less a "pushing down" than a "turning away" from experience, thus closer to what contemporary clinicians call "dissociation" (Bromberg, 2003). In analysis, one "remembers" that *dis*-sociated feelings, thoughts, desires, and situations are in fact *a*-ssociated, and does so by "facing" what we have turned away from.

Imagine a child who learned that when they break a rule, their parents become angry. An association forms, "*If* I am bad, *then* my parents are mad"—at a more gut level, something like "*If* I = bad; *Then* parent = mad," or, "bad = mad." Suppose the parents have a hostile divorce. In trying to understand the situation, the child's psyche works backwards from their experience—"*If* my parents are mad, *then* I must be bad" or "*If* parents

= mad; *Then* I = bad," or "mad = bad." The child represses these painful thoughts to cope with their (undeserved) guilt. Yet in adulthood they struggle with a "disproportionate" sense of guilt they cannot explain.

If this individual entered psychotherapy, they might "not *remember* anything of what he has forgotten and repressed, but *acts* it out. He reproduces it not as a memory but as an action; he repeats it" (Freud, 1914, p. 150, emphasis original). This repetition often makes itself known in the beginning of treatment. Once the patient is invited to say what comes to mind, "one expects him to pour out a flood of information, but often the first thing that happens is that he has nothing to say. He is silent and declares that nothing occurs to him" (p. 150). Or, as Ferenczi observed, the patient talks about everything *except* the problem which brought them to treatment (see Chapter 3). In either case, the patient repeats—in contemporary jargon, *enacts*—a stereotyped way they protect themselves from unwanted feelings. It is both a resistance against remembering, *and* how they remember through action. Free association evokes resistance not as an obstacle, but the very vehicle by which the patient's struggles become vividly known.

Freud (1914) noted that in the therapeutic relationship the patient both "shows" and "tells" us their problems. A patient talks about their low self-esteem when they suddenly cut themselves off, declaring their problems are "not that important" and the therapist "probably" wants to help people who "really" struggle. The patient behaves as someone with "lower value," positioning the therapist as someone who has "better things to do" than listen to them. Freud referred to this repetition as the "transference" of the past into the present, an association formed between the therapist and others in the patient's life—an association is in effect *a relationship*. In the same way as "a dog has four legs" but so does a chair, so too are superficial features of the therapist—their behavior, gender, race, sexuality, class—associated with others in the patient's experience. These associations can be "real," imagined, or something in between.

Repetition, Safety, and Working Through: Psychoanalytic Treatment as an Experience

The transference is a repetition of the patient's symptoms, "not as an event of the past, but as a present-day force," repeating those fears and the avoidances they use to protect themselves (Freud, 1914, p. 151). With the therapist's help, the patient comes to understand that the symptom serves a purpose "which has a solid ground for its existence" (p. 152). We honor the symptom's purpose so that freedom can be renewed. "The way is thus paved," he writes, "for a reconciliation with the repressed material which is coming to expression in his symptoms, while at the same time place is found for a certain tolerance for the state of being ill" (p. 152). To bear the anxiety that emerges from facing the symptom is a difficult but necessary component of recovery. We not only work within the patient's window of tolerance, we try to *expand* it.

Listening to the patient's free association, and redirecting them when they deviate from speaking freely depends on "the attachment through transference" (Freud, 1914, p. 153). The therapist is put in the role of a significant other from the past, an object of love as well as frustration, even trauma. But in contrast to the original attachment figure, the therapist does not punish the patient for their feelings but welcomes them. Like any relationship, the transference requires specific boundaries and a "frame," including the hour and frequency of sessions, the fee, and the fundamental rule. But it may also involve other requirements depending on the case, such as a plan for safety and clinical emergencies (see Yeomans et al., 2015). At the same time, Freud (1914) maintained one should "[leave] untouched as much of the patient's personal freedom as is compatible with these restrictions, nor does one hinder him from carrying out unimportant intentions, even if they are foolish" (p. 153). With some humor, he quips this too has utility, "only through his own experience and mishaps that a person learns sense" (p. 153).

The frame creates a safe enough space for the patient to have a new experience, whose "main instrument" is the "handling of the transference":

We render the compulsion [to repeat] harmless, and indeed useful, by giving it the right to assert itself in a definite field. We admit it into the transference as a playground in which it is allowed to expand in almost complete freedom and in which it is expected to display to us everything in the way of pathogenic instincts that is hidden in the patient's mind. (Freud, 1914, p. 154)

The patient repeats those behaviors that cause problems in their relationships with the therapist. For example, while the patient pulls others to reject them, the therapist aims to understand their behavior without the same response. The transference "creates an intermediate region between illness and real life through which the transition from the one to the other is made" (p. 154).

It bears repeating that for Freud (1914) psychoanalysis is no cognitive exercise, but a deeply affective, experiential treatment to move the soul. As the patient talks about the presenting problem, and this is repeated in the transference, the anxiety fueling the problem "heats up," evoking the impulse to avoid. The therapist here supports the patient to "*work through*" the resistance, "to overcome it, by continuing, in defiance of it, the analytic work according to the fundamental rule" (p. 155). Put differently, to continue talking openly *even when anxiety makes the patient want to turn away from their feelings.*

As anxiety rises so does resistance, which is not a "bad thing," but the very vehicle of the work. Freud (1914) writes:

> Only when the resistance is at its height can the analyst, working in common with his patient, discover the repressed instinctual impulses which are feeding the resistance; and it is this kind of *experience* which convinces the patient of the existence and power of such impulses. (p. 155, emphasis added)

By "insight," we mean the surprising experience of avoided thoughts and feelings within a safe enough relationship that expands our range of emotional freedom, our sense of "I" reimagined by accepting those feelings previously marginalized as "it." Remember that emotions *drive* us to action and "get us in motion," freeing our bodies toward satisfaction and satisfying action.

"Neutrality" and Beginning the Treatment: Clarifying the Psychodynamic Stance

There are many debates about "neutrality" in contemporary psychoanalysis (e.g., Hart, 2022 and other papers in this special issue). Neutrality is generally described as an "aspirational" stance of objectivity in which one avoids "taking sides" in the patient's conflicts, or, as Anna Freud formulated it, an "equidistant" position (almost geographically "neutral") between the id, ego, and super-ego. The term itself, however, does not appear in Freud's writings. In what follows, I describe the psychodynamic stance based on Freud's writings *and* his actual practice.

In describing his stance, Freud (1912) is clear that his is not the only one, and other clinicians could take a different stance that works for their patients (p. 111). He describes the therapist attending to the patient's free association with "evenly-suspended attention," remaining open without becoming "fixed" on any single interpretation of the patient's words. When we assume we "know" what the patient means or what to focus on we become more selective in our listening, "one point will be *fixed* in [our] mind... and some other will be correspondingly disregarded" (p. 112, emphasis added). The analyst also strives for openness toward what the patient's speech evokes in them, turning their "own unconscious like a receptive organ towards the transmitting unconscious of the patient" (p. 115). Hence, we work through our resistance to the patient, listening for our unconscious blind spots as well.

The idea of the analyst's openness to the patient (see Hart, 2022) seems to make Freud nervous. While he (1912) cautions against playing the part of a "savior" toward the patient, he insists on a "purification" of our feelings, putting them aside to the point of "emotional coldness" so we may "[perform] the operation as skilfully as possible" (p. 115). To that end, he advocated against the therapist disclosing their feelings out of concern the patient will "reverse roles" and analyze *them*, and also thought it "wrong to set a patient tasks," e.g., homework (p. 119). However, Freud either changed his mind or did not fully practice this way (see below).

In discussing how to begin the treatment, Freud (1913) again stresses he is offering guidelines, not iron laws (p. 123). He recommends a consultation period for patient and therapist to get to know each other, and if they decide to work together establish the frame (e.g., meeting times, the fee, safety plan). He advocates for the patient lying on the couch out of personal preference (he did not like to be stared at) and to not bias the patient with his facial expressions, but again acknowledges others work differently (e.g., sitting face to face). He may take a formal history of the patient's struggles or childhood, or wait for them to emerge organically. But early on he introduces free association with the quality of a mindfulness exercise, "Act as though… you were a traveller sitting next to the window of a railway carriage and describing to someone inside the carriage the changing views which you see outside" (p. 135). Lastly, Freud asks the patient to not avoid speaking something because it is unpleasant.

How does the therapist intervene as the patient is free associating? Freud (1913) introduces what is today known as the principle of working from "surface to depth." He reverses his call from a year prior for emotional coldness, arguing that the therapist's non-judgmental presence, "serious interest" and "empathy [*Einfühlung*]" for the patient helps establish an attachment bond (pp. 139–140). With this rapport the analyst avoids premature interpretations, waiting until the patient is *just* a step away from arriving at an understanding of something themselves (p. 140). We work with material that is *just* outside the patient's awareness and their window of tolerance, evoking a level of arousal that allows them to experience their feelings without being fully overwhelmed. What facilitates the patient being willing to "touch" these painful feelings is their desire to overcome the resistance and get better. Borrowing again from Du Bois, the recognition that the cost of liberty is less than the price of freedom.

Was Freud a Freudian? A Different Account of His Clinical Practice

There is a contradiction in Freud's thinking between being a distant "surgeon" who coldly administers a technique (his 1912 paper) and being an engaged, empathic presence (his 1913 paper), a tension contemporary Freudians like Steven Ellman (1991/2018) struggle to reconcile in light of Freud's actual practice (p. 285). Ellman's otherwise erudite review of Freud's technique neglects an important speech he gave in 1918 that recenters how he understood analytic work. While I review this paper below, it is important to take a broader view of his cases and practice. In a study of 43 cases Freud treated from 1907 to 1939, Lynn and Vaillant (1998) found Freud deviated from "neutrality" in *86%* of the cases, and abandoned the anonymous "blank screen" in *100%* of them. Freud was *actively* engaged with patients, often disclosing his thoughts and feelings while assigning homework as befit the case, consistent with his 1918 paper (see below).

Freud's clinical practice—combining empathy, self-disclosure, and occasional use of homework—is supported by contemporary research, as Lynn and Vaillant (1998, p. 169) also recognized. Other studies of Freud's cases such as Lohser and Newton (1996) show that his deviation from "the rules" often had a *positive* impact on his patients. Against that backdrop, the argument that we should follow the "rules" of abstinence and emotional distance is akin to saying "Don't do as Freud did, do as he *said*." If psychoanalysis is based on Freud, then students and practitioners would benefit from learning how he actually worked. This is not a polemic, but a natural extension of examining the historical record. I do not claim a spurious objectivity, only that his writings and practice present a more nuanced picture of clinical practice than is often recognized.

What then of neutrality? Instead of imagining the analyst as "equidistant" between id, ego, and super-ego, keeping different perspectives at arm's length as if we are somehow Switzerland—literally neutral—I argue we understand what Freud pointed to as a proper "psychodynamic stance." If we recall the etymology of the term—*psyche* meaning "mind," *dynamic* meaning "force in motion"—we are talking about how the analyst "keeps their mind in motion." Rather than a distant observer, our role is one of *moving* dynamically toward and away from different perspectives without becoming one-sidedly "fixed." This assumes times when we *will* become "stuck" on a given point of view or feeling and must do the hard work of working through this stuckness—our resistance—to restore our capacity to be open to different feelings, perspectives, self-states, and values in the patient.

To insist on neutrality risks the very problem Freud warned us about—if one is perfectly "equidistant" from different points of view, one is in effect *fixed* to a singular position. As Wachtel (2017) once said, you "can't go far in neutral." We must be able to "flow" between different positions, perspectives, feelings, and points of view. To paraphrase the actor and martial artist Bruce Lee, clinicians must "be like water."

For example, the issue is not whether we are unilaterally "quiet" or "conversational," help the patient "figure things out on their own" or suggest a course of action, but whether we flexibly shift between these positions depending on each case. With respect to culture and identity, the problem is not whether the patient's difficulties are wholly intrapsychic, relational, or sociocultural, but whether we can entertain these possibilities without becoming fixed to them in a rigid way. It is not "neutrality" but openness and flexibility that lies at the heart of technique and the psychodynamic stance—or if one prefers, the psychodynamic *dance*.

Freud's Clinical Work in Action: The Case of the "Rat Man"

Freud's (1909) treatment of the "the Rat man" illustrates his practice. To tell this patient's story beyond this appellation, I use an acronym Freud himself used—"L." L was a young man with severe obsessions, compulsions, and suicidal thoughts. After a consultation, Freud introduced the fundamental rule to say what came to mind. L began describing the obsession that he was a criminal, recalling the sexual encounters he had as a child by his nanny, who later married a *Hofrat*, a German term for a government council member, "so that to-day she is a Frau Hofrat [lit. Mrs Councillor]. Even now I often see her in the street" (p. 161). Though the encounters were "in secret," L feared his father "knew what he did" and could hear his sexual thoughts.[1] He also struggled with the fear his thoughts could become reality, taking strenuous efforts to prevent acting them out. Among these was the thought his father would die.

Over time Freud (1909) formulated L's conflict in terms of the relationship between (a) his wishes, (b) the anxiety of a catastrophic outcome, and (c) the "*protective measures*," or defenses used to prevent the catastrophes he feared (p. 163, emphasis original). For example, L wished to be intimate with a woman, which he was barred from as he could only have sex if he

---

[1] Neither L nor Freud truly considered that boys could be victims of sexual abuse within their patriarchal culture.

were married, and could only marry if he could afford it. Associated with L's wish was a fear that something "dreadful" would happen. This took many forms, with Freud discerning over time an underlying contingency with an "*If*, *then*" quality, "If I have this wish to see a woman naked, [then] my father will be bound to die" (p. 163). The patient's defenses functioned as a kind of "*therefore*," as in "*therefore* I must punish myself for this wish, disavow my desires, etc."

In their second session, L discussed the experience that brought him to treatment. During his training in the army he lost his glasses, but pushed forward without them to show the officers he "had what it takes" to be a soldier, wanting to impress a captain he admired but also dreaded, who was "*obviously fond of cruelty*" (Freud, 1909, p. 165, emphasis original). During an argument about physical punishment—which the captain approved of— the captain told L about a torture technique used in the backwaters of the Austrian empire. The patient suddenly jumped from the couch, begging Freud "to spare him the recital of the details" (p. 165). Freud "assured him" he had no taste for cruelty and "had no desire to torment him," but stressed it was important he finish his thought. Seeing L struggle with his anxiety, Freud offered "I would do all I could... to guess the full meaning of any hints he gave me" (p. 166). Freud showed a willingness to give L room, not by forcing him to say what was on his mind but making it safe enough to do so:

> Was he perhaps thinking of impalement?—"No, not that... the criminal was tied up..." —he expressed himself so indistinctly that I could not immediately guess in what position—"... a pot was turned upside down on his buttocks ... some *rats* were put into it ... and they ..."—he had again got up, and was showing every sign of horror and resistance—"... *bored their way in...*" —Into his anus, I helped him out. (p. 166, emphasis original)

As Freud helped L work through his anxiety, he noticed L's conflicted facial expressions—horror, which made sense, but also a sense of pleasure? A thought flashed across Freud's mind, "*horror at pleasure of his own of which he himself was unaware*" (p. 167, emphasis original).

Another thought then crossed L's mind—a person close to him was being subjected to this torture. After some prompting by Freud, L disclosed it was a "lady he admired." The patient again "broke off his story" to reassure Freud (1909) he found these thoughts alien and "repugnant." L shared he often repudiated these thoughts by saying to himself "*but* they don't deserve that," or "whatever are you thinking?" and in the end, "succeeded in warding off *both* of them" (p. 167, emphasis original). "Both?" Freud was confused. L spoke about *one* thought, of the lady being tortured. Paying close atten- tion to his words, Freud asked what was the *other* thought that crossed his mind? L admitted this second thought was of his father being tortured. The young man stressed this did not make sense—his father had died years ago. He continued, sharing that the evening after the argument with the captain, the latter informed L that one of the lieutenants had paid for his new set of glasses, and that L should pay him back. In that moment, L found himself owing a *debt*. The thought came to mind that he *should not* pay the lieutenant or else the rat punishment would befall his father and the lady he admired. He fought this idea by saying out loud, "You *must* pay him back," concocting an intricate scheme to do so.

Freud (1909) needed to ask L to repeat the story several times, at which point he realized it was extremely convoluted. At the end of session, L seemed disoriented, referring to Freud as his "captain." Freud realized L was *contrasting* him to his sadistic captain, "probably because at the beginning of the hour I had told him that I myself was not fond of cruelty like Captain N., and that I had no intention of tormenting him unnecessarily" (p. 169). Freud, surprising L's expectations, reassures him that he is not here to torture him, and does not chastise L but patiently helps him express his fears. In effect, Freud passed a "test"—by not punishing L he allowed the "testing" to which L's psyche subjects his thoughts and feelings *to relax*. In their third session, Freud gets into the weeds of L's complex scheme for paying back the lieutenant. *Contradictions* kept popping up, which Freud pressed L to clarify. In the end, L realized he knew all along the captain was mistaken, and that it was a woman who worked at the post office who paid for his glasses. She was attracted to L, and paying for his glasses was a pretext to see him. Why such a convoluted story? He realized he vowed himself to "pay back" the lieutenant so he *did not* have to go see the woman, creating an opportunity to pursue romance with someone who liked him—a betrayal of the lady he admired, yet whom he imagined being tortured.

In their fourth session, Freud (1909) prompted L with a question therapists to this day find tried and true—"And how do you intend to proceed to-day?" (p. 174). The patient talked about his father, who had passed away nine years prior. When his father became sick, L asked the doctor "when the danger [would be] over." The doctor replied probably the day after tomorrow, but L did not realize he meant his father would *die*. Tragically, he awoke one evening to learn of his father's death, and reproached himself for not being present, his shame growing when he found out his father uttered his name in his final moments. L struggled to mourn, expecting his father to walk through the door any minute. A year and a half later, his guilt tormented him, and he began to treat himself "as a criminal," falling into a depression impacting his ability to work.

Freud (1909) at this point provided more psychoeducation, explaining that when there is a "false connection" between a feeling and an idea (L's self-reproach and his father's death), one might say the feeling does not fit the facts. But psychoanalytically, "The affect is justified," (p. 175), serving some other purpose or meaning. The "known" thought ("I am a criminal *because* I was not by my father's bedside") serves as a substitute for an unconscious thought. The idea that the symptom is a false connection helps us account "for the powerlessness of logical processes to combat the tormenting idea" (p. 176). There is a non-logical but *justified* sense L feels he committed a "crime" against his father. L doubted whether he could overcome feelings that resisted logic, to which Freud replied that although he did not dispute the severity of his struggles, L was still young and capable of change, reassuring him with "a word or two upon the good opinion I had formed of him, and this gave him visible pleasure" (p. 178).

At their sixth session, L described a childhood episode from age 12, when he fell in love with a friend's sister who did not reciprocate his affections. The idea came to L that if something bad happened to him, *such as his father dying*, she would be kinder to him. He at once rejected the idea, denying to Freud (1909) he ever wished his father's death, dismissing it as just a "train of thought" (p. 178). Freud challenged L's defense, asking "why, if it had not been a wish, he had repudiated it" (pp. 178–179). L replied the idea his father should die so he could be loved by a girl was *preposterous* and *offensive*. They went back and forth, with Freud pointing out that L's refusal, "It is irrational that *I wish my father would die* so this girl will love me," carries within it, linguistically, the very wish he fears—"I wish my father would die" (remember our example about *not* thinking about pink elephants). Realizing they were at an impasse, Freud takes a different approach. He remarked, "I felt sure this had not been the first occurrence of his idea of his father's dying" (p. 179). This was shrewd in that L did not have to *accept* the idea, only reflect on whether it came to mind at other times. By helping L talk about another occasion where this thought came to mind, Freud helped him approach this wish in a safer, indirect way. The very nature of associations made it so that the act of saying "Here is another situation where *I* had the *wish my father* died" includes, again linguistically, "I wish my father died."

L replied that in fact, "a precisely similar thought had flashed through his mind a second time six months before his father's death" (Freud, 1909, p. 178). Ten years ago L was in love with the lady he admired (the other "victim" of the rat torture), but he was not able to marry her due to financial difficulties. It was then that his childhood thought came back, "*his father's death might make him rich enough to marry her*" (p. 179, emphasis original).

L defended against the idea by wishing his father left him nothing. Other thoughts flooded to mind, which "*surprised him very much*, for he was quite certain that his father's death could never have been an object of his desire but only of his fear" (pp. 179–180, emphasis added). The surprise of a direct experience of his unconscious wishes challenged L's identity.

It was after this experience that Freud (1909) offered interpretations, explaining to L how a wish is repressed due to a fear of losing someone he loves—he wished for his father to die, but "it was precisely the intensity of his love that would not allow his hatred… to remain conscious" (p. 181). L saw his father as his best friend, just as his grandfather was his father's. But he began to recognize his father also interfered in his romantic life, and if he could somehow get rid of him he could find the love he desired. To disavow these feelings, he engaged in increasing self-reproaches, to which Freud interpreted, "That is because you derive pleasure from your self-reproaches as a means of self-punishment" (p. 184). By punishing himself for his desires, L played the role of a "moral" person punishing a "criminal's" misdeeds, itself a form of pleasure.

In their seventh session, L described an incident from when he was eight years old. He loved his brother, but was also jealous of him as the more attractive sibling. Freud (1909) remarked that L had already shared a scene of jealousy—his nanny "leaving" him to marry a wealthy councillorl, a *Hofrat*. On one occasion, L took a toy gun, tricked his brother to look down the barrel, and shot him. Although his brother was not hurt, L *meant* to hurt him. As a child he threw himself on the ground, berating himself for his hostile wish. Freud pointed out a contradiction in L's narrative—"If he had preserved the recollection of an action so foreign to him as this, he could not… deny the possibility of something similar" (p. 185). L became aware of other aggressive feelings toward the lady he loved, acknowledging for the first time she did not love him back, harboring a fantasy he would one day grow wealthy and marry another woman to make her jealous. As L expressed shame about his fantasies, Freud reassured him he was not responsible for these childhood feelings, "and he must know that moral responsibility could not be applied to children" (p. 185). He was not absolving L of responsibility, only expressing empathy toward him so he could have some empathy toward himself.

Over the course of subsequent sessions, Freud (1909) and L reconstructed his family history. His father was a soldier from a working-class background who "moved up" by marrying into a wealthy family, a source of contention for L's mother; he once overheard an argument in which he learned that before meeting his mother his father "had made advances to a pretty but penniless girl of humble birth" (p. 198). Realizing his father gave up a relationship with a working-class woman to marry his mother had an impact on L. After his father died, his mother told him she had arranged for him to marry one of his cousins after he finished school, a connection to help him "move up" in his profession. This "family plan" was a source of intense conflict for L, "whether he should remain faithful to the lady he loved in spite of her poverty, or whether he should follow in his father's footsteps and marry the lovely, rich, and well-connected girl" (p. 198). L "resolved" this conflict between his love and his father's wishes by falling into a deep depression, "by falling ill he avoided the task of resolving it in real life" (p. 199).

To be clear, Freud (1909) is not accusing L of "faking" his depression. Quite the opposite, by tracing how L's symptoms resolve a problem even as they cause another, he comes to understand its function. So long as L does not finish school, he will not have to confront his family's wishes, "what appears to be the *consequence* of the illness is in reality the *cause* or *motive* of falling ill" (p. 199, emphasis original). This is L's resistance in the fullest sense of the word—resistance against a wish that does not belong to him, the wish of a family navigating an economically stratified society that demands a sacrifice of one's desire in exchange for status and position. Freud's initial interpretation along these lines was rejected out of hand. Only when L experienced these feelings in the transference would they feel truly vivid.

Over the course of treatment, there were similar moments when Freud (1909) encouraged L's working through in word or deed. For example, Freud noticed that although he spoke glowingly about the lady he admired, he did not have any sense of her as a person, and so requested he bring a photograph of her to overcome his reticence to share more about her. In another session, L shared the "most frightful thing" that came to mind. He did not want to share it, as the treatment "would not be worth such a sacrifice" (p. 281). L said Freud should throw him out, for it concerned *him*, and why should he put up with his violent thoughts? After going back and forth, L disclosed he had vengeful feelings toward him, and Freud told him "by refusing to tell me and by giving up the treatment he would be taking a more outright revenge on me than by telling me" (p. 281). Something about this compelled L, who implied it had to do with Freud's "daughter."

L had met a woman on the stairs of Freud's (1909) house, and fantasized she was his daughter. He found her attractive and imagined the reason Freud was kind and patient with him was because he wanted him as a son-in-law, "At the same time he raised the wealth and position of my family to a level which agreed with the model he had in mind" (p. 199). Freud "moved up" in L's fantasy, in which he dreamed he married Freud's (fantasized) daughter for her money (p. 200). In exploring these fantasies, L remembered that years after his father's death, when L had sex for the first time, "an idea sprang into his mind: 'This is glorious! One might murder one's father for this!'" (p. 201). This evoked another memory, in which L remembered his father *had* interfered in his relationship with the lady he admired, advising him "to keep away from her, saying that it was imprudent of him and that he would only make a fool of himself" (p. 201).

Soon after, L's demeanor toward Freud (1909) shifted, "heaping the grossest and filthiest abuse upon me and my family" (p. 209). For example, he made a pun off Freud's name by calling his "daughter" a *Freudenhaus-Mädchen*, a girl from a "house of joy," (i.e., a prostitute). Still, Freud weathered these attacks and continued to treat L with care and respect. In one session, the young man was hungry and Freud had him fed (p. 303). Over the course of the session, Freud pointed out that L "was playing the part of a bad man in relation to me" (p. 314) to confirm he was the criminal he feared he was. L retorted it was *Freud* who was the criminal, as giving him time to eat was his ploy to prolong the treatment, and set about settling his "debt" by paying the fee and for the meal as well (p. 314).

L's attacks alternated with supplication, "'How can a gentleman like you, sir... let yourself be abused in this way by a low, good-for-nothing fellow like me? You ought to turn me out: that's all I deserve'" (Freud, 1909, p. 209). In quick succession L denigrated Freud, only to shift into a self state in which *he* was the lowly one. L paced around the room, with Freud encouraging him to keep putting his anxiety into words. Eventually L realized another reason he paced around the room—he feared Freud would beat him (p. 209). As Freud patiently listened, the young man remembered his father had "a passionate temper, and sometimes in his violence had not known where to stop" (p. 209). Freud's openness to L's wishes—to torture him *and* earn his love—helped him overcome his anxiety and connect how the father he loved was also a source of abuse. Then something unexpected arose. "Now it happened by chance," Freud writes, "—*for chance may play a part in the formation of a symptom*, just as the wording may help in the making of a joke—that one of his father's little adventures had an important element in common with the captain" (p. 210, emphasis added).

When L's father was a soldier he lost his money gambling—he was a *Spiel-ratte*, or "play-rat," German slang for "gambler." His father became indebted to a friend who paid his debts, but never paid the friend back, a lack of character that weighed heavily on L's image of him. These money troubles were what led his father to marry a woman of wealth rather than a woman he loved. Freud reasoned that when L's captain told him to "pay back" his debt, his unconscious heard it like an allusion to his father's unpaid debt—remember, it was L's captain who told him the story of the rat torture, and erroneously told L he owed another officer for his glasses. This created a conundrum. If L paid the debt, he would be "more moral" than his father, hence his father should be "punished" with the rat torture. Paying his "debt" also meant paying the woman at the post office. Pursuing a romance with her was akin to "punishing" the lady he admired for not loving him by pursuing a woman who *did*.

Freud (1909) realized L formed an association between rats (the rodents) and money. L hinted at this once when he reacted to the German word *Ratten* (rats) with the association *Raten*, meaning installments paid to fulfill a debt. Freud later learned that when he told L his fee, the patient said to himself "So many florins [a form of money], *so many rats*." By asking him to pay an imagined debt, L's captain inadvertently triggered his anxieties around his father's gambling debts, mediated by the word *Spielratte*. He felt abandoned by his nanny, who "moved up" in station by marrying a wealthy *Hof-rat*. L's conflicts, expressed through these linguistic associations, stemmed from anxieties around class and social position, around who his father married, and whom *he* was supposed to marry—the German word "to marry" being hei*rat*en.

The signifier *rat* was associated with how debt and the pressure to "move up" in status distorted such intimate matters as one's choice of partner, the relationship between parents and children, and whether one is at the mercy of others' wishes, and others' debts. L's obsession around the "rat torture" was an unconscious communication to his world: "Stick your money, your debts, and your wishes up your ass!" When L worked through these feelings—love and hate toward Freud, his father, his romantic interest—his obsessions abated. Something Freud (1909) said in passing, that "chance may play a part in the formation of a symptom" (p. 210), will have implications for how we conceive of the analytic cure. If we fall ill due to such chance encounters, then perhaps it is a new chance encounter that leads to change, loosening the core beliefs, fantasies, and associations that constrain our freedom.

Freud's Clinical Work Reconsidered

Freud was an active clinician who helped his patients feel safe enough to put their feelings into words, using techniques conversant with clinical work today such as empathy, reassurance, challenging distortions, repeating back evocative words, and even homework—such as requesting that L bring a photo of his lady. In the transference, Freud encouraged the patient to express their feelings toward him openly to draw out their fantasies in the here and now. He also understood how critical it is to not reinforce the patient's expectations of others. Although he did not theorize about this explicitly, we see examples of him behaving in ways that contrast with and disrupt his patient's transference expectations—a surprising, "chance" encounter with something *other* than their existing mappings of self and other.

Freud's attention to L's intergenerational, social, cultural, and linguistic context is also notable, illustrating a foundational precept for decolonial psychoanalysis—if we pay close attention to the patient's language, what at first appears like a personal drama reveals its embeddedness in a wider sociocultural network. Freud also centers the intergenerational transmission of trauma from father to son, where the illusion of harmony hides an abusive reality, with anxieties around love and class mobility texturing the transference, mediated by specific associations embedded in German language and culture. Freud could not have helped L without exquisite attention to the social, cultural, and linguistic context of treatment.

Active Therapy, The Principle of Frustration, and A "Psychotherapy for the People"

In the post-World War I world, Freud further evolved in his understanding of race, culture, and class amidst the rise of social democratic governments across Europe, while expanding the scope of technique in his paper at the 1918 Budapest Congress, "Lines of advance in psycho-analytic therapy" (Freud, 1918). Freud realized that a patient may "understand" their anxiety around certain feelings and why they avoid them, but if they do not work through their anxiety inside *and* outside the transference, they will struggle to change.

Freud (1918) points to Sandor Ferenczi's "active therapy" as a "unobjectionable and entirely justified" contribution in these efforts (p. 162). We will discuss active therapy in the next chapter in more detail. Active therapy stipulates that while much work takes place in the transference—through the therapeutic relationship—there also needs to be a "working through" outside in the patient's life. Inspired by active therapy, Freud discusses the principle of frustration, that "treatment should be carried through, as far as is possible, under privation—in a state of abstinence" (p. 162). Freud is emphatic he does not mean depriving the patient of warmth, referring instead to "the dynamics of falling ill and recovering" (p. 162). "[It] was a frustration that made the patient ill," Freud reminds us, "[and] his symptoms serve him as substitutive satisfaction" (pp. 162–163). He underscores that it was a frustration (e.g., trauma, loss, rejection) that led the patient to avoid in order to survive, producing a symptom that provides relief from a pain that is feared.

Freud's logic is "that the patient's suffering… not come to an end prematurely" (p. 163). Exposure to the patient's underlying anxiety then becomes central for change.

For example, if a patient with fears of intimacy is able to experience vulnerability and express their wish to be cared for (a) *without* avoidance, and (b) *without* their fear coming to pass (i.e., they are not abandoned), this will lead "to the symptoms having been taken apart and having lost their value" (p. 163). Treatment is effective when the patient learns to abstain from (i.e., chooses to not act out) their habitual ways of avoiding problems, so that new learning that allows greater freedom for their desire is possible, a reiterative process which requires working through in different areas of life in and outside the transference. In the process, older patterns of being, behaving, and relating are no longer needed.

The Supportive-Expressive Continuum: Helping the Patient Face Their Fears

Freud (1918) also noted that the patient may try to "compensate himself" for their traumas in the analyst, seeking the perfect parent they never had. "Some concessions must of course be made to him," he clarifies, "greater or less, according to the nature of the case and the patient's individuality" (p. 164). While Freud's practice shows he often did behave as the parent the patient "needed," he also believed it is not good to let these satisfactions "become too great." To cite a passage that sets the groundwork for connecting Freud and Fanon, he writes that any analyst who "out of the fullness of his heart" and desire to heal the patient

> extends to the patient all that one human being may hope to receive from another, *commits the same economic error as that of which our non-analytic institutions for nervous patients are guilty.* Their one aim is to make everything as pleasant as possible for the patient, so that he may feel well there and be glad to take refuge there again from the trials of life. In so doing they make no attempt to give him more strength for facing life and more capacity for carrying out his actual tasks in it. (p. 164, emphasis added)

Freud's point is that a clinician cannot be "everything" the patient needs. To attempt this risks providing a compensation that keeps treatment "stuck" in a split between the "bad" world "out there" and the microworld of the therapeutic relationship where the patient finds the *one* person who understands them. Ferenczi's counterpoint (see Chapter 3) is that sometimes people *do* need to feel the therapist is that "one person," using the experience to relearn how to do relationships.

I ask the reader to keep in mind the italicized fragment above for our discussion of Ferenczi and Fanon. Freud compares a therapist who protects the patient from "the trials of life" to inpatient units where patients are removed from the contexts that they struggle with. Without exposure to their conflicts under safer conditions the patient is deprived of the "strength for facing life." Freud (1918), perhaps being hyperbolic, argues the therapist should leave the patient "with unfulfilled wishes in abundance… [denying] him precisely those satisfactions which he desires most intensely" (p. 164). At the heart of Freud's insistence is a tension we refer to today between "being supportive" (e.g., creating a safe space) and "being expressive" (e.g., knowing when to push for change by exploring deeper, painful feelings) (Luborsky, 1984), also known in cognitive-behavioral circles as the tension between "acceptance" and "change" (Linehan, 2018)—with Freud and Ferenczi emphasizing different sides of this dialectic.

Freud (1918) also cautioned against analysts making "projects" out of their patients, turning them "into our private property, to decide his fate for him, to force our own ideals upon him, and with the pride of a Creator to form him in our own image and see that it is good" (p. 164). While he did not think sharing the same identities to be an absolute necessity, "I have been able to help people with whom I had nothing in common—neither race, education, social position nor outlook upon life in general" (p. 165), one should not be opposed to at times being a peer, teacher or mentor to the patient, though he again cautions, "the patient should be educated to liberate and fulfil his own nature, not to resemble ourselves" (p. 165).

Turning back to Ferenczi's active technique, Freud (1918) recognized the limitations of the "talking cure" in treating phobias: "One can hardly master a phobia if one waits till the patient lets the analysis influence him to give it up" (p. 166). In agoraphobia, for example, "one succeeds only when one can induce [the patient]… to go into the street and to struggle with their anxiety while they make the attempt" in progressive, incremental steps (p. 166). Freud applies this principle to compulsions, recommending a "counter-compulsion forcibly to suppress [them]" (p. 166), similar to contemporary treatments for obsessive–compulsive disorder such as exposure and response prevention. Privation and frustration, then, are Freud's words for exposing the patient to warded-off feelings while redirecting them from avoidant behavior. Freud here is not only "directive," but advocates for the role of *homework* in facing fears outside the session.

Freud (1918) closes by advocating for the widening of psychoanalysis toward the public good, calling for universal mental health care and a "psychotherapy for the people" that combined analytic treatment with other interventions such as Ferenczi's active therapy. He maintained that despite this integration, "its most effective and most important ingredients will assuredly remain those borrowed from strict and untendentious psychoanalysis" (p. 168). To the extent this entails working through resistance in the transference *and* the patient's life, we should indeed experiment freely with interventions that help patients feel less afraid of their experience.

Freud's Theory of Racism as Psychological Compensation

After 1918, Freud (1921) writes more about the role of culture, society, race, and class, recognizing that in the psyche "someone else is invariably involved, as a model, as an object, as a helper, as an opponent; and so from the very first individual psychology… is at the same time social psychology as well" (p. 69). The psyche is relational and communal, bound by intersecting identifications, "those of his race, of his class, of his creed, of his nationality, etc." (p. 129). It is here that Freud explores how we are defined not just by relationships, but by our social context.

Freud's (1927) critique of religion, *The Future of an Illusion*, has a critique of racial capitalism quietly nestled within it. He observes society is something "imposed on a resisting majority by a minority which understood how to obtain possession of the means to power and coercion" (p. 6). Social structures reflect "all the regulations necessary in order to adjust the relations of men to one another and especially the distribution of the available wealth" (p. 6). Humans themselves "come to function as wealth… in so far as the other person makes use of his capacity for work, or chooses him as a sexual object" (p. 6). Given the relationship between satisfaction and wealth, society develops various forms of control to "aim not only at effecting a certain distribution of wealth but at maintaining that distribution" (p. 6).

Ideology, which Freud (1927) calls society's "mental assets," works to "reconcile men to [society] and to recompense them for their sacrifices" (p. 10). Although Freud thought privation to be a part of life, he distinguished between "privations which affect everyone and privations which … [affect] only groups, classes or even single individuals" (p. 10). He names something Lacan drew from Marx—the "surplus of privation" of the oppressed results from the "surplus of enjoyment" of the oppressor (see Chapter 4). The oppressor's societal desires and laws are internalized in our super-ego, turning us "from being opponents of civilization into being its vehicles"

(p. 11). Inequality leads the working class to "envy the favoured ones their privileges and will do all they can to free themselves from their own surplus of privation" (p. 12). Exploitation yields an understandable response among the exploited, "an intense hostility towards a culture whose existence they make possible by their work, but in whose wealth they have too small a share" (p. 12). Such a society, Freud concludes, "neither has nor deserves the prospect of a lasting existence" (p. 12).

To manage class tensions, substitutive compensations are needed, such as providing comparisons with other cultures: "every culture claims the right to look down on the rest" (Freud, 1927, p. 13). Racism facilicates a cross-class pleasure the working class can also enjoy, "since the right to despise the people outside it compensates them for the wrongs they suffer within their own unit" (p. 13). Freud uses the same metaphor Marx drew upon when discussing racism: "No doubt one is a wretched plebeian, harassed by debts and military service; but, to make up for it, one is a Roman citizen, one has one's share in the task of ruling other nations and dictating their laws" (p. 13). Racism thus facilitates an identification between the exploited and the ruling elite, "in spite of their hostility to them they may see in them their ideals" (p. 13).

Freud (1927) turns to religion as the example *par excellence* of the illusions society serves up to compensate the privations of its working class. Focusing on "white Christian civilization" (he does not mince words), he argues that authoritarian religion attempts to "compensate them for the sufferings and privations which a civilized life… has imposed on them" (p. 18). In exchange for suffering on earth, the working class are rewarded by "going up" to Heaven. The power of oppressive religion comes from this compensation, a wish for "life everlasting" within a racial capitalist world that drains one of life. Alongside religion, race plays a powerful role for Freud (1921, p. 101), serving as a compensatory pleasure for whites, extracted through the privations visited upon the other—Jews and Black people among them.

We have here a direct connection between Freud's theory of symptoms as compensations and the sociopolitical that allows us to formulate how systems of oppression provide substitutive compensations in exchange for the deprivation and trauma they cause. Borrowing Freud's (1927) words, if we were to give up these substitutive compensations and concentrate our "liberated energies" on building a world for all, we can achieve "a state of things in which life will become tolerable for everyone and civilization no longer oppressive to anyone" (p. 50).

Race, Class, and Culture in Freud's Clinical Work

As stated earlier, there is a gap or "broken circuit" between Freud's social and cultural texts, and his clinical and theoretical writings. To repair this gap, I draw on some of his unpublished cases, the first of which is his treatment of Clarence Oberndorf, illustrating how he addressed race informed by his theory and technique. The second will focus on writer and poet Hilda Doolittle, whom Freud treated near the end of his life and where cultural differences played a central role in their therapeutic relationship. Through these examples we begin to integrate psychoanalysis' clinical and critical theory with its technique.

Love Between Whiteness, Jewishness, and Anti-Blackness

Clarence Oberndorf was an American Jew raised in Alabama, the son of Joseph Oberndorf, a Jewish emigré from eastern Europe, and Augusta Hammerstein, the sister of Broadway impresario Oscar Hammerstein (see Ginsburg, 2015). His father emigrated to the United States as a teenager to Alabama, where he lived with relatives from Bavaria who opened a small store. When his relatives went off to serve in the Confederate Army during the American Civil War, Joseph stayed behind to "mind the store" until his family returned and established a larger business in Selma. Oberndorf's mother Augusta emigrated from Germany to New York and later Selma, where Joseph became a successful businessman, an emblem of the "American Dream" in the shadow of Jim Crow. The two married and wanted to start a family, but experienced difficulties with their pregnancies—three of their children died post-partum. The pregnancy with Clarence also resulted in a complicated birth leaving him with facial deformities.

The infant Oberndorf struggled to recover from his injuries. According to his (1958) autobiography, he "remained alive during my first year chiefly because of the devotion of a Negro wet nurse and a conscientious small-town doctor" (p. 8). As he grew older he struggled to connect with his mother, who was "unpredictable, versatile and restless" (cited in Kubie, 1954, p. 547). By contrast, he fondly remembered the care he received from his Black wet nurse and other Black adults in his home in the Old South (Ginsburg, 2015). Oberndorf's (1958) early years were marked by a "Southern atmosphere colored in both senses by the Negroes of the household, to whom one habitually resorted for solace and advice" (p. 9).

After Oberndorf's father died, his mother moved them to New York where he attended Cornell University. He entered medical school in 1904, earning his MD in 1906 and pursuing psychoanalytic training, landing on Sigmund Freud's doorstep in 1921 for a personal analysis (Ginsburg, 2015). After the analysis, Oberndorf became a prolific clinician and scholar, serving as president of the New York Psychoanalytic Society, the American Psycho-analytic Association, and vice-president of the International Psychoanalytic Association (Isay, 1997, p. 136; Kubie, 1954). Oberndorf, who identified with his Jewishness (1958, p. 17), also helped organize the Committee for Mental Health among Jews in 1919—which later became New York's Hillside Hospital. The organization integrated psychoanalytic ideas with an understanding of how immigration, anti-Semitism, and economic disloca-tion impacted the mental health of the Jewish community (Goldstein, 2006, p.126), alongside a therapeutic home for children (Kubie, 1954).

Sharing a Jewish identity with Freud, Oberndorf felt at home with the elder analyst, suggesting they could conduct the analysis in German (Butts, 1975, p. 58). He was eager to learn from Freud, and be part of the first cohort to introduce psychoanalysis in community settings in the States. Here, the story becomes complicated—the analysis was broken off after five months.

By Oberndorf's (1958) account, he shared with Freud his childhood history, then committed himself to the fundamental rule. In one session, he shared a dream with Freud. In the dream, "I was on the driver's seat of an old-fashioned country wagon drawn by a white horse and a black horse" (p. 9), pulling in different directions toward somewhere unknown (cf. Butts, 1975, p. 59; Kardiner, 1977, p. 76). Oberndorf was shocked by Freud's response. Freud interpreted "that my life had unconsciously been under the influence of two fathers, a white father Joe, and a black father Joe" (p. 9). In this telling, Freud pointed out to Oberndorf that he was conflicted between his love for his biological father and for their coachman, who "had been a slave but taught me many things besides currying a horse and riding bareback" (p. 9). Obern-dorf does not go into detail as to why this interpretation ended the analysis. Abraham Kardiner (1977), in his memoir of his analysis with Freud, told another version of the story Freud shared with him (not a great move from a confidentiality standpoint). The dream "hit" one of Oberndorf's "weak spots," as Freud interpreted that he "could never marry because he didn't know whether to choose a white woman or a black woman, and so he was in a quandary" (p. 76). Kardiner noted, in passing, that Oberndorf remained single until his death. According to Kardiner, the interpretation "infuriated" Oberndorf, and they argued about it for months until *Freud* discontinued the analysis.

In her analysis of this episode, June Dobbs Butts (1975) unpacks how Freud's interpretation hit on an unresolved conflict between competing forces in Oberndorf's psyche:

> On the one hand there was his biologically real white Mother whom society esteemed but whom he found to be personally withdrawn as a Mother; on the other hand there was his caretaker since birth, a Black Mammy whom society devalued as a woman but whom he found to be personally warm and invaluable as a mother figure. (p. 59)

Butts notes how Oberndorf's version in his autobiography may have been symptomatic, feeling it preferable to share a conflict between two fathers than between two mothers. She frames his conflict as one between competing, racially reified images of love, status, and power, turning white women but especially Black women into stereotyped *images* (cold but valued, warm and devalued, respectively) which impeded his ability to relate to women as real people.

Oberndorf enacted an intergenerational transmission of contradictions. Both sides of his family were Jews who immigrated from Germany's anti-Semitic milieu, and he was no stranger to the struggles of Jewish emigrés fleeing Europe. Yet, his family also fought in the Civil War *on the side of the Confederacy*, benefiting from the South's concentration of capital as business owners. This societal context facilitated his family's ascent into whiteness, punctuated by the fact that between childhood trauma, his father's death, and his mother's unpredictability, he felt love and care from a Black woman and the Black staff in his house. This too is punctured by social realities, as many of them were emancipated from slavery before his birth and likely suffered the violence of Jim Crow that subjugated them and privileged *him*. The love he received operated within the logics of continued anti-Black domination (see Hartman, 1997).

We have here a unique example of Freud taking race, culture, and context into account, integrating his clinical theory, critical theory, and clinical technique contextualizing the psychic in the social, with a symbol in a dream (a carriage drawn by black-and-white horses) interpreted back to its unconscious, racialized context. Oberndorf's indecision in choosing a romantic partner fulfilled a racist compromise formation. If he married a white woman, he would be in a "socially sanctioned" relationship yet his "template" for white women, derived from his experience with his mother, was that they are cold and erratic. If he married a Black woman, his "template" predicted someone who could love him *yet* would be socially devalued. In both versions, Freud draws attention to the psychological function of Oberndorf's racism.

However, we also find the enactment of *Freud's* blind spots when he fought Oberndorf over this interpretation for months, eventually breaking off the treatment. As a Jew navigating an anti-Semitic world that associated Jewishness with Blackness (see Chapter 1), Freud likely saw *too much* of himself in Oberndorf, identifying with his position as a Jew as a source of ongoing anxiety. Although Freud would speak ill of Oberndorf, his estimation of the treatment's impact is interesting—"he made an experience which will do him some good" (Freud, 1921/1993, p. 458). How did the analysis impact Oberndorf's life? As Kubie (1954) noted, Oberndorf returned from Europe an evangelist for community psychoanalysis and social justice, as reflected in his writings.

In a paper entitled "Co-Conscious Mentation," Oberndorf (1941) wrote about splitting, dissociation, and de-personalization, "The coexistence [sic] of *double consciousness* or of two fairly distinctly formed superego streams… strives to drive the ego in opposite directions" (p. 52, emphasis added). The language here is striking (had he read Du Bois?), citing Ferenczi's work on how the psyche is "split" between "two antagonistic superegos … [who] regard each other intensively, vigilantly and belligerently" (p. 52). He compares this "double consciousness" to a horse being ridden by two riders— one in white, the other in black—"the clashing riders attempt to direct the horse oppositely" (p. 53). The black horse is confused by these two riders, leaving the horse helpless and "not itself." Oberndorf identifies this analogy of unconscious conflict in cases of "indecision," an internal debate that leaves the patient unable to take action in accord with coherent wants and values. Note Oberndorf's metaphor for "double consciousness" as a mind split by conflict and indecision pulled in opposite directions. It seems the motif of "black" and "white" riders and horses made an impression following his analysis with Freud.

His (1954) other works focus on race and the therapeutic relationship. He talks about the antidemocratic nature of racism, and the need to oppose legalized segregation, writing that segregation "is disadvantageous to those who are excluded and probably ultimately automatically harmful to those who are presumably privileged" (p. 754). He called for a psychoanalysis "For the sick without regard to race, creed or color," advocating for cultural competence in psychoanalytic therapy through close attention to the patient's language, culture, race, and ethnicity, alongside addressing one's blind spots and biases (pp. 754–756). Oberndorf argued that attending to culture was an important component of building trust across difference in successful treatment, but was also aware that there were cultural affinities and a sense of safety that Black, Latinx, and indigenous patients might experience with clinicians who shared their cultural background—which they may not experience with him as a white Jewish man.

Oberndorf (1954), a past president of the American Psychoanalytic Association, was especially sensitive to how psychoanalysis turned away from social concerns in America and toward "capitalistic thinking" among private practitioners (p. 756), along with the rise of the image of the "neutral" Freud popular among Americans. While he acknowledged that Freud theoretically "was inclined to avoid decisions of an ethical or moral nature in the treatment of social problems which enter into all mental illness," speaking from personal experience with "Freud's procedure and actual practice, he deviated *frequently* from this scientific, impersonal conception" (p. 758, emphasis added).

Oberndorf (1954) contrasts the aspiration to neutrality and "objectivity" with Freud's practice, which he notes is closer to the "sensitive Ferenczi" who "abandoned the cool, passive technique in favor of actual encouragement of the patient in one direction or the other, giving consideration to moral and ethical factors" (p. 758). Presciently, Oberndorf predicted that clinicians of color might "apply the Ferenczi technique with a very different slant" (p. 758). Given how—with the exception of Lacan's adherents—the early decolonial analysts leaned toward a relational-interpersonal stance (see Chapter 1), Oberndorf had a point, and one which applies to Fanon as well. He concludes by drawing attention to the relationship between mental health and sociocultural pressures with the dominant culture, stressing that "The concept of an autonomous individual is imaginal" (p. 758).

Judging by Oberndorf's commitment to desegregation, cultural competence, and bringing psychoanalysis to the poor and marginalized it seems the analysis with Freud had quite an impact on him. Although he never married, he sublimated his conflict by working to end segregation in psychiatric units and advocating for social-cultural factors in psychoanalysis (Ginsburg, 2015, p. 2). In contrast, Oberndorf's assessment of American psychoanalysis converged with Lacan's, in that it had "become legitimate and respectable… sluggish and smug, hence attractive to an increasing number of minds which found security in conformity" (cited in Isay, 1997, p. 136).

Freud's Broaching of Cultural Difference: The Case of Hilda Doolittle

The last case we review integrates many of the aforementioned themes— Freud's clinical theory, critical theory, and clinical technique. Hilda Doolittle was a white American poet born in Bethlehem, Pennsylvania in the late 1800s, a prodigious writer who struggled with unresolved trauma from the First World War, dissociation, splitting and conflict in her relationships (Lohser & Newton, 1996, p. 41). The loss of her brother during the war, her father soon after, and a miscarriage led her into a deep depression. She then had a second pregnancy which survived to term, but she and her child were infected by the Spanish flu, a traumatic brush with death. Although they survived, the repeated loss and trauma in her life was too much to bear.

Doolittle tried psychoanalysis with two other analysts in as many years before calling on Freud, arriving at 19 Berggasse in 1933 anxious and over-whelmed. Freud's kindly invitation, "Enter, fair madam," did not assuage her, and she actively thought about leaving the appointment. Doolittle regulated herself by focusing on Freud's art collection, or distracting herself with his dog Yofi who greeted her in his office. Freud listened to her story, then invited her to lie on the couch. Noting the previous treatments she had abandoned, he was direct: "I see you are going to be very difficult… I will tell you something: YOU *WERE* DISAPPOINTED, AND YOU *ARE* DISAPPOINTED IN ME" (Lohser & Newton, 1996, p. 41). Doolittle was struck, screaming at him, "do you not realize you are everything, you are priest, you are magician." She came to see the father of psychoanalysis. How could he think she was disappointed in him? "No," he replied, "It is you who are poet and magician" (p. 41).

This simple intervention highlighted that although Doolittle sought Freud as the great "priest and magician," she tended to reject her therapists, abandoning them to prevent being abandoned *by* them. Freud pointed out her non-verbal behavior, noting that since entering his office she "had preferred to look at the art objects rather than at him" (Lohser & Newton, 1996, p. 41). Doolittle protested, noting his dog Yofi welcomed her, and that Freud must like her as well. He laughed, saying "Like me and you like my dog." Doolittle corrected him. Perhaps he meant to cite the saying, "Love me, love my dog"? Made aware of how he misspoke, Freud apologized and broached their cultural differences, offering that it must be difficult for someone with a gift of language such as her to listen to his bad English (p. 41).

This made Doolittle anxious, replying, "in looking at antiquity [the art in his office] I was looking at [you]," commenting on their similarity as lovers of history (Lohser & Newton, 1996, p. 41). In discussing her losses in the war, Freud commented again on their differences—he remarked that she was English woman from the United States, and asked what that "made him." Doolittle replied, "he was a Jew." "That too was a religious bond," Freud responded, "as [the] Jew was the only member of antiquity that still lived in the world" (p. 42). Freud intuited that Doolittle, a white American woman, might have some feelings about his Jewishness, and broached the subject to make it safer for linguistic and ethnic differences to be present "in the room." This made her feel safe enough to acknowledge that she *did* feel disappointed—as she was taller than him. She felt uncomfortable with her height as a tall woman, and did not want to be the "grown-up" in the room. With humor, Freud asked her to stand next to him, joking she was not that much taller than him. As she was leaving the session, Freud pointed out her bags were still on the couch, implying her desire to stay. This moved Doolittle, who decided to come back and continue treatment (p. 42).

At their next session, Freud noticed Doolittle's anxiety and invited her into the next room, walking alongside her while they connected again over their love of art and mythology to help her calm down. He broached the subject of religion and culture in Doolittle's family, noting the meaning of her place of birth, Bethlehem, and her family's Moravian background. The Moravian church was persecuted by the Catholic church and, coincidentally, Moravia is where Freud and his family were from. "You were born in Bethlehem?" Freud asked, "It is inevitable that the Christian myth..." he stopped himself. He realized his assumptions as an atheist might be disrespectful to her, who seemed sensitive to their cultural differences, so he checks in: "This does not offend you?" "Offend me?" she replies in surprise. "My speaking of your religion in terms of myth?" Doolittle (1956) replied that she was not offended but appreciated his curiosity about her faith (p. 123). Reading the text of her memoir, it also seems possible she was moved by a sensitivity and care on Freud's part she likely had not experienced before from another person. As she delved deeper into her losses, she talked about her daughter surviving the Spanish flu, which moved Freud. He disclosed he remembered the Spanish flu all too well, having lost his daughter Sophie to it. He showed her a picture of his daughter kept close in a locket attached to his watch chain (Lohser & Newton, 1996, p. 45).

Freud's vulnerability had an impact on Doolittle, further closing the gap between them. She shared more freely, describing how after the Spanish flu and the dissolution of her marriage (her husband had an affair), she met the English novelist and poet Annie Winifred Ellerman, known by the pen name Bryher. The two fell in love, starting an open relationship. At the same time, Doolittle also met the sexologist Havelock Ellis, toward whom she had unrequited feelings—and found her dissociative episodes worsening. Freud commented on what a vivid storyteller she was, "Ah, you tell this all so beautifully" (p. 45). There was not a hint of judgment as he discussed the possibility Doolittle was bisexual, and perhaps alongside her losses was also struggling with her identity in a rejecting world. As Lohser and Newton (1996) relate, Freud asked her at the end of the session "whether she was feeling lonely" (p. 45). At another session, Doolittle showed him a picture of Bryher, of whom he approved (p. 46).

After Doolittle disclosed her worsening dissociative episodes, Freud no longer insisted she use the couch and started working face to face, which helped her stay regulated as she processed her trauma. He was always aware, however, that she was holding something back. In one session he commented she had an interesting expression on her face but could not read it. She broke down in tears, becoming aware there *was* a subject she avoided since the beginning. Freud picked up that her anxiety may be related to his being Jewish, but changed gears thinking perhaps it was his age, wondering if she kept her distance because she feared he would "abandon" her by dying from old age, "The trouble is—I am an old man—*you do not think it worth your while to love me*" (cited in Lohser & Newton, 1996, p. 48, emphasis original). To address her fears of abandonment, Freud committed to seeing her even when he was seriously ill with cancer.

But this was not quite it either. Doolittle realized she was avoiding talking about the German atrocities being committed against the Jews, and how the Nazi fervor spread to Vienna itself. One day, on the way to her session she saw pamphlets strewn across the ground, "Hitler gives bread," "Hitler gives work." Also drawn across the pavement were chalk swastikas: "I followed them down Berggasse as if they had been chalked on the pavement especially for my benefit. They led to the Professor's door…" (Doolittle, 1956, p. 59). In a sense, they *were* to her benefit as a white gentile woman, and a threat to Freud as a Jewish man. Doolittle was not rejecting Freud because he was Jewish. She *attached* to him as someone who showed her kindness as a trauma victim and was accepting of her as a bisexual woman. She feared Freud's death not of old age, but of him being murdered by fascists as a Jew. Still, Doolittle met Freud's commitment to the treatment with her own, *working through* her fears of abandonment.

Freud continued to nip at the edges of her resistance with questions, reflections, gentle inquiries, and challenges. In another session, he said he could tell that there was something she did not want them to analyze. Doolittle feared he would find out about her ever-present fear of the Nazis taking his life. She had built a relationship where she did not fear that Freud as a person would disappoint or abandon her, but as Lohser and Newton (1996) write, she "was constantly worried that death would end their relationship. She still could not talk about this fear. But Freud understood what was on her mind" (p. 47). He started alluding to the theme of death in the room. She began to open up, saying she was afraid as death had touched many of her relationships. Freud replied that "the process of psychoanalysis itself was like death" (cited in p. 48).

Finally, Doolittle shares a fantasy that she and her fears are like a tiger, ready to pounce. What if it were to attack the "frail and delicate old Professor?" She begins to express her "*terrors of the present situation*; the lurking 'beast' may or might destroy him," (emphasis added) then catches herself, saying this is just a childhood fantasy. What if her fears were to come true? Although the truth was left unsaid overtly, Freud received the message. He replies, "'I have my protector.' He indicates Yofi, the little lioness curled at his feet" (cited in Lohser & Newton, 1996, p. 50; cf. Doolittle, 1956, p. 150). Doolittle's fantasy of the Nazis as a tiger or "lurking beast," and Freud's remark that his dog Yofi is a "little lioness" who will protect him is not an accident. We will return to this motif of Freud's associating race and devouring lions (see Chapter 6). For now, what Doolittle could not put into words was expressed indirectly. Freud read between the lines, and communicated between them as well.

On May 1, 1933, Doolittle made her regular commute to Freud's office even as the Nazis occupied Vienna. She was interrogated by soldiers on the way to the opera the previous night, which worried him, and he warned her not to go outside. Still, she ventured out. When she arrived, she discovered she was the only patient to come that day. "But why did you come?" Freud clamored, "No one has come here today, *no one*" (cited in Lohser & Newton, 1996, p. 64, emphasis added). She realized she "made a unique gesture" that surprised Freud. "He could not be thinking, I am an old man—*you do not think it worth your while to love me*," she thought, "Or if he remembered having said that, this surely was the answer to it" (p. 65, emphasis original).

Doolittle was able to accept her sexuality and find peace, her poetry helping her process the splits between her many selves. She wrote to her partner Bryher, "the conflict consists partly that what I write commits me— to one sex, or the other, I no longer HIDE" (cited in Lohser & Newton, 1996, p. 74). Doolitle felt valued by Freud and came to value him, but she also surprised Freud, her love shaking a vulnerable part of him. Though Freud mused that "the secret of therapy is to cure through love," he did not theorize on how the patient can move the therapist as part of therapeutic action, something elaborated by his prodigal son, Sandor Ferenczi.

Coda

Harumi Setouchi was a literary force in 1960s Japan, but now she was in crisis as her romantic difficulties took their toll on her (see Harding, 2022). Her friends intervened, referring her to a retired doctor who trained with Freud in the 1930s. Setouchi knocked on the door of Heisaku Kosawa, who came out of retirement for one last analysis. She remembered his gentle demeanor as he listened intently to her troubles. He invited her to recline on the couch, sitting just behind her head. "Now that your eyes are closed," he guided her, "you'll be seeing images floating up in front of you. I want you just to name each one as it appears. As though you're on a train looking out of the window, watching the scenery pass before you" (p. 50).

Setouchi felt a lightness after each session, experiencing Kosawa's technique of "melting" defenses with a tender voice and a caring attitude (Harding, 2022, p. 51). She "lived through" a new relationship which helped her feel *seen*, an experience she brought to her later work as a Buddhist monk, reflected in the name she chose for herself—Jakuchō, which means "silent, lonely listening." Although she was a vocal anti-war activist and advocate for women's rights, she also became a renown counselor. Whenever people came to her for counseling, she listened intently and at the end of the session offered a little compliment, just as Kosawa often did. "When people are suffering," she shares, "they need someone to notice them, simply to recognise them. So when someone… comes to me now, I think to myself, 'What was it that Kosawa did for me?'" (cited in p. 52).

Decades earlier, in a 1931 letter to Freud, Kosawa described the repetition compulsion as the "redemption of Buddha," reflecting on how patients are not just stuck in vicious cycles of behavior, but seek a "complete death" beyond them—a life beyond repetition (Harding, 2022, p. 53, fn. 62). If to be "Freudian" is to be an empathic and culturally responsive presence who works with the unconscious to seek this life beyond death, then every clinician in this book is a Freudian. Decolonial psychoanalysis uncovers this "Freud from below," but it is not always found in the overt discussion of politics and culture, class and race, gender and sexuality. Decolonial psychoanalysis is often found in moments of tenderness, moments of meeting, moments—as Fanon once wrote—in which another feels heard and understood, perhaps at last (see Chapter 6).

Reflection Questions

- Compromise formations are patterns of thinking, feeling, and behavior we develop to survive and get our needs met, often a balance between different benefits and costs. Thinking of yourself, what patterns do you notice help you in some ways but not others? Thinking of your patients, how can formulating their behavior as serving a function that helps them survive help you empathize with their difficulties?
- Freud could be direct, but also used the dynamisms of speech to "talk around" certain topics (see the case of L above). Are there moments in treatment where you "talked around" difficult topics to help your patients approach them? What was that like for you? If you have not tried it before, what would it be like to phrase your interventions this way? For example, instead of "How did that make you feel?" saying, "I wonder what came up for you."
- Freud was more direct in addressing culture and race with Oberndorf compared with Doolittle, with whom he was more indirect and tentative. How do we make clinical decisions on how and when to address culture and identity in psychotherapy? When does it make sense to bring it up directly? When is it more effective to be more cautious and exploratory?

Further Reading

Contemporary Freudian Perspectives
- Christian, C. (2015). Intersubjectivity and modern conflict theory. *Psychoanalytic Psychology, 32*(4), 608–625.
- Ellman, S. (1991/2018). *Freud's Technique Papers*. Routledge.
- Robinson, K., & Schachter, J. (Eds). (2020). *The contemporary Freudian tradition: Past and present*. Routledge.

Contemporary Freudian Approaches to Culture and Identity
- Padrón, C. (2022). Other Lullabies: Attacks on Blackness, Confusion of Tongues, and the Loss of Play. *Journal of Infant, Child, and Adolescent Psychotherapy, 21*(2), 97–107.
- Moskowitz, M. (2022). How I came to understand white privilege. In B. Stoute & M. Slevin (Eds.), *The Trauma of Racism: Lessons from the therapeutic encounter*. Taylor & Francis.

References

Bettelheim, B. (1984). *Freud and man's soul*. Vintage.

Bromberg, P. M. (2003). Something wicked this way comes: Trauma, dissociation, and conflict: The space where psychoanalysis, cognitive science, and neuroscience overlap. *Psychoanalytic Psychology, 20*(3), 558–574.

Butts, J. D. (1975). Inextricable Aspects of Sex and Race. Paper presented at the Five College Black Studies Seminar Series.

Doolittle, H. (1956). *Tribute to Freud*. New Directions.

Ellman, S. (1991/2018). *Freud's Technique Papers*. Routledge.

Falzeder, E. (2019). *Psychoanalytic filiations: Mapping the psychoanalytic movement*. Routledge.

Fanon, F. (1952/2008). *Black Skin, White Masks*. Pluto Press.

Freud, S. (1895/1950). Project for a scientific psychology. In *The standard edition of the complete psychological works of Sigmund Freud I (1886–1899): Pre-Psycho-Analytic Publications and Unpublished Drafts* (pp. 95–397). Psychoanalytic Electronic Publishing.

Freud, S. (1909/1955). Notes upon a case of obsessional neurosis. In *The standard edition of the complete psychological works of Sigmund Freud X: Two case histories (Little Hans and The Rat Man)* (pp. 151–318). Psychoanalytic Electronic Publishing.

Freud, S. (1911). Formulations on the two principles of mental functioning. In *The standard edition of the complete psychological works of Sigmund Freud, Volume XII (1911–1913): The case of schreber, papers on technique and other works* (pp. 213–226). Psychoanalytic Electronic Publishing.

Freud, S. (1912). Recommendations to physicians practising psycho-analysis. In *The standard edition of the complete psychological works of Sigmund Freud, Volume XII (1911–1913): The case of schreber, papers on technique and other works* (pp. 109–120). Psychoanalytic Electronic Publishing.

Freud, S. (1913). On beginning the treatment (Further Recommendations on the Technique of Psycho-Analysis I). In *The standard edition of the complete psychological works of Sigmund Freud, Volume XII (1911–1913): The case of schreber, papers on technique and other works* (pp. 121–144). Psychoanalytic Electronic Publishing.

Freud, S. (1914). Remembering, repeating and working-through (Further recommendations on the technique of psycho-analysis II). In *The standard edition of the complete psychological works of Sigmund Freud, Volume XII (1911–1913): The case of schreber, papers on technique and other works* (pp. 145–156). Psychoanalytic Electronic Publishing.

Freud, S. (1915). The unconscious. In *The standard edition of the complete psychological works of Sigmund Freud Volume XIV (1914–1916): On the history of the psycho analytic movement, papers on metapsychology, and other works* (pp. 159–215). Psychoanalytic Electronic Publishing.

Freud, S. (1918/1955). Lines of advance in psycho-analytic therapy. In *The standard edition of the complete psychological works of Sigmund Freud, Volume XVII (1917–1919): An infantile neurosis and other works* (pp. 157–168). Psychoanalytic Electronic Publishing.

Freud, S. (1920/1955). Beyond the pleasure principle. In *The standard edition of the complete psychological works of Sigmund Freud, Volume XVIII (1920–1922): Beyond the pleasure principle, group psychology and other works* (pp. 1–64). Psychoanalytic Electronic Publishing.

Freud, S. (1921). *Group psychology and the analysis of the ego*. W. W. Norton.

Freud, S. (1921/1993). December 9 letter to Ernest Jones. In R. A. Paskauskas (Ed.), *The complete correspondence of Sigmund Freud and Ernest Jones, 1908–1939* (pp. 446–447). Harvard University Press.

Freud, S. (1924). The economic problem of masochism. In *The standard edition of the complete psychological works of Sigmund Freud 19* (pp. 155–170). Psychoanalytic Electronic Publishing.

Freud, S. (1925). An autobiographical study. In J. Strachey (Ed.), *The standard edition of the complete psychological works of Sigmund Freud, volume XX (1925–1926): An autobiographical study, inhibitions, symptoms, and anxiety, the question of lay analysis and other works, 1–292* (pp. 1–74). Hogarth Press.

Freud, S. (1927). The future of an illusion. In J. Strachey (Ed.), *The standard edition of the complete psychological works of Sigmund Freud, volume XXI (1927–1931): The future of an illusion, civilization and its discontents, and other works* (pp. 1–56). Hogarth Press.

Ginsburg, L. M. (2015, October 22). An elegy for Clarence P. Oberndorf, M. D. (1882–1954). Posted on inter nationalpsychoanalysis.net. Retrieved on May 20, 2018.

Goldstein, J. S. (2006). *Inventing Great Neck: Jewish Identity and the American Dream*. Rutgers University Press.

Harding, C. (2022). The therapeutic method of Kosawa Heisaku: "Religion" and "the Psy Disciplines." *The Journal of the Japanese Psychoanalytic Society, 4*, 42–58.

Hart, A. (2022). Neutrality as a "White Lie": Discussion of Gabbard, Holmes, and Portuges. *Journal of the American Psychoanalytic Association, 70*(2), 335–349.

Hartman, S. V. (1997). *Scenes of Subjection: Terror, Slavery, and Self-making in Nineteenth-century America*. Oxford University Press.

Isay, R. (1997). *Being homosexual*. Avon.

Kardiner, A. (1977). *My analysis with Freud: Reminiscences*. Norton.

Kubic, L. S. (1954). In memoriam: Clarence P. Oberndorf, M. D. (1882–1954). *Journal of the American Psychoanalytic Association, 2*, 546–552.

Linehan, M. M. (2018). *Cognitive-behavioral treatment of borderline personality disorder*. Guilford Publications.

Lohser, B., & Newton, P. M. (1996). *Unorthodox Freud*. Guilford.

Luborsky L. (1984). *Principles of psychoanalytic psychotherapy: A manual for supportive expressive treatments*. Basic Books.

Lynn, D. J., & Vaillant, G. E. (1998). Anonymity, neutrality, and confidentiality in the actual methods of Sigmund Freud: A review of 43 cases, 1907–1939. *American Journal of Psychiatry, 155*(2), 163–171.

Oberndorf, C. P. (1941). Co-conscious mentation. *Psychoanalytic Quarterly, 10*, 44–65.

Oberndorf, C. P. (1954). Selectivity and option for psychiatry. *American Journal of Psychiatry, 110*(10), 754–758.

Oberndorf, C. P. (1958). *An Autobiographical Sketch*. Cornell University Infirmary & Clinic.

Siegel, D. J. (2012). *The developing mind: How relationships and the brain interact to shape who we are*. Guilford Publications.

Wachtel, P. L. (2017). The ambiguities of neutrality: Comment on Gelso and Kanninen. *Journal of Psychotherapy Integration, 27*(3), 342–349.

Yeomans, F., Clarkin, J. F., & Kernberg, O. F. (2015). *Transference-focused psychotherapy for borderline personality disorder: A clinical guide*. American Psychiatric Publishers.

3

The Promises and Limitations of Relational-Interpersonal Psychoanalysis: Returning to Ferenczi's Legacy

Fanon (1965) was exquisitely attuned to the therapist's participation in ruptures, moments of tension between patient and therapist that can take the form of overt confrontation, but often are subtle corrosions of trust and safety leading both to withdraw in the relationship. Fanon calls on clinicians "to analyze, patiently and lucidly, each one of the reactions of the colonized, and every time we do not understand, we must tell ourselves that we are at the heart of the drama" (p. 125). Fanon's recognition of the therapist as an active participant, especially in therapeutic impasses, reflect his immersion in Sandor Ferenczi's work on the therapeutic relationship as a source of trauma and transformation. Ferenczi (1933/1994c) teaches us that patients are often deeply attuned to "the wishes, tendencies, whims, sympathies and antipathies of their analyst, even if the analyst is completely unaware of this sensitivity" (p. 157). The therapist enacts their biases, prejudices, and reactions in subtle behaviors signaling what is and is not allowed, an unconscious world the patient must adapt to in order to be loved. Ferenczi calls on us to listen not just for the patient's past but also their traumatic present with the therapist—something Fanon resonated with.

Sandor Ferenczi's thinking is foundational to contemporary psychotherapy writ large, foreshadowing developments in British object-relations theory (Gutiérrez-Peláez & Herrera-Pardo, 2017), humanistic psychotherapy (Hoffman, 2003), self-psychology (Rachman, 2013), and relational and interpersonal psychoanalysis (Dimitrijević, Cassullo, & Frankel, 2018). Even Lacan—who was critical of Ferenczi—was engaged by his writings (Gutiérrez-Peláez, 2015). In this chapter I review Ferenczi's clinical theory,

D. J. Gaztambide, *Decolonizing Psychoanalytic Technique*, https://doi.org/10.1007/978-3-031-48476-6_3

political thinking, and evolution as a clinician culminating in his posthumous *Clinical Diary*, and trace how Ferenczi's clinical theory gestures toward a theory of the social he struggled to integrate into his clinical practice. By connecting the "circuits" between his theory, critical thinking, and clinical work, we consider the promises and limitations of relational and interpersonal approaches, laying the groundwork for how Fanon reimagined clinical work beyond the two-person interaction.

Political Ferenczi: From the 1900s to the 1920s

Ferenczi's early work was surprisingly attentive to race, gender, sexuality, and class. In 1902 he was actively involved in the treatment of poor and displaced people at St. Elizabeth's Hospital in Hungary, including gay, lesbian, and gender-nonconforming people facing marginalization and persecution, leading him to advocate for queer rights (Rachman, 1993). Ferenczi was also an active participant in Jung and Freud's 1910 correspondence on anti-Semitism and anti-Blackness as psychological compensations, leading to a related 1910 letter to Freud in which he argued that sociopolitical tensions are enacted in analytic work. "[W]e investigate the real conditions in the various levels of society," he wrote, "cleansed of all hypocrisy and conventionalism, just as they are mirrored in the individual" (Brabant et al., 1994, p. 153). To illustrate his point, he told Freud about the treatment of a print shop owner which exposed "all his swindles" to get around worker protection policies, marking the earliest recognition in psychoanalysis of how society is "mirrored" in the psyche.

In a later paper, Ferenczi (1922/1994b) analyzed the hollow life of a middle-upper-class woman who sought to "enliven" herself by exotifying the workers who served her family as well as those outside her ethnicity—for example, marrying a Jewish man to spite her parents. Ferenczi analyzed how people fantasize about "rising" or "sinking" in social status, associating those "lower" on a hierarchy as being closer to "nature," both desired and despised (p. 416). He (1922/1994c) also commented on the analyst's relational and political power in his review of Freud's book *Group Psychology*, writing that in treatment "the physician is the representative of the whole of human society... he has the power to loose or bind" (p. 376). Ferenczi suggests that relational and political dynamics are enacted with the therapist who, as an authority figure, can either help loosen or bind—i.e., render more rigid—the patient's mappings of self and world.

Politically, Ferenczi advocated for redistribution and taxing the rich (Erös, 2014), and like Freud contributed to a theory of "surplus repression" under capitalism, alongside a critique of fascism that became central to Freudo-Marxist thinking (Erös, 1990). Ferenczi (1909/1994c) also wrote about how education can be a source of psychic and social repression, examined the relationship between capitalist accumulation, money, and pleasure (1914/1994a), and drew attention to the relationship between psychic and social "diseases," advocating for a socialism that "cares also for individual welfare as well as for the interests of society" (1913/1994b, p. 433). His politics informed his clinical thinking on the victim's identification with the aggressor, an idea foundational to liberation and decolonial psychology (Gaztambide, 2019). By the mid/late-1920s, however, Ferenczi's work became more "clinical," moving away from this political emphasis for reasons underscored by the rise of the Nazis and his growing vulnerability as Jewish man.

Reckoning with Pain and Pleasure, Love and Hate, Self and Other

In a paper entitled "The problem of acceptance of unpleasant ideas," Ferenczi (1926/1994b) explores the dynamics of pleasure and pain that organize the psyche. Our need to protect ourselves often leads us to choose a more manageable pain we feel is safer than another, more catastrophic pain, so that "the less painful becomes relatively pleasurable" (p. 369). The relative *absence* of pain due to the "avoidance of a still greater 'pain'" underlies the mechanics of compensation (p. 369). Understanding that symptoms serve a function, a *purpose*, in our "psychical mathematics" (p. 370) sheds light on our investment in behaviors that cause suffering.

In discussing early attachment, Ferenczi describes the infant as "reckoning" or "testing" the environment's capacity to meet their needs. A child may have their needs met consistently, yet suddenly finds herself experiencing hunger and thirst. After a period of uncertainty, the parent arrives with nurture and nourishment. The parent's timely arrival constitutes them as a *real*, separate other with their own autonomy, no longer an extension of the child. The parent becomes "an object of love and hate, of hate because of its being temporarily unobtainable, and of love because after this loss it offers a still more intense satisfaction" (p. 371). Ruptures are not obstacles to love per se. Rather, they serve a function to let the other know something is not working. They are love's very vehicle when repair arrives in good-enough time. Paraphrasing a well-known relational-interpersonal mantra, it is not the presence of rupture but the absence of repair that is the determining factor, whether for parent and child or patient and therapist.

That which satisfies our needs we reckon as part of our sense of "I," while what we perceive as hostile we deny or erase (Ferenczi, 1926/1994b, p. 371). But those whom "we love because they bring us satisfaction, and hate because they do not submit to us in everything," we reckon as *real*, "we are glad when we find them again in reality, i.e. when we are able to love them once more" (p. 371). Reckoning with reality involves the pain of integrating our love and hate for the same person, for love as such is on the other side of that pain. "[T]he mutual binding of attracting and repelling forces," Ferenczi writes, "is… in every compromise-formation and in every objective observation" (p. 372). For Ferenczi (1988) love and hate parallel Freud's aggressive and life instincts; he calls them "drives for self-assertion and conciliation" (p. 41).

The symptom reflects not only our choosing a more manageable pain to cope with a more painful reality, but also how that symptom helps resolve an interpersonal quandary. For example, the same experience of neglect and abandonment could lead one person to be more interpersonally dominant and controlling to "prevent" loss, whereas another person may become increasingly submissive and conciliatory, in the hopes that if they placate and take care of others their needs will be met. In both cases, the boundary between self and other becomes porous, having the "paradoxical" effect of pushing others away.

Reckoning With the World, Renouncing Our Dominance, Negating Our Negation

To recognize the external world is to realize that what is "good" does not belong to me, others have good in them too. We also learn that something unpleasant or "bad" is part of "me," and that we are not "all good." A further step is made when the child recognizes their unrealistic wishes and compensations must be "renounced" (Ferenczi, 1926/1994b, p. 374), including the desire of control over the other. This recognition of others as separate beings is made possible by love, an act of vulnerability, "a sacrifice of our narcissism" (p. 377; cf. 374).

Ferenczi (1926/1994b) is cognizant about his use of the word "reckon," and his reference to the psyche as a "reckoning-machine." When we give up repression, we have a *reckoning* with the world. We engage in unconscious "tests" of the world, perceiving it moment to moment based on the pleasure principle, i.e., the degree of safety we feel, the costs and benefits of a situation, etc. Reckoning also includes choosing between different "modes of action that can result in either more or less unpleasantness" (p. 378). These unconscious calculations guide behavior through the body, with only the result of these operations entering consciousness. Ferenczi surmises these "unconscious reckoning-operations" employ forms of "arithmetical simplification (algebra, differential calculus)," and that "thinking in speech-symbols represents the ultimate integration of this complicated reckoning-faculty" (p. 378). The unconscious draws on bits and pieces of speech, sound, and images in a symbolic, associative form, *speaking in code*, yielding a contingent series of "*If*, *then*" schemas of increasing complexity.

"Recognition of the surrounding world, i.e. affirmation of the existence of something unpleasant," Ferenczi (1926/1994b) writes, " is... only possible after defence [sic] against objects which cause 'pain' and denial of them are given up" (p. 379). When we give up our defenses we accept what was warded off as part of ourselves. If repression is a negation of reality, then for negation to be undone "a fresh effort has to be made *to negate this negation*" (p. 368, emphasis added). If avoidance negates a painful reality, then negation of avoidance leads to *acceptance*. Put concretely, imagine a patient with the following schema: *If* I feel the need to assert myself, *then* I will be rejected, *therefore* I become agreeable to prevent rejection (negation of a painful outcome). Change would entail *not* being agreeable and asserting myself, to say "no" and open the possibility others can value my needs. The negation of negation—its *refusal*—is itself a form of love ("eros," p. 379). Love is never simply a "yes," it must also be a "no."

Ideally, child development is a process of coming to accept painful realities in the context of a loving environment. In "The adaptation of the family to the child," Ferenczi (1928/1994c) argues, conversely, that it is the relational surround—parents, family, community—that makes the "first adaptation... to understand the child" (p. 61). When a caregiver has the capacity to reflect on their own mind, this is expressed in their responsiveness to the child, whose experience of care fosters a sense of trust that allows ruptures to be tolerated (p. 62). For example, the child's capacity for play and control over their environment often encounters their caregivers' limitations and boundaries. Ferenczi gives the example of his nephew, who once took advantage of his leniency by hitting him. "Psycho-analysis," Ferenczi writes, "did not teach me to let him beat me ad infinitum" (p. 75). He took the boy in his arms and restrained him from punching his uncle. The child told Ferenczi he hated him, to which he replied, "All right, go on, you may feel these things and say these things against me, but you must not beat me" (p. 75).

Ferenczi's theory of child development informed his approach to treatment, insofar as facing difficult feelings is possible only after trust and safety are established. Like Freud, Ferenczi explored the importance of a) facing feelings, thoughts, and behaviors that are painful (being *expressive*), b) in a context in which it feels safe enough to do so (being *supportive*). Wrestling with this tension took him—and psychoanalysis—in radical new directions, transforming his thinking on the therapist's role in the therapeutic relationship.

The Fundamental Rule, Defenses, and the Therapist's Intervention

In an earlier paper, "On the technique of psychoanalysis," Ferenczi (1919/ 1994b) explored how free association can be defensively "misused," such as when an obsessional patient goes "on and on" in a ruminative fashion, or when the patient reports that "nothing" comes to mind, even though they actively reject their thoughts as silly, stupid, or not important. Ferenczi shows a nuanced attention to the "little peculiarities" in speech revealing the patient's defenses, such as responding with "I think that…" when asked about feelings. In such cases, the patient inserts "a critical examination between the perception and the communication of the idea" (p. 180). Likewise, "Many prefer to cloak unpleasant ideas in the form of a projection," saying, "'You are thinking that I mean that…' or 'Of course you will interpret that to mean…'" (p. 180). The patient may stop their sentences mid-speech with a "by the way," shifting to a different topic. Ferenczi realized such speech reflects a *turning away* from where the original sentence was going, often something unpleasant. He learned "to insist that the patient should always complete any sentence he had begun" (p. 181). What was important was "the complete utterance of what had been thought" (p. 181), regardless of whether what is spoken is understood or "made sense."

For a moment, Ferenczi (1919/1994b) seems *more* expressive than Freud, writing that "one must not spare patients the effort of overcoming the resistance to saying certain words," by letting them write it or express it in another manner, as this goes against the "continuous and progressive practice" of being exposed to anxiety around feelings (p. 182). When the patient is trying to remember something they "must not just be helped out at once" (p. 182), allowing space to work through their resistance. "Of course," he changes course, "this withholding of help… cannot be absolute" (p. 182). If it is more important to render the patient's feelings safer to say, "one simply puts into words the ideas one supposes him to have, but which he lacks the courage to utter" (p. 182). His other recommendations are familiar to practitioners, such as exploring questions about the therapist, or helping the patient come to their own conclusions.

An important recommendation offered by Ferenczi (1919/1994b) addresses when patients talk in an abstract, generalized manner. He argues that moving from the general to the "particular dominates the whole of psycho-analysis" (p. 184). Helping patients describe their experience in detail is more likely to get them in touch with unacknowledged desires and feelings. For a patient addressing their dating difficulties to say "Aren't we all looking for different things in a partner?" avoids the question of what specifically *they* are looking for, if those expectations are reasonable, etc. "[T]he phrase 'for example'," Ferenczi writes, "is really the proper technical method for guiding the analysis from the remote and unessential to the imminent and essential" (p. 185). Specific examples help us move from the intellectual to the affective.

Ferenczi then moves to a subject that was testier for Freud—the management of the countertransference. The mirror of the patient's transference, the countertransference is the oft-unconscious feelings, thoughts, and reactions the therapist has toward the patient. They are the associations we have to the patient based on our own relational history, cultural background, and social biases. Like Freud, Ferenczi refers to the "double task" of observing the patient during their free association while tracking and noticing our own thoughts, feelings, and behavior toward them. At this point in 1919, however, he believes the goal is for the therapist to "control" their reactions, and to seek supervision and personal analysis to prevent enacting them. His turn toward the therapist's subjectivity as a determining factor in treatment would define Ferenczi's contributions, and have him excommunicated for over half a century.

Active Therapy as a "Behavioral," Experiential Intervention

Alongside countertransference, Ferenczi's (1920/1994b) "active therapy" has also received derision for its "behavioral" flavor. We should remember, however, that it was Freud who approved of this technique to begin with (see Ferenczi, 1920/1994b, ft. 1, p. 201). Active therapy takes a mechanism of change—working through—and applies it to the world outside the therapy room. Ferenczi did not think active therapy was the "be all end all" of psycho-analysis, discovering important caveats in its application commensurate with Freud's (1937/1964) own.

Ferenczi (1920/1994b) recognized that certain patients could not get beyond "dead points" in treatment despite "deep insight" into their problems. It was not until they were "compelled" by the analyst "*to expose themselves experimentally* to the situation they had avoided because of its painfulness" (p. 201, emphasis original) that treatment could progress. Although exposure "brought with it an acute exacerbation of the anxiety," the patient "overcame the resistance to hitherto repressed material that now became accessible" (p. 201). For phobias and other anxiety-related conditions, "the task consisted in the carrying out of painful activities" (p. 201). Recalling Freud's 1918 speech, Ferenczi reiterated the importance of abstinence—not of the therapist but of *the patient*. "[T]he same renunciation that led to the symptom formation," he writes, "must be preserved throughout the whole treatment as the motive for the desire to get well" (p. 202). Treatment recreates the conditions in which the symptom formed, but in a manageable and safer way. And in that context, help the patient "abstain" from their typical patterns of avoidance so they can spontaneously develop a new solution to old problems.

Ferenczi's (1920/1994b) classic example of active therapy involves the case of a Croatian musician with performance anxiety and shame around her body size. Although she had much *cognitive* understanding of her dynamics, the treatment stalled for weeks until a song came to mind which her abusive older sister used to sing. After some trepidation she recalled the lyrics, with some hints of what the melody was. Without delay Ferenczi asked her to *sing* the song. Similar to his recommendation on helping patients finish incomplete sentences, he noticed his patient "was so embarrassed that she broke off repeatedly in the middle of a verse," (p. 203). He encouraged her to continue, until her voice became "an unusually beautiful soprano" (p. 203). When memories came to mind of her sister singing this song with a dance, Ferenczi asked her to "get up and repeat the song exactly as she had seen her sister do it" (p. 203). Moving her body evoked memories of shame which proved pivotal, allowing her to truly accept herself as she was.

He (1920/1994b) stated that at first the patient had to be "commanded to carry out [activities] contrary to inclination" (p. 205), meaning, she had to work through her inclination to avoid. Simultaneously, there were obsessional activities that had to be "prohibited." The result of these "commands" and "prohibitions" was that previously repressed feelings, thoughts, and associations became conscious "as desires, as ideas agreeable to herself" (p. 205). Akin to Freud, Ferenczi's patient could not "deny neither to herself nor to the doctor that she had recently actually *experienced* these activities and their accompanying affects" (p. 206). This led him to recognize that inviting the patient to engage in action, "works... 'against the grain,' that is against the pleasure principle" (p. 208). This is analogous to "opposite action" in Linehan's (2018) dialectical behavior therapy, doing the opposite of one's avoidant (or confrontational) urges. Ferenczi (1920/1994b) cautions, however, that one should not rush patients toward action as this may provoke too much anxiety and premature termination. At the same time, "'The end-game' of the analysis is seldom successful without active interferences or tasks… the patient must perform beyond the exact adherence to the fundamental rule" (p. 209).

Ferenczi (1920/1994b) wrote that the aim of analysis is for:

[the] patient not only to own deeply concealed impulses to himself, but to *enact them before the doctor*, and, by setting him the task of *consciously controlling* these impulses we have probably subjected the whole process to a revision that was despatched at some other time in a purposeless fashion by means of *repression*. (p. 216, emphasis original)

Ferenczi realizes, like Freud, that the analytic "cure" involves a surprising experience of one's disavowed feelings—insight not as a cognitive statement, but an irruption enacted before the other that "revises" the patient's maps of self and world. But why should "expressions of emotion or motor actions" (p. 216) evoke unconscious associations? Ferenczi points to "the reciprocity of affect and idea emphasized by Freud" (p. 216). Talking about feelings and moving one's body are both actions in line with what drives and emotions do—*drive* and *move*.

Therapeutic Responsiveness, Empathy, and the Psychodynamic Stance

Eight years later, Ferenczi (1928/1994c) concludes that the decision of when to address avoidance, stay silent, or invite the patient to engage in experiments "is above all a question of psychological tact… the capacity for empathy" (p. 89). By empathy he means listening closely to the patient's words and how they imply, allude to, or signify feelings, thoughts, and associations they are not aware of. It is also attuning to how much affect arousal the patient can tolerate. Ferenczi (1920/1994c) writes that empathy protects the treatment:

from unnecessarily stimulating the patient's resistance, or doing so at the wrong moment. It is not within the capacity of psycho-analysis entirely to spare the patient pain; indeed, one of the chief gains from psycho-analysis is the capacity to bear pain. But its tactless infliction by the analyst would only give the patient the unconsciously deeply desired opportunity of withdrawing himself from his influence. (p. 90)

Empathy helps us navigate "staying" within the patient's window of tolerance or inviting them to explore painful experiences outside of awareness. It is not a dichotomy between challenging or being empathic—empathy helps us negotiate *how* and *when* to be challenging. Respecting the patient's experience *and* bringing it into question can both be empathic acts.

Ferenczi's (1920/1994c) refrain to the patient is that "you must decide for yourself whether or not the amount of suffering which your difficulties are causing you is sufficient to make the experiment [of facing one's pain] worth while" (p. 92). It is sometimes necessary to explicitly frame the fundamental conflict between what the symptom offers to resolve (its benefit), the suffering it causes (its cost), *and* what the patient ultimately desires (their values, wishes, goals). Facing their fears must be grounded in their values, not the therapist's. Empathy is distinct from what Fredrickson (2017) calls "pseudoempathy" or "psychosyrupy," where the therapist centers their discomfort around the patient's pain and performs a facsimile of empathy to mask their countertransference. Empathy, then, is about (a) attuning to the patient's "comfort zone," (b) an opacity that exists outside that comfort zone, and (c) deciding when to invite them to step *just* beyond it—not so far it is dysregulating and unbinding, but just enough to facilitate change. Empathy is not just about attending to conscious experience, but cultivating an openness to parts of ourselves that are opaque, unknown, and unknowable.

Repeating, Relating, and Remembering: The Corrective Emotional Experience in Relational and Social Context

This shift in Ferenczi's thinking started after the 1918 Budapest Congress, when he collaborated with Otto Rank on a monograph on technique. That text, *The Development of Psychoanalysis* (Ferenczi & Rank, 1925), was a response to Freud's call for a "psychotherapy for the people" and a foundation to interpersonal and relational thinking, as well as humanistic psychology. They called attention to the "increasing confusion" in technique, with analysts adhering "too rigidly" to Freud's recommendations (p. 2). They scrutinized the intellectualizing emphasis on the patient "remembering" memories to the neglect of repetition, echoing Freud's stance that repetition was a vehicle for experiencing the past as a lived reality in the here and now. Repetition is a "form of communication, the so-called language of gesture" (p. 3), a "showing," not a "telling."

Through repetition, there is a "gradual *transformation of the reproduced material into actual remembering*" (Ferenczi & Rank, 1925, p. 4, emphasis original). Although inviting the patient to talk freely according to the fundamental rule can evoke repressed material, it is often necessary to "intervene 'actively,' behaving... as a sort of catalyzer" (p. 8). The therapist's activity makes them a "lightning rod" for the patient's transference, giving them "the opportunity to 'experience' these wishes intensely for the first time," (p. 10). Ferenczi and Rank evoke Freud's approach to case formulation, identifying (a) the patient's wish or affect (the *if*), (b) the anxiety produced by a feared outcome (the *then*), and (c) the interpersonal and internal defenses used to ward off their wishes and anxieties (the *therefore*). If the patient's anxiety, fear, guilt, and shame can be gradually reduced by experiencing them *without* the feared outcome (rejection, judgment, shaming, etc.), "the libidinal tendencies [affect, wishes, etc.], venture forth in the form of the transference" (pp. 10–11). The patient is allowed to experience intimacy and closeness with a safe other for the first time, or express the anger typically disavowed, leading their underlying action potentials to "be elaborated by the actual ego in a new and more useful way" (p. 11).

Like Freud, Ferenczi and Rank (1925) maintain that resistance "is actually a requisite and acts as a mainspring" (p. 15) of treatment. Resistance is a relational act carrying within it the seeds of change, with the analyst's response to it allowing the patient to re-experience their wishes in a way that renders the symptom "useless" (p. 18). Psychoanalysis is an alloy between providing a corrective "satisfaction" and a frustrating "privation" that allows the patient:

> to relive, partly even for the first time to live through to the end, the original infantile libidinal situation with a partial satisfaction under the condition of consciously giving up its unadjusted realization... it is this ability to stand a partial giving up, at the same time avoiding an *en bloc* repression, which on the whole enables a person to seize the possibilities of substitute satisfactions which reality offers. (p. 19)

Tolerating a more manageable frustration in the context of a *partial* satisfaction of the patient's needs (after all, no therapist can provide *all* we need), *without their avoidance*, opens up room to pursue satisfactions in reality as opposed to compensatory fantasy.

Ferenczi and Rank (1925) write that the therapeutic relationship "really *exposes* the patient a second time to his infantile trauma by offering... the actual old object" (p. 20, emphasis added). In some respects the therapist is *just* as limited as the old object, yet is responsive in a surprising way the patient had not experienced before, which along with their insight brings them "to a new and more fortunate conclusion" (p. 54). Harkening back to Freud's 1918 speech, Ferenczi and Rank argue that greater technical clarity will help "shorten and simplify the treatment" (p. 63), and allow other treatments to be "legitimately combined with psycho-analysis," (p. 64). Today, we call this "psychotherapy integration."

Power, Epistemic Humility, and Not-Knowing in the Psychodynamic Stance

Echoing Ferenczi's review of Freud's *Group* book, Ferenczi and Rank (1925) argue that psychotherapy is a fundamentally "social process, a 'mass structure of two,' according to an utterance of Freud," in which the therapist takes on the role "of the whole heterogeneous environment, particularly of the most important persons in the surroundings of the patient" (p. 27). The therapist, then, stands in for both (a) significant attachment figures in the patient's life, and (b) a *social* position inhabited by intersecting identities and dynamics of power. In recognition of this fact, Ferenczi and Rank stress a *decentering* of the analyst's knowledge, with humility as a counterbalance to the power dynamics of the therapeutic relationship—an insight Lacan popularized by framing the analyst as a "subject supposed to know" (see Chapter 4).

"The analyst should, according to [Freud]," Ferenczi and Rank (1925) write, "always proceed from what is at the time the mental surface" (p. 30). The analyst works with what is readily observable to the patient, rather than scrounging for hidden meanings. Working "from surface to depth" ensures a collaborative relationship, protecting the treatment from the "the analyst having too much knowledge" (p. 34). Humility and holding one's theories lightly is key. If your theory is that *everything* is about "attachment issues," then you will be biased to listen *only* for relational conflict instead of other themes in the material, such as issues around culture and identity. Likewise, it is "also a mistake, while neglecting the individual… to make cultural and phylogenetic analogies at once, no matter how fruitful the latter might be" (p. 36). Reducing *everything* to culture is no less problematic than reducing *everything* to sex and relationships.

Ferenczi and Rank (1925) emphasize that not all transference is projection, as it includes reactions to the therapist's actual behavior (which may also mirror figures from the past). It is imperative for the therapist to attend to "the delicate indications of criticism, which mostly only venture forth hesitatingly, and helping the patient to express them plainly." To this end a healthy level of self-criticism, "a certain overcoming" of their own resistance is required (p. 42). The therapist must also be wary of erring too much on the side of activity, enacting their "zeal to heal" by overwhelming the patient with their interventions without also rigidly adhering to a passive stance which inadvertently spares the patient "the pain of necessary intervention" (p. 43). There is a time for the therapist to confront, and a time to shut up and let the patient speak.

Therapeutic Humility and Elasticity within the Therapeutic Window

After his collaboration with Rank, humility becomes even more central to Ferenczi (1928/1994c). He cautions against a "schoolmasterish" attitude, arguing that what we say to patients should be phrased "in the form of a tentative suggestion and not of a confidently held opinion… there is always the possibility that we may be mistaken" (p. 94). He gives the example of an interpretation a patient raised objections to. Working through his "immediate impulse" to reject their objections, he realized upon reflection the patient was *right*. Ferenczi wades into waters Freud struggled with—the patient may intervene *on the therapist*, with the latter's receptivity itself part of the cure. "[T]he analyst's modesty," Ferenczi writes, "must be a reflection of the limitations of our knowledge," allowing "an alteration in the attitude of the doctor to the patient" (p. 94). The therapist works through *their* countertransference: "One must never be ashamed unreservedly to confess one's own mistakes" (p. 95). Humility signals our openness to being moved by the patient, especially when we are wrong.

One of Ferenczi's (1928/1994c) patients referred to the "elasticity" of technique, a metaphor that stayed with him (p. 95). "The analyst, like an elastic band," he writes, "must yield to the patient's pull, but without ceasing to pull in his own direction" (p. 95). One does not "give in" to every demand by the patient, but figures out when and where to be flexible. Similar to Freud's "evenly-suspended attention," Ferenczi argued the therapist allow the patient's associations to "play" with their own fantasies. As they listen, their "mind *swings* continuously between empathy, self-observation, and making judgements" (p. 96, emphasis added). Maybe what the patient says took place as they report it, but maybe there is a different perspective. Maybe that is just from the therapist's point of view and cultural background. Maybe it is "both/ and," and so on. Such elasticity facilitates exploration from different points of view.

This is a beautiful encapsulation of the psychodynamic stance, in which the therapist keeps their mind in motion, "swinging" between different positions without becoming one-sidedly fixed to any single one. This stance, or more accurately *dance*, helps the therapist keep their mind open and develop a "humble hypothesis," an empathic conjecture about the patient's conscious and unconscious experience. Empathy is central to the psychodynamic dance, attuning to what is explicit, conscious, and within the patient's "comfort zone," while recognizing an opacity that lies just beyond it, inviting the patient to reflect on the implicit, unconscious, anxiety-provoking, unsaid, and unknown. By modeling this dance, we help the patient develop skills of openness, flexibility, and self-observation, so that by the end of treatment they do "the work of interpretation practically unaided" (Ferenczi, 1928/1994c, p. 96).

The same applies to active therapy. Through experience, Ferenczi (1928/1994c) learned never to order or demand the patient to engage in behavioral change, instead presenting these interventions as suggestions and being ready to empathically explore the patient's resistance to action without insisting on change. Analytic work, then, includes "interpreting the patient's concealed tendencies to action and supporting his feeble attempts to overcome the neurotic inhibitions" (p. 96). Further, he observed that after much working through, "the patient will himself sooner or later come up with the question whether he should risk making some effort, for example to defy a phobic avoidance" (p. 97), at which point the therapist can encourage and support the activity. Active therapy becomes a *collaborative negotiation* where the patient decides their readiness for behavioral change. Ultimately, the goal is for the patient to cultivate "precisely that elasticity which analytic technique demands of the mental therapist" (p. 99). Psychoanalysis nurtures the patient's humility and openness toward their own opacity and inscrutability, the flexibility with which to hold multitudes.

The Principle of "Indulgence": Therapeutic Responsiveness and the Role of Trust

A year later, a turning point became a sea change. In his "The principle of relaxation and neocatharsis" (1929/1994c), originally entitled "Progresses in Psycho-Analytic Technique," Ferenczi argued that the field rigidly adhered to the "principle of frustration" Freud derived from "active therapy" (see Chapter 2), such that one-sidedly compelling the patient to face warded-off feelings led the therapist to have a "didactic and pedantic attitude" (p. 113).

Sensing his patients' dissatisfaction whenever he behaved this way, he advocated for therapists to invite their patient's feedback, alongside humility in admitting their mistakes. This led him to complement the "principle of frustration" with the "principle of indulgence (*Nachgiebigkeit*)" (p. 114).

Some scholars (Rachman, 1998; Soreanu, 2016) note the impreciseness of the translation "indulgence" from the original German, which suggests a non-reflective "giving in" to the patient (often, to shut them up or quell the therapist's anxiety). The dynamism of the term *Nachgiebigkeit* implies compliance, but in the sense of being pliable to the other's needs and giving "permission" for their being met, showing softness while also being "resilient," and having a certain "springiness" into action in responding to the other. If "frustration" means "depriving" the patient of a defense that harms them, then *Nachgiebigkeit* implies a "willingness to give," a tenderness that gives permission *to be*. Per Kosawa, defenses *melt* instead of being "deprived" or yanked away. This optimal responsiveness is not just a complement to the principle of frustration, but recontextualizes the very function of frustration itself.

Ferenczi (1929/1994c) thought frustration worked by heightening the patient's anxiety within the bounds they could tolerate, and in many cases this was true. He once noticed aloud how a patient seemed to have a "stiff posture" and invited her to relax her body. He noticed not a heightening of anxiety, but a lessening of tension in her body—she was *too anxious to begin with*. His responsiveness to her needs allowed her to *relax*. He concludes that psychoanalysis "employs two opposite methods: it produces heightening of tension by the frustration it imposes and relaxation by the freedom it allows" (p. 115). He sees these two principles—being "expressive" and "supportive"— at play in free association, where the patient is *compelled* to express unwanted truths and *permitted* a freedom of speech not possible in other areas of life.

How does one apply these principles tactfully? One patient may experience being challenged as the imposition of an authoritarian parent's will they must rebel against to maintain their autonomy. A different patient might experience being challenged as a show of care, and never being questioned as a lack of real interest by the clinician. No therapist can know in advance what will be effective for each patient, but their willingness to be elastic (flexible) and responsive (open to shifting gears) provides not only a "technical" guide to intervention but is itself curative—the experience of being heard, of someone owning their mistakes and being willing to share power in the relationship. Ferenczi (1929/1994c) still thinks it important for patients to "learn to endure the suffering which originally led to repression. The only question is whether sometimes we do not make him suffer more than is absolutely necessary" (p. 118).

Ferenczi (1929/1994c) points to cases of severe trauma, where only after "an atmosphere of confidence" is created could patients enter deep regressions in which the trauma could be relived (p. 119). In such cases, he supported the patient's fragmented, dissociated self-states by having an "infantile conversation," speaking softly and tenderly as if to a child who needs safety and care, so that they could tap into experiences that had not been encoded verbally but existed only in somatic, "physical memories" (p. 122). Through conversations with Anna Freud, Ferenczi learned that his work with adults resembled her work with children. In some cases, what patients need is "*to be adopted and to partake for the first time in their lives of the advantages of a normal nursery*" (p. 124, emphasis original). Of note for our discussion of Fanon (see Chapter 5), Ferenczi points to the role of psychoanalytically informed inpatient treatments as potential havens of safety where such experiences of care could be had (p. 125).

Helping patients feel safe enough is not the same as "coddling" them, nor should we gratify extremely hostile behavior or unreasonable demands. Rather, Ferenczi (1929/1994c) advocates for "the tactful and understanding application" (p. 123) of *both* frustration and relaxation. A caring attitude does not leave the patient's compromise formations "off the hook." On the contrary, proper empathy lies in our ability to intervene with tact and humility, making room for the patient's unconscious underside, dancing across the line between when to "push" and when to "stroke" (as my advisor Nancy Boyd-Franklin was fond of saying).

Referring to a patient who was particularly challenging, Ferenczi (1929/1994c) discovered that using the relaxation/empathic approach allowed her "to discriminate the present from the past," experiencing powerful emotions evoking remembrance of childhood traumas in the context of an accepting relationship. "[W]*hile the similarity of the analytical to the infantile situation impels patients to repetition,*" Ferenczi concludes, "*the contrast between the two encourages recollection*" (p. 124, emphasis original). Harkening back to Freud with a twist, it is not sufficient for the therapist to *tell* the patient that they are not like their parents. If the patient's repetition in the transference is how they *show* the therapist their symptoms, then the therapist must also *show* a contrast with the traumatogenic situation through their own behavior.

Ferenczi's Thinking in Comparative Context: "Corrective Experiences" By Another Name

How one shows such a contrast is a matter of technique, as there are many "roads to Rome." This contrast might be demonstrated in the therapist's genuine and spontaneous gesture of kindness, or simply offering an interpretation in a non-defensive, "neutral" but engaged tone that does *not* reproduce a punitive reaction from a past object (Strachey, 1934). For Ferenczi (1929/ 1994c), the patient's experience in treatment "may be compared with that of the playwright whom pressure of public opinion forces to convert the tragedy he has planned into a drama with a 'happy ending'" (p. 125). Although after his death Ferenczi was banished from the psychoanalytic canon, it is interesting to put his ideas in dialog with James Strachey (1934), whose work was lauded by the Freudian establishment of the time.

Following Freud in a manner resonant with Ferenczi, Strachey (1934) espouses a functional view of the symptom in which it (a) defends against an unconscious trend (wish, desire, affect) deemed unacceptable, and (b) provides some compensatory gratification. In helping the patient face these unconscious wishes, "the whole *raison d'être* of the symptom would cease and it must automatically disappear" (p. 67). Naturally, resistance emerges in the process of approaching these feelings, with the key to addressing them lying in the transference. The transference, by making the core problem alive in the here and now, offers the patient the opportunity to choose "a new solution instead of the old one" (p. 68).

What is at stake for Strachey (1934) is how to breach the "vicious circle" the patient finds themselves in. If the patient could be made less afraid of the anxieties tied to a catastrophic outcome, then they will have less need to project it outward pre-emptively to avoid pain. Think, for example, of someone who goes on the attack to defend themselves due to the expectation of being attacked. If this person were less afraid and more open, they might evoke openness in others as well: "a *benign* circle would be set up instead of the vicious one" (p. 71, emphasis original). To initiate this process, the therapist allows themselves to become an "auxiliary super-ego" that contrasts with the patient's internalized super-ego. This also leads to a dilemma.

At first, the therapist's more benign super-ego gives permission for the patient to say what comes to mind. The patient's super-ego, however, answers back: "You must *not* say what comes to mind, *if* you do, *then* you will be punished." Emotionally, the therapist's benign invitation is filtered through this projection. While the content is different ("say what comes to mind and it will be accepted"), its *quality* is heard as punitive: "*If* you *don't* say what comes to mind, *then* I will punish you." What shifts the impasse is not the *content*, but the *process* of a mutative intervention. Strachey (1934) gives the example of interpreting a patient's unconscious anger. As a new attachment figure, the therapist's interpretation "gives permission" for the patient's anger to enter awareness (p. 73). The treatment comes to a head:

> the patient's ego will become aware of the *contrast* between the aggressive char-acter of his feelings and the real nature of the analyst, who does not behave like the patient's "good" or "bad" archaic objects... The interpretation has now become a mutative one, since it has produced a breach in the neurotic vicious circle. (p. 73, emphasis added)

This new experience is internalized, leading to a reconfiguration of the super-ego while bringing into awareness the original traumatic situation as re-experienced with the therapist.

Strachey (1934), like Ferenczi, stresses these are not one-and-done "aha" moments, but a series occurring "upon a small scale. For the mutative inter-pretation is inevitably governed by the principle of minimal doses" (p. 74). The patient often assimilates the therapist to their past object relations, such that reassurance that one is not like the "old object," while sometimes helpful, is often heard through the "voice" of the old object (a conundrum Lacan wrestled with as well). As Frieda Fromm-Reichman intuited years later, the patient needs an experience, not an explanation. Strachey concedes that "non-interpretive" behaviors "may be dynamically equivalent to the giving of a mutative interpretation" (p. 76). Sometimes the therapist triggers the patient's expectations of others yet behaves in a way that shocks them, leading to "the necessary distinction between an archaic object and a real one" (p. 76). Many changes may occur "due to *implicit* mutative interpretations of this kind" (p. 76, emphasis original).

I discuss Strachey's paper at length to illustrate the "narcissism of smaller differences" often at play in psychoanalysis. While Ferenczi's thinking on how the therapist provides a contrast to the patient's feared expectations of others has been historically derided as "non-analytic"—much like his descendant Franz Alexander (see Chapter 4)—I would be hard pressed to identify a meaningful difference between this and Strachey's conceptualiza-tion of a mutative interpretation as a contrast between the therapist and the patient's archaic objects. Given the recognition that mutative interpreta-tions can occur *implicitly* through the therapist's behavior—without a verbal explanation ("interpretation" in the classical sense)—this difference narrows further, bringing Freudian thinking in line with both Ferenczi and Lacan (see

Chapter 4). A decolonial approach melts these distinctions, and advocates for fitting the technique to the patient and not the other way around.

The way Ferenczi (1929/1994c) works through the intricacies of therapeutic work reminds us that no single technique is a magic bullet, nor should it be discarded as useless: "we must constantly be prepared to find new veins of gold in temporarily abandoned workings" (p. 120). In that spirit, we turn to Ferenczi's final paper, often thought to have caused a rupture with Freud, injuring the development of psychoanalysis for decades to come. This will lead us to Ferenczi's (1988) *Clinical Diary*, which formed the inspiration for that fateful paper.

Between Rupture and Repair: The "Confusion of Tongues" Paper and its Aftermath

Ferenczi's (1933/1994c) "Confusion of tongues between adults and the child" is a cornerstone of interpersonal and relational psychoanalysis. It is also a paper he read aloud to Freud at their last meeting before the outbreak of World War II, rupturing their relationship and psychoanalysis for decades to come. Ferenczi recognized that sometimes the repetition central to analysis "turned out to be too good" (p. 157). The therapist was not experienced *like* a figure from the past, but *as* them in a way that was overwhelming and retraumatizing. The patient might withdraw or attack the therapist as cold and cruel, alternating with panic: "Help! Quick! Don't let me perish helplessly!" (p. 157). He began to consider ruptures are more than projections of the past, "I began to test my conscience in order to discover whether, despite all my conscious good intentions, there might after all be some truth in these accusations" (p. 157).

He (1933/1994c) realized patients were exquisitely attuned to his unconscious wishes, desires, and negative feelings toward them, but instead of calling him out they suppressed their own feelings to protect their relationship. Periodically, however, patients "pluck up enough courage to make a protest" (p. 158), experimenting with the wish to evoke a different response from the analyst that reconstitutes the relationship in more a freeing way. Ferenczi's understanding of resistance here shifts from something occurring *within* the patient as a defense against feelings, to a relational process taking place *between* patient and therapist.

Identification with the Aggressor, Identification with the Oppressor

Ferenczi (1933/1994c) theorizes that trauma disrupts attachment, leading the child to feel anxious about losing the love of the adults around them—including those abusing them. To maintain their safety and regulate their anxiety the child identifies with the adult, compelled to *"subordinate themselves like automata to the will of the aggressor, to divine each one of his desires and to gratify these"* (p. 162, emphasis original). Through identification the aggressor is "taken inside" and subjected to the primary process, "according to the pleasure principle it can be modified or changed by positive or negative hallucinations" (p. 162). Through splitting, the abuser may be transformed into a savior to preserve their goodness, while the child takes all the badness unto themselves (*I* made them violent). The child becomes an "automata," an object bound to the abuser as subject, torn between two wills, "enormously confused, in fact, split—innocent and culpable at the same time... his confidence in the testimony of his own senses is broken" (p. 162). As the child grows into adulthood, they may become overly submissive, or aggressively defiant but unable to understand their hostility. The victim holds in mind themselves and their abuser—splitting as Du Boisian double consciousness (see Chapter 1).

He (1933/1994c) describes how early, chronic trauma can result in deep fragmentation of the child's self, lacking the emotional regulation to tolerate distress, and finding it "unbearable to be left alone" (p. 163). Yet behind the extreme submissiveness or aggression of such patients lies an "ardent desire" to heal, "to get rid of this oppressive love" (p. 164). Even with "difficult" patients, one must remember that behind their "difficult" behavior lies a wish to overcome their difficulties, and that their behavior may manifest an attempt to "replay" an older attachment story to bring about a new ending. Acts of defiance especially represent the patient's attempt to *have an impact* on others so they may learn from the patient's wisdom (p. 165). The key to maintaining our attunement to the patient's wisdom lies in our countertransference.

Beyond "Neutrality" or "Empathy": Countertransference, Rupture and Repair

The countertransference as a resistance of the analyst takes center stage in the form of their "professional hypocrisy." The patient is invited to speak freely in the presence of the analyst's non-judgmental listening. And yet, the analyst struggles with aspects of the patient—their physical features, background, behavior—that evoke negative feelings. Ferenczi (1933/1994c) drops the first bomb that chilled Freud: "I cannot see any other way out than to make the source of the disturbance in us fully conscious and to discuss it with the patient, *admitting it perhaps not only as a possibility but as a fact*" (p. 159, emphasis added). The therapist discloses and owns their feelings while taking responsibility for their behavior as the first step out of the impasse, offering a repair that "[frees] the tongue-tied patient" (p. 159).

Whether the therapist aspires to being unconditionally accepting *à la* Carl Rogers, or an abstinent "blank screen," both are "neutral" in that they presume the therapist is not "nudged" by the patient's behavior into being not-accepting or punitive. It may seem odd to describe unconditional positive regard as neutral, but it is—as Wachtel (2007, 2018) would say—a "default position." Ferenczi discovers something of an open secret—therapists lapse in their empathy and "neutrality" *often*, whether due to their personal reactions and/or the patient's "pull" for behaviors that confirm their fears. We are neither everflowing waterfalls of empathy nor bastions of objectivity—there is *no* default position to hide behind. We can only ever be in motion betwixt positions in the psychodynamic dance, recognizing the limits of our knowledge, empathy, and objectivity, ever willing to look at ourselves in the process. This is not a call for "anything goes," as that would also be a *fixed* position that limits our technique. My larger point is that "unconditional positive regard" can *also* be a mask for one's professional hypocrisy, hiding one's negative counter-transference—including bias and prejudice—toward the patient behind a veneer of kindness.

What does Ferenczi recommend when the therapist's empathy and objectivity falters and this ruptures the therapeutic relationship? He (1933/1994c) writes,

> The setting free of [the patient's] critical feelings, the willingness on our part to admit our mistakes and the honest endeavour to avoid them in future… create in [them] a confidence in the analyst. *It is this confidence that establishes the contrast between the present and the unbearable traumatogenic past…* (p. 160, emphasis original)

It is the patient expressing their feelings of injury and the therapist admitting their misstep and taking responsibility in a way the patient did not expect that establishes a mutative contrast. As contemporary research attests, such cycles of rupture and repair may be more salubrious to outcome than "perfect," unwavering empathy (see Muran et al., 2023).

In his posthumous *Clinical Diary*, Ferenczi (1988) shares the realization that ruptures are inevitable. No matter how "good" or empathic the therapist is, "the time will come when he will have to repeat with his own hands the act of murder previously perpetrated against the patient" (p. 52). The therapist will inevitably fall short of what the patient needs, or hurt them as others have in the past. Yet through repair—a shift in the therapist's thinking, feeling, and behaving—this offers up a new possibility for the patient. In a sense, this places the subjectivity of the therapist front row and center in therapeutic change. Ferenczi's vulnerability seemed to shock and dismay Freud. As his friend finished reading his paper, Freud turned around and walked away in silence. The psychoanalytic establishment turned its back on Ferenczi, until relational and interpersonal thinkers claimed him as an ancestor (Aron & Harris, 1993). We return to Ferenczi anew through Fanon's eyes to build on his contributions, and uncover the promise and limitations of interpersonal and relational approaches.

Hidden in Plain Sight: Race in Ferenczi's *Clinical Diary*

Ferenczi's (1988) *Clinical Diary* is rich in insights with which contemporary therapists can resonate. His brilliance notwithstanding, we can also gleam the limitations of relational thinking regarding social context through two of his patients: "R.N.," known to be Elizabeth Severn, herself a pioneer in the study of trauma (Rachmann, 2017), and "S.I.," Harriot Sigray, an heiress and multimillionaire (Brennan, 2015). Severn was also a psychoanalyst who suggested they engage in "mutual analysis" to work through their relationship. Ferenczi's insights on enactments, ruptures and their repair, and trauma can be traced in large part to their collaboration as patient and therapist (Rachman, 2017). Two facts about both women are worth noting. Both reported multiple early childhood traumas, difficulty tolerating distress, interpersonal difficulties, dissociation, stress-induced paranoia, and transient psychotic symptoms. The other is that they are both white Americans—Severn was born in 1879 in Milwaukee, Wisconsin (Rachman, 2017), while Sigray was born in 1884 in Butte, Montana (Brennan, 2015).[1]

The Pleasures of Colonial Cannibalism and Recognition of One's Value in Physical Space

In their treatment, Sigray reported visual hallucinations of being attacked by ghosts of different ethnicities, "especially so Chinese people" (Ferenczi, 1988, p. 76). As they attack her, she lets out a violent cry, "They are hitting me! They will smash my head in! They are killing me!" (p. 76). After several minutes, her dissociation deepens: "she claims that she is no longer inside but outside her body, the body itself is dead, murdered" (p. 76). Sigray and Ferenczi traced these attacks back to her mother, whose domineering behavior prompted the impulse to self-harm. She describes this as an "alien will" forcing her personality out of her body (p. 75).

Ferenczi (1988) theorized that the abuser cannibalizes the victim's mind by "implanting" their own psyche within them, causing the victim pain to extract pleasure. "Hence," he writes, "the soothing effect on an enraged person… when he succeeds in causing pain" (p. 77). By cannibalizing the victim, "the aggressor annexes the naive state of peaceful happiness, untroubled by-anxiety in which the victim had existed until recently" (pp. 77–78). Ferenczi compares this to someone who suffers and envies the joy of another, and kicks them. The *jouissance* or pleasure violence ensures "the other suffers too, something that will inevitably ease my pain" (p. 78). The victim is "poisoned" by the aggressor, forming "wish-fulfilling hallucinations" to protect from the fact that a beloved figure has invaded their mind and body like an alien will—in Sigray's case, through fantasies of violent, "dirty" racial others to protect her family's purity (p. 82). In a related entry, "All hate is projection, in fact psychopathic," Ferenczi comments on how racism displaces one's suffering onto another to ease one's pain, where "hatred is extended to a whole family, a whole nation, a whole species" (p. 78).

In a section entitled "Awareness of personality (awareness of one's own size, form, value) as a result of recognition from the environment," Ferenczi (1988) reflects on a later session with Sigray. He describes Sigray's family

---

[1] There are many layers of complexity to the treatments of Elizabeth Severn (R.N.) and Harriet Sigray (S.I.). For example, Sigray was originally a patient of Severn whom the latter referred to Ferenczi, something that likely impacted their transference to Ferenczi, which he himself reflected on (Brennan, 2015; Ferenczi, 1933/1988, pp. 139–140). While there is much comment on here, it is beyond the scope of the present chapter to do so.

as wealthy and well-to-do, "puritanical… kept away from anything 'dirty'" (p. 127). Beneath this image of a "pure" white American family lay the scenes of sexual decadence and drug addiction Sigray was exposed to, especially on a globe-trotting trip with her sister and a governess (p. 127). During their stay in China, the rickshaw Sigray and her family were riding passed a town square where an execution had taken place. The executioner frightened Sigray by throwing a severed arm at her. She told Ferenczi of dreams in which large ghosts (apparently, of Chinese people), approached her in an intimidating fashion.

Ferenczi (1988) makes an interesting comment here. He writes

> the recognition and assertion of one's own self as a genuinely existing, a valuable entity of *a given size, shape, and significance*—is attainable only when the positive interest of the environment… guarantees the stability of that form… (p. 129, emphasis added)

When made to feel small, "the individual tends to explode, to dissolve itself in the universe, perhaps to die" (p. 129). Ferenczi interprets Sigray's ghosts as representing how small she felt, coping with her mother's domination and her family's moral hypocrisy through dissociation with race as a substitutive symptom—projecting the violence she experienced onto Chinese people as dirty and dangerous to maintain her family's "purity." Although heavily implied, Ferenczi does not comment theoretically on the role of race despite its prevalence in the material.

Later on, Sigray reports a dream in which she had fungi over one ear that "do not belong to her body," and removes them. Ferenczi (1988) comments that this dream reflects her insight "that her colossal terror stems only from the incorporation of hatred that is in fact foreign to her" (p. 139), and her wish to liberate herself from her family's toxicity. Although Ferenczi implies a connection between the ghosts of Chinese people threatening Sigray and her family's hatred, this is never stated outright. Sigray then reflects on her preoccupation with "the wishes and moods of people important to her," and how she is forced to "swallow" them (p. 140).

The dream symbolized her family's wishes attempting to reassert themselves, "but the greater independence acquired in analysis refuses to accept the exogenous substance" (Ferenczi, 1988, p. 140). Yet just when Sigray was in touch with the pressure to "swallow" her family's wishes she suddenly cries out loud, "Please eat it yourself! Deal with it yourself! I will not let myself be tortured instead of you" (p. 140). Struck by these words, Ferenczi inquired further, leading Sigray to remember the connection between her family's imposition of their wishes and a grotesque murder, in which "she was forced to swallow the severed genitals of a repugnant black man, who had just been killed" (p. 140). This was not an isolated incident, as castration was a recurrent form of sexual violence against Black men during lynchings in America (Carter, 2012). This entry ends abruptly without further commentary. Did Ferenczi not recognize the humanity of this victimized Black man, or see his lynching as deserving discussion?[2]

The Curious Case of Elizabeth Severn: Do'er and Done-To

This is not the only case of a lynching in Ferenczi's (1988) *Clinical Diary*. Although little is known about Severn's biography, Ferenczi's notes and her family's testimony suggest her father was a violent criminal who tormented her and her mother throughout her childhood (Rachman, 2017). She told Ferenczi (1988) her story of abuse and her "ostracism from a society in which no one wants to believe me innocent" (p. 14). The hypervigilance she developed to survive was active in their relationship, with moments of aggression and mistrust making it difficult for Ferenczi to stay empathic. Severn picked up on his hypocritical displays of care when he in fact felt angry toward her, and suggested—being a clinician herself—that they engage in "mutual analysis" to address *his* resistances. Ferenczi agreed, and in the process, opened a new horizon for psychoanalysis. At the same time, inadvertently foreclosed another.

In reflecting on his "mutual analysis" with Severn, Ferenczi (1988) associated to his own childhood experience of sexual assault by a housemaid, tracing to this trauma and his mother's hostility his unconscious hatred of women: "I want to dissect them for it, that is, to kill them. This is why my mother's accusation 'You are my murderer' cut to the heart," (p. 61). Ferenczi defended against the emotional and sexual abuse he faced as a child by developing a passion to help anyone who is suffering, *especially* women, while avoiding situations in which he would have to assert himself or be aggressive. This behavior served to reinforce Ferenczi's "feeling that in fact I am a good chap," (p. 61), while dissociating his tendency to explode with rage at even minor affronts, followed by intense guilt and a desire to make a repair. Ferenczi took Severn's feelings seriously as a response to his own unacknowledged countertransference. By reflecting on his childhood traumas and unconscious bias toward women, his openness to validating Severn's

---

[2] I should note, for the sake of clarity, that on page 139, Ferenczi (1988) makes mention of "R. N.," Elizabeth Severn, and how she used to interpret "S.I.'s", Harriet Sigray's, experience in terms of sexual symbol. On page 140 where this lynching is reported, Ferenczi clearly refers to "S.I.," Sigray, as the one relating this experience.

experience had a profound effect in the treatment leading to her recovery (Rachman, 2017). This is part of the genius that drew relational and inter-personal psychoanalysts to his work (Aron & Harris, 1993), and inspired a whole body of research on ruptures in the therapeutic alliance (Muran et al., 2023). However, Ferenczi also reveals profound limitations in interpersonal and relational perspectives around social justice.

Karen Maroda (1998) wrote an extensive critique of Severn's treatment, arguing it represented a malignant enactment caused by Ferenczi overly accommodating her demands that *all* her emotional needs be met. Severn's charge that he was psychologically "murdering" her whenever he set a boundary or did not respond in an optimally empathic way hit a soft spot in Ferenczi's own psychology (see above). It is likely she *did* pick up on Ferenczi's unconscious aggression towards women, though at the same time the treatment seemed caught in what Benjamin (2004) calls a "do'er done-to" enactment—*one* of us must be the "bad" perpetrating do'er, the other the "good" victimized done-to, with each side taking turns accusing and hurting the other.

Ferenczi's (1988) commentary understands Severn's accusation of him "murdering" her partly as a response to his missteps, but also as her internal-ization of the perpetrator's "alien will." Whenever she alternated with hostility toward him, her protest that "the person who does these things is not me," symbolizes a dissociated awareness that the internalized aggressor is "behind" her more destructive behavior. "Hence," Ferenczi writes "[Severn's] extraor-dinary, incessant protestations that she is no murderer, *although she admits to having fired the shots*" (p. 17, emphasis added). What is this repeated, "inces-sant" protest referring to? Perhaps this is a metaphor, capturing his sense that Severn positions herself as all good ("she is no murderer") while being hostile toward him and others ("she… fired the shots"). The truth is more horrible, and it is striking how it has remained without comment in the psychoanalytic literature.

Rudnytsky (2002) cites an interview with Severn's daughter, who disclosed that her mother's admission that she "fired the shots" refers to her "having been forced… to participate in the murder of a black man" as a child (ft. 12, p. 136). This suggests that among the horrors to which Severn's father subjected her, these included making her shoot and kill a Black man. That Ferenczi's *Clinical Diary* includes the treatment of two white American women who were witness, bystander, victim, and *perpetrator* of the lynching of two Black men demands commentary on his blind spots regarding race and society in psychotherapy. Although he articulated brilliant insights birthing a "two-person" model in psychoanalysis, I argue he was sorely limited by this frame, which risks constraining relational and interpersonal practitioners as well. In what follows I read his theory of race in light of Freud's conceptualization (see Chapter 2), and use it to suggest how race could have been woven into the treatment.

Ferenczi's Forgotten Theory of Psychic Colonialism: Addressing a Relational "Blind Spot"

In his *Clinical Diary* Ferenczi (1988) developed a theory of how abusers "colonize" the mind of the abused to derive pleasure and soothe their own suffering, a psychic parasitic cannibalism. In an almost passing comment, Ferenczi extends this process beyond the intimacies of the family or interpersonal relations into "hatred [of] a whole nation, a whole species" (p. 78). Ferenczi underscores how the environment's recognition of the self in spatial terms determines one's value—if I am not valued I feel "small" and "lesser," dissolving to the point of "death." But if I can make *the other* feel small, I enlarge my value and position.

But how did Ferenczi go from critiquing racism, calling for socialist reform, and pointing out how in psychoanalysis "we investigate the *real* conditions in the various levels of society… mirrored in the individual" (see Chapter 1) to almost avoiding—or at least, struggling—to address race in his clinical work? Erös (1990, 2014) tells us how by 1932 Ferenczi had become increasingly disaffected with politics. As a Hungarian Jew, he experienced the collapse of Left-progressive governments, giving way to anti-Semitic fascism across Europe—Hitler in Germany, Mussolini in Italy, and Gömbös in his native Hungary—remarking to Freud on the "imminent collapse of our old political world" (cited in Erös, 2014). The post-World War I social democratic movements that inspired the sociopolitical turn in psychoanalysis came to an end.

Ferenczi, like Freud, could think deeply and cogently about race, class, and the sociopolitical. But by 1932 he was turning away from the social toward the exigencies of clinical care. While American psychoanalysis abandoned the social to focus on the intrapsychic, the founder of relational and interpersonal psychoanalysis turned from the social to the *dyadic* (cf. Layton, 2018). Although his exploration of the transference–countertransference relationship gave us groundbreaking tools for "bread-and-butter" clinical work that stand the test of time, he focused so narrowly on the therapeutic relationship as only "two people in a room" that it foreclosed his insight that psychoanalysis reveals the social as it is mirrored in the individual. While we appreciate that Ferenczi, like Freud, was trying to survive literal fascism, we should not turn away from examining where the foundations of relational-interpersonal theories fall short.

Reimagining the Foundations of Relational Psychoanalysis

This leaves us with the "broken circuits" of relational and interpersonal psychoanalysis—a theory of mind and clinical technique *disconnected* from its critical theory and potential decolonial insights. In what follows I "reconnect" these circuits in Ferenczi's work, outlining how race and class could have been integrated in his treatments and how the foundations of contemporary relational psychoanalysis can better account for race, class, gender, and sexuality.

As reviewed above, Ferenczi had some insight into the role of race in his treatment of Sigray. Her mother's imposition of her wishes reflected both an interpersonal dynamic (a parent dominating her child) and the transmission of specific values along the lines of race, gender, culture, and class. On the surface, they were a well-to-do family, but underneath that veneer was emotional abuse, drug addiction, sexual hypocrisy, and racist violence. Her hallucinations of "large" Chinese people attacking her represented the internalization of her family's racism, and a racist projection putting the "dirty" and "bad" outside of her family to maintain their "purity." By helping Sigray free herself from her mother's will, Ferenczi evoked an association encapsulating the trauma of "swallowing" her family's racism—being forced to participate in a lynching. The story ends there, with gratuitous violence visited on a Black man left without commentary. In a sense, Ferenczi restores Sigray's "innocence" as a white woman and victim of a puritanical middle-class family.

Without question, Sigray was viciously abused as a child. But what would it have been like if Ferenczi had drawn attention to the fact that the very same patriarchal, racist society that ended the life of another human being both brutalized *and* privileged her? What would it have meant to process the complexity of being a victim, a bystander and, perhaps, a perpetrator? To address how racism was an expression of her suffering and a *salve* through which to maintain a relationship to an abusive family she loved? To expand the analysis beyond the dynamics of parent and child and into the broader systemic violence that contextualizes the two? To think with and *beyond* the twosome, whether parent and child or patient and therapist?

Similar questions abound in Ferenczi's treatment of Severn. Without question, as a survivor of childhood physical, emotional, and sexual abuse, and as a woman in a patriarchal world she was oppressed and "murdered" by her father and society. Understandably, she was hypervigilant based on her life experience, picking up on Ferenczi's sexist bias. His *Clinical Diary* gives us the earliest example of a therapist wrestling with their own trauma and unconscious bias against women, and the earliest example of a patient doing their best to "coach" their therapist into intervening in a way that is helpful. Processing countertransference, taking ownership of one's bias, and making a repair is part and parcel of clinical work today.

But the two-person frame erases an underlying tension in the treatment. The two-person perspective, by definition, prioritizes "two people in the room," which risks excluding how racism, patriarchy, and the sociopolitical played a role in Severn's struggles. What if Ferenczi reflected on his sexism not just in terms of his personal, dyadic experiences with his mother but in terms of patriarchal structures and gender norms? What would it have been like to not only reflect on gender, but also race? What if he not only owned his unconscious sexism and made a repair, but also explored Severn's guilt and shame over being complicit in the murder of a Black man? What would it have been like to talk about a sexist and racist world that murdered Severn as a white woman and Ferenczi as a white Jewish man, while also making murderers of them both? Such an exploration could have broken out of the impasse in which one is either a victim or a perpetrator by repositioning the two-person field within a wider sociopolitical world that enlists individuals to function—per Freud—as *vehicles* for its violence and maintenance.

Returning to Ferenczi's paper on accepting unwanted ideas, if love brings "reality" into view by recognizing the "bad" in ourselves and the "good" in the other, then love that includes "the two of us in the room" but points "outward" may bring social realities into perspective. By surrendering their narcissism—Ferenczi's need to be a "good" male therapist, Severn's need to be an "innocent" white woman—and recognizing how as non-Black people they are complicit in a system of anti-Black violence, they could have shifted the conflict from being *essentially* a two-person problem into what it is, a sociopolitical problem. This would necessitate a love that counts beyond two, extended to those whose humanity has not been recognized, whose pain has had no redress, whose suffering is not the same yet is structurally related to their own, and has been left without a reckoning.

The Relational-Interpersonal Tradition Post Ferenczi: The Social, Decolonial Turn

There is a political potential in relational and interpersonal approaches (Cushman, 2015; Layton, 2018, 2020). There are many ways that an abusive relationship between parent and child can be analogized to the relationship between oppressor and oppressed. There are applications of Klein's theory of paranoid-schizoid positions to understand the splitting at play in racism (e.g., Dalal, 2013; Dennis, 2022), interpersonal approaches to understanding class, race, and culture (e.g., Frie & Sauvayre, 2022), and relational perspectives on intersectionality, gender, and sexuality (e.g., Belkin & White, 2020). It must also be recognized that relational approaches have "democratized" psychotherapy, with patient and therapist relating on more equal ground while recognizing the asymmetry in their roles (Aron & Harris, 2013). Relational psychoanalysis has built on Ferenczi's attention to therapeutic impasses by articulating how to overcome them through a "third position" that holds both the therapist and the patient's experience (Benjamin, 2017), and expanded on how the intersubjective "third" can intersect with the "social third" of race, class, gender, and sexuality (Altman, 2000; Chang et al., 2021).

Relational and interpersonal approaches are right to address ruptures—including ruptures around culture and identity—that emerge between patient and therapist (the intersubjective third), and suggest that addressing such ruptures is a pathway to discussing the sociopolitical (the social third, see Altman, 2000). But what does one do in the absence of a clearly delineated rupture? Does one wait for the patient to bring cultural topics up? Maybe the therapist bringing them up makes the subject matter safer to talk about, or maybe that is an imposition of the therapist's own agenda, feelings of guilt, and values. Maybe the therapist waiting for the patient to bring them up places an undue burden on them that reproduces the silencing of their experience elsewhere.

And so on and so forth.

To be clear, processing transference–countertransference enactments and the repair of ruptures is a staple of my own clinical work, as it is for many interpersonal and relational clinicians who center identity, culture, and power in their practice. My problem with these debates and with many relational theories is that they depend on primarily interpersonal, *dyadic* logic. *Either* the therapist brings it up or the patient does, creating an impasse that obfuscates how to have organic explorations of the sociocultural in treatment. This is where Lacan and Fanon become critical, as both centered the role of speech as a "third term" which cultural, social, and political forces "slip through," helping us move past the "confusion of tongues" that often bogs down conversations about the social in clinical work.

Sandor Ferenczi Interrupted

As a relational practitioner, I am mindful of being especially critical of Ferenczi and the relational-interpersonal traditions descended from him. Ferenczi put the therapeutic relationship front row and center as a lived encounter between two people. Perhaps no figure has had as lasting an impact on psychoanalysis—and humanistic traditions beyond it—than him. At the same time, his "relational turn" enacted a "turn away" from his earlier socialist, anti-racist, and political insights. This is not to diminish his legacy, but contextualize it in terms of its promises and limitations. While many of us work to "extend" interpersonal and relational frameworks to the sociocultural, they do not inherently account for them as central to their theories.

While one can appreciate the work of Erich Fromm, Harry Stack Sullivan, Karen Horney, and Clara Thompson as sensitive and open to the social, we find the same "broken circuits" as with Freud and Ferenczi—a theory of mind and clinical technique disconnected from critical theorizing—something that is beginning to be remedied (Frie & Sauvayre, 2022). I cannot conceive of a Freudian without a theory of the unconscious, but I can think of relational and interpersonal practitioners without a theory of the sociopolitical. It is not *integral* to the foundations and basic principles of its theories or practices. What I offer is an attempt to think through the "early Ferenczi" attending to social context and the "later Ferenczi" centering the intersubjective process between patient and therapist, so we no longer have to choose between one or the other.

Coda

In the fall of 1937, four years after Ferenczi's death, the Japanese army occupied Beijing, China. That same fall Bingham Dai received a most curious patient (Dai, 1944). "Li" (pseudonym) was a college student who had been tortured by Japanese soldiers for insurgency activity in another territory five years before. After release, he started learning Japanese and making Japanese friends, which surprised his family. At the same time, he struggled with compulsions and trauma symptoms that worsened whenever he encountered Japanese soldiers.

In treatment, Li related a story in which his father brutally beat him into submission, with the feelings of hatred and anger he felt disavowed by his culture which demanded their suppression. The transference reflected this, as Li treated Dai with deference while harboring intense hostility toward him as a paternal figure. While these interpersonal dynamics were important, Dai (1944) pointed out to Li that he was not only relating to him as his father, but his behavior toward him was "similar to his attitude toward the Japanese" (p. 336). Although a proud insurgent, after being tortured Li behaved obsequiously toward the Japanese to survive the occupation, in the hopes that submission offered love and protection. As Li processed this political enactment with Dai his symptoms abated, and he began to reimagine how to engage the Japanese and the anti-imperial struggle in a more conscious way.

As an interpersonal psychoanalyst inheriting Ferenczi's innovations, Dai (1944) was attentive to the role of early childhood as it manifests in the here and now of the therapeutic relationship. At the same time, he critiqued how psychoanalysis "tends to ignore the conflicts of the patient in the present life situation," including their social, cultural, and political context (p. 337). Although his lessons were not heeded by the broader psychoanalytic establishment, his work points to the importance of considering the relational and sociopolitical as two distinct but intersecting dimensions of human experience, something we now develop over the subsequent chapters.

Reflection Questions

- Ferenczi named empathy as a tool to guide us on when to establish emotional safety versus challenging the patient. In what ways do you notice "being empathic" and "being confrontational" put in opposition to each other? Can they be complementary? If so, how? What feelings come up when you think about being direct with patients?
- Ruptures—moments of conflict or misunderstanding—in the therapeutic relationship often evoke anxiety among clinicians. What kinds of ruptures do you notice most challenge you or are harder to pick up on? Are there times when culture and identity become involved? How do you broach or address impasses related to difference?
- Parent–child relations—and drawing parallels to the two-person therapist–patient relation—are a staple of psychoanalytic treatment. What would it mean to think about relationships and the therapeutic process outside of a two-person frame? Are there other factors that impact a two-person

relationship? Are there other ways relationships are organized outside of a two-person model?

Further Reading

Relational and Interpersonal Theory and Practice

- Barsness, R. E. (2021). Therapeutic practices in relational psychoanalysis: A qualitative study. *Psychoanalytic Psychology, 38*(1), 22–30.
- Hirsch, I. (2014). *The interpersonal tradition: The origins of psychoanalytic subjectivity*. Routledge.
- Safran, J. D., & Muran, J. C. (2000). *Negotiating the therapeutic alliance*. Guilford Press.

Relational and Interpersonal Approaches to Culture and Identity

- Belkin, M., & White, C. (Eds). (2020). *Intersectionality and relational psychoanalysis: New perspectives on race, gender, and sexuality*. Routledge.
- Eng, D. L., & Han, S. (2019). *Racial melancholia, racial dissociation: On the social and psychic lives of Asian Americans*. Duke University Press.
- Frie, R., & Sauvayre, P. (Eds). (2022). *Culture, politics and race in the making of interpersonal psychoanalysis: Breaking boundaries*. Routledge.

References

Altman, N. (2000). Black and white thinking: A psychoanalyst reconsiders race. *Psychoanalytic Dialogues, 10*(4), 589–605.
Aron, L., & Harris, A. E. (1993). *The legacy of Sandor Ferenczi*. Analytic Press, Inc.
Aron, L., & Harris, A. E. (2013). *Relational psychoanalysis, volume 2: Innovation and expansion*. Routledge.
Belkin, M., & White, C. (Eds). (2020). *Intersectionality and relational psychoanalysis: New perspectives on race, gender, and sexuality*. Routledge.
Benjamin, J. (2004). Beyond doer and done to: An intersubjective view of thirdness. *The Psychoanalytic Quarterly, 73*(1), 5–46.
Benjamin, J. (2017). *Beyond doer and done to: Recognition theory, intersubjectivity and the third*. Routledge.

Brabant, E., Falzeder, E., Giampieri-Deutsch, P (eds). (1994). *The correspondence of Sigmund Freud and Sandor Ferenczi, 1908-14, vol. 1,* transl. Peter T. Hoffer. The Belknap Press of Harvard University Press.

Brennan, B. W. (2015). Decoding Ferenczi's clinical diary: Biographical notes. *The American Journal of Psychoanalysis, 75*(1), 5–18.

Carter, N. M. (2012). Intimacy without consent: Lynching as sexual violence. *Politics & Gender, 8*(3), 414–421.

Chang, D. F., Dunn, J. J., & Omidi, M. (2021). A critical-cultural-relational approach to rupture resolution: A case illustration with a cross-racial dyad. *Journal of Clinical Psychology, 77*(2), 369–383.

Cushman, P. (2015). Relational psychoanalysis as political resistance. *Contemporary Psychoanalysis, 51*(3), 423–459.

Dai, B. (1944). Divided loyalty in war: A study of cooperation with the enemy. *Psychiatry, 7*(4), 327–340.

Dalal, F. (2013). *Race, colour and the processes of racialization: New perspectives from group analysis, psychoanalysis and sociology.* Routledge.

Dennis, E. (2022). The Paranoid-Schizoid position and envious attacks on the black other. *Psychoanalysis, Self and Context, 17*(2), 141–153.

Dimitrijević, A., Cassullo, G., & Frankel, J. (Eds.). (2018). *Ferenczi's influence on contemporary psychoanalytic traditions.* Routledge, Taylor & Francis Group.

Erös, F. (1990). Technique as politics: Sandor Ferenczi's contribution to analytical social psychology. Presented at the Second Congress of the International Association for the History of Psychoanalysis, London, July 20–22.

Erös, F. (2014). Freedom and authority in the *Clinical Diary. The American Journal of Psychoanalysis., 74*, 367–380.

Fanon, F. (1965). *A dying colonialism.* Grove Press.

Ferenczi, S. (1988). *The clinical diary of Sándor Ferenczi.* Harvard University Press.

Ferenczi, S. (1994a). *First contributions to psycho-analysis.* Karnac Books.

Ferenczi, S. (1994b). *Further contributions to the theory and technique of psycho-analysis.* Karnac Books.

Ferenczi, S. (1994c). *Final contributions to the problems and methods of psycho-analysis.* Karnac Books.

Ferenczi, S., & Rank, O. (1925). *The development of psychoanalysis.* Nervous and Mental Disease Publishing Co.

Fredrickson, J. (2017). *The lies we tell ourselves.* Seven Leaves Press.

Frie, R., & Sauvayre, P. (Eds). (2022). *Culture, politics and race in the making of interpersonal psychoanalysis: Breaking boundaries.* Routledge.

Freud, S. (1937/1964). Analysis terminable and interminable. In *The standard edition of the complete psychological works of Sigmund Freud, volume XXIII (1937–1939): Moses and monotheism, an outline of psycho-analysis and other works* (pp. 209–254).

Gaztambide, D. J. (2019). *A people's history of psychoanalysis: From Freud to liberation psychology.* Lexington Books.

Gutiérrez-Peláez, M. (2015). Ferenczi's anticipation of the traumatic dimension of language: A meeting with Lacan. *Contemporary Psychoanalysis, 51*(1), 137–154.

Gutiérrez-Peláez, M., & Herrera-Pardo, E. (2017). Environment, trauma and technical innovations: Three links between Donald W. Winnicott and Sandor Ferenczi. *Revista Colombiana de Psiquiatría, 46*(2), 121–126.

Hoffman, D. (2003). Sandor Ferenczi and the origins of humanistic psychology. *Journal of Humanistic Psychology, 43*(4), 59–86.

Layton, L. (2018). Relational theory in socio-historical context: Implications for technique. In *De-idealizing relational theory* (pp. 209–234). Routledge.

Layton, L. (2020). *Toward a social psychoanalysis: Culture, character, and normative unconscious processes*. Routledge.

Linehan, M. M. (2018). *Cognitive-behavioral treatment of borderline personality disorder*. Guilford Publications.

Maroda, K. (1998). Why mutual analysis failed: The case of Ferenczi and RN. *Contemporary Psychoanalysis, 34*(1), 115–132.

Muran, J. C., Eubanks, C. F., & Samstag, L. W. (2023). *Rupture and repair in psychotherapy: A critical process for change*. American Psychological Association.

Rachman, A. W. (1993). Ferenczi and sexuality. In L. Aron & S. Harris (Eds.), *The legacy of Sándor Ferenczi* (pp. 81–100). Analytic Press.

Rachman, A. W. (1998). Ferenczi's relaxation principle and the issue of therapeutic responsiveness. *American Journal of Psychoanalysis, 58*(1), 63–81.

Rachman, A. W. (2013). Sándor Ferenczi and the evolution of a self psychology framework in psychoanalysis. In *Conversations in self psychology* (pp. 341–365). Routledge.

Rachman, A. W. (2017). *Elizabeth Severn: The "evil genius" of psychoanalysis*. Routledge.

Rudnytsky, P. L. (2002). *Reading psychoanalysis: Freud, Rank, Ferenczi, Groddeck*. Cornell University Press.

Soreanu, R. (2016). Ferenczi's times: The tangent, the segment, and the meandering line. *American Imago, 73*(1), 51–69.

Strachey, J. (1934). The nature of the therapeutic action of psychoanalysis. In *Classics in psychoanalytic technique* (pp. 361–378).

Wachtel, P. L. (2007). Carl Rogers and the larger context of therapeutic thought. *Psychotherapy, 44*, 279–284.

Wachtel, P. L. (2018). What must we transcend to make progress in psychoanalysis?: Tribal boundaries, the default position, and the self-defeating quest for purity. In S. Axelrod, R. Naso, & L. Rosenberg (Eds.), *Progress in psychoanalysis* (pp. 36–55). Routledge.

4

Lacan atop a Mango Tree: Retrieving the Decolonial Lacan

Fanon (1952/2008) saw language as central in understanding the relationship between the individual, interpersonal, and the social, insofar as learning a language means "to assume a culture, to support the weight of a civilization" (p. 8). It is no surprise, then, that he held Lacan's theory of language as a vehicle for the sociocultural in high regard. For Lacan (1953/2006), the human subject "goes far beyond what is experienced 'subjectively' by the individual," including those intergenerational and collective traumas that form the background of their lives. While the patient "knows only his own lines," the language he speaks is fundamentally "transindividual" (p. 219). When we speak entire traditions, discourses, ideologies, and norms speak through us, our individual "lines" embedded in a larger "script." To understand Lacan's importance for decolonial thinking requires an engagement with the Lacan that Fanon read, as well as insights Lacan developed later in his career which dovetail with Fanon's independent theorizing.

To be clear, I am not a Lacanian… but I am "Lacan-curious." In that spirit, I want to acknowledge how Lacanians talk about the analytic process in terms of analyst and the "analysand." The term analysand underscores the *patient's* active participation in the treatment—the analysand *analyzes* (Fink, 1999, 2007). However, not all Lacanian practitioners are institute-trained psychoanalysts—some are therapists drawn to Lacan (e.g., M. J. Miller, 2011). Similarly, there is no one Lacanian approach but a plurality of approaches (Svolos, 2018). In respect of this diversity, I use "therapist" and "analyst" interchangeably while retaining the term "analysand."

D. J. Gaztambide, *Decolonizing Psychoanalytic Technique*, https://doi.org/10.1007/978-3-031-48476-6_4

Although Lacan is derided as obtuse (his works *are* difficult to read), we examine both the theorist and the practitioner, drawing on his *Ecrits* or "writings," his seminars, and first-person accounts of his clinical work. I note that Lacan's works—like Fanon's—were often dictated instead of written, speaking to something central to psychoanalysis: the beauty of the spoken word. When we read Lacan and Fanon we are in effect reading poetry. We turn to Lacan's poems, recited to a psychoanalysis in the throes of conformity.

The "Mirror Stage" as a Reflection of the Social Link

We begin with the paper Fanon most cited from Lacan's work (1949/2006), "The mirror stage," where Lacan describes the infant's experience of motor incoordination, bodily fragmentation, and dependence on the other for survival. In relating to the child's distress, the caregiver forms a mental image of their bodily state, providing a verbal reflection (mirror) of this image: "Aw, are you hungry?" This image is offered to the child as something to *identify* with, such that their internal experience acquires meaning and coherence, turned into a sense of "I" (i.e., "I am hungry"). The child's identification with this image is ambivalent, facing the image in the "mirror" like an unwanted intruder (p. 77). The social surround transforms the child's fragmented body into a kind of "'orthopedic'… armor," an image that alienates them from their immediate experience, now seen through the external point of view of the other (p. 78).

The body's fragmented nature, however, seeps in from time to time in dreams of falling teeth or exposed organs (Lacan, 1949/2006, p. 78). The "I" may be represented in dreams as "a fortified camp," whose depths "symbolizes the id [it]" (p. 79). The "it" is a source of shame as it does not fit the image provided by the other, leading to the feeling that we are *lacking* and can never live up to the image reflected by our parents and society. We come to *hate* this image, even as we fit ourselves to it to procure love. We go to war with this image, projecting it on others who become uncanny doubles to be vanquished—only then will I be "whole." Regardless, the lack remains, requiring greater Quixotic charges against a litany of windmills.

The subject's identification with the image places them in a state of constant anxiety, oscillating between submission and competition with the other: "a freedom that is never so authentically affirmed [as] within the walls of a prison… [or when] satisfied by Hegelian murder" (Lacan, 1949/ 2006, pp. 79–80). Between "nature and culture," psychoanalysis examines "the knot of imaginary servitude that love must always untie anew or sever" (p. 80). This suggests that analytic love is an unbinding (un-tying, loosening, severing) of the knots that get us tongue-tied, freeing us from the clash of power and domination. It is interesting to recall again Du Bois' double consciousness, caught between the image seen through the other's eyes and one's own immediacy, a parallel that underscored Fanon's use of Lacan as well.

The mirror stage is central to what Lacan calls the "imaginary register," an interpersonal struggle for wholeness in which we try to "fit" one another to the images we hold, while wanting others to recognize us. What Lacan calls the symbolic order intervenes in this conflict through language as a "third term" that regulates the self–other relation, pointing beyond the "twosome" of the interpersonal dyad toward societal rules, values, laws, and norms. The symbolic provides a "shared language" that facilitates intersubjectivity and dialogue through cultural conventions. In chess, for example, the players are in an "imaginary" relation trying to form an image of what the other player is thinking, what move they will make, etc., in order to win—the symbolic establishes the rules of the game, such as taking turns, the knight moves in an "L" shape, etc.

Lacan alternates between the lowercase "other" to refer to interpersonal relations, and the uppercase "Other" to depict an otherness beyond our imaginary constructions. Language functions as this third "Other" in relation to the interpersonal dyad, giving rise to Lacan's dictum, "desire is desire of the Other." Meaning, what is it that others, society, etc., want of me? Who do they want me to be? Imagine a parent who raises their child to "be a doctor" because they were unable to. The child becomes a doctor, achieves success, yet struggles with an ever-present anxiety that they will fall short. No matter how hard they work to fulfill their parent's desire, a lack remains. The desire to "become a doctor" is not only the burden of a familial desire, but something society deems *desirable*. The (interpersonal) other's desire becomes a vehicle for the (social) Other's desire.

Initially, Lacan conceptualizes psychoanalytic work as the use of the symbolic (language and speech) to articulate a reality that cannot be captured by rigid, imaginary conceptions of the world, freeing desire from its oppressive entanglement with the Other. Over the course of his career, he recognizes the role of what he calls "the Real," a traumatic excess beyond words, reimagining analytic work less as putting experience into words, and more as a spontaneous encounter with something outside our mappings of self and world that *shatters* them, unbinding tightened knots so they can be quilted anew. Imagine as you are playing chess a hurricane suddenly appears, blowing away the pieces and board, "clearing the table" for something new. We trace this trajectory in Lacan, concluding with case examples illustrating his work.

The Symbolic Order: Language as a Transindividual Associative Network

In "The Instance of the Letter," Lacan (1957/2006) describes how before we are born we are "already inscribed" in a discourse that precedes us, a tradition passed down unconsciously though "inconceivable apart from the permutations authorized by language" (p. 414). Culture is in a dynamic relation to language, in that words signify something beyond themselves, a presence that is also an absence. A formula Lacan uses to illustrate this is

$$\frac{S}{s}$$

This formula means, "signifier [S] over signified [s], 'over' corresponding to the bar separating the two levels" (p. 415). Lacan reinvents Saussure's distinction between the *signifier*, the phonology or sound of a word such as "tree," and the *signified*, what a word points to, i.e., the wooden thing in a forest with branches. The "bar" separating the two denotes that signifier and signified have no direct correlation, as the signifier is primarily related to *other* signifiers—for example, the word "wait" sounds like the word "weight." It is based on sound that jokes and dreams derive meaning. Consider this cringy "dad" joke, "How do you follow Will Smith in the snow? You follow the fresh prints." When you say this aloud, "fresh *prints*" sounds like "Fresh *Prince*," the reference to the iconic 90's sitcom delivering the punchline. Hence, associations between signifiers are arbitrary but not strictly illogical, mediated by language and cultural context.

Earlier we said that language and words are "a presence that is also an absence." If you are an English speaker, think of the expression "what goes up..." and in very short order your mind fills in the blank, "...must come down." The phrase "what goes up..." is a presence that signifies the second phrase, which is an absence—it is not literally there except through the link formed through language and culture. And yet, that very "absence" ("...must come down") is itself a ghostly presence haunting the uttered phrase. Language and its associations are opaque in that you cannot know in advance what it signifies unless you are immersed in its sociocultural context. Culture is exactly such an absence that is also a presence, texturing what we say, do, believe, etc.

Phonemes, the perceptually distinct units of sound in language, are one medium for associations (Remember L's "rats" from Chapter 1). A related dynamic is metonymy, using the name of one thing for another linked by an abstract, superficial reference. For example, using "suits" to refer to people in business (they wear them), or "shrinks" for therapists (they "shrink" your head). Phonemes, metonymy, rhyme, and the structure of words (e.g., "house" and "mouse"), are linguistic traits that structure signifiers in an associative network, linked "according to the laws of a closed order," within given cultural and linguistic practices (Lacan, 1957/2006, p. 418).

The unconscious is thus "structured like a language," a code, "a web of... formulas for connection and substitution," using speech "to signify *something altogether different* from what it says" (Lacan, 1957/2006, pp. 421, 434, emphasis original). We are metaphorical creatures, playing with words in counterintuitive ways: "I'm *not* mad at you, I *just* felt like screaming." Lacan shows how the substituting of one word for another through metaphor "shows the mechanism's connaturality with poetry" (p. 425). We might play with Lacan's dictum and say that "the unconscious is structured like a poem," taking bits and pieces of sound and metaphor to write "the Other" a rhyme we secretly *hope* they will decipher. Given the concealing *and* expressive nature of speech, we can speak concretely about defenses as "figures of style... rhetoric... the analysand actually utters" (p. 433).

Lacan advocates for closer attention to what the analysand actually says—like Freud and Ferenczi, to be more "superficial." A defense is a rhetorical device that *says something* otherwise *difficult* to say. For example, an analysand court-mandated for a DUI asserts "I *don't really* have a problem with my drinking, I *just* enjoy a *little* drink *now and then*," their body swaying under the influence. Remove the italicized words, listen to what their body is "saying," and the message becomes clearer. Another analysand says "We don't really have problems, *but* my boyfriend *sometimes* talks over me." The statement, meant to minimize the idea the relationship has some difficulties, inadvertently *insists* on them. The therapist repeats back a fragment of this sentence, "he sometimes *talks* over you," triggering associations between "talks" and "walks," leading the analysand to verbalize for the first time how their partner "*walks* all over me."

Lacan's Critique of Object Relations and Ego Psychology: Speech as a "Transindividual" Force Beyond the Relational

In "The Function and Field of Speech," Lacan (1953/2006) notes an aversion to language in object-relational and ego psychological approaches of the 1950s—Ferenczi and Freud's descendants, respectively—criticizing what he calls the "imaginary" turn toward countertransference responsiveness (p. 202). Lacan characterizes responsiveness as "imaginary" in that it creates an image of the analysand's "needs," then compels them to identify with it, foreclosing any reality outside the therapist's "understanding." This leads to "an activism motivated by charity" privileging caregiving over the analysand putting their experience into words, the therapist undertaking a "Samaritan-type aid" emphasizing their "mastery," *adapting* the analysand to their values and beliefs, and reigning sociocultural conventions (p. 202).

Lacan (1953/2006) argues for a "return to Freud," recentering the analysand's speech. The analysand's speech always "calls for a response" in the presence of another: "this is the heart of its function in analysis" (p. 206). Speech is a "testimony" the analyst tries to decipher: "he takes the description of an everyday event as a fable... a simple slip of the tongue as a highly complex statement" (p. 209). Lacan acknowledges that the analyst's instrument for hearing the analysand *is* "the imaginary relation that links him to the subject qua ego; and although he cannot eliminate it, he can use it to adjust the receptivity of his ears," (p. 211). One cannot "eliminate" the imaginary but find ways of attuning within it not captured by traditional notions of "empathy," so far as this means "knowing what the other person feels" (see Chapter 7).

For Lacan, it is not by looking for "deeper meaning" that one hears, but by listening to "what" the analysand actually says, "how" they say it, and "who" is speaking through them—the unconscious, Lacan (1953/2006) tells us, "is the Other's discourse." Meaning, that the analysand's speech betrays a "transindividual reality... which is not at the subject's disposal" (p. 214). When we speak, we have access to the "lines" available to us as part of a broader story, a script full of characters and collective histories—multitudes speak through us. This is why Lacan argues that seeing treatment "in merely dyadic terms is as inadequate to it in theory as it is damaging to its technique" (p. 220). To wit, there is no such thing as "one person" in the sense of an isolated individual devoid of context, and *there are never just two people in the room*.

The Structure of the "Law" in Language: *Le Nom Du Père* Beyond the Father

If language functions like a "law," a collective set of contingencies, prohibitions, and associations, then it requires a symbolic mediator, a function Lacan calls "the name of the father," (Lacan, 1955–1956/1988). I ask the reader's patience in unpacking this concept. Lacan was emphatic that this does not refer to an actual father, nor is this function limited to a specific gender, though he nonetheless opens himself up to critiques of a tacit patriarchal trend.

The original French illustrates Lacan's wordplay, alternating between *le nom du père* (the *name* of the father) and *le non du père* (the *no* of the father). The term captures a psychosocial function through which meaning, tradition, and symbols of the "law" (shared associations in language and culture) are transmitted intergenerationally and "names" one as part of a community and lineage. Think of Thor from the movies of the same name. He is "Thor, son of Odin," or "Odin-son," named *by* his father and bearing his name as part of Nordic culture, much like in Latin American cultures a person's primary last name is usually their father's followed by their mother's. The function of the name, *le nom*, allows one's identity to be constituted. But just as important is *le non*, "the no," outlining what associations and meanings *are not* allowed.

Remember our earlier discussion of psychosis (see Chapter 2), where there is a disruption of the function of "the no," as in "*no*, a dog is *not* god." Without this regulatory "no"—this *cut*—psychotic thought proliferates, "a dog *is* god," resulting in hallucinations of persecutory canine gods. In a different cultural context such as ancient Egypt, these associations are not psychotic but "fit" within their linguistic milieu (e.g., the dog-headed god Anubis). The "no" of that symbolic order allows certain associations to be formed (a dog-headed god) but render others alien—for example, that a Hebrew, once enslaved by Pharaoh, could be God. What is "crazy" in ancient Egypt feels true for a Roman Christian. The "name/no" allows certain symbols, associations, and meanings while curtailing others. For a less patriarchal formula, we could call it "the no of the yes," *le non du oui* in French. In English we can also read it as "the no of the *we*" to underscore its communal character (*oui* sounds like "we"). Though a societal function, it can also be performed at an interpersonal level. Imagine a child who scrapes herself and cries, "It hurts, I'm going to die!" The mother caresses the child, "I know it hurts, sweetie, but you're ok. You're *not* going to die."

To anticipate our reading of Fanon, I share an example of how the "no of the yes" operates socially. Isabel Wilkerson (2020), an African American journalist, tells the story of an interview with a businessman she was going to conduct for the *The New York Times*. He arrived in a rush, saying he did not have time to talk as he was "running late for an appointment." Wilkerson was confused. "I think I'm your appointment," she said. "No," he replied, "this is a very important appointment with *The New York Times*." Wilkerson insisted, "But I am with *The New York Times*." Even after showing him her ID, he was unfazed. "She must be running late," he said, "I'm going to have to ask you to leave so I can get ready for my appointment." Wilkerson realized that his notion of who *is* and *is not* a *New York Times* reporter blinded him, "it seemed not to occur to him that a *New York Times* national correspondent could come in a container such as mine, despite every indication that I was she" (p. 60).

Punctuation: Reflecting, Repeating, and "Remixing" the Analysand's Speech

Mirroring Ferenczi's insight that the analysand perceives in the analyst the whole of the social surround with the power to "bind or loosen," Lacan (1953/2006) sees the analyst as performing the symbolic function of the "name/no" to establish a *difference* between the analysand and their "narcissistic relations… with the image" (p. 230). In practice, the analyst "plays on the power of symbols by evoking them in a calculated fashion in the semantic resonances of his remarks" (p. 243). Put simply, the analyst uses language to disrupt the analysand's speech. When the analysand says, for example, "I was sad when my mom abandoned me as a child, *but* I'm over it now," the therapist reflects back "…over it?" with an inquisitive tone, tacitly inviting the analysand to expand on how exactly they are "over it." A simple rearrangement of words can evoke other meanings, reflecting back the unspoken yet present phrase, "sad child," leading the analysand to release a deep sigh, "I feel like if I don't get over it, I'll never forgive my mother and have a good relationship with her in her final days."

The analyst "plays back" the analysand's free association like a tape recorder—a DJ really—"punctuating" it, cutting and editing the tape by reflecting or remixing choice words, phrases, or motifs in their speech (Lacan 1953/2006, p. 258). In the same way punctuation in writing "establishes… meaning; changing the punctuation renews or upsets it" (p. 258). Punctuation or "scansion" of the analysand's words and phrases can involve rearranging them, adding a comma or period, a different intonation, or just inviting the analysand to "play back the tape." The analyst works with speech like an editor working with a text, generating "a renewed technique of interpretation" (p. 243). As we will unpack below, by interpretation Lacan does not mean a didactic explanation, but saying or doing something that provokes the analysand to interpret *him*, writing "the function of language in speech is not to inform but to evoke" (p. 247).

It was not only words that Lacan (1953/2006) punctuated, but sessions themselves. The technique that made Lacan an *enfant terrible* in psychoanalysis (not unlike Ferenczi), the "variable-length session," involves the analyst picking a poignant or surprising statement by the analysand to punctuate by ending the session early. Why such a potentially disruptive intervention? Lacan noticed that some analysands fill sessions with "empty speech," circuitous stories or intellectualizing as part of their "evasive maneuvers," running out the clock "as [one] would [run] for a place of shelter" (p. 258). But if he ended sessions early, this disrupted the avoidance, and like Ferenczi's "active" interventions accelerated the production of meaningful material.

Lacan (1953/2006) gives the example of how punctuating sessions evoked a cisgender male analysand's fantasies of becoming pregnant "in a time frame in which I would normally still have been listening to his speculations on Dostoyevsky's artistry" (p. 259). As another of his analysands put it, the shortened sessions enhanced his free association, saying what comes to mind "almost immediately, with *spontaneity*, for there is no time to mull them over, to find the nicest formulation" (cited in Roudinesco, 1997, p. 388, emphasis added). Yet another analysand, a Jesuit priest wrestling with his faith, shared there were "Few interpretations, but interventions which led to decisions… The shorter sessions allowed me to avoid obsessionalizing my therapy" (cited in Roudinesco, 1990, p. 233). Lacan (1953/2006) compares this to Zen practices "to bring about the subject's revelation," though he cautions against "extremes," advocating for "a discreet application of its basic principle… insofar as [it] does not in itself entail any danger of alienating the subject" (p. 260). The variable length can also mean extending sessions. For example, Lacan would visit patients who were hospitalized to continue the treatment (see Weiss, 2001). Whether punctuating words or sessions, what is essential for Lacan (1953/2006) is technique that "shatters discourse only in order to bring forth speech" (p. 260). Put colloquially, to disrupt the voice of all those familial, cultural, and social Others so our own voice can breathe—a voice that says "no."

The Ethics of Not-Knowing: The Analyst as the Subject Supposed to Know

Psychoanalysis disrupts the imaginary oscillation between submission and domination by introducing a third option—to *refuse* the intersubjective struggle altogether, allowing desire to "[refind] in negation a final triumph" (Lacan, 1953/2006, p. 263). This negation frees the subject from the ego's mask and the Other's desire by saying "'No!' to this darting game of intersubjectivity in which desire gains recognition for a moment only to lose itself in… the other's will" (p. 263). Out of this process emerges a reckoning, a negation, a "No" from the analysand toward those interpersonal and societal "others" that have structured their life. Paving the way for this refusal—this act of agency—is the analyst's refusal to inhabit a position of knowledge and power. Lacan returns to Ferenczi's recommendation to place the analyst's knowledge in "a subordinate position; authority that knows not to insist…true modesty regarding one's knowledge" (p. 283), stressing the surrender of the analyst's ego.

To decenter the analyst's power is to center the analysand's speech, and recognize "in [the analyst's] knowledge the symptom of his own ignorance," (Lacan, 1953/2006, p. 297). The therapist is not a keeper of truths to be deposited in the analysand, but a master of "nonknowledge, which is not a negation of knowledge but rather its most elaborate form" (p. 297). Calling the analyst the "subject *supposed* to know," Lacan agrees with Ferenczi on the role of humility and addressing one's resistance to the analysand (p. 298), except that for Lacan the analyst does not make a repair to the patient directly—which risks recentering their experience—but explores their resistance in supervision or their own personal analysis.

While the role of self-disclosure, countertransference, and repair form a fault line between relational and Lacanian approaches today (see Fink, 2007, 2010), Lacan was not a "good Lacanian," much like Freud was not a "good Freudian." Lacan's clinical work gestures toward something complex yet complementary to Ferenczi. For example, Ferenczi stressed empathy as a guide for engaging the analysand within their "therapeutic window," while Lacan draws attention to the limits—and colonizing effects—of "understanding," insofar as it risks reducing the analysand to an image in the analyst's mind. Both stress the importance of not-knowing with different emphases in ways that proved useful to Fanon's clinical work.

Speech and the Transference as Vehicles for the Social

Lacan (1953–1954/1991) asserts that if analysis takes place within a wider frame of language and culture, then there is a "necessity for a third term… which is speech" (p. 261). Free association is a medium not just for the analysand's familial drama, but the ideologies and cultural values of their wider surround. Resistance, as both vehicle and obstacle, symbolizes the interruption of the analysand's speech by another voice. When we listen to free association or resistance in treatment we must ask ourselves, "*who is speaking?*" (p. 41, emphasis original).

Just as the analysand is about to say something they never shared with anyone, they suddenly "break off" their speech and address the therapist, "Oh, well I don't really mean that," "But, you don't think…" "I feel like I'm boring you…" etc. Behind this break is another voice, perhaps the caution of an early caregiver ("don't say *that*, that's not nice") or a criticism from one's community ("*we* don't think that way, that's shameful"). Alongside those inner voices is also the analysand's realization, "*I am aware all of a sudden of the fact of your presence*" (Lacan, 1953–1954/1991, p. 40, emphasis original). Transference is the recognition that there is someone else *here*, like a horror movie when the protagonist turns and faces a ghost. The Other emerges not only in the analysand's speech but in the presence of the analyst, a presence that brings with it a "bit of Real," a traumatic excess that mark the analysand's history.

The Analysand as Interpreter of the Transference

In "The direction of the treatment," Lacan (1958/2006) argues that verbal interpretations are not terribly useful, for "the analyst's speech is still heard as coming from the transferential Other" (p. 494). If an analysand fears the analyst will abandon them, simply reassuring them "I will not abandon you" offers little relief, as it is still heard as coming from someone who is transferentially feared *will* abandon them. A tug of war may ensue, in which the analyst anxiously tries to convince the analysand of their good intentions. By insisting on the "correctness" of our interpretation or empathy, understanding becomes a form of violence reducing the other to our image of them. Lacan makes a connection between enactments in which analyst and analysand attempt to "fit" one another to their imaginary conceptions, and a Darwinian "struggle for life," a survival of the fittest where only one perspective can "live" (cf. Benjamin, 2016). Lacan (1953–1954/1991) again cautions us against "understanding" too much, for it is through a "refusal of understanding that we push open the door to analytic understanding" (p. 73). His (1958/2006) words should be taken to heart, "When you don't understand... don't blame yourself immediately, say to yourself—the fact that I don't understand must mean something" (p. 228).

Earlier we mentioned the analysand's refusal of the intersubjective game of domination and submission. Citing Ferenczi, Lacan (1953–1954/1991) argues that just as the wisdom of the child can emerge "out of nowhere" to disrupt the parent's mistreatment of them, so too the way out of imaginary enactments can arise from "whatever is verbalised in an irruptive fashion" (p. 219). If we remain non-defensive and invite the analysand to tell us more, we create an opportunity for something else to come through in their speech, a truth that emerges *spontaneously*.

Even when the analysand seeks to undo their own speech by distancing themselves from it, the therapist must "link the subject to his contradictions, to make him sign what he says, and to pledge his speech" (Lacan, 1953–1954/1991, p. 230). To kindle the emergence of this irruptive speech in the transference, Lacan (1958/2006) draws on the card game bridge, in which the analyst "enlists the aid of... the dummy *[le mort]*... to bring out the... player who is to be the analysand's partner here, and whose hand the analyst, by his maneuvers, strives to get the analysand to guess" (p. 492). The opacity of the therapist's mind keeps the analysand guessing, facilitating the irruption of the analysand's actual partner—the subject of their unconscious. By reflecting on the analyst's mind, the analysand is guided toward reflecting on their own. From this position, Lacan does not so much *make* an interpretation as offer the analysand an opportunity to interpret *his* behavior. This inverts the power relation—the analysand becomes the interpreter of the analyst's mind as well as their own.

Lacan (1958/2006) emphasized that interpretations operate on "the function of the signifier" (p. 495) meaning they do not aim for a singular, conclusive meaning but open up a plurality of possibilities leading to more journeys, fewer destinations. The best "interpretation" the therapist can offer is one *the analysand must interpret*, generating possibilities beyond what they thought imaginable. There is an interesting "family resemblance" here with relational theorizing on the analysand as interpreter of the analyst's subjectivity (Aron, 1991; Hoffman, 1983), reinforced by Lacan's (1969–1970/2011) later reformulation of this reversal of power as a change in discourse, where discourse refers to a particular kind of relationship. For the sake of space, we focus on three of these discourses—the master, the hysteric, and the analyst.

The discourse of the master refers to a relationship in which an agent puts the other "to work" to produce a "surplus enjoyment," a "theft" of the other's enjoyment to satisfy their own (Lacan, 1969–1970/2011, pp. 5, 53). In the analytic relationship, this can manifest as the therapist behaving like a "master" of knowledge, emplacing the analysand in a position similar to Ferenczi's abused child who attunes to the abuser's needs, wants, and desires to survive (p. 9). Such moments come up in treatment whenever the analyst attempts to assert their knowledge and power over the patient's. Instead of asserting mastery, the therapist should seek to create the ideal conditions for "the hystericisation of discourse" (p. 9).

What is this discourse of the hysteric? If, as Lacan (1972–1972) asserts, "love is the sign… that one is changing discourse" (p. 78), then the analyst surrendering their power is itself an act of love, allowing space for the analysand to interrogate themselves, asking "Who am I?" while posing to the analyst "Who do *you* want me to be?" This is a critical moment, as the analyst may be tempted to retake the position of the master and tell the analysand "who they are" according to their whims and desires. The analyst's mastery is (rightly) questioned by the analysand as it does not "fit" them—the analyst keeps offering windmills for the analysand to charge. What is needed is a turn toward the discourse of the analyst, which "ought to find itself at the very opposite of any will for mastery" (1969–1970/2011, p. 103). The discourse of the analyst communicates that it is the analysand's knowledge that is centered: Lacan's invitation is to "*say everything that goes through your head… What you produce will always be accepted*" (p. 103, emphasis original). This is the curvature of the analyst's desire—to the extent the analysand desires to know what it is the analyst desires (as desire is always desire of the Other), the analyst deploys their desire to *redirect* the analysand toward their own unconscious as a source of value, worth, and meaning.

To give a concrete example, a young adult analysand of color discusses their options between different graduate schools: "I think I'm gravitating to this school, since they are offering me a full ride." Suddenly they ask me, "Where do *you* think I should go to school?" Struck by this question, I reflect back his words with a twist, "Between these different options you are gravitating toward this school, but you're asking *where* you should go to school?" The analysand insists on my answer; I insist on their knowledge with an edited punctuation: "You are gravitating to *this* school, but you're asking *where* you should *go*?" He sighed deeply, expanding on his underlying anxiety, "If I go there, I will be far away from my family." They knew very well what they desired but feared acting on it, turning their ambivalence into a question for me to fill with my mastery, with what *I* would want him to do. My desire to know, sincerely, what it was *they* truly wanted redirected us back toward my patient's desire and the anxieties orbiting it.

The Power of the Treatment: A Chance Encounter with The Real

In Lacan's (1964/2018) seminal *The Four Fundamental Concepts of Psycho-analysis*, he studied how we repeat certain patterns of behavior to the point of pain, borrowing from Aristotle the term *automaton* to describe the automatic, almost mechanical tendencies of the repetition compulsion, juxtaposing it to another Aristotelian word, *tuché*, which he interprets as a "chance encounter" with the traumatic Real (p. 52). Remember here Freud's remark that chance plays a role in the symptom (see Chapter 2). The Real—that traumatic presence beyond words—lies "behind the automaton" (p. 53), with the repetition compulsion an attempt to master but also run away from an original *tuché*, a chance encounter with a trauma that follows close behind. Transforming this trauma involves "the duty of the analyst in the interpretation of the transference," meaning again an encounter the analyst offers for the *analysand*'s interpretation (p. 63).

One only goes so far in detoxifying the Real through the symbolic, that is to say, by putting trauma into words—something beyond words is needed. "If development is entirely animated by accident, by the obstacle of the *tuché*," Lacan (1964/2018) concludes, "it is in so far as the *tuché* brings us back to the same point" (p. 63). If a chance encounter with the Real led to a rigid binding or "knotting" of the subject, then a more manageable encounter with that "origin point" opens this knot to be restructured in a new way. Lacan argues that what the analysand needs "is not adaptation, but *tuché*, the encounter" (p. 69). Remixing interpersonal analyst Frieda Fromm-Reichman once again, we might say the analysand does not need an explanation but a chance encounter with what Lacan (1964/2018, p. 69) calls "a being capable of choice," *outside* their mappings of the other. He imagines a different role for the analyst's "presence" which dovetails with relational-interpersonal thinking.

The analysand's repetition compulsion leads to a "missed opportunity… The appointment [with the Real] is always missed" (Lacan, 1964/2018, p. 128). The role of the analyst is to help the analysand "keep" this appointment, and encounter the traumatic Real of the Other's enigmatic desire. If the analysand's "fundamental fantasy" is their attempt to decipher what the *Other*—their parents, family, society, etc.—wants, then the analyst through an act beyond words *reintroduces* enigma and opacity to "traverse" and shatter this fantasy. The analyst becomes not a silent figure but an *enigmatic* one, an opaque "provocateur" who responds in a spontaneous fashion. In precise terms, Lacan states, "I am a clown. Take that as an example, and don't imitate me!" (cited in Nobus, 2016, p. 37).

The analyst behaves in a way that is not contrived, cannot be pre-planned, and is unique to each analysand, contrasting so jarringly with their understanding of how people are "supposed to be" that it cannot be assimilated within their imaginary or symbolic coordinates. As some have commented, this is a kind of "therapeutic traumatization," not in the sense of traumatizing the analysand but of re-exposing them to a manageable fragment of the Real: "If the analyst to a certain extent embodies what may be Real to a person—unpredictable, impossible, shocking—this allows the traumatic experience to be worked over within the transference" (Cauwe et al., 2017, p. 626). At the risk of being provocative to my Lacanian colleagues, this reminds me of a relational-interpersonal idea—the "corrective emotional experience."

The Corrective Emotional Experience, A Bit of Real, and the *Sinthome*

Alexander and French (1946) define the corrective emotional experience thusly: "to re-expose the analysand, under more favorable circumstances, to emotional situations which he could not handle in the past... to repair the traumatic influence of previous experiences" (p. 66). Reflecting Ferenczi's influence, they argued it is secondary whether this "takes place... in the transference relationship, or parallel with the treatment in the daily life of the patient" (p. 66). The analyst provides a contrast with the analysand's experience, a radical difference breaching their transferential similarity to earlier traumatic situations. This difference gives the analysand "an opportunity to face again and again, under more favorable circumstances, those emotional situations which were formerly unbearable and to deal with them in a manner different from the old" (p. 67). A final element of this corrective experience is that it must be surprising, "*overwhelming* and *unexpected*" (p. 68, emphasis added).

Similarly, Lacan's discussion of the analyst's Real presence suggests that what is mutative is to re-expose the analysand time and again, under different circumstances, to a manageable "bit of Real," a disruptive, sometimes overwhelming contrast that shatters their expectations of self and other so a new space can be created. *How* we accomplish this is a matter of which road we take to Rome. There lies the genius of Lacan's remark, "don't imitate me!" A contrived, pre-planned provision of a "corrective experience" is indeed an imaginary construction—folding the analysand into an image the therapist already has. Hence why Lacan stressed the character of spontaneity, improvisation, surprise, even a bit of the comedic, hence "I am a clown." In this respect, Lacan comes close to relational theorizing on the "safe surprise" enacted by the analyst's behavior (Bromberg, 2003).

Lacan (1957/2006) hinted at the analyst's Real presence earlier in his work, in that

> a *calculated vacillation* of the analyst's 'neutrality' may be more valuable… than any number of interpretations—provided, of course, that the *fright* this risks bringing about in the analysand does not lead to a breaking off of the analysis, and that the analysand is convinced by what follows that the analyst's desire was in no way involved in the matter. (p. 698, emphasis added)

This is why the analyst's spontaneous response is so important, so long as the "fright this risks" operates within what the analysand can tolerate. Lacan is clear this is "not a recommendation regarding technique" as it would defeat the spontaneity of a chance encounter. Rather, we must cultivate "an ever renewed ignorance so that no one is considered a typical case" (p. 699). Our intervention, then, must be unique and improvised with each new patient, even as we follow certain clinical principles and technical "rules of thumb." But should even your thumb lead you to err as a clinician, it might be fortuitous to "pluck it out."

Related to the concept of *tuché* is the *sinthome*. Gherovici (2017) points to a shift in Lacan's later work to supporting the analysand's identification with the symptom. What does this mean? Lacan (1975–1976) draws on an archaic spelling of "symptom" which sounds the same when spoken aloud—*sinthome*—which he defines as what "allows someone to live by providing an organization of *jouissance*" (p. 142). *Jouissance*, again, refers to how pain and pleasure—cost and reward—are structured in how we live. And for Lacan, life is structured through a kind of Borromean knot bound by three interconnected rings—precisely the imaginary, the symbolic, and the Real. If one of the rings is "cut"—due to trauma or loss—the structure risks falling apart. The *sinthome* is the analysand's unique solution to this crisis to keep the chain linked. Lacan's use of a different spelling, *sinthome*, delinks symptom from pathology and redefines it as the person's creative solution to life's struggles. Symptoms are not simply maladies, but the patient's attempt to heal and live. In the patient coming to "identify" with their symptom, to understand it (as Freud said) not merely as an adversary to be gotten rid of but as something with a "solid ground for its existence" (as well as ours), they can begin to honor, mourn, and reposition the symptom in a new way.

The Real as Decolonial Shattering: Lacan on Joyce

The symbolic nature of language inserts a cut to "tame" the Real, but such bindings can become rigid, stuck in imaginary reifications. Where the symbolic likes to "bind" with words, the Real shatters with a radical "unbinding." "Analysis," Lacan (1975–1976) writes, "is a matter of suturing and splicing" (p. 80), a controlled unbinding that opens new paths toward the *sinthome*. Lacan draws on the Irish author James Joyce, asking "was Joyce mad? Which is: what was it that inspired his writing?" (p. 112). Through Joyce's subversive approach to the English language—notable as an Irish author upending language of his colonizer—Lacan defines the *sinthome* as "a way of repairing" breaches between the symbolic, imaginary, and the Real. Related to this is his preoccupation with "the proper name." He interprets that Joyce writes to compensate for his lack "by wanting a name for himself" (p. 128). Relatedly, analysis is an act of renaming—*claiming* a name with and beyond one's heritage.

Lacan makes a peculiar comment relevant to decoloniality—which he may have siphoned from Fanon, who was a contemporary (see Richards, 2021). Lacan (1975–1976) argues the very words we depend on are often *imposed* on us. Thinking of English invading Joyce's native Gaelic language, Lacan writes, "the word is a parasite… a form of cancer with which the human being is afflicted" (p. 128). In his seemingly "mad" writing Joyce decomposes the English word itself, writing as "a matter of liberating oneself from the parasite" (p. 131). In the act of writing as *sinthome*, Joyce repairs the rupture colonialism wrought in his Borromean knot. Lacan cautions that in such a repair "you will not get the same knot [as before]" (p. 132). The *sinthome* is a novel creation, a cut of the old knot, a death to be mourned. Critical to this again is a "a bit of Real" (p. 150).

"The fire is the Real," Lacan (1975–1976) writes, "[setting] fire to everything" (p. 152). It is a "cold fire… on the side of absolute zero" (p. 152). The Real is in "the lower limit" where there is no beyond, "no progress except that marked by death" (p. 156). An encounter with the Real is like hitting "rock bottom," the absolute zero where death looms, yet from it also emerges what Fanon called an "authentic upheaval" (see Chapter 6). Per Lacan, the advent of the *sinthome*. To the extent the symptom protects against death, the *sinthome* tallies with death itself. The symptom seeks to be reduced to knowledge, whereas the *sinthome* resists knowledge. Hence, "a sinthome [is] such that there is nothing that can be done to analyse it" (p. 157). It defies words.

This is not to imply opposition between symptom and *sinthome*—the latter emerges when we cease being at war with the former. Gherovici (2017) comments on the *sinthome* as "*a corrective device* to repair a fault, a slip of the knot" (p. 143, emphasis added). Similar to *tuché*, Gherovici argues this "corrective device" involves dealing with "chance and spontaneity… turbulence, creating vortices and eddies… the creation of new bodies; it is the spontaneous creativity of matter" (p. 143). The analytic cure is not about "decoding" the unconscious per se, but calling forth the *sinthome* to wrap the Real in a symbolic carapace, "transforming the economy of jouissance" (p. 145). Facing our pain does not entail the end of suffering per se. We face it because on the other side is something of value that makes our brush with death worth it.

For example, we fear the loss of love, running from it only to find ourselves in suffering's clutches. But if we work through this fear, instead of a pleasure in pain that deprives us of love we discover the pleasure in pain that *is* love itself. Love involves a brush with the Real that restructures *jouissance*, risking death itself so that we may live, love, and be loved. The analyst facilitates this brush, introducing a "bit of Real" to disrupt the symptom so the *sinthome* can play in the gap between registers. Lacan (1976–1977) invites the analysand to *identify* with the symptom "while taking… a kind of distance" (p. 3). Meaning, to understand its function so it can be deconstructed and reshaped in a new way. "Knowing how to deal with your symptom," he writes, "is the end of analysis" (p. 4). Playing with Gherovici's (2017) reading we might say that surviving the "Real" and enjoying our *sinthome* in a new way is a… corrective experience.

Lacan as Clinician across Culture and Difference

We have discussed Lacan's theory and technique in broad strokes, yet throughout his work are moments where what is implicit in his theory of language and culture is made more explicit. For example, Fanon and other decolonial thinkers have drawn attention to how the imaginary recognition struggle of the mirror stage can help us understand the psychodynamics of oppression (see Chapter 6). In speaking of the imaginary as a Darwinian "struggle for life," Lacan (1953–1954/1991) makes clear this is not a metaphor, "If it was Darwin who wrought it, that was because he came of a nation of privateers, for whom racism was the basic industry" (p. 177). Hatred, whether based in race or other identities, "is not satisfied with the disappearance of the adversary" (p. 277). The other is needed to constitute one's subjectivity, perennially degraded as a form of enjoyment. Lacan and his colleagues identify "Western moralism" as the culprit, where "Hatred… discovers how to *feed* on everyday objects" (p. 277, emphasis added).

There is no detour here—Lacan (1958/2006) was aware that treating the analytic relationship only as a two-person encounter opens the door for the imposition of the therapist's ego and wider cultural values (p. 494). Not only can the analyst "feed" on the analysand like an abusive parent (see Chapter 3), they can also become the vehicle for societal discourses like racism, cisheterosexism, and classism that cannibalize their chosen object of derision.

Lacan (1953–1954/1991) draws on Ferenczi to unpack the role of the analyst's presence in the transference, speaking of the analysand's experience of "the gaze," referencing Sartre much like Fanon did (see Chapter 6). "I can feel myself under the gaze of someone whose eyes I do not even see," Lacan writes, "From the moment this gaze exists, I am already something other, in that *I feel myself becoming an object for the gaze of others*" (p. 215, emphasis added). The parallel with Du Bois' double consciousness is again notable. The other enjoys the self's horror at being caught in the image of their gaze, not unlike the pleasure a perverse child derives from burning ants under a magnifying glass. The imaginary is "the gaze" while the symbolic provides the magnifying glass, directing the sun's "Real" rays to its victims. Lacan relates this to Hegel's master–slave dialectic, where the intersubjective imaginary that results in the master's prestige "establishes the relation between pleasure *[jouissance]* and labour" (p. 223). The symbolic order transforms the subjugation of the slave into propositions, associations, and rules imposed as a form of law: "It is not sufficient for him to plea for mercy, he has to go to work" (p. 223), the "work" of fulfilling the master's enjoyment. One person's imaginary fantasy becomes another's symbolic order.

At the conclusion of the imaginary conflict, the Hegelian master subjugates the slave, with the social context turning the master's imaginary fantasy into the slave's symbolic reality—sociopolitical structure grants the oppressor's fantasies "objective value" (Wilderson, 2010), as if to say "today a White fantasy, tomorrow a new law" (p. 145). This constitutes how systems of oppression—patriarchy, white supremacy, and capitalism—must transform the imaginary anxieties, fantasies, and desires of cisheterosexual men, white people, and the rich into the symbolic, ontological nightmare of cis and trans men and women, people of color, and the poor. The other's pain becomes the source of our compensatory enjoyment, our *jouissance*.

Lacan (1959–1960/1992) follows Freud's analysis of the *jouissance* of inequality in *Civilization and Its Discontents*: "it is suffering because it involves suffering for my neighbor" (p. 184). The link is very clear in how he cites Freud, in that human beings try

> to satisfy his need for aggression at the expense of his neighbor, to exploit his work without compensation, to use him sexually without his consent, to appropriate his goods, to humiliate him, to inflict suffering on him, to torture and kill him. (cited in p. 185)

We must remember two uses of *jouissance* here: (1) our attachment to defenses that provide us with the "least suffering" even if this is destructive in the long run (p. 185), and (2) how we displace our suffering onto others so that they do the "labor" of suffering for our enjoyment.

This ties the personal and sociopolitical for Lacan. What does capitalism do, if not instill an urgency to work oneself to death to put food on the table and enjoy "the good life?" An urgency to "keep climbing" for a higher position or income that will keep hunger at bay and prestige overflowing from one's cup? Even if we are left feeling empty, anxious to climb the next rung in the ladder lest we fall to the bottom? Repetition is bound up with *jouissance* (Lacan, 1969–1970/2011, p. 33), which capitalism colonizes for profit. Lacan borrows from Marx the notion of "surplus value," the profit the capitalist extracts from the worker's labor, the difference between the sale of a product and worker's wages. Lacan saw Marx as having invented the notion of the symptom, defining *jouissance* as a "surplus enjoyment," *plus-de-jouir* (p. 38). Lacan reasons, "What makes repetition necessary is enjoyment... *that there is produced something*" (p. 79, emphasis added). Even where repetition leads to harm, it always renders *a profit*, a surplus of enjoyment. At the same time, it reproduces a loss requiring its own compensation, in the end resulting in a failure, "a waste of enjoyment" (pp. 80, 85).

Jouissance at the neighbor's expense reduces them to a "credit" traded and used in pursuit of surplus enjoyment. For Lacan (1969–1970/2011), "What Marx exposes in surplus value is the plundering of enjoyment" (p. 115), that the extraction of wealth is both a plundering of wages and a plundering of pleasure. The surplus of privation experienced by the populace results in hostility, which is then colonized and *redirected* toward plundering another's life and pleasure—the racial, gender, and sexual other in particular.

The dynamics of love and power are enacted in the transference through the analysand's desire to either submit to or usurp the analyst's position. By surrendering mastery while operating as an enigmatic, provocative, opaque figure, the analyst disrupts the analysand's habitual imaginary and symbolic coordinates through a "bit of Real" that frees up the analysand's desire. In this sense, dynamics of power and oppression enacted in the transference similarly open themselves up to be challenged. Lacan's theory and practice, then, offers up the possibility of a decolonial technique, which was useful to Fanon as well.

Lacan as Clinical Practitioner: Case Examples

Though Lacan rarely discussed his cases, there are testimonies from former analysands in Roudinesco's (1997) biography of Lacan, Gerard Haddad's (2006) and Betty Milan's (2014, 2021) memoirs, and documentaries of his work. I begin with Lacan's treatment of Houda Aumont, who became a psychoanalyst herself (Roudinesco, 1997). Aumont was raised in France until she returned to her native Algeria as an adolescent. As she did not speak Arabic and struggled with Algeria's patriarchal norms, she left her home as a young adult to attend college in France, where her experience with racism, immigration, and sexism led her to become involved in activism. Over time she discovered that her father, who was absent in her childhood, lived just nearby. Their first meeting was awkward as he was a quiet man, a retired worker of few words. Aumont felt ambivalent about reconnecting with him, given she had left their family in Algeria for France when she was still young, and so decided to enter analysis to sort through her feelings. She reached out to the École Freudienne de Paris and, after trying a few women analysts who were either unavailable or not a good fit, she made an appointment with Lacan.

Their initial interview lasted an hour, with Lacan expressing an interest in working with her, setting a low fee to take her situation as a student into account (Roudinesco, 1997, p. 393). Right away Lacan pointed out her tendency to arrive late for sessions. Aside from maintaining a clear frame, he would ask her "questions in a language I could understand." True to his technique, "He repeated my own words and expressions, without any jargon," but he was more than a "tape recorder." She recounts a session in which she tried to show she was a "good pupil" by talking about Lacan's theories, when he suddenly "asked me what I meant and told me there was no point in my bothering with all that" (p. 393). This shocked her at first, but ended up making her feel freer to speak as herself without trying to impress her French white analyst. "[Lacan] had a fantastic ear for listening to people, a human approach that was very tactful and sensitive," she recalled, "I always felt he understood my suffering and wasn't looking down on me" (p. 393).

The caring, paternal ambiance Lacan provided made Aumont more curious about her own father's past. Why was he so quiet? Why was he absent in her life? Talking to her brother, she discovered their father was a member of the revolutionary *Partie Populaire d'Algerie* (or PPA), a rival to the *Front de Libération Nationale* (FLN, coincidentally, Fanon's party), leaving the family to work as an undercover operative. He was eventually arrested after assassinating an FLN member who sold out a comrade to the French police. Aumont did not know the truth as she lived with her mother while he served time in prison. Upon release he was disabled by a debilitating lung disease, at a loss for words from the police torture he had endured, his silence carrying the colony on his lips. Her transference with Lacan helped her work through her complex feelings toward her father, as well as understand how her history of activism mirrored his own, "with [Lacan] I encountered a possible father—pleasant, courteous, glad to see me, and encouraging me to be active in the real world: for example, to see my father more often" (cited in Roudinesco, 1997, p. 393).

Although it was important for Lacan to not "get stuck" in the imaginary, the imaginary transference is not in itself an obstacle to analytic work unless one relinquishes their duty to the symbolic—to working with the signifiers in speech. By inserting a "cut" in Aumont's attempt to impress him, Lacan's "calculated vacillation" in neutrality disrupted her association to him as the French white "master" analyst, setting her on the path to free association. His managing of the transference also comes through in his demeanor in contrast to the image of the "expert." Despite her experience with immigration, colonialism, sexism, and racism, she experienced him as a caring person who did not "look down" on her—a father figure who was present.

Another example of Lacan's clinical work comes from the documentary *Rendez-vous chez Lacan* (G. Miller, 2011). Suzanne Hommel, born in Germany in 1938, witnessed the rise of the Nazis as a young girl. She lived through World War II in a state of constant horror, hungry even as Hitler "promised bread," wishing to run away from the terror that haunted her dreams. In her first session with Lacan, she asks "if it was possible to cure me of this suffering," to which he responded with his first "interpretation." Lacan looked at her "in this way that made me understand I would have to live with this for the rest of my life." A later session in which she recounts the dreams tormenting her bears quoting at length,

> … I told him, 'I wake up every morning at 5 o'clock… [when] the Gestapo came to get the Jews in their houses.' At that moment Lacan jumped up from his chair… and gave me an extremely gentle caress on my cheek. I understood it as *'geste à peau'* [gesture to skin] … a very tender… extraordinarily tender gesture. And that surprise, it didn't diminish the pain but it made it something

else… years later, when I recall that gesture, I can still feel it on my cheek. It was a gesture as well which was an appeal to humanity…

Lacan's tenderness came through not in words, but action. What makes this an interpretation evoking a "chance encounter" is his non-verbal use of the signifier. The Real irrupts into Hommel's experience and Lacan springs, the Ferenczian in me would say, *spontaneously responds*, with a gesture that transforms the traumatic association. She is struck with *surprise*—a bit of Real—deriving a new association, "*geste à peau*," or "gesture to skin," which phonetically in French sounds like "Gestapo." Lacan's surprising responsiveness did not erase her pain but allowed her to bear it through her *sinthome*, a memory of tenderness restoring her humanity.

There is an interesting convergence between Lacan's *tuchè* and Ferenczi's *Nachgiebigkeit*—a willingness to give to the other that must be spontaneous and at times even provocative. As Roudinesco (1997) observed in first-person accounts of Lacan's clinical work, he "behaved at once like a willful child and a devoted mother, though this was contrary to his theory" (p. 387). Perhaps not so contrary if we consider his thinking on "a bit of Real" and its paradoxical nature. Earlier we mentioned a Jesuit analysand. When he decided to leave the order and get married, Lacan tried to stop him, "He said that in marriage, my superego would be worse than in the Church," as if saying, tongue in cheek, he was trading one "oppression" for another—the church for a married life. Lacan's provocation pushed him "to abandon my robe and to make a decision on my own" (Roudinesco, 1990, p. 233). Lacan seemed to alternate between maternal care and serving as a paternal figure to be challenged and overcome.

My point is not to assimilate one thinker to the other but show the ground is ripe for a long overdue dialogue (Lugrin, 2015), including an integration of Lacan and Ferenczi's views on language (Gutiérrez-Peláez, 2015), and how Lacan offers a corrective to relational theories of therapeutic action and emphasis on "empathic" understanding as a form of knowing (Fink, 2010; Kirshner, 2015). As we saw in Chapter 2, a narrowly dyadic perspective also risks viewing the analysand's struggles in only interpersonal terms. A perspective that takes speech—and the sociopolitical world speaking through it—as a third term structuring the relational suggests a decolonial strand in Lacan's thinking (Obiwu, 2015; Rahmat, 2021; Richards, 2021).

Decolonial Thought in Lacan's Circle, Practice, and Politics

Anti-colonial thinkers in France kindled Lacan's (2006) insight into colonialism as capitalist *jouissance*, "the tree of the bourgeoisie... acquired wealth by trading staples from the colonies" (p. 628), and his children—like his step-daughter Laurence Bataille—were actively involved in the communist party, raising funding to support Algerian revolutionaries (Obiwu, 2015). After this led to her arrest in 1958, Lacan visited his step-daughter frequently while she was in prison, entertaining her by reading and discussing transcripts of his seminars (p. 92). Across his seminars and a television interview, Lacan called out the rise of racism in Europe, and the hypocrisy of its attempts to "save" Africa by denigrating it as an "underdeveloped" continent to be rescued and remade in Europe's image (Obiwu, 2015, p. 92).

Rahmat (2021) alerts us to remarks Lacan (1969–1970/2011) made about colonialism in his clinical practice, discussing three African doctors who entered treatment with him while studying medicine in France. He noted that they related to their culture with an almost intellectual detachment, describing their experience as if they were colonial ethnographers. He realized their alienation from their culture was by colonial design, forcing them to "make their way into the medical hierarchy of France" (pp. 123–124). Lacan observed that "their unconscious functioned according to the good old rules of the Oedipus complex" (p. 124), not because the Oedipus complex was universal but because they were "sold along with the laws of colonisation, an exotic, regressive form of the discourse of the Master, in the face of the capitalism described as imperialism" (p. 124).

Lacan's analysands, born under French colonialism, assimilated the language of the colonizer to navigate the racial hierarchy of French society and its medical establishment. This included learning how to speak "psychoanalese," retroactively reimagining their childhood to "fit" a nuclear family drama, and fulfill the fantasized desire of their white analyst. Lacan set about the task of disrupting his analysands' attempt to please him as the white guru so they could speak from their own desires, not those of the European unconscious. In working across cultural lines, he recognized that sociopolitical dynamics could speak through (i.e., be enacted in) the transference, and argued it is imperative the analyst relativize their knowledge both in general and when working across lines of difference, power, and identity.

Rediscovering One's Roots: The Case of "Seriema"

A rich example of Lacan applying this in practice is his work with Brazilian psychoanalyst Betty Milan (2014), who wrote about her analysis under the pseudonym "Seriema," in a novel which was later adapted into a movie (Ledes, 2022). For convenience, I provide translations from the Spanish version of the text. "Seriema," a Brazilian medical student, traveled to Paris to deliver Lacan a letter from her colleagues requesting a training analyst—a pretext to ask him to become her analyst. Lacan intuited this, asking Seriema to return tomorrow to draft a reply. The next day, Lacan's "My dear" greeted her, and after some pleasantries he broached the subject. "And this analysis, Seriema," he asks, "when do we begin?".

Seriema was struck by his bluntness. She was unsure on when to start, as this would mean relocating from Sao Paolo to Paris. Her thoughts wandered to Maria, an Afro-Brazilian woman who served her family and raised her: "How will I live without Maria, who is more mother than my mother?" (Location 205). Her ambivalence toward Maria as mother figure and *servant*, toward race and ethnicity, and toward Brazilian culture and her family, became central to her work with Lacan. But at the moment she got cold feet. She told Lacan she would return after finishing medical school to undertake analysis for four months. Lacan sensed her ambivalence but responded that he wouldl wait until then, "Do not forget to write" his only request. Years later, Seriema wrote back to Lacan but did not hear back. Worried he had forgotten about her, she wrote again, receiving a response, "At your service. I will receive you when it is most convenient for you. Please confirm the date of your arrival. Yours" (Location 417). "*Yours*," Seriema was thrilled by his personal tone. She fantasized about working in French with Lacan, remembering her mother's quip that French is "where civilization exists" (Location 425). With excitement came anxiety, as she would have to leave Maria's care. She became aware of the relationship between her dependence on Maria and her power over her, "Maria do this... Maria do that... forgetting to add *please*." Her family had only taught her "the art of issuing orders" (Location 459).

Having to figure things out on her own for the first time, Seriema returned to France to meet with Lacan, fantasizing about what treatment would be like, and her wish to be accepted unconditionally. "Come," Lacan beckoned her into his office. They sat face to face in their first sessions. "Tell me," he beckoned, "I am here to listen." "Yes, I can stay for four months." "*What?*" Lacan exclaimed (Location 581). "The four months we agreed to," Seriema continued, knowing well she had set that limit so she would not commit to the treatment. Lacan sensed this, as to say "I *can* stay" is not the same as

"*I want* to." "French will be a problem," Lacan replied. "Give me a bit of time," she pleaded. "I could refer you to a Portuguese-speaking colleague." "From *Portugal?*" "The country of your discoverers, no?" Lacan was being provocative and Seriema knew this. "If not [analysis] with you, I will take a flight back tonight," she threatened. "Well then, until tomorrow," Lacan stood and opened the door.

Seriema left perplexed. Had suggesting a Portuguese-speaking analyst from Portugal—her country's colonizers—meant to provoke her commitment to treatment? Their second session drew out some of her central concerns. In hearing more about her family background, Lacan broached the question of her heritage, "Is there indigenous blood in your family?" Seriema was surprised by this question. Did Lacan see her as a naked savage, climbing on European ships seeking Heaven? The question provoked a very old anxiety. Swallowing her saliva, she replied, "*Only* Lebanese immigrants." Lacan's tone shifted, "What else?" "Now I am here in France, a stranger." He became animated, "The country, home, family… a great adventure from one continent to another, as if you came to discover America!" Seriema resonated with his words. She had come to rediscover Brazil through Lacan, a home that had not felt like home.

Seriema was a third-generation Lebanese immigrant whose grandparents fled Lebanon due to war and exploitation, and now faced recurrent racism in their adoptive country of Brazil. Her family harbored shame about their origins, reinforced by racist remarks by non-Arab Brazilians referring to them derisively as "Turks." Within the racially and economically stratified Brazil, her brown skin and straight black hair often led to her being read as indigenous. Lacan's broaching of her ethnic-racial background triggered a deeper anxiety—as a child of the Arab diaspora, she did not "fit in" within Latin American *mestizaje* blending whiteness, Blackness, and indigeneity. Her family felt their own racial resentment toward Brazilians, while seeking upward mobility through Brazil's hierarchies as *mektub*, destiny or fate. This was enacted, for example, in how she dominated Maria even as she depended on her for care. Seriema, in turn, felt that becoming a doctor was the only way of "moving up" as a Brown woman: "The diploma was indispensable. I needed that title to rise to the highest rung on the podium, as my father would have wanted" (Location 317). Her father's, and Brazilian society's, wish for wealth and lighter skin weigh heavy on her like the chains of fate.

And yet, living in France and working in French was not all it was cracked up to be either. Seriema felt just as alienated in French as she did in Brazilian Portuguese, except now the microaggressions she experienced were coming from white French men and women. In a later session, she expressed her despondency. "I don't understand anything," she exclaimed. "Truly?" "Truly." "Aha… tell me, tell me." "I do not know why or for what I am here. But something made me come." "That's it," Lacan leaned closer in his chair. "But what is it that forces me to come?" "Tell me, my sister," Lacan invites gingerly. "If only I knew… unfortunately to want is not enough." "This is true, until tomorrow," Lacan ends the session. Session by session, Seriema felt she was beginning to lose herself—what would she find in the lack that remains? She felt tremendous anxiety, concocting a two-week trip to Brazil to escape. She wished Lacan would forbid her to travel as her father did when she was young, "To not become an orphan, I reinvented the censor" (Location 778). "Well, my dear," Lacan did not play ball, "when do I see you again?" "*What?*" Seriema responded in shock. After a silence she answered, "In about fifteen days." "Fifteen," Lacan repeated as if placing himself in her hands. Seriema was struck he did not try to dissuade her or force her to pay for the missed sessions.

While Seriema was driven to repeat a relationship in which care was exchanged at the cost of freedom, Lacan's openness and surrender before *her* desire created a new space. Her family spoke the language of control, feeling her father's love to the extent she submitted to his will. Seriema could extract love from Maria to the extent she controlled *her*, domination texturing the language of love. During her trip Seriema's mind was preoccupied with Lacan, drawn by the enigma of his analytic desire—"my sister," "come," "tell me" (Location 814).

"Come in," Lacan welcomed her as if time had not passed between them. "Tell me," he began. Does she disclose he had been in her thoughts? "Tell me," he repeated anew. "The only thing I have to tell you is I saw you." "*Where?*" he asked with surprise. "Dreaming," she replied, "You were in my land, atop a mango tree eating *zapote*, and I atop another branch drinking *guarana*, our national drink." She dreamt of him feeding others fruit while singing "She who wanted me, took me with her." He flew away, accompanied by angels and green birds. "To what better world I might have gone!" he exclaimed (in reality). Before his joy Seriema felt a deep attachment, not wanting to separate from him though she had contrived the four-month limit. "There are only fifteen days left," she said. "Until tomorrow," he bade her, as if the separation was of little consequence.

At their last session, Seriema expressed loss at the treatment's end, "What was not done can no longer be done." "That is very true," Lacan replied. "I still do not know why I came and why I am leaving." "Is that so?" Lacan asked. "How will the doctor's renown [*renommeé*] serve me?" she asked, wondering how an analysis with Lacan will confer her status as an analyst, even if it did not answer the questions she struggled with. "Aha," he replied with a flash of insight, yet kept his restraint, "What else?" "Three times I dreamt that I asked you to read me the name of a street." "Yes, yes, very curious," Lacan replied, mulling over an interpretation, "Name, renown … perhaps you will make a name with my renown" (Location 869). He stood and ended their last session for the time being. Was Lacan making a pun in French between "name" (*nom*), "renown" (*renommeé*), and "rename" (*renommer*)? Was he implying that Seriema sought analysis to give her renown as a psychiatrist, but deep down hoped he would help her read her name, meaning, decipher her complex identity? Was his pun a counterproposal of sorts, not to read her name (*nom*), but to help her *rename* (*renommer*) herself on her own terms?

Years later, Seriema returned to Paris to resume her analysis with Lacan following a breakup with a cheating boyfriend. She did so on her mother's orders, which led her to feel like a "yoyo from one place to the next… without knowing what I myself wanted" (Location 903). "Yes, come in," Lacan received her calmly. She wondered if he cared for her. "Tell me," was the answer. "What?" "Whatever you wish to say." Seriema worried about being judged for her absence, enshrouding herself in silence. "Nothing you say will leave this room," he reassured her. "I had no choice but to return," she answered. "The risk is all yours," he said, "Here I cannot answer for what you do, nor provide a guarantee." "I do not need a guarantee, I accept the risk." "Well, until tomorrow" (Location 930). She tested Lacan by negating her choice to return to treatment, but in returning responsibility for the treatment to her, Lacan "passed."

In a latter session, Seriema wore a crystal eye necklace which caught Lacan's attention. "What is that you have around your neck?" "The eye?" "Might that be a fetish?" he offered. "[That] had never occurred to me," she replied with surprise. After the session, Seriema was intrigued by his comment. The necklace was a gift from Maria to ward off evil, one she never left home without. She laughed at herself, "So faith was not only a thing for servants" (Location 994), suddenly realizing how much she degraded Maria even as she loved her. Although she did not believe in Maria's Afro-Brazilian spiritual traditions, they were central in her upbringing:

> It was so inscribed on my body I could not imagine myself without [the] amulet. I was a pure blooded Arab, yet *mestiza*, taken by the rituals of the earth… not all white, half Black perhaps, *mulata* by upbringing. The country I tried to get away from continued to bungle my ideas and embarrass me… [Lacan] aimed at what I could see and hit on the target of what I could not. (Location 994)

As a Spanish speaker, I note an ironic dimension to the translation. "The target" is from the Spanish *en el blanco*, which would translate in English to "on the white." My association is that Lacan "hit on the *white*" of what Seriema could not see—the wish among many Latin American cultures to "move up" and become white.

In another session, Seriema spoke about her new home in Paris, which was filled with mirrors. "I want *more*," she regaled Lacan, "more mirrors." "Oh yes?" "Yes! Versailles, the gallery of mirrors, Louis XIV dreamt it only for me." "What?" he said in a raised voice prompting her to hear herself speak. "The sun king, your great Louis…" she repeated with surprise as he suddenly stood up, ending the session (Location 1078). Afterward, walking through the streets of Paris, her mother's fantasies came to mind, of France as "where civilization is." Seriema realized she was raised to dream about royalty, opulence, and power. "Yes," she reflected, "Seriema was a false princess."

As she put into words how her upbringing colonized her psyche, Seriema yearned for home, dreaming not of thrones or mirrors but mangos and palm trees. "Tell me," Lacan insisted after a silence. "If only I could…" Seriema struggled. "[Why] not?" Lacan reassured her, "I will not censure you." "In your language I lack the word." With a sweet tenderness, Lacan invited her, "What word, my sister?" "*Saudade*," she replied in Brazilian Portuguese. "This means nostalgia, no?" he interpreted, ending the session to underscore the message. On her way home, her thoughts went to Maria, remembering how she would disappear to celebrate *Carnaval*, returning with gifts and stories. "Do you want me to read your fortune?" Maria said once, holding a statue in hand, "she is *Pomba Gira*," an Afro-Brazilian spirit of unrelenting desire.

"Tell me, my dear," Lacan invited her thoughts anew. "Would you under-stand," Seriema began, "if I talked about *Pomba Gira* and… Maria?" "Inter-esting," Lacan took a deep drag of his cigar, nudging her to proceed. She spoke about missing Brazil, Maria, her tongue, and yet, something kept her in Paris. "What happens is that I… that I…" "Tell me," Lacan refrains. "… I am here for *you*" Seriema let out at last. "Aha," Lacan answered. "I miss my country… here in turn, *you* are my country." Seriema was so moved by her words she rushed from her chair to lie on Lacan's couch, her eyes "nailed" to the ceiling, avoiding his gaze while moved by a profound sob (Milan, 2021). "Now now, my dear," he sat on the chair behind the couch, "there is no reason to be sad." He marked her triumph with pride: "Is the couch not now yours? You have taken to it at last, in majestic fashion" (Milan, 2014, Location 1279). Seriema recommitted herself to the work: "Like it or not, I would face my origins."

After taking to the couch, Seriema had a hallucination in Lacan's waiting room. "What?" Lacan's typical refrain had a mixture of curiosity and surprise. She saw "Rats, but then there wasn't anything there." "What?" "Rats, I tell you." "*What?*" he insisted. Thinking he had not heard her, Seriema said it again, inadvertently elongating the word, "Ra-ats." Hearing herself utter the first syllable, she heard the name she had avoided uttering since her teenage years. Lacan urged her to speak, "Say it…" "*Raji*, my father's name." She recounted her father's experience of discrimination in Brazil, internalizing the racism he faced and which he expressed toward other Brazilians, imbuing Seriema with a desire to move up within Brazil's hierarchy. "[In] order to not be a victim of others' xenophobia," she relates, "I exercised mine over all, including my own [family]" (Location 1324). Her father raised her to erase their origins as immigrants, seeking entry into a Brazilian society founded on its history of indigenous genocide and anti-Black slavery. In many respects that collective history facilitated her family's attempt to integrate into their host country. This became apparent in a subsequent dream.

In the dream Seriema was in a mansion. Outside she sees a glass horse-drawn carriage. She opens the door and sees two black bulls charging at the horses. One of the horses lies wounded on the ground with the carriage shattered to pieces. Seriema sees her sister dead on the ground. "What else?" Lacan asks. She continues associating, "My sister was myself… I looked at her as Narcissus looks upon water. Dead, but why?" "Tell me," Lacan urges. "If only I knew… only the broken pieces remain. [my sister], the glass carriage… Cinderella maybe." "What?" "… [my sister] is in Cinderella's place… dead… because the illusion is gone." "What illusion?" "Of being Cinderella." "Interesting…" Lacan reflected. "I'm left with having to accept this olive color," Seriema raised her hand, showing him her brown skin. "Well, my dear," and with that, sent her on her way without a glass slipper (Location 1359). Seriema was not able to see herself in the image of white Cinderella, a broken mirror distorting her existence. In a retelling of this dream, Milan (2021) explained that the bulls destroyed "the white, blond, civilized woman… the woman I wanted to be" (p. 59). Their sessions explored the broken fragments of her identity, caught between different racial identifications, coming into her own voice.

In one session, Seriema realized she lost her necklace. "Another pendant," Lacan urged her, "go find another pendant!" Seriema was again surprised by Lacan's behavior. He seemed to understand the necklace's importance, cementing her connection to Maria and Brazilian culture. In this show of care, "The doctor incarnated the saintly father, offering me his protection in conceding me the [necklace]. There was no mask he adhered to completely"

(Location 1619). Seriema wonders, "Was it not natural I became so attached to the Doctor? In accepting magic, he opened a path for me to be what I was: Brazilian" (Location 1672).

Seriema had another dream, traveling across palm trees from a beach to the top of a mountain, the breaking waves shifting to the beat of drums. "*Egun* [the spirit of the ancestors] awaits you," she hears in the dream. Lying on the couch, she teased Lacan. "What can I tell you? Nothing, because you would understand nothing." "Are you sure?" he asked calmly. "Almost." "Then speak." "Would you like me to tell you what I heard about *Egun*, called *Babá* [father in Arabic]?" "What did you say?" Lacan did not need to understand, but be humble and allow space for Seriema to speak her truth, including what emerged from her cultural context. "*Egun Babá*, the ancestor of the Africans appeared in the dream repeating 'Seriema.'" "Yes?" he nudged her. "He said... Ser-i-ema." "What?" Lacan prodded. "Ema, eme, emi..." she repeated until it hit her like lightning, "Emi—my God—in Arabic means mother! 'Ser,' of the verb 'to be,' and mother! 'To be a mother!'" "That's it, Seriema, my sister. Until tomorrow." Lacan ended the session, underscoring her desire to raise a family of her own.

Over subsequent sessions, Seriema worked through her fear of being abandoned by her father if she asserted herself, but now in the transference to Lacan. In another session, he happened to lean on the couch while situating himself in his chair. "With what right?" Seriema protested, as if he was getting too close for comfort. "Right?" he repeated, confused. "Yes, exactly." "Huh!" "If you allowed yourself to be seduced," Seriema warned, "I would have no choice but to leave and break forever." "That is true," he said with a smile. This was, after all, *her* couch. Seriema setting this boundary between Lacan and *her* couch, her *no*, her body, her separateness was mutative in her separating from her family's toxic beliefs, leading her to write and put into words how she is Lebanese but also "no more than a Brazilian. A Brazilian like any other" (Location 2156). This desire to rewrite her story called forth her *sinthome*. The end of the analysis drew nearer. "What else?" Lacan prompts. "I have nothing more to say." "Truly?" "Truly what? What I say is not what matters to you. You are only interested in what I have *yet* to say." "So it is... come see me again, my dear. Until tomorrow." "What is left for me to answer but *no*?" "Tomorrow," Lacan replies, "and then never again" (Location 2240, emphasis added). She was ready to return to the "sweet cadence of my tongue," to Brazil.

A thought came to Seriema as she commuted their last session. Why *did* she choose to work with an analyst who did not speak Portuguese? It dawned on her that her father treated her like a princess, bound for whiteness and success as an extension of himself. She realized she sought Lacan not only as a "great man" of psychoanalysis, the language of "civilization," but also *because* he did not know Portuguese. The language barrier protected her from having to say everything that came to mind, allowing her to stay loyal to her father, whose "little girl should not reveal herself to others" (Location 2336). She felt caught between two fathers—the one who compelled her to hide, the one who invited her to bare all. Her *sinthome* took form as new knot, a *no* to both fathers. She would decide what to share and what to dream on her own terms. "Quijote died when cured of his madness," she told Lacan at their last session. "This is very true," he answered. "Died for not dreaming." "This is so." "I do not want to be cured of the desire to dream…" "What else, my dear?" "I think we have told everything." "What?" "This analysis has ended." "If you say so," Lacan consented (Location 2344). Years later, Millan (2021) testified her analysis "did not definitively cure me of anguish, but it changed my life" (p. 8).

A "Relational" Lacan? Gerard Haddad's Testimony

There is more to Lacan's technique than popular discourse gives credit for. Gerard Haddad's (2006) account of his analysis is illuminating (translations from the Spanish version are my own). In one session, Haddad was anxious he would fail his medical school exam, to which Lacan replied with a warm smile, "Take it easy. You are going to pass this exam!" Haddad was taken aback by how naturally he intervened, reflecting "the intense transferential relation that bound us" (p. 159). When his mind went blank during the exam, Lacan's words came to mind, "Take it easy. You are going to pass." He felt soothed by these words, and as he relaxed fragments of what he had studied came back to him, helping him pass. Lacan could also be confrontational when needed. In another session Haddad—who experienced problems in his marriage—challenged him, "Isn't it true that you desire my divorce?" "*Me*?" Lacan replied, "You are mistaken. You are the only one who desires a divorce. You!" (p. 168). This confrontation helped Haddad work through his conflicts with his wife and save his marriage.

Haddad (2006) gives examples of how Lacan cut sessions to underscore the irruption of a surprising utterance, but sometimes he underscored the importance of new behavior or insight with his own joy. Haddad—a secular Tunisian Jew—once described how his father overstepped his bounds, trying to impose religion on his son and planning a *bar mitzvah* behind his back. He confronted his father and set limits, deciding *he* would take charge of his son's *bar mitzvah* on his own terms. Haddad worried Lacan would disapprove of him owning his Jewish heritage and hide this behind a "neutral" mask. "Extraordinary!" Lacan exclaimed to Haddad's surprise, as the senior analyst stood to shake his hand. From that day, Haddad felt greater freedom to explore his cultural roots and process feelings of loss as an immigrant from Tunis. At the end of analysis, he expressed to Lacan, "There is no element of my existence… that has not been elaborated by your side… You have been, in my transference, my father and my mother" (p. 209), an assertion Lacan approved of. Years after Lacan's death, Haddad (2006) was asked if Lacan did not intervene "too much," transgressing the "sacred rule" of neutrality. "Without a doubt," he replied, adding that without Lacan's active intervention he would not have survived medical school, saved his marriage, or reconnected with his heritage (p. 246). The treatment changed his life, and was mutative beyond its end. Haddad remarked on how "strange" psychoanalysis is: "In each crisis I experienced later on, Lacan would appear in my dreams, and this nostalgic call bringing his memory to mind would help me overcome the moment" (pp. 283–284).

In one of these dreams—the first Haddad (2006, p. 284) had since Lacan's death—Lacan sat at the foot his bed, old and gray, his feet barely touching the floor, with tears streaming down his cheek. In the dream, Haddad asks what brought him so much pain. "I did not fix *all* of your problems," he answered. Haddad reassured him, "But you did fix a few of them." Lacan then utters a phrase that shocked him: "You are my adoptive son." Despite Lacan's protests against the idea of analyst and analysand developing a close, intimate relationship, it is possible his underlying attentiveness—never spoken, but *interpreted* by his analysands—left an impact on their ability to remain open to life's possibilities without foreclosing them into rigid images. Haddad was not only shocked, but *perturbed* by Lacan's words in the dream. The encounter with someone who genuinely cares and is willing to love us is often painful and disruptive—it is *Real*.

To Play on Symbols of Power: The Centrality of Speech

Lacan's emphasis on speech—and how our familial, sociocultural, and political worlds speak through it—provides us with an important tool for clinical practice from a decolonial point of view. The practice of punctuating (i.e., reflecting, cutting, editing, remixing, underscoring) select words or phrases provides another path for drawing out meaning, stimulating the broader associative network they are embedded in, allowing other associations to be expressed. What I focus on through a Fanonian lens is how we can pick up on bits and pieces of speech signifying the analysand's sense of their location within their immediate symbolic order, punctuation as an invitation to put into words the relational and sociopolitical world implied in their speech.

If the analyst's role for Lacan (1953/2006) is to "[play] on the power of symbols by evoking them in a calculated fashion in the semantic resonances of [their] remarks" (p. 243), then a Fanonian lens reimagines that analytic function—to play on the *symbols of power, identity, and culture* that emerge organically in the analysand's speech, evoking them through the semantic resonance of the clinician's remarks. Another aspect of Lacan's technique useful to a decolonial perspective is his emphasis on the therapist's not-knowing stance (Fink, 2007, 2010). Not only is this an important corrective to the tendency among therapists to engage in near Herculean feats of "under-standing," but it also makes room for the analysand to articulate their own knowledge. A Lacanian position of not-knowing is conversant with contemporary notions of cultural humility stressing a not-knowing, other-oriented stance, as opposed to the therapist's "cultural competence" which "knows" the analysand's identity ahead of time (see Chapter 7).

There is much that is clinically useful in Lacan. His recentering of speech as a "third term" that binds the individual, intersubjective and social informed later theorizing—including within relational and interpersonal psychoanalysis—on the "social third" between analysand and therapist, contributing important tools to a politically conscious practice (e.g., Altman, 2011; Cushman, 2018; Layton, 2020). It is unquestionable that Lacan had a major influence in the humanities and critical theories of race, gender, sexuality, and class (e.g., George & Hook, 2021; Gherovici, 2017; Žižek, 2019), including Fanon's work (Richards, 2021; Stephens, 2018).

While one may debate the utility of variable-length or "cut" sessions, it cannot be denied that many therapists extend sessions past the hour, or offer additional sessions as needed when the analysand is in crisis. Conversely, ending the session "on time" at the end of the hour, right as the analysand starts talking about something they alluded to the entire session, can also insert a "cut" that keeps the analysand reflecting until the next appointment. In that sense, non-Lacanian clinicians are *already* inserting cuts in their sessions. Although it is beyond the scope of this book to deliberate on the variable-length session, research suggests it is optimally effective in the context of a positive therapeutic alliance, for analysands who have an organized personality structure (i.e., are non-psychotic), without an extensive history of trauma, and not in an active state of mourning a loss (Radiszcz et al., 2019).

Coda

We should take Lacan's invitation to "not imitate" an *image* of his practice to heart. While this chapter provides an introduction to Lacan as a stepping stone to Fanon's work, there is a diversity of Lacanian approaches today (e.g., M. J. Miller, 2011; Svolos, 2018). In that spirit, I end on a related story. Although Lacan helped Houda Aumont meet many of her goals, things changed in 1978 when Lacan was around 77 (Roudinesco, 1997). Aumont's father died of cholera that October, and she arrived for her session "still shattered," sharing the news in a state of shock: "My father's dead." Lacan, however, was silent and unresponsive. Aumont considered whether he was making an "interpretation" through his silence, but worried he was not understanding her words. "That day I didn't wait for the end of the session; I just got up and left," (p. 394). Aumont was shaken, but continued the treatment in disbelief that the man who helped her find a new direction in life was so erratic. She was used to Lacan ending sessions, but now he was cutting them after a few minutes, leaving her in tears.

"Then I understood what was happening to me," Aumont realized, "I could no longer see Lacan as the great analyst he had been before" (cited in Roudinesco, 1997, p. 394). She ended treatment with Lacan, who died months later of colon cancer. She mourned him deeply, processing the loss of her father, and of the father she had found in Lacan. She let go of her image of the great psychoanalyst, recognizing he was not able to help her as he once had. In a tragic way, she took Lacan's advice to heart—"I changed my practice, avoiding all imitation: for example, I abandoned short sessions" (p. 394). Different strokes—or cuts—for different folks. Paraphrasing Milan's (2014) remembrance of Lacan's words, the couch is *ours*—let us take it in magisterial fashion without imitation.

Reflection Questions

- Lacan theorizes that when we speak different social, cultural, and political discourses "speak through" us. How do you notice different ideologies, cultural values, and associations "slip" through speech in daily life? Think

of yourself, your patients, or politicians and celebrities on TV or social media.
- Lacan and Lacanians caution against seeing "empathy" or "understanding" as central to treatment. What is your reaction to this position? Are there ways we try to understand patients (and others) too much? Can empathy have its downsides? How can "not-knowing" create more space for patients?
- Punctuating, reflecting back, or "remixing" key words or phrases in speech is a key Lacanian intervention. What would it be like to experiment with this technique in your practice? For example, noticing an evocative word or phrase that seems fraught, loaded with meaning, then reflecting those exact words back? If you pay close attention to speech in everyday life, in what ways do you notice the words people use and how they use them serving to mask, cover over, or evoke meaning?

Further Reading

Lacanian Psychoanalysis
- Fink, B. (2007). *Fundamentals of psychoanalytic technique: A Lacanian approach for practitioners.* Norton & Company
- Miller, M. J. (2011). *Lacanian psychotherapy: Theory and practical applications.* Routledge.
- Moncayo, R. (2020). *The practice of Lacanian psychoanalysis: Theories and Principles.* Routledge..

Lacanian Approaches to Culture and Identity
- George, S., & Hook, D. (Eds). (2021). *Lacan and race: Racism, identity, and psychoanalytic theory.* Routledge.
- Gherovici, P. (2003). *The Puerto Rican syndrome.* Other Press.
- Žižek, S. (2011). *How to read Lacan.* Granta Books.

References

Alexander, F. G., & French, T. M. (1946). *Psychoanalytic therapy: Principles and applications.* Ronald Press.
Altman, N. (2011). *The analyst in the inner city: Race, class, and culture through a psychoanalytic lens.* Routledge.
Aron, L. (1991). The patient's experience of the analyst's subjectivity. *Psychoanalytic Dialogues, 1*(1), 29–51.
Benjamin, J. (2016). Non-violence as respect for all suffering: Thoughts inspired by Eyad El Sarraj. *Psychoanalysis, Culture & Society, 21*(1), 5–20.

Bromberg, P. M. (2003). Something wicked this way comes: Trauma, dissociation, and conflict—The space where psychoanalysis, cognitive science, and neuroscience overlap. *Psychoanalytic Psychology, 20*(3), 558–574.

Cauwe, J., Vanheule, S., & Desmet, M. (2017). The presence of the analyst in Lacanian treatment. *Journal of the American Psychoanalytic Association, 65*(4), 609–638.

Cushman, P. (2018). *Travels with the self: Interpreting psychology as cultural history.* Routledge.

Fanon, F. (1952/2008). *Black skin, white masks.* Pluto Press.

Fink, B. (1999). *A clinical introduction to Lacanian psychoanalysis: Theory and technique.* Harvard University Press.

Fink, B. (2007). *Fundamentals of psychoanalytic technique: A Lacanian approach for practitioners.* Norton & Company.

Fink, B. (2010). Against understanding: Why understanding should not be viewed as an essential aim of psychoanalytic treatment. *Journal of the American Psychoanalytic Association, 58*(2), 259–285.

George, S., & Hook, D. (Eds.). (2021). *Lacan and race: Racism, identity, and psychoanalytic theory.* Routledge.

Gherovici, P. (2017). *Transgender psychoanalysis: A Lacanian perspective on sexual difference.* Routledge.

Gutiérrez-Peláez, M. (2015). Ferenczi's anticipation of the traumatic dimension of language: A meeting with Lacan. *Contemporary Psychoanalysis, 51*(1), 137–154.

Haddad, G. (2006). *El dia que Lacan me adopto.* Letra Viva.

Hoffman, I. Z. (1983). The patient as interpreter of the analyst's experience. *Contemporary Psychoanalysis, 19*(3), 389–422.

Kirshner, L. (2015). Ferenczi with Lacan: A missed encounter. In *The legacy of Sandor Ferenczi* (pp. 271–283). Routledge.

Lacan, J. (1953–1954/1991). *The seminar of Jacques Lacan: Book I. Freud's papers on technique (1953–1954)* (J.-A. Miller, Ed., J. Forrester, Trans.). Norton.

Lacan, J. (1955–1956/1988). *The seminar of Jacques Lacan: Book III, The psychoses* (J. Miller, Ed., R. Grigg, Trans.). Norton & Company.

Lacan, J. (1959–1960/1992). *The seminar of Jacques Lacan: Book VII. The ethics of psychoanalysis.* Routledge.

Lacan, J. (1964/2018). *The four fundamental concepts of psychoanalysis.* Routledge.

Lacan, J. (1969–1970/2011). *The seminar of Jacques Lacan: Book XVII, The reverse side of psychoanalysis* (C. Gallagher, Trans.). Retrieved July 1, 2022, from http://www.lacaninireland.com/web/translations/seminars/

Lacan, J. (1972–1973). *The seminar of Jacques Lacan: Book XX, Encore* (Trans. C. Gallagher). Retrieved October 10, 2022, from http://www.lacaninireland.com/web/translations/seminars/

Lacan, J. (1975–1976). *The seminar of Jacques Lacan: Book XXIII, The Sinthome* (C. Gallagher, Trans.). Retrieved October 10, 2022, from http://www.lacaninireland.com/web/translations/seminars/

Lacan, J. (1976–1977). *The seminar of Jacques Lacan: Book XXIV: L'insu que sait de l' une-bévue s 'aile a mourre* (C. Gallagher, Trans.). Retrieved October 10, 2022, from http://www.lacaninireland.com/web/translations/seminars/

Lacan, J. (2006). *Ecrits: The first complete edition in English.* W.W. Norton & Company.

Layton, L. (2020). *Toward a social psychoanalysis: Culture, character, and normative unconscious processes.* Routledge.

Ledes, R.C. (2022). *Adieu Lacan* [Film]. Good Soup Media.

Lugrin, Y. (2015). Lacan and Ferenczi: paradoxical kinship?. *The American Journal of Psychoanalysis, 75*(1), 86–93.

Milan, B. (2014). *El loro y el doctor* [Spanish edition]. Homo Sapiens.

Milan, B. (2021). *Lacan ainda: testemunho de uma análise.* Editora Schwarcz-Companhia das Letras.

Miller, G. (2011). *Rendez-vous chez Lacan.* France 3. Retrieved July 25, 2022, from https://www.youtube.com/watch?v=VA-SXCGwLvY

Miller, M. J. (2011). *Lacanian psychotherapy: Theory and practical applications.* Routledge.

Nobus, D. (2016). Psychoanalysis as *gai saber:* Toward a new episteme of laughter. In P. Gherovici & M. Steinkoler (Eds.), *Lacan, psychoanalysis and comedy* (pp. 36–59). Cambridge University Press.

Obiwu. (2015). Jacques Lacan in Africa: Travel, Moroccan cemetery, Egyptian Hieroglyphics, and other passions of theory. In M. Nwosu & Obiwu (Eds.), *The critical imagination in African literature: Essays in Honor of Michael J. C. Echeruo* (pp. 75–93). Syracuse University Press.

Radiszcz, E., Reyes, P., Reinoso, A., & Pulido, R. (2019). The use of variable length sessions. Qualitative study from Lacanian psychoanalysis perspective. *Revista Argentina de Clínica Psicológica, 28*(5), 901–914.

Rahmat, F. A. (2021). The anti-colonial knot: The significance of decolonization in Lacan. *Lacunae, 23,* 52–85.

Richards, S. (2021). The logician of madness: Fanon's Lacan. *Paragraph, 44*(2), 214–237.

Roudinesco, E. (1990). *Jacques Lacan & co: A history of psychoanalysis in France, 1925–1985.* University of Chicago Press.

Roudinesco, E. (1997). *Jacques Lacan.* Columbia University Press.

Stephens, M. (2018). Skin, stain and lamella: Fanon, Lacan, and inter-racializing the gaze. *Psychoanalysis, Culture & Society, 23*(3), 310–329.

Svolos, T. (2018). *Twenty-first century psychoanalysis.* Routledge.

Weiss, E. (2001). *Quartier Lacan* (film). Centre Georges Pompidou, Michklan World Production.

Wilderson III, F. B. (2010). *Red, white & black: Cinema and the structure of US antagonisms.* Duke University Press.

Wilkerson, I. (2020). *Caste: The origins of our discontents.* Random House.

Žižek, S. (2019). *The sublime object of ideology.* Verso Books.

5

A Caregiving Psychiatrist—Reconstructing the Clinical Fanon

While Fanon's life as a revolutionary is an important part of his legacy, his friend and supervisee Marie-Jeanne Manuellan reminds us that "he was also a CAREGIVER, A CAREGIVING PSYCHIATRIST" (Manuellan & Cofiant, 2017–2018, caps original). Given his tragic passing at 36 years old from cancer, he did not leave behind a systematic model of his theory and technique. Hence, what follows is a reconstruction of his clinical work drawing on his recently translated psychiatric writings in *Alienation and Freedom* (Fanon, 2018), *Écrits sur l'aliénation et la liberté* in French—Fanon's *Écrits* analogous to Lacan's—as well as other collections (Fanon, 1965, 1988). His more popular books, *Black Skin, White Masks* and *The Wretched of the Earth*, will be considered in the following chapter. Lastly, first-person testimonies of his clinical work by Alice Cherki (2006) and Marie-Jeanne Manuellan (2017) help trace the influence of Freud, Ferenczi, and Lacan, laying the foundations for a psychoanalysis "from below."

Psychoanalysis as a "Science of the Collective"

Fanon's original dissertation, *Black Skin, White Masks*, was rejected by his advisors as "too subjective," forcing him to produce—in short order—a new work that was no less powerful. At the heart of it is Fanon's (1952/2018) advocacy for societal factors in psychiatry over biological reductionism, noting that human beings are always in relation to an otherness that constitutes their existence. "A key advance of psychoanalysis," he writes, "was

© The Author(s), under exclusive license to Springer Nature Switzerland AG 2024
D. J. Gaztambide, *Decolonizing Psychoanalytic Technique*,
https://doi.org/10.1007/978-3-031-48476-6_5

precisely to have unveiled this side of the personality, since called the unconscious" (p. 218). The unconscious is an encounter with "the other's face,"
an alterity that "reveals me to myself" (p. 219). Echoing Freud's saying that
individual psychology is at the same time social psychology, Fanon writes
that "psychoanalysis… establishes itself as the science of the collective par
excellence" (p. 219).

Fanon (1952/2018) examines Rorschach data—associations to images on
a card—and case notes on a sample of patients to illustrate how mental illness
is not only or primarily a biological dysfunction but a rupture in "the 'social
constants of the personality'" (p. 219). With each patient, Fanon picks up
on the "*If, then*" quality of their relational schemas and projections: "If I
feel odd, [then] other people can only confirm me in my mutation… If I
find others odd, [then] this observation will confirm my difference" (p. 224).
His patients not only had a distorted view of self and other but behaved in
ways that pulled others into reinforcing those unconscious beliefs. Assessment
and intervention, then, must address two components, "alteration of the ego,
alteration of the relations between the ego and the world" (p. 224).

He (1952/2018) concludes that "*the mad person is someone who can no
longer find his place among people.* Either he *feels* superior to them, or he *feels*
unworthy of entering the category of the human" (p. 224, emphasis original).
Whether we cope by acting superior to others or through self-denigration, our
coping styles reflect the symptoms of a maddening world. Fanon here draws
on Lacan's dissertation as "an unremitting defence of the nobility rights of
madness" (p. 263). He describes how symptoms serve a function in social
context, reading Lacan's understanding of desire as a "cycle of behavior" in
which we mobilize our body in pursuit of an object (p. 264). "Object," again,
refers to a relationship (an object relation), a goal we are trying to achieve,
or a catastrophe we are trying to avoid. As Fanon (1953/2018) wrote elsewhere, "To desire something is to want to desire it no longer… desire sees
further than the thing desired: the desired thing is always a limit" (p. 281).
We seek the object not only for itself, but to achieve a limit-setting, regulating
function to our desire. Put differently, we are not just seeking confirmation
of the schemas we develop to cope with a fragmented world. We also seek,
desperately so, for these associations to be *disproven* so we can rest.

Language and Relationality in Fanon

Following Lacan, Fanon (1952/2018) argues that behind seemingly incomprehensible psychotic speech lies symbol and metaphor with "a human
comprehensible meaning" (p. 266), a fundamentally social experience whose

fragmented language is a symptom of alienation from the community (pp. 266–267). He removes psychosis from a purely biomedical frame and places it in a world of relationality, citing Lacan again: "madness is not separable from the problem of meaning for being in general, that is to say, of language for human beings" (cited in p. 267). Interestingly, Fanon here describes the process of "cure" as "the liberation from a conception of oneself and the world, illusory in that it depended on unknown affective drives… accomplished *through a shock with reality*" (p. 266, emphasis added).

We will return to how he conceives of therapeutic action over the course of this chapter. For now I want to note Fanon's (1952/2018) appreciation for "the Lacanian theory of language," (p. 268), which resonated with other theories of language he was familiar with. In his copy of Jean-Paul Sartre's *Situations*, Fanon marks passages on the poet's use of language, "*which considers words as things and not as signs*" (cited in p. 754, emphasis original). Meaning, that poetry treats words not as signifiers pointing to a concrete signified but—like Lacan—as primarily related to *other* signifiers (see Chapter 4). Fanon et al. (2018) underlines another passage:

> Thus, regarding language: *it is our shell and our antennae*; it protects us against others and informs us about them; it is a prolongation of our senses, a *third eye* which is going to look into our neighbour's heart. We are within language as within our body. (cited in p. 754, emphasis added)

Language is a fundamentally relational act. Fanon comments on the margins of the book how speech conveys indirect meanings, significations implied in the use of specific words and a specific syntax. Keep in mind Sartre's description of language as our "antennae" and a "third eye," which is relevant to Fanon's thinking (see below; see Chapter 6).

In his clinical practice, Fanon (1952/2018) notes that psychic suffering "is ultimately expressed, that is to say, spoken," and thus "the best way of analysing [sic] a delusion or an abnormal psychic process is still to squarely face the making explicit of that delusion" (p. 268). Instead of simply challenging distortions, delusions, or hallucinations, we invite them to be spoken freely in the presence of a caregiving therapist, establishing the central mechanism of the cure—a relationship that reintroduces a sense of shock and surprise. As a relational process, language "breaks the silence and the silences" though it always involves a risk, "The neighbour… is always an accomplice. An accomplice who can betray" (Fanon, 1953/2018, p. 282). Rupture and difference bring us face to face with the *otherness* of the other, which can either lead to a new relationship or to a breach in the self's continuity

(p. 282). The symptom emerges here as the person's best available solution to repair this breach between self and other.

Compromise Formation as The Price of Freedom

Borrowing Lacan's understanding of madness as a "stasis of being," Fanon (1952/2018) writes that "[the] madman, facing the disorder of the world… wants to establish the law of his heart" (p. 268). He notices two solutions a patient can arrive to: "either he breaks the circle through outward violence or else he strikes a blow to himself" (p. 268). Either the tension one feels is turned inward so that one "disappears," or is expressed outward as an act of defiance. The patient's solution to the challenges posed by adversity, loss, and trauma constitutes the "law of their heart," though it comes with a cost, "the price of freedom" (p. 268). The symptom is the person's best attempt to maintain their freedom, even as it places limits on their freedom, as Freud also observed (see Chapter 2). The patient accepts this cost because they "accepted to inventory all the abysses that freedom offers" (p. 268)—the "psychical mathematics" Ferenczi spoke of and Lacan codified as *jouissance*.

Fanon's (1952/2018) dialectics of freedom are tied to his conception of cure. He writes that "with psychoanalysis, the 'singular' colloquium [of the patient] risks taking the aspect of a confession" (p. 271). In this confession the patient issues "a call" to the therapist, whose responsiveness Fanon compares to "the *appeasement* that the doctor brings to ulcerous pain by prescribing bismuth [Pepto Bismol]" (p. 271, emphasis added). Fanon implies that responsiveness has a soothing effect that allows the patient to heal. He is not idyllic on this point, however. "Psychoanalysis entails a pessimistic view of humanity," he writes, "The medicine of the person presents itself as a deliberate choice for optimism in the face of human reality" (p. 271). The psychoanalytic process, for Fanon, entails placing the patient in a position to make a deliberate choice for freedom in the face of adversity.

Shock, Surprise, and the Psychoanalytic Cure

Fanon's thinking resembles Antonio Gramsci's (1977) phrase "pessimism of the intellect, optimism of the will," a dialectic Lewis Gordon (2020) captures beautifully in his analysis of Fanon. Gordon (2020) describes how both optimism and pessimism relinquish responsibility: "Optimists expect intervention from beyond. Pessimists declare that relief is not forthcoming.

Neither takes responsibility for what is valued" (p. 77). Both are neurotic in that one "knows" the outcome in advance, foreclosing possibility. The fundamental issue is not what tomorrow holds, but "the realization that whatever is done will be that on which the future will depend. Rejecting optimism and pessimism, there is a supervening alternative… political commitment" (p. 77). Put differently, the patient is freed by a shock that "clears the table" of pessimism or optimism, centering the drive to act on what is valued without knowing what tomorrow brings—even *regardless* of a tomorrow, yet laying down tomorrow's possibility.

Fanon's conception of cure integrates the role of an encounter—a "shock"—that challenges the patient, and a supportive, empathic presence that allows them to explore reality outside of rigid conceptions of self and world, reconsidering freedom amidst adversity and oppression. Fanon's use of "shock" here is interesting, as it is also a term he uses to refer to trauma, whether childhood trauma, war trauma, or structural traumas such as racism (Fanon 2018, ft. 3, p. 720). This belies a logic we have encountered so far—if a shock is what made us ill, then another, "safer shock" reactivates capacities for change. It notable that Fanon also conducted electroshock therapy, although he and his supervisor de Tosquelles argued this must be integrated with psychotherapy and a healing millieu (Tosquelles & Fanon, 1953a/2018; 1953b/2018). Electroshock alone would be like giving a patient ketamine without talk therapy.

Tosquelles and Fanon (1953a/2018) give the example of a French white nun with paranoia, emotional lability, aggression, and condescension toward others that caused difficulties in her convent, leading her fellow nuns to trick her into an inpatient admission. As she was not in immediate crisis, Tosquelles and Fanon refused to admit her without giving an explanation of her colleagues' concerns. Although she had some insight into her behavior, she only acquiesced to please her superiors. Observing her in the unit, Tosquelles and Fanon noticed she avoided relating to others and was at times haughty: "I refuse to have anything to do with *those* girls." Eventually, they learned her family struggled with mental health, including the suicide of a beloved brother, a trauma that informed her anxieties around closeness. They also learned she was a highly skilled worker but her "very proud character" created difficulties in her convent, who sent her away on a mission to Africa, where she was rejected due to her contempt and racism.

When the treatment team spoke to the nun about her mission trip she was initially evasive, talking about Africa's climate until she let it "slip" that Black people "were naked," and she "never lowered herself to their level and their dirty way of living" (Tosquelles & Fanon, 1953a/2018, p. 288). It is not clear from the paper who was her therapist in the treatment. Tosquelles might have wanted to protect Fanon from working with a racist patient, but it is also likely Fanon chose to work with her. In either case, "one of us" undertook "active intervention psychotherapy [notice the call back to Ferenczi] aimed at unveiling to the patient the meanings of her conduct and the psychological interpretation of her behaviour" (p. 288). The treatment was intense, including "frank discussions, almost aggressive ones" about how she treated others.

Over time her defensiveness—"my subconscious belongs to God only"—thawed, leading her to reflect on how her arrogance and "self-sufficiency" prevented closeness with others. Complementing individual therapy, she was referred to electroshock therapy, after which the therapist re-engaged her in a tender manner evocative of "mother–child relations" (p. 289). As she allowed herself to build bonds with others on the unit, she remembered an episode from childhood in which she felt jealous of her mother's pregnancy, stating she "had no need of another brother (the one, precisely, who committed suicide)" (p. 290), bringing to the forefront feelings of envy and competition toward the beloved brother she lost. In participating in a hospital workshop as a typist, she realized this had been her first job at the convent, but was fired from that role because of her pride, and was rehired only because they could not find a better typist. As she integrated her feelings of jealousy, defensive narcissism, and loss, she become more open toward others. After three months of "active" psychodynamic therapy, milieu therapy, and electroshock, she was discharged back to her community.

In a follow-up paper on the integration of psychodynamic and electroshock therapy, Tosquelles and Fanon (1953b/2018) cautioned against depending on electroshock due to its risks and the tendency of inpatient units to abuse it to "manage" aggressive patients. For patients who are agitated, they advocate for less dangerous psychotherapeutic interventions, such as group therapies, vocational training, and making the inpatient unit a therapeutic environment: "the social life of the entire hospital is just as essential as the stage of active, interventionist analysis preceding the treatment" (p. 295). Without these "therapeutic linkages" between a healing relationship and a healing system, electroshock on its own was "complete nonsense" (p. 295).

Interestingly, Tosquelles and Fanon (1953b/2018) cite Delmas-Marsalet's theory of "dissolution-reconstruction" to explain the efficacy of "active" psychoanalytic therapy. In their view, psychodynamic therapy works by inducing a controlled, manageable dissolution or "unbinding" of the defended, conflicted, torn aspects of the personality so that they can be reconstructed in a way that is more freeing to the patient. They argued that *all* aspects of the inpatient unit must empower the patient to expand their awareness of their illness: "Gradually demystifying the 'approximative' conceptions that the patient forms of the morbid event and of his-/herself, the psychiatric hospital must be an institution of disalienation" (p. 298).

There is another angle for understanding this "shock" that promotes the dissolution and reconstruction, unbinding and binding, of the personality. From his residency to his psychiatric practice, Fanon was consistently recognized by his supervisors and supervisees as having an exquisitely attuned "third ear" (Cherki, 2006, p. 121; Manuellan, 2017, p. 124; Tosquelles, 1975/2017). Tosquelles (1975/2017) spoke candidly about his former supervisee: "He was clairvoyant, but an even better listener... his third ear, allowed him to weave a web out of the products emanating from the suffering of 'his' patients" (p. 227, my translation). These accounts reference Theodor Reik's (1948/1983) *Listening with the third ear*, the practice of listening for what is not said but implied in the patient's speech—another phrase for "empathy" or analytic listening. Another of Reik's (1933) contributions is pertinent here, in which he writes, "The essence of the analytic process consists in the series of *shocks* experienced as the subject takes cognizance of his repressed processes... essentially a *surprise*" (p. 322, emphasis added). Further, this "element of 'surprise' lies in the *encounter, at an unexpected moment or in unexpected circumstances... [with] something long known to us but now become unconscious*" (p. 322, emphasis original).

I have no evidence Fanon read Reik, but want to note a connection that follows from Freud and contemporary research (see Chapter 7). To the extent psychopathology results from (a) a traumatic shock, surprise, or unbinding of our bodily integrity that leads us to (b) develop rigid and contradictory bindings of our assumptions about others and the world, then (c) a *different*, manageable shock, surprise, and unbinding "frees up" our psyches to develop new connections, understandings, and ways of being. From Freud to Fanon, this implies an encounter with our unconscious, an otherness simultaneously inside and outside—like a mobius strip.

Therapeutic Responsiveness and Sociocultural Context

In "The therapeutic role of engagement," Fanon (1953/2018) underscored the "constant concern to refer a patient's every word, every act and every facial expression to the illness affecting him or her" (p. 283). The patient's speech and body language are a guide to their underlying affect, including the unarticulated need or wish expressed in the guise of withdrawal or aggression. "*Do* something," Fanon hears the patients' plea beneath their behavior, an attempt to get him to respond in a way that is helpful and healing (p. 284). If the clinician is not able to fulfill their role as a "vigilant guardian for the patient," then the patient is labeled "nasty… irksome, disagreeable," not considered someone "to be looked after and treated; there is no psychotherapeutic tension" (p. 284). The patient is given up on as "unchanging," relinquishing one's clinical responsibility, "no longer heeding the activity of psychotherapy" (p. 284). A central component of this activity is close attention to the patient's sociocultural context.

As chief attending at Blida-Joinville, Fanon (1954a/2018) developed innovative programs integrating culture and religion into the life of the unit. He wrote about how decontextualizing the patient from their community after a trauma or psychotic break further destabilizes their sense of self. Over the course of treatment "[one] needs to rediscover one's dimensions… to stabilize one's positions," (p. 318). In longer-term admissions, there can be "a total forgetting of one's previous life, an indifference concerning time," (p. 319) destabilizing one's sense of continuity. He recommends active intervention to establish "against this background of inertia and indifference, some tasks, occupations and timetables," integrating patients into the life of the unit by learning skills, contributing to the running of its affairs, etc., transforming them from passive recipients of care into active participants (p. 319).

In a series beginning with the article "Patients' relations with the outside world," Fanon (1954a/2018), emphasized the importance of culture in maintaining psychic continuity. He addresses another complaint that Ramadan was not celebrated in the unit, leaving the predominantly Muslim population culturally and religiously unmoored. He shares his fondness for the expression "*prise en charge*," to "provide care and nursing," writing that "To care for someone is not only to give him or her the possibility not to die, it is above all to give him or her the chance to live" (p. 321). And for his Muslim patients, "to live" includes celebrating Ramadan, keeping the rhythms of prayer alongside culturally congruent norms and relationships. Cultural humility is not distinct from relational care but is its most expansive expression.

Fanon's attention to the sociocultural context led him to adapt Tosquelles' social therapy. In a paper co-authored with Jacques Azoulay (Fanon & Azoulay, 1954/2018), they reported on what they learned from the experiment. "By virtue of what impairment of judgement," they ask, "had we believed it possible to undertake a Western-inspired social therapy in a ward of mentally ill Muslim men?" (p. 362). Initial attempts to engage their Muslim patients were unsuccessful, in part because many of the activities (a film club, a music club, etc.) were undergirded by tacit white European values. Hence, "it was necessary to go from a position in which the supremacy of Western culture was evident, to one of cultural relativism" (p. 363).

"It was necessary to change perspectives or at least supplement the initial ones," Fanon and Azoulay (1954/2018) write, "to try to grasp the North African social fact" (p. 363). This included recognizing that films, literature, and music in the unit betrayed French ways of seeing the world. Offering media that was linguistically and culturally legible to their patients was an important intervention, such as establishing "a Moorish café in the hospital, the regular celebration of traditional Muslim feasts, of periodical meetings around a professional 'storyteller'" (p. 371). Although the first attempt was a failure, "this failure was not worthless, to the extent that we have understood its reasons" (p. 371). The failure to understand a people's culture need not be the end of treatment, so long as one remains open and restores a relation in which the other's values *are valued*. In that vein, Fanon developed an understanding of religiously and culturally contingent understandings of mental illness (Fanon & Sanchez, 1956/2018), and recommended culturally specific adaptations of the Rorschach (Fanon & Geronimi, 1956/2018).

Psychotherapy as a Process for Relearning Freedom

In an article published after Fanon's report on social therapy, a fellow doctor observed that the intervention is "an excellent terrain for relearning gestures of the outside world" (cited in Fanon 1955a/2018, p. 331). Fanon was moved by this comment: "To relearn. I find this expression very beautiful" (p. 332). To help a patient "relearn" is to help them "reprise, to begin again by helping him or her to understand better… to grasp him- or herself better again" (p. 332). Treatment recreates a relational and social context that empowers the patient "to rediscover the meaning of freedom, which is the first milestone on the way to responsibility" (p. 332). If the symptom is a result of strategies we develop to protect our freedom—even if its price is freedom itself—Fanon envisions change as our relearning to be free.

"Relearning" likely resonated with Fanon's engagement with Lacan's colleague Merleau-Ponty. In his copy of Merleau-Ponty's *La Structure du comportement*, Fanon (2018) underlines this sentence, "To learn is thus never about becoming able to repeat the *same* gesture, but to provide the situation with *an adapted response by different means*" (cited in p. 745, emphasis added). To relearn how to be free is to repeat the old behavior in a new way that breaks the vicious cycle of repetition. This idea, evocative of Freud, Ferenczi, and Lacan's theorizing, also comes through in Fanon's (1959/2018) paper "Day hospitalization in psychiatry: Value and limits." Noting that the psychiatric day programs (in his time) are in "technologically advanced countries," he reports on the efficacy of the day program in Tunis with the goal of promoting similar centers across Africa (p. 475). I do not have evidence Faladé and Fanon crossed paths, though it is interesting to note their commitment to building a wider mental health infrastructure in Africa.

Fanon (1959/2018) argues that in terms of treatment intensity, day programs are "in between" outpatient and inpatient treatment. Inpatient hospitalization removes patients from their "conflictual milieu," leading to the false impression that their symptoms are "under control." Echoing Freud and Ferenczi's comments on hospitalization, Fanon writes "internment effects some relaxation" (p. 474). However, during visits by family members, or when the patient is discharged back to the same environment, their symptoms worsen, revealing "the neurotic attitudes remain present" (p. 474). What is needed is "to create a neo-society… akin to the outside world, in which the patient could *repeat* the neurotic attitudes such as they were to have existed before" (p. 475, emphasis added). Patients repeat patterns of relating not only with their therapists, but also with institutions, collectives, and groups. "The point is thus not to remove patients from the circuitry of social life," Fanon concludes, "but to set in place a therapy that is part of the setting of social life" (p. 475). Though repetition and re-exposure to conflictual situations is important, he is careful not to push patients beyond their limits. Hence, his guiding principle is "that consciousness is to be affected as little as possible," avoiding deep regression, building awareness, putting experience into words, and strengthening the sense of self (ego) (p. 493).

Fanon (1959/2018) integrated psychoanalytic and behavioral approaches in individual and group therapies to meet patients' needs on a case-by-case basis. In group therapy, patients are invited to talk about their difficulties, while therapists note "their projections or identifications," alongside other patients' reactions to their stories (p. 478). Fanon also draws inspiration from "drama therapy," insofar as the patient re-enacts their difficulties, except instead of depicting a fiction they enact their life history. As the patient shares and enacts their story, other group members ask questions, point out contradictions, and "take a position" for and against alternative points of view. The patient "tries to justify him- or herself through his or her behaviour, which reintroduces the priority of reason over fantasmatic and imaginary attitudes" (p. 493). Reflection on one's behavior and its impact on others provides a corrective to distortions in the group space.

Countertransference and Therapeutic Openness in Systemic Context

Fanon (1959/2018) drew on "the psychoanalytic method" at the day center to treat anxiety disorders, depression, and sexual disorders, among other conditions. The frequency of his sessions with patients is notable, "one session daily, except Sunday. The length of a session is forty minutes" (p. 494). He remarks, "As the patients do not pay the doctor, the transference neurosis is especially atypical" (p. 493). As I argued elsewhere (Gaztambide, 2021), Fanon is uncomfortable with deep transference regression, an aversion he overcomes in his later work (see below). It is also interesting to note that he "often intervened to activate a counter-transference dynamism" (p. 493). How he thought about countertransference responsiveness played a major role in his clinical work and his supervision of residents, nurses, and social workers.

Fanon (1959) observed how "acute problems" periodically arose among unit staff who enacted highly conflictual and destructive "sadomasochistic relations" with patients (p. 476–477). He intervened at a systems level, providing training to help staff be more aware of transference-countertransference reactions. Cherki (in Gibson & Beneduce, 2017) shares how nurses remarked on the change this brought about:

> they stopped being repressive guards, and became instead active agents in their relationship with the alienated person. One nurse, who is now very old, tells the following anecdote: "In the refectory, I was eating a piece of bread when [Fanon] arrived. I felt like I'd been caught red-handed and tried to hide the bread. [He] said, there is no reason for you to hide… you can share this bread with your patient." (p. xii)

Sometimes, per Freud and Margaret Lawrence, the patient is hungry and needs to be fed. Fanon values moments between patient and therapist where care can be shared—even the breaking of one's bread. Following de Tosquelles and Ferenczi, Fanon asserted that clinicians and the social context need to be cured alongside the patient, promoting tenderness in his relations with staff.

Cherki (2006) shares the testimony of a psychiatric nurse and ward supervisor, Makhlouf Longo. "I would like to know who you really are," Fanon told him in their first meeting, "I would like us to help one another for the welfare of the patients" (cited in p. 70). By building trust, Fanon created change in a system that had become rigid and cold, developing trainings informed by a Ferenczian sensibility. "Remain open… remain honest, be sincere" he instructed clinicians (cited in p. 70). "The patient," Fanon explained, "is able to perceive the doctor's attitude, and a proper welcome can lay the ground for the prospect of recovery" (cited in p. 71). Displaying a "proper welcome" to the patient's reactions to the therapist was fundamental to Fanon, who conceived of the transference-countertransference dance on two levels—an *interpersonal* axis focused on their ways of relating, and an axis of *power and position.*

The Therapeutic Relationship as a Political Encounter

In a piece entitled "Medicine and colonialism," Fanon (1965) describes how cross-cultural therapeutic relationships in an unequal society complicate clinical work. We not only bring unconscious scripts about relatedness to the patient–therapist encounter, but also templates and identities organized around power in a given society. When patient and therapist are from the "same" group—or share a predominance of identities—the assumption of basic trust is more likely, tempered by early attachment schemas. Under unequal conditions, basic trust may not be assumed so readily. For example, court-mandated treatment creates a structural antagonism between patient and therapist, exacerbated when their cultures and positionalities reinforce hierarchies of power. The patient may become compliant and passive, leading the therapist to behave like a "technician" intervening in a stereotyped, objectifying manner. The patient's body becomes rigid, their muscles contracting in the presence of "a technician and a colonizer" (Fanon, 1965, p. 127). The colonized awaits the end of the hour as an escape.

The mistrust experienced across difference is not reducible to a projection of childhood attachment, but reflects the symptom of a societal tension, "an opposition of exclusive worlds... a vehement confrontation of values" (Fanon, 1965, p. 131). Fanon advocates exploring and conveying respect for the patient's culture and experience, enlisting their indigenous values and healing practices alongside attending to ruptures due to cultural differences or the therapist's biases (pp. 130–131). Reflecting his reading of Ferenczi, Fanon argues we have to analyze "patiently and lucidly" the patient's reactions to us, and "every time we do not understand, we must tell ourselves that we are at the heart of the drama" (p. 125). This is Ferenczi beyond the two-person dyad, attending both to the relational dynamic between patient and therapist and what social positions, values, or power dynamics may be enacted, with the therapist exploring their unconscious biases and taking ownership of them in a spirit of openness.

Psychoanalytic Treatment as an Encounter Between Two Freedoms

As director of the Tunis day program, Fanon discussed the role of psychoanalytic therapy in a paper co-authored with Charles Geronimi (Fanon & Geronimi, 1959/2018). They underscore the *freedom* afforded to the patient, who attends treatment during the day and returns to his community without inpatient admission—such intensive outpatient programs being novel for the time. Inpatient internment communicates that the patient must "give up the fight" and surrender to the doctor in an unequal relationship. The day program, by contrast, is a "transient support" that equalizes the relationship. "The *a minima* master/slave, prisoner/gaoler dialectic created in internment," Fanon and Geronimi write, "is radically broken… the doctor-patient encounter forever remains an encounter between two freedoms" (p. 497). This condition, of two subjectivities having an encounter on equal ground "is necessary for all therapy" (p. 497).

Fanon returns to a theme of his dissertation, that "mental illness is… a veritable pathology of freedom" (Fanon & Geronimi, 1959/2018, p. 498). The patient's freedom is already "broken" by their symptoms and anxieties, with hospitalization further restricting their movements. Under psychiatric domination, "the patient feels free only in his opposition to the doctor who has withheld him" (p. 497). To the extent symptoms are compromise formations, the patient's best available solutions to protect their freedom, the therapeutic relationship offers a renewed possibility for exploring freedom's contours. In treatment the patient enacts their "need to verbalize… to explain himself, to take a position" (p. 498). In the process, psychotherapy "wrests patients from their fantasies… to confront reality on a new register" (p. 499).

Fanon and Geronimi's (1959/2018) discussion draws on psychoanalytic principles while critiquing the limitations of the inpatient setting. The inpatient setting, like psychotherapy, "reactivates delusional and hallucinatory processes. It provokes new dramatizations and enables the doctor to understand better what may have 'happened outside'" (p. 500). But inpatient treatment is limited as it removes the patient from the very situations in which healing must happen. Hence, the "veritable social-therapeutic milieu is and remains concrete society itself" (p. 500). For Fanon, psychoanalytic treatment is not a relationship that exists in a pocket universe outside the world—it exists *in* the world. Hence, "in-session" work may be complemented by work between sessions in the patient's daily life, even in the form of homework. In some cases, it may involve the patient's intervention in the world itself.

By engaging the contexts that are constitutive of the patient's conflict there emerges an "obviously fruitful" opportunity to practice what is learned in therapy (Fanon & Geronimi, 1959/2018). Through repeated exposure within and between sessions, the conflictual situation "experienced as threatening prior to the psychiatrist's intervention, progressively loses its traumatizing character" (p. 500). The patient's communal context is no longer "an arena in which liberty is perpetually trampled, but instead a place for exercising and deepening freedom" (pp. 500–501). This exercising of freedom requires that the patient's life is not "fundamentally overturned, but… provisionally *shaken*" (p. 501, emphasis added).

Fanon's "General Theory" of Mental Illness and Treatment: Optimal Responsiveness Between Confrontation and Appeasement

Fanon and Geronimi (1959/2018) advocate for a psychoanalytically informed "existential" approach to diagnosis assessing "reactional formations, inhibitions, and identifications" in the therapeutic relationship and day program's milieu. Through these observations one arrives at "a dynamic understanding of the structure involved, the indigence of the ego," to inform treatment. He argues against focusing on a narrow list of symptoms, preferring "a global tackling of a form of existence, a structure, a personality engaged in current conflicts" (p. 502). While the therapist respects the patient's fundamental value as a human being, their intervention requires a "simple confrontation… a progressive calling into question of forms of existence" (p. 502).

"Progressive" is an important word for Fanon and Gheronimi (1959/2018), in that the therapeutic process involves a sequential, titrated confrontation balanced with support to prevent "phantasms of bodily fragmentation or the crumbling of the ego" (p. 503). They cite Klein and Ferenczi to underscore "the importance of the care for one's own body as a mechanism for avoiding anxiety," with extreme ego-dissolution putting the patient "on the path of regression, danger and anguish" (p. 503). Echoing Lacan and the French existentialist tradition—the body is implicated in our schemas of the self, and the question of who we are in the eyes of the world. "[Is] not the question that the illness supports one about the foundation of being qua subject?" Fanon and Geronimi (1959/2018) pose, "Who am I, ultimately? Is that not the nagging question that the mental patient repeats to us at multiple levels and on different registers?" (p. 503). Hence, at the heart of the psyche are fundamental questions of *being*. Who am I in relation to others?

What position, role, or *status* does my body occupy in space? Am I loved? Am I valued? Fanon seeks to question the distorted (though understandable) answers we arrive at.

Fanon and Geronimi (1959/2018) here offer a "general theory" of mental illness. If the symptom reflects an underlying conflict, then protecting the patient from the "conflict's conditions" is counter-productive. In psychiatric internment, there can be a "thingification... of the patient," reducing them to a diagnostic label without recognizing how the symptom "contains the conflict and the elements of its overcoming" (p. 504).

The patient not only has symptoms and defenses but also a desire and capacity for change (an unconscious "plan" for change, see Chapter 7). They have some tacit desire to act, and it is in recognition of that desire that Fanon and Geronimi (1959/2018) write, "Action upon reality... is unifying" (p. 504). Empowering the patient to take action in their life is centered as a treatment goal, which opens up the possibility of the patient's political action as a therapeutic act. In treatment, this action occurs under "limited contact" with the conflict so that emotional intensity "is diminished and the ego is reinforced with a view towards imminent and daily confrontations" (p. 505). Within safe enough conditions, "the personality effectuates its restructurations, its updating" (p. 505). The patient facing their traumas in a new way allows their growth to be actualized, "updating" their assumptions about self and world, to then change that world.

I want to end our review of Fanon and Geronimi's (1959/2018) paper by noting again the role of individual therapy, "from commonplace so-called support psychotherapy to the psychoanalytic cure, as well as psychotherapies of psychoanalytic inspiration" (p. 506). In these treatments "we practice *appeasement*, we foster fantasy reconstruction and, as a rule, adopt an active attitude in Ferenczi's sense" (p. 507, emphasis added). Ferenczi's influence— from appeasement (responsiveness), elasticity, to active therapy—is palpable in Fanon's theory and technique, including how he conceptualizes the role of early relationships.

Fanon's Object-Relations Theory: Language, Attachment, and Culture

Fanon's thinking on child development is an interesting amalgam of Ferenczi and Lacan (see Ben Salem, 1959–1960, in Fanon, 2018). He sees the mirror stage as the child misrecognizing him or herself in the image reflected by their social surround. "The fact that I am me," he states, "is haunted by the existence of the other" (p. 521). Alongside the family is the social milieu, haunting the self with stereotypes in the form of relational blueprints of inter-personal others, and caricatured images of outgroup others. The child takes in the "atmosphere" of their social world, navigating "a constant tension between the ego and society" (p. 521). If the social milieu "does not authorize me to reply… a conflict occurs" (p. 521). This suggests we can think of conflict as being given a language while deprived of a voice.

For Fanon (1956/2018), parents are the "custodians of tradition," whose values and rules are the vehicle for communal law, culture, society, their methods of discipline—whether strict or permissive—serving as the "[herald of] all other punishments" (p. 343). Fanon recognized the intergenerational transmission of trauma, with parents "continuing on the tradition" of their own parents (p. 343). Hence, understanding the adult's experience of parental discipline as a child sheds light on how they relate to systems of authority (hospitals, penal systems, etc.). While Fanon stresses the sociogenic origins of mental illness, he recognized how families internalize sociocultural norms and reinforce them. Connecting object relations to treatment, Fanon draws attention to the etymology of the term patient as "one who suffers," and asks for relief: "In hours of great suffering, the adult again has need of a consoling mother"—the soothing of infancy, or the love lacked but desired. The therapist fulfills this "maternal" role alongside a "paternal function" that sets boundaries and distinguishes fantasy from reality (p. 345).

The Patient's "Testing" of the Treatment's Limits: Enactments as an "Expressive Style"

Fanon (1956/2018) used this developmental and societal perspective to understand the tendency of staff to become authoritarian toward patients, transforming the hospital "into a barracks in which children-boarders tremble before parent-orderlies" (p. 346). This was the result of how patients turn toward clinicians as sources of care and authority while also *pulling* them into these roles (p. 346). Without a system that supports reflection on these roles, clinicians are more likely to enact them, mirroring how the patient is controlled and punished by institutions and others in the community. Regardless of the systemic lack that underpins such struggles, we must take accountability, "when we give up our attitude of understanding… we are mistaken" (p. 346). And when we err, like Ferenczi, we must be willing to own our mistakes.

Fanon (1956/2018) cautions against raising limit setting into an iron law, erasing the fact that different patients need different kinds of boundaries: "we must necessarily *adapt* to each" (p. 347, emphasis added). Rigidity impairs the therapeutic relationship, right when we need to adapt ourselves to a new dimension of the patient's needs. This theme re-emerges in a paper co-authored with Slimane Asselah (Fanon & Asselah, 1957) on "The phenomenon of agitation," in which they address a similar repetition between staff and their "aggressive" patients. Although psychosis and mania may involve agitation, they argue that one must distinguish these from a rupture in the therapeutic relationship, stressing "benevolent neutrality" in examining one's countertransference for impatience, anger, and hostility the patient is responding to (p. 439).

If the clinic is to be therapeutic, it must be an environment "for de-alienating encounters," providing an experience in which treatment is "lived by the patient as that which 'understands at last', and not as that which amputates, that which castrates" (Fanon & Asselah, 1957/2018, p. 439). To this end, treatment "must be able to absorb pathological manifestations" without collapsing or breaking down (p. 439). Such moments of tension "*tests* the service's degree of resistance, simultaneously probing its plasticity and its solidity" (p. 440, emphasis added). The testing of our elasticity serves a therapeutic function, exploring the boundaries of the treatment and the patient's freedom. When we survive the patient's aggression without rejecting them, we begin to understand their "anxieties linked to infantile frustrations" (p. 441).

Fanon and Asselah (1957/2018) are not advocating for loose boundaries, as extreme permissiveness is as counter-productive as the "passionate over-statement" of rules and limits (p. 440). Using isolation, restraints, and other forms of punishment as a vehicle for sadism "provoke… and deepen the [patient's] regression" (p. 442). The enactment of destructive countertransference often lays blame on the patient, ignoring "the *reciprocal foundation* that exists between each of the sides. It thus appears within a human framework—the clinical service itself" (p. 444, emphasis added). Rather than framing the patient's behavior as internal pathology, we understand ruptures as relational and systemic phenomena, noting that "agitation diminishes in accordance with staff training and the environment's dis-alienation" (p. 444). Working through ruptures is not a function of the clinician's personal "goodness," but of their being supported in a community and institution that provides ongoing training and supervision.

When systems of care do not provide support that humanizes therapists and patients, what results is "putrefaction," a decay in helping relationships where ruptures and misunderstanding are the norm (Fanon & Asselah, 1957/

2018, p. 444). But if the treatment setting "forms a knot of social relations," then agitation becomes comprehensible as a functional human act (i.e., it serves a purpose in relationship). From a relational point of view, "agitation then enters into the primordial cycle of the reflecting-reflected mirror: you give to me, I receive, I assimilate, I transform, I render to you" (p. 445). Agitation is how the patient expresses something about their relationship to the world. It is part of a language, a system of "significations" (p. 445), "a modality of existence, a type of actualization, an expressive style" (p. 447).

In trying to find out who they are, the patient encounters a disordered world that entraps them, arriving at a solution that secures *some* relief at the cost of freedom. Yet they have some unconscious sense of how the symptom limits their freedom, and so they test freedom's boundaries. Will the other free or dominate me, accompany or abandon me, kiss me or kill me? Are they willing to risk a repair that frees us both? Fanon and Asselah (1957/2018) write,

> This is why the 'madman-who-knows-what-he-is-doing' meets in the isolation unit with 'the madman-who-does-not-know-what-he-is-doing'. In actual fact, the agitated individual at once does and does not know what he is doing. Or if you will, he does not know what he is doing but he is trying to find out. (p. 447)

Providing a twist to Lacan's "subject supposed to know," they made a reversal in which the patient is both seeker and source of knowledge who in some sense does and does not "know" the meaning of their behavior. In turn, the therapist becomes a madman who does *not* know, and if they can surrender to that not-knowing, they may yet provide the patient with "the benevolent and realistic (*actualisant*) help of another (*autrui*)" (p. 442). The translation here is interesting, in that *actualisant* can mean "realistic" but also refers to "modifying" or "updating." In Fanon's case, an-other who helps the patient "update" their sense of self in the world.

The Clinicians' Implication in Systems of Oppression: The Role of Humility

The therapist as a benevolent other or a carceral "gaze" is a tension in Fanon's (1952/1988) earliest essay, "The 'North African Syndrome'," embedding diagnosis and treatment in sociocultural context. He takes aim at white French psychiatrists in Algeria, who when faced with Arab and African patients reporting pain without a discernable medical origin, all too often conclude that "the North African is... a liar, a malingerer, a sluggard, a thief" (p. 7). The French clinician could not comprehend that what is not allowed to be named by one's society finds another path through the body. When we are tongue tied, the body speaks.

Fanon (1952/1988) stressed the fundamental role of relationship: "Without a family, without love, without human relations, without communion with the group, the [colonized's] first encounter with himself will occur in a neurotic mode" (p. 13). Without a society that values one and one's relationships, the colonized "will feel himself emptied, without life, in a bodily struggle with death... A daily death" (p. 13). The death Fanon speaks of echoes Ferenczi's—that of not being valued by one's social environment. This daily death is enacted whenever the colonized's symptoms are dismissed, or when the physician concludes the colonized is unreachable. The "conservative" doctor may look down on the oppressed as "dirty" and lesser than, while the "liberal" doctor rationalizes their lack of care with a kind of pseudoempathy, stating that "it's hard for them being the way they are... [but] you can't say it's our fault" (p. 14). "But that's just it," Fanon interjects, "it is our fault. It so happens [it] is YOUR fault" (p. 14).

Fanon (1952/1988) calls on the therapist to remain open in negotiating difference, lest they turn the patient into a *thing*, an objectified, imaginary "they," as in "that's just how *they* are." Fanon's call is one of accountability and humility, a reminder that diagnostic difficulties and therapeutic impasses are not solely located within the patient, but the therapist–patient relationship. While Fanon emphasizes the therapist's responsibility, he does not locate bias and prejudice as something wholly internal to them, but places it in the context of societal forces.

Society and political economy are the bedrock of the psychic for Fanon (1952/1988). He criticizes the colonizer—and the acculturated middle class of the colonized—who prescribes moving out of the colony as the solution to seeking better living conditions. If conditions are better for the North African in France this is not a failure of the oppressed, but a reflection of the colonial relationship that impoverishes the global south. While Fanon believes in the power of psychotherapy, the essential answer to oppression is not primarily therapeutic but political:

> ... there are houses to be built, schools to be opened, roads to be laid out, slums to be
>   torn down, cities to be made to spring from the earth, men and women, children and children to be adorned with smiles. This means that there is work to be done over there, human work, that is, work which is the meaning

of a home…there are tears to be wiped away, inhuman attitudes to be fought, condescending ways of speech to be ruled out, men to be humanized. (p. 15)

He demands that the humanity of the oppressed be recognized not in "thoughts and prayers" but in policy and political action. Being "a good therapist," even a "good" culturally competent therapist, is insufficient without action in the world. If therapeutic action is not complemented by political action, even the most empathic work amounts to mere words.

Fanon (1952/1988) demands a sacrifice of one's narcissism—"if YOU do not sacrifice the man that is in you so that the man who is on this earth shall be more than a body, more than a Mohammed, by what conjurer's trick will I have to acquire the certainty that you, too, are worthy of my love?" (p. 16). Recognition for Fanon is less an act of "seeing" the other, than an act of *not-seeing* oneself, a level of self-denial, a witnessing of the "no" of the other. It is not that their "no" is absolute, but that we allow their refusal to shake us up and unbind our ways of "seeing."

Resistance as Refusal of the Colonial Order

We finish our review with Fanon's (1955c/2018) forensic writings. At the crux of these papers is the question of the "insanity" of the accused person. In the reasoning of French forensics at the time, to confess to a crime allows the criminal to reintegrate back into society, a logic Fanon questions, as it depends on "a reciprocal and prior recognition of the group by the individual and of the individual by the group" (p. 414). The law of a society "has value only as ratified by the ego" (p. 414), so to *not* condemn one's misdeeds is "an act of aggression vis-à-vis the superego" (pp. 414–415) as a representative of internalized authority. To not recognize the law is a condemnation turning the collective upside down, suggesting *it* is being judged on another set of terms. If confession validates the social contract, what Fanon notices when conducting forensic evaluations of detained Algerians is that "Eight times out of ten, the accused absolutely denies any wrongdoing… he will not explain his detention" (p. 416).

Fanon (1955c/2018) observed the accused admit their guilt, only to later retract their confession. In other cases the accused "does not try to prove his innocence. He *claims* his innocence" (p. 416, emphasis added). Even when the evidence is "extremely hefty"—witnesses point to the accused, the murder weapon is revealed, etc.—Fanon found himself "in the presence of a lucid, coherent man, whose judgement is unimpaired and who claims his innocence" (p. 416). He (1955b/2018) poses the question thus: "Was the accused in a state of insanity at the moment of the act?" (p. 409). His task is to render the accused's behavior coherent before the court, but their retraction wrongdoing "becomes definitive and unshakeable, the accused does not actively try to prove his innocence" (p. 411). As the "expert," he is disarmed of the tools to assess the accused's "insanity," who in turn deprives the colony of "assent" to its sanctions.

Fanon (1955b/2018) asks whether the colonized is bound by a social contract within the colony. If the colonized has never been recognized as a *subject* of the social contract to begin with, their assent is moot, "there can thus be no reintegration if there has been no integration" (p. 412). Repair is nonsensical if the subject is *always already accused*, rendered a criminal prior to the act—an experience Black and Brown people are all too familiar with. Fanon realizes the truth behind the accused's behavior—the sanction is meaningless. "By denying, by retracting," Fanon concludes, "does the North African not *refuse* this?" (p. 412, emphasis added). Is refusal, then, not an act of resistance? In one of his earliest writings, a play entitled *The Drowning Eye*, Fanon (1949/2018) refers to life as a series of "hard blows," which lead us to develop "a compromise between life and death" (p. 97). We face life's troubles because we exist, resisting fate by offering "a constant insult to destiny" (p. 97). In the face of adversity we refuse so-called fate not so much in denial of death, but as an "acceptance of life" (p. 96). In the transference, the patient renegotiates the boundaries of freedom of such acts of refusal—a "no" that can be a raging wind or a quiet whisper, testing the therapist through a risk that enlarges freedom for both.

In relation to Fanon (1955b/2018) as "the expert," the accused he is supposed to diagnose *refuses* to participate in a rigged game. He concludes that the accused's "*refusal to authenticate… the social contract proposed to him*, means that his often profound submission to the powers-that-be… cannot be confounded with an acceptance of this power" (p. 412, emphasis added). Fanon—as an agent of the powers-that-be—realized that despite his forensic patients' compliance to his questions they did not accept his authority, exercising their "first right," the right to refuse the choices before them (see Harney & Moten, 2013). If we return to the question Fanon is charged with, "Was the accused in a *state* of insanity at the moment of the act?", the answer is a resounding *yes*—during, after, and prior to the act, the state hospital, the state of the colony, the state of racial capitalism writ large. If the patient's "no" is a test of their freedom, then the transference-countertransference matrix is a laboratory not only for interpersonal relations, but for exploring practices of refusal toward sociocultural structures and authorities.

The Testimony of Marie-Jeanne Manuellan

We turn now to a beautiful testimony of Fanon as a psychoanalytic therapist by his supervisee and confidante, Marie-Jeanne Manuellan (2017). As it is currently only available in French, I provide translations in English. Manuellan, like Alice Cherki, is unique in that she had direct experience working with and being supervised by Fanon while bearing witness to his political commitments. Through her testimony, we will learn about cases Fanon either treated or supervised, getting a closer look at his clinical practice. Hers is the story of a clinician and a supervisor, but also an evolving relationship with a man she called friend.

Manuellan (2017), originally from French Correze, struggled with her post at the neuropsychiatric day center in Tunis, but more so with how to relate to her new boss. She sensed Fanon kept his distance, having heard he wanted no relationships with white people as the Algerian revolution raged. Over time, however, she and her husband Gilbert became friends with Fanon and his wife Josie. When Manuellan, who became Fanon's transcriber, learned that he had not so much written but "spoken" *Black Skin, White Masks* to Josie, she realized that behind the façade of his rough exterior he had an incredible desire for connection: "Fanon's words had to fall into the ear of another human he felt close to" (p. 15).

Manuellan Discovers the Unconscious in Fanon's Technique

When she took up her post in 1958, Manuellan (2017) struggled to adapt to her new surroundings. Si Aissa, the head nurse and ward supervisor, showed her to her "office," more of a cubicle with a table and a couple of chairs, opposite Fanon's office. Without any patients to tend to, she sat down at her desk and simply waited. Periodically, a trio of residents—Lucien Levy, Charles Geronimi, and Alice Cherki—would enter Fanon's office for supervision, and afterward exchanged pleasantries with Manuellan, especially Geronimi who became a friend. She formed relationships with the nurses, orderlies, and residents on the unit, but Fanon would come and go without a word, offering a distant greeting if at all. Often after work she went home flustered, complaining about Fanon to her husband, who urged her to resign. It so happened, however, that Manuellan and Fanon had friends in common who urged her to *stay*. Her friends told her about how Fanon had been deported from Algeria after he resigned his position at Blida-Joinville to join the FLN, a source of intense pressure for him as he split his time between psychiatry and revolution. "Right now you hate him," they told her, "but give it time, you will grow to love him" (p. 63). She scoffed, but agreed to give him a chance.

In subsequent weeks, Geronimi invited Manuellan (2017) to co-lead process groups in the women's unit with him, opening other opportunities to provide vocational rehabilitation and occupational therapy. One morning, Fanon suddenly "saw" her, noticing her anxiety to have more responsibilities in the unit. To her surprise, he showed up in the doorway to her office and gruffly asked, "Do you want to work?" She nearly fell over herself "Yes!" "So," he replied, "you are going to follow me on my rounds, noting down everything the patient says and everything I say" (p. 64). She scurried around her desk grabbing paper, pencil, and pad, and accompanied him as he sat by his patients' bedsides in the inpatient unit, conducted assessments, discussed cases with colleagues, conducted supervision, and engaged in psychoanalytic therapy multiple times a week—the patient on the couch, Fanon behind it, and Manuellan to the side transcribing the session. At first she struggled with the medical jargon, worrying about misspelling a technical word and feeling ashamed of her ignorance. But more so, that Fanon would be upset with her. Yet she noticed that Fanon never made a critical remark or corrected her spelling. He studied her transcripts diligently after sessions and rounds, conveying a quiet appreciation for her work.

"I had a privileged place," Manuellan (2017) notes in her memoir, "right next to the boss, to hear well. And I noted, noted, opened my ears wide and as much as possible my brain, to understand" (p. 65). Listening to Fanon listen to his patients, she experienced "astonishment after astonishment" as she encountered a "hidden story" behind the patient's sincerely told story—the unconscious, "Fanon and his colleagues worked… with the *id* [lit. "*ça*," the French translation of Freud's "*es*/id/it"]" (p. 65). She began to learn psychoanalytic theory by observing his clinical practice, more and more thawing the image of the "gruff," distant Fanon in her mind. A few weeks later he again passed by her office, asking her "always in a rough tone" if she "wanted to learn." "Of course!" she answered, hungry to better understand what she witnessed on their rounds together. Fanon sent her to a local bookstore with a list of "Nothing but books by Freud and the first psychoanalysts" (p. 65), including Stekel, Helene Deutsch, and Alfred Adler (p. 70).

Fanon and Manuellan (2017) used psychoanalytic theory to understand patients' symptoms and how to treat them, something they also drew on in supervision together. He came to depend on her, requesting she "be almost constantly behind him, close to him, at his disposal," (p. 66), writing down everything that took place between him and his patients. On one occasion,

Fanon treated an Algerian revolutionary on leave from the front line. As Manuellan began to transcribe, the patient announced he did not want to talk "in front of this lady." She gathered her things to leave when Fanon said to the young man, "This lady is not a lady, she is a tape recorder, I need it to do my job" (p. 67). Manuellan receded into the background, *witnessing* the patient talk about his arrest by the French police, the torture he suffered, the daring escape to the Tunisian border he barely pulled off, and the headaches and nightmares that haunted him.

Manuellan (2017) felt incredible guilt and shame as the one French white woman in the unit: "I had there, before my very eyes, a man… my country had almost massacred" (p. 67). Fanon encouraged the man to speak, just as he compelled her to *listen*. As she listened, the soldier's trauma left "wounds… in my narcissism" (p. 67), leading her to question her presumed innocence as a white woman implicated in the colonial system. She also became aware of the enactment taking place in the room: "Fanon somehow forced him to speak in front of me, the Frenchwoman, as his torturers had done, just as he had forced me to hear from the mouth of a tortured man, what my country, France, was practicing" (p. 67). As the session came to a close, the man gave Manuellan "a heavy and long look" before he turned to leave. Afterwards in supervision, Fanon reassured her that if this work was too overwhelming, he would not insist on her accompanying him. She acknowledged her discomfort, but said it was nothing compared to this man's suffering. She remarked that in Fanon's engaged listening to the patient he "showed a certain humanity, and even a certain humanity towards me" (p. 68). By seeing Fanon's tenderness and willingness to invite and sit with patients' pain, she began warming to him.

In their work together, Manuellan (2017) was struck by the exquisite recall Fanon had for his patients, each seen as a person and not a number (p. 68). As they grew closer, Fanon decided that Manuellan would conduct intakes for patients who entered the service, using her assessment reports to guide his case formulation and intervention. Between the presenting problem the patient reported to her, and what emerged in the sessions with Fanon, Manuellan came to realize that he "was deciphering in the patient's speech a completely different story than the one [they] sincerely told" (p. 70). As she wrote down their exchanges, she too began to "tune in" to certain "frequencies," certain details that seemed to be "talking" to her—the patient's relationship with their conflict, with significant others, the memories that emerged in therapy, the ways they defended against and avoided painful topics, and so on. She came to learn that "Fanon was spotting *knots* in what the patient said" (p. 69, emphasis added).

Listening to Fanon raise questions, form hypotheses, make interpretations, and address defenses helped Manuellan (2017) pick up "a certain 'tune,' as they say from a song." The readings Fanon assigned her took on life before the clinical material, referencing de Tosquelles' discussion of how listening psychoanalytically involves picking up on a certain "'poetry'…the rhythm of what [patients] say and where they hesitate," a way of being present with others "that little by little made its way into my brain and my own unconscious. That's probably what I call 'the tune'" (pp. 69–70). When she saw Fanon ask patients about their dreams—something she never saw in her training—she decided to "tune into" her own, learning she dreamt quite often but tended to "forget" them! She started taking notes on her dreams and discussing them with colleagues. When Fanon found out, he encouraged her interest in dream work by sending her back to the bookstore for a copy of Freud's *The Interpretation of Dreams*. Theory was discussed as a part of practice: "talking on the job. But in the light of Freudian theories" (p. 70).

A Friendship Across Rupture and Revolution

Manuellan (2017) noted how Fanon engaged in "scholarly interpretations," grounded in his patients' speech while guided by psychoanalytic theory. That was how she learned, by listening to patients, observing Fanon's interventions, and reading theory. Little by little, her "own psyche… began to function differently. 'It' was moving in me" (p. 70). But what impacted her the most was "what *came alive* in the relationship between the patients, the team, Fanon and my eagerness to know more," (p. 71, emphasis added). She became aware that she was no longer behaving—as her friend Geronimi once observed—like a delicate "flower," keeping to herself and paying little attention to how her mind worked (p. 71). As her mind blossomed, so too did her relationship with Fanon. They started carpooling and getting to know each other's families across work events and parties. Sensing the closeness growing between them, Fanon reiterated that as an active FLN member he did not maintain close relationships with white people. This hurt Manuellan, who complained to her husband that Fanon was "a pretentious sadist!" (p. 76).

By talking about the incident with some of their friends, Manuellan (2017) again gained some perspective in understanding why Fanon kept his distance. As a French white woman, "I had forgotten that I was part of the enemy's camp" (p. 76). Although they began to cultivate a relationship, her privilege and their racial difference within a colonial situation—of active warfare between France and Algerian revolutionaries—was something she needed to wrestle with. Nevertheless, they continued working together. Weeks later

Fanon suddenly remarked "Your husband must be a good person because you are a good woman" (p. 77). These words comforted her, signaling there was room for friendship if she remained open and willing to hold space for their differences. Their relationship helped her appreciate how she was discovering "the world of psychic functioning according to psychoanalysis… I became a student again" (p. 77). She recognized Fanon was a trainer of therapists, committed to turning nurses and residents into "full-fledged healers" (cited in Cherki, 2006, p. 119; Manuellan, 2017, p. 77).

In December 1959, Fanon asked Manuellan about her Christmas plans, to which she replied that she and her husband were hosting a holiday party. Fanon was hurt! Why had she not invited him? "There will be French people there," she replied, "and you don't hang with them" (see Aubenas, 2017). "Well," he said with good humor, "if they are like Sartre, I'm not against it." Fanon invited himself, which terrified Manuellan and her husband. To their surprise, he came with his wife and became the life and soul of the party, cracking jokes, drinking Johnny Walker while mingling with guests, and dancing with Manuellan to the tune of Sidney Bechet (on a personal note as a Johnny Walker fan, I always knew Fanon was "my guy"). After that night the two families grew closer, sharing Sundays at the beach, playing cards, watching movies together, talking politics, and singing Martiniquan songs. Manuellan became one of the few people Fanon talked with about his past, sharing his experience of joining the French army to fight for freedom "whether one was white, black or yellow" (see Aubenas, 2017).

Fanon's Supervision of Manuellan's Child Therapy

After a time, Fanon assigned Manuellan (2017) some child cases in the outpatient service for psychoanalytic play therapy, including a North African Arab girl, "M" (pseudonym) who only walked on her tiptoes, which seriously deformed her feet. M developed this symptom shortly after finding out her mother was pregnant with a second child. Initially her parents threatened and disciplined her to "walk normally," which did not work. Her doctors ruled out a biological cause, and referred the family to Fanon's outpatient service. He asked Manuellan to "reconstitute" the child's family system using toy dolls to better understand her world, letting M play with the dolls without saying a word, only writing down everything she said and did. Si Aissa, the ward supervisor, joined Manuellan's sessions along with a nurse who translated whenever M alternated between French and Arabic. And so they began their treatment, twice a week, in Manuellan's office. Apart from the instruction to be silent and note everything M said, she at first did not understand what was transpiring between the M, the dolls, and herself.

Along with the dolls, Manuellan (2017) brought some modeling clay (play dough) that she left on the table for M to play with. M started playing with the dolls, with different characters (the mom, dad, children) alternating between punishing each other and providing care, especially for the doll that seemed to "represent" herself. Manuellan jotted down M's behavior and speech, later bringing the transcript to Fanon's office for supervision. She felt a little "lost" in understanding the process but diligently, for the most part, carried out his instructions. In one of their supervisions, which Si Aissa once happened to attend, Manuellan remembered that M often spoke about a "bird," or a "whistle" that was hiding in her mother's womb, and had kissed her hand (Cherki, 2006, p. 116; cf. Manuellan, 2017, p. 83). Si Aissa was struck, sharing that in Arabic the word for "bird" is also slang for "penis." Fanon leaned closely over her notes (he had a visual impairment he hid from others), and became angry upon realizing she had not written about it in her notes! Alluding to their Freudian readings, he chided her, "You know perfectly well that this little girl's mother is pregnant" (cited in Cherki, 2006, p. 116).

In their next session, after Manuellan (2017) had set up the toy family and clay on the table, Fanon entered her office and asked M what the bird in her mother's womb was. She started playing with the dolls while seemingly paying him no attention. Sensing his presence might present an obstacle, Fanon left Manuellan and M to their session. As soon as he left, M dropped the dolls, turned around, and started playing with the clay she had up to this point never touched. Manuellan was stunned as the little girl "began with ardor to make the most suggestive forms, male and female sexes, interlocked with each other" (p. 84). In subsequent sessions M played only with the clay, enacting a "dialogue" between her "mother's belly" and the "bird or whistle" that entered it. The "bird" was sometimes beaten and sometimes cuddled by the mother, with M stating she could sometimes "hear" the bird/whistle in her mother's belly if she put her ear to it.

As she began to put into words her feelings of envy, sadness, competition, and anger toward her mother's pregnancy, M started to no longer walk with her feet "erect" on tiptoe. At first she struggled with her balance, due to the deformity of her feet, but quickly "sailed" on her own two feet, flat on the ground. Manuellan (2017), the nurse, and Si Aissa were perplexed, but witnessed in real time as the somatic expression of M's conflict—her "erect" feet in competition with her mother's womb and her father's "whistle"—dissipated, her feet beginning to heal. Weeks later, Fanon was injured in an FLN operation and needed to stay in bed with a cast. He asked Manuellan to come visit him at his home, where he proposed a new project—he wanted to write a book, and for her to help him write it. She was stunned at the request! As she considered his proposal, she shared with anxiety and excitement that her little patient was walking "flat" again. It was then, despite his severe injuries, that Fanon smiled for the first time. "You've cured her," he said warmly, recognizing Manuellan's growth as much as her patient's.

Humility and Confrontation in Fanon's Stance

Fanon's praise meant the world to Manuellan. The contrast between his warmth and the image she had of him made her aware of unconscious feelings affecting how she perceived him. Her perception of his coldness and distance, her fear of upsetting and disappointing him, her at times urgent desire to close the gap between them—all of this evoked the fear she felt toward her father, and her deep yearning for his love (see Aubenas, 2017). Her relationship with Fanon was not only teaching her to be a therapist, but also helping her grow as a person. In becoming more open and less withdrawn, she came to see the respect and care Fanon had for her, a quality she observed in his relationship to patients. "Fanon respected patients infinitely," she (2017) writes, "[he] had to be entirely at their service" (p. 90). When he made an interpretation to patients or shared a hypothesis with colleagues, he avoided taking on an air of superiority or using technical jargon: "On the contrary, he constantly explained," taking his time to unpack terms and ideas for his trainees while speaking to patients in a manner close to their experience, "He liked to teach, do, 'To grow brains' [so] that everyone understands" (p. 90).

According to Manuellan (2017), although Fanon rarely suffered fools he was incredibly sensitive and attuned to his patients. She recalled a young Algerian hospitalized for depression. Fanon, who was conducting rounds with his team, sat down at the edge of her bed, taking her hand in his own as she spoke about her difficulties with her husband and her conflicted feelings toward her brother-in-law, whom she had fallen in love with. As her eyes welled with tears Fanon focused on her, as if everyone else had disappeared. Manuellan overheard him whisper to himself, "Before the sick, we are filled with humility" (p. 93). In contrast to the image of Fanon as a revolutionary who fetishized violence—a misreading of his revolutionary texts—Manuellan stressed his "calls for humility, modesty, solicitude. *To tenderness!*" (p. 94, emphasis added).

That is not to say, per his writings, that Fanon was shy of being confrontational. A high-profile patient struggling with headaches once presented to the outpatient service, leading the attending nurse to tell Fanon that she was the mother-in-law of a prominent minister. Fanon invited her to lie on the couch so he could conduct a neurological examination. In applying the Babinski reflex (stroking the bottom of the foot with a pin) the patient begins to scream and threatens to end the examination. Given the language barrier, Fanon turns to the nurse, demanding, "Tell this lady that I have no time to waste, that she remain quiet, I am here to take care of the poor, not the mothers-in-law of ministers" (cited in Manuellan, 2017, p. 95). As the patient understood French, she quickly got the message and calmed down, allowing Fanon to conduct the examination as he would for any other patient.

There are limits to confrontation, of course, and it is not always successful without a foundation of empathy and tact. In another case, a young woman was brought to the hospital's emergency room after suffering her first psychotic break. Fanon asked to speak with her family to discuss and plan her treatment post discharge. The woman's father was initially reticent, as the mother had a "condition" that prevented her from leaving her home. When Fanon asked about this condition, he was told that she struggled with relentless burping. Nevertheless, Fanon asked to interview the entire family. When both parents arrived, he was astounded. The father was passive and silent as the mother controlled the session, pontificating on how their daughter was not really sick, but just needed a good husband to settle down with and give up her education. All the while, she constantly burped and spat into a box she carried. Without reflecting on his countertransference Fanon replied, "But madam, *you* are married, and that doesn't stop you from being sick" (Manuellan, 2017, p. 97, emphasis added). Not surprisingly, the family took their daughter to another hospital. Although Fanon might have correctly ascertained that the family played a role in this young woman's illness, his lapse in empathy derailed the therapeutic alliance.

Fanon's Psychoanalytic Therapy: The Case of a Young Man

"The truth," Manuellan (2017) tells us about Fanon's approach, "is often therapeutic" (p. 98). He hoped to grow people's awareness by dislodging the social norms and childhood deprivations that result in repression, affecting us outside of our awareness, aiming to "dealienate everyone, make them free so that they are full subjects" (p. 103). As shown above, Fanon's conception of freedom was informed by psychoanalysis alongside Sartre, Marx, Merleau-Ponty, and his supervisor de Tosquelles, of whom he spoke often as someone who "taught me my job" (p. 103). Despite his lack of formal training at a psychoanalytic institute, his peers recognized that Fanon was clairvoyant, having a kind of "second sight" that allowed him "not only to listen, but to hear. Through words but also be observing the ways of being, detecting pretenses, reach the truth of things" (p. 105). This was apparent in his diagnostic skills as well as how he listened to patients, adding to his reputation as a "sorcerer."

Fanon protested this characterization, explaining he had no such "'second sight,' but experience" (Manuellan, 2017, p. 106). Listening closely to patients helped him "unmask their bad faith (in the Sartrian sense), the masks with which they dressed to value themselves in the eyes of others" (p. 104). At the same time, he stressed the importance of humility and reflecting on one's blind spots and limitations, citing two of Freud's sayings—from *The Interpretation of Dreams*: "it is instructive to become familiar with the much raked-up soil from which our virtues proudly arise," and from *Studies in Hysteria*, "…much has been gained if we succeed in turning your hysterical misery into common unhappiness" (paraphrased in p. 106). Fanon (2018) was clear-headed in appreciating where Freud was insightful without ignoring how he could also be a "bastard" (Fanon's words) in how he talked about people of color as "primitives" (p. 734).

As mentioned earlier, Fanon was severely injured during an FLN assignment, having his spine severed. During his recovery he called Manuellan (2017) to his home, greeting her in a full body cast. Worried, she asked how he was, to which he answered with good humor, "You can see. But *you* seem to be ok!" As she put some "get well soon" chocolates on his desk, he stated that he would need her help to write a book. Although Manuellan did not own a typewriter, she enthusiastically said she would learn. She went ahead and bought one, bringing it with her every morning to type up his dictation of the new book. Her early attempts were less than successful as her typing speed could not keep up with Fanon's dictation.

Eventually, he became frustrated and told her he would find another secretary. Manuellan, now used to his bellicose nature—especially while recovering from an injury—left him to his own devices. A few months later, however, he poked his head into her office, complaining about the secretary he had hired and how he would have to find a new one. Manuellan took the hint, telling him that if he dictated the book and she wrote it by hand she would be much quicker, and would type up the text in the evening. And with that, they wrote *L'An V de la révolution algérienne*, or as it is known in English, *A Dying*

Colonialism (Fanon, 1965), with Fanon engaging in his "spoken word," and Manuellan writing assiduously at his desk.

One of the psychoanalytic treatments Fanon conducted and Manuellan (2017) transcribed was of a young adult, 27-year-old Tunisian man seen five times a week for psychoanalytic psychotherapy for a year, from 1958 to 1959. As usual, she sat at his desk and transcribed everything "said between the chair behind the couch, in which Fanon was sitting, and the couch on which the patient was lying" (p. 123). Fanon again explained Manuellan's role as a "tape recorder" to quell the young man's anxiety, then they embarked on the analysis together. Although Fanon was not trained at an institute, Manuellan observed that he had "surprising intuitions" about the patient, recognizing in his technique that he worked in a manner similar to the first psychoanalysts gathered around Freud, experimenting with different interventions while maintaining an active curiosity and openness toward the patient.

The young man worked in administration as a public official, and had recently experienced severe disturbances at work. Specifically, whenever he handed important documentation to a co-worker or delivery man he was suddenly "invaded by a paralyzing fantasy of being sodomized" (Manuellan, 2017, p. 123). The anxiety and panic attacks he experienced led him to avoid work, becoming withdrawn in ways that affected his personal and professional life. In the sessions that followed the patient talked about his life history, with Fanon intervening often, using, as he explained to Manuellan, "the 'active method' in the manner of Ferenczi" (p. 124). After a few months, the young man felt more comfortable and began to talk about how in childhood he went on walks with a family friend "whom he loved very much" (p. 124). This friend, who was very religious, would ask him to pick up any paper or piece of bread on the street, "because it was holy." As a child, the young man placed these objects on the edge of a window to "save" them from "filth." Fanon, listening with his "third ear," offered an interpretation connecting this memory with his symptom, "a link totally absent from the patient's conscious thinking" (p. 124)—could the act of "bending over" to pick up these items in front of this friend he "loved very much" have a relationship to his fears of being sodomized? Surprised by this comment, the young man became aware of desires he had previously warded off as filthy and unclean.

Over time, it was not only Fanon who inhabited a transferential place in the patient's fantasies, but also Manuellan (2017). On one occasion, the patient showed up at her office before his appointment with Fanon, asking her to wear his wristwatch. She asked Fanon what to do, to which he responded she should agree to wear his watch for a couple of days and then return it to him. He clearly sensed that transference was at work, wanting to offer the patient some flexibility with his wish yet with a clear limit. In short order, the patient reported dreams alluding to Manuellan's presence as a silent observer. In that sense, the patient was being treated by both an active, relational therapist *and* a Freudian "blank screen!".

Manuellan (2017) produced a thick volume of Fanon's cases, an archive that remained in her drawer for years. After Fanon died, she could not bring herself to throw the papers away, with the "psychoanalysis" he conducted becoming intimately precious to her. It was undergoing her own analysis in France that led her to retrieve and re-read this case, and then pass it on to Alice Cherki with whom she had crossed paths at a psychoanalytic seminar (p. 127). It was Cherki (2006) who continues relating the process of this "unorthodox" psychoanalysis. In her analysis of the transcripts, she recognizes a resemblance between Fanon's technique and Freud's, in particular the latter's treatment of L, the "Rat Man," alongside Ferenczi, whom Fanon discussed often in their supervisions and didactics (p. 121). Cherki remarks on Fanon's "extremely attuned ear as well as considerable theoretical grounding," attending to the young man's "desired and negated homosexuality" alongside "the repetitive pattern of signifiers… the denials and the lapses" in speech, following Lacan (p. 121). She observes, however, a certain discomfort he has with the transference. Fanon's countertransferential avoidance, per Lacan, his *resistance* to the young man's transference only deepens it, with his dreams and associations making greater reference to Fanon as the father he wished he had.

Fanon avoids addressing the transference either by redirecting the young man to talk about his past, or by insisting "I cannot be your father, I am your doctor" (cited in Cherki, 2006, p. 121). Eventually, he realized that by paying such close attention to the patient's speech, by showing that he was truly and deeply listening to him, he was evoking both a great tyrannical figure of his past—his father—alongside the wish for a father that loved and accepted him. Having "found his way to Freud by way of Ferenczi," Fanon decided to intervene using "a third voice," his own, to provide a contrast so that "these figures could be made to retreat or take on another aspect" (p. 121). He stops avoiding the patient's wish, "I would have liked you to be my father," and displays a "willingness to give," welcoming their wish with great tenderness. "The young man in question made incredible progress," Cherki tells us, "As did Fanon" (p. 121).

Frantz Fanon: The Once and Future Psychoanalyst

Near the end of this treatment, Manuellan (2017) tells us that Fanon was getting ready to depart for Accra for the African People's Conference, and afterward leave his post at Tunis to return to Algeria as a full-time FLN combatant. It was then Manuellan teased him that it was a pity he was abandoning psychiatry for politics. Fanon was appalled, declaring "Never in my life. As soon as I'm done with the Algerian revolution, I will undergo an analysis and resume my psychiatry" (cited in p. 126). This was no contradiction, as psychiatry—and psychoanalysis—were "a primordial area in his very life, an instrument of struggle in the fight against alienation, for the liberation of human psyches" (p. 126). Fanon turned to her, remarking on her work with children, "*You* should be a psychoanalyst." He quickly balked at the idea of her training in France, telling her to come to Algeria instead, "I will train you myself" (p. 126).

In another instance, Fanon and Manuellan went to the cinema to see Alain Resnais' film, *Hiroshima my Love*. In the film, a traveling white French actress hooks up with a Japanese man. They are both married, but the man wishes to continue the affair, while she refuses and plans to return to France. The woman later reveals she fell in love with a German soldier occupying her hometown of Nevers during the war. They planned to escape the war, but her lover was shot on the day Nevers was liberated from the Nazis. After liberation, her neighbors found out about the relationship and shaved her head as punishment. She disclosed she was keeping her distance from the Japanese man to avoid being hurt again. After discussing her fears, they reconcile and resume their affair. Afterward, Fanon asked Manuellan what she thought of the movie. She said the film reminded her of psychoanalysis, recalling the scene in which Emmanuelle Riva says that Nevers is a city she does not think about during the day, but dreams about at night. After her meeting with the Japanese man, the actress says "little runner of Nevers, I give you to oblivion." It was this latter phrase, "I give you to oblivion" that stood out to Manuellan.

Manuellan (2017) offered Fanon a psychoanalytic reading of the film, noting the parallels between the actress having a chance encounter with the Japanese man, much like her German lover from Nevers, a stranger "passing through." "She remembers what she had repressed but dreamed of every night," referring to the death of her German lover and the shaving of her hair:

From now on she will be able to 'forget,' that is to say, she will no longer dream of

Nevers at night, and will be able to evoke the past trauma that will have lost its traumatic character... to forget, you have to be able to remember... the repressed is there, alive, but only in dreams. (p. 154)

Fanon was overjoyed. Reminiscing over their work together and discussions of psychoanalytic ideas he tells her, "You make me happy. I taught you something" (p. 154).

Fanon encouraged Manuellan to resume her studies in psychology and undertake psychoanalytic training, going so far as to recommend an analyst for her. She found this odd, wondering if this analyst was for her or for *him*. Then, one morning in 1961, Fanon rang the doorbell at Manuellan's (2017) home one last time, who was surprised by the sudden call. He tells her to grab a seat. She sits on her couch and watches anxiously as he takes out a set of documents. "I have leukemia," he tells her, "these are the analyses..." She leaps up from her couch, crying out, "It's not true, you're wrong!" "You have to help Josie," he asks his friend, "But I will defend myself." "How?!" she asked in disbelief. He pointed to his forehead with that smile of his: "With my brain" (p. 164). Tragically, Fanon lost that fight later that year.

Manuellan mourned the supervisor, colleague, and friend who had taught her about her own unconscious: "Fanon had made me free" (see Aubenas, 2017). In 1967, six years after Fanon's death, Manuellan returned to Paris, where she did indeed pursue advanced studies in psychology and made an appointment with a psychoanalyst—entering analysis for herself, but also on behalf of her friend. On her first session, Manuellan was beckoned to enter the consulting room, where she sat and looked squarely at her analyst. A wave of emotion came over her, a combination of love and sorrow, mourning and melancholia, guilt and gratitude, bursting deep within her soul as she broke down in tears. Her analyst sat with her, patient, present, listening. When she was finally able to speak through her tears, the words came—"I thought that you would be Black."

Cherki (2006) reminds us that Fanon was not "technically" a psychoanalyst, as he did not undergo formal analysis. But what appears at first to be a shortcoming becomes, "on closer analysis, further proof of the unwitting contemporaneity of Fanon's ideas" (p. 214). He was one of psychoanalysis' greatest innovators, the "most disputatious heir" of not only Freud, but also Ferenczi and Lacan. Fanon read Freud to think about the intrapsychic, "was very much taken" by Ferenczi's thinking on trauma and relationality, while engaging Lacan's claim that the act of entering language as a speaking being "is always structurally traumatic" (p. 215). To the extent the practice of psychoanalysis is "to listen for the gaps, the lapses, the search for words and meaning," so that patients may "[transform] walls into passageways, not only for themselves but for their predecessors as well as their descendants" (pp. 215–216), then Fanon comes to us as contemporary psychoanalysis' most disputatious ancestor.

Coda

One wonders if the restrictiveness of psychoanalytic training would push Fanon to break with analysis. Or maybe, as suggested in his offer to train Manuellan, it would lead him to formally inaugurate a new school of decolonial psychoanalysis. Such a gesture presumes authority as a psychoanalyst—analysts, after all, train future analysts. Perhaps becoming a psychoanalyst is a relational venture, a co-creation of analyst and analysand, supervisor and supervisee. When Manuellan faced her analyst for the first time, she was moved by a transference that first developed with Fanon. Her experience was textured by her fear and yearning for her father, activated in her relationship with Fanon. As she witnessed the humility he exhibited with his patients and with her, a new set of associations formed in her mind.

She became aware of how whiteness textured her experience while becoming more reflective about her own mind, coming to love Fanon as a colleague and friend. Her transference to her analyst—"I thought you would be Black"—is a gift, an image of who could be a psychoanalyst, and what psychoanalysis *is*, that was intimately bound up with Fanon. Put differently, when she thought psychoanalysis, she thought Fanon, an association born out of their relationship. If, as Cherki (2006) tells us, Fanon worked "to transform the real of the camp, to reinstate temporality to life and inscribe the dream" (p. 217), then let us take hold of Manuellan's transference as that dream, and accept the charge to become Fanon's most disputatious heirs.

Reflection Questions

- Fanon thought about the therapeutic relationship within the context of its institutional, social, cultural, and systemic world. How has the institutional or social context in which you work impacted your clinical practice? Your own relationships living through the times we are living in? How have you managed these conflicts or tensions? What do you think this tells us about the relationship between interpersonal dynamics and the social, cultural world?

- Fanon was an integrative thinker and practitioner who drew on relational and Lacanian thinking alongside community work, individual and group therapy, and even behavior therapy. What kind of training have you had about the value of different theoretical orientations to mental health? What are the pros and cons of choosing a single school of thought versus working with different models, even integrating them? How can learning different tools help treat different populations?
- Fanon stressed the role of the therapist's humility and responsiveness as much as the patient's right to challenge and refuse their authority, whether interpersonally or as representative of different identity groups. In what ways do you negotiate humility and authority with your patients? Co-workers? People in your daily life? Is balancing self-assertion and yielding to others more complex across lines of difference?

Further Reading

Fanon's Clinical Work and Papers
- Gibson, N. C., & Beneduce, R. (2017). *Frantz Fanon, psychiatry and politics.* Rowman & Littlefield.
- Turner, L., & Neville, H. (Eds). (2020). *Frantz Fanon's psychotherapeutic approaches to clinical work: Practicing internationally with marginalized communities.* Routledge.

Decolonial Approaches to Psychology
- Bhatia, S. (2020). Decolonizing psychology: Power, citizenship and identity. *Psychoanalysis, Self and Context, 15*(3), 257–266.
- Goozee, H. (2021). Decolonizing trauma with Frantz Fanon. *International Political Sociology, 15*(1), 102–120.
- Maldonado-Torres, N. (2017). Frantz Fanon and the decolonial turn in psychology: From modern/colonial methods to the decolonial attitude. *South African Journal of Psychology, 47*(4), 432–441.

References

Aubenas, F. (2017). In the shadow of Frantz Fanon. Retrieved March 31, 2020, from https://www.versobooks.com/blogs/3491-in-the-shadow-of-frantz-fanon.

Cherki, A. (2006). *Frantz Fanon: A portrait.* Cornell University Press.

Fanon, F. (1952/2008). (1965). *A dying colonialism.* Grove Press.

Fanon, F. (1988). *Toward the African revolution: Political essays.* Grove Press.

Fanon, F. (2018). *Alienation and freedom.* Bloomsbury Publishing.

Gaztambide, D. (2021). Do black lives matter in psychoanalysis? Frantz Fanon as our most disputatious ancestor. *Psychoanalytic Psychology, 38*(3), 177–184.

Gibson, N. C., & Beneduce, R. (2017b). *Frantz Fanon, psychiatry, and politics.* Rowman & Littlefield.

Gordon, L. R. (2020). *Freedom, justice, and decolonization.* Routledge.

Gramsci, A. (1977). *Selections from political writings, 1910–1920* (Vol. 1. J. Mathews, Trans., Q. Hoare, Ed.). Lawrence and Wishart.

Harney, S., & Moten, F. (2013). *The undercommons: Fugitive planning and black study.* Minor Compositions.

Manuellan, M. J. (2017). *Sous la dictée de Fanon.* l'Amourier.

Manuellan, M. J., & Cofiant, R. (2017–2018). Conversations on Fanon. Retrieved November 8, 2022, from https://www.montraykreyol.org/article/marie-jeanne-manuellan-assistante-de-frantz-fanon-a-tunis-decede-dans-la-92e-annee-de-son

Reik, T. (1933). New ways in psycho-analytic technique. *International Journal of Psychoanalysis, 14*, 321–334.

Reik, T. (1948/1983). *Listening with the third ear.* Macmillan.

Tosquelles, F. (1975/2017). Frantz Fanon en Saint-Alban (1975). *Teoría y Crítica de la Psicología, 9*, 223–229.

6

Sociogenic Foundations of Theory and Practice: Revolutionizing Psychoanalysis

Fanon's original dissertation, *Black Skin, White Masks* (1952/2008), is a "clinical study" (p. 14) comprising his most detailed analysis of the colonial situation from a psychoanalytic perspective. It is *the* decolonial text and, I argue, the foundation of decolonial psychoanalysis. I will unpack Fanon's theorizing on colonialism, race, and class while drawing out critiques of psychoanalysis immanent in the text—specifically, of Freud and Ferenczi. At the heart of the work is his concern with the "vicious cycle" that maintains the colonial situation—the desire to "rise upwards" in the hierarchy. Fanon's goal, politically and clinically, is to "extricate ourselves" from this cycle, asserting "only a psychoanalytical interpretation of the black problem can lay bare the anomalies of affect that are responsible for the structure of the complex" (p. 3).

For the majority of this chapter, we work through *Black Skin, White Masks* to unpack Fanon's theorizing on how hierarchies of inequality structure our desire in ways that lead us to protect those hierarchies in the hope of enjoying their privileges, and end by drawing on case examples from his practice reported in his final work, the revolutionary treatise *The Wretched of the Earth* (1963). I want to note that while Fanon's theorizing centers race, class, and colonialism, questions of hierarchy and positionality are no less relevant for gender and sexuality as well. Similarly, while I do not assume the conditions of colonial Martinique or Algeria are universal, Fanon's analysis of these conditions reveals certain principles about the human psyche and hierarchy that I believe are cross-culturally applicable (see the research in Chapter 7).

Psychoanalysis is certainly not the only lens in Fanon's work, though it is a central one. *Black Skin, White Masks* features recurrent citations of Sigmund and Anna Freud, Adler, Jung, Bonaparte, and Lacan, among others. It is also clear that Fanon has a Marxist critique of colonialism as a capitalist, racist structure (Gibson, 2020), arguing that the "inferiority complex" of colonized peoples results from a "double process: primarily, economic, subsequently, the internalization—or, better the *epidermalization*—of this inferiority" (Fanon, 1952/2008, p. 4, emphasis original). Socioeconomic structures create conditions of inequality which are then inscribed in the body. What does the work of inscribing sociogeny on the body is language.

The Social Unconscious Is Structured Like a Language

As in Fanon's other work (see Chapter 5), Lacanian ideas on language occupy a central place. Speech is fundamentally addressed both to "the other" on the level of an intersubjective relation, as well as the "big Other" incarnated in the social, political, and economic world grounding that relation. "To speak means to be in a position to use a certain syntax," Fanon (1952/2008) writes, "to grasp the morphology of this or that language, but it means above all to assume a culture, to support the weight of a civilization" (p. 8). Fanon is not simply speaking of the imposition of the French language on Martinique, or the imposition of Spanish and English on Puerto Rico, though it includes that. He is speaking more broadly, more *psychoanalytically*, about language and culture as such.

If to use a "certain syntax" is to adopt a set of rules for how to arrange and put words together in certain clauses or phrases, and to "grasp a morphology" is to adopt how those words, prefixes, and signifiers are associated within the linguistic universe of a culture, then "to assume a culture" means to assume those *associations* encoded in that culture's unconscious (think of Lacan's "symbolic order"). Hence, "a language consequently possesses the world expressed and implied by that language" (Fanon, 1952/2008, p. 9). Language positions us in relation to others and the world, tacitly communicating what values, peoples, and things are "higher" or "lower," to be approached or to be avoided.

Fanon (1952/2008) speaks about, for example, African immigrants who "pretend" to be Antilleans, or Antilleans who are offended by being mistaken for Africans, "because the Antilles Negro is more 'civilized' than the African, that is, he is closer to the white man" (p. 15). Hierarchies of value among colonized peoples, such as colorism (lighter = more valued), find their way into everyday language, structured by implicit associations between Blackness and what is "lower" or "violent" that "slip" through our speech with "a hidden subtlety" (p. 26). Foregrounding research on microaggressions—subtle speech or behavior that consciously or unconsciously communicate a "put-down" to a person or group (Sue, 2010)—Fanon (1952/2008) identifies how such slips communicate to the oppressed "You'd better keep your place" (p. 21).

Fanon (1952/2008) underscores the verticality of the language of oppression. If one desires to "move up," one is "getting *up*pity," just as one can easily "sink" to the "bottom." Still, "there are climbers, 'the ones who forget who they are,' and, in contrast to them, 'the ones who remember where they came from'" (p. 24). Notice the spatial and motoric metaphors of movement. To say to a person of color "You speak English so well!" communicates that they are speaking "above" their "station." "You're not like the others, you seem nice and sweet," implies that those in your group are "unsafe," whereas *you* are not threatening. These experiences impact our psyche even if we reject them, worming their way into our speech and behavior. For example, Fanon recalls how being "talked down to" by white men as "feeble-minded" impacted his clinical work. During a session with an old woman with dementia, he was "suddenly aware of the collapse of the *antennae* with which I touch and through which I am touched" (p. 20, emphasis original). He noticed how he "talked down" to her as if she was "slow," revealing "the stigmata of a dereliction in my relations with other people" (p. 20).

Remember how Fanon underlines Sartre's book *Situations* on how language functions as our "antennae" for relatedness (see Chapter 5). The rupture with his patient was embedded in his microaggressive speech toward her, and through that rupture the social unconscious—those unspoken associations of who is and is not human, deserving, worthy of care—*spoke through* him, revealing how the racism he internalized was enacted in the therapeutic relationship. In reckoning with that which spoke through him, he was able to shift his behavior and restore his patient's humanity, alongside his own. The social unconscious "slips" through our utterances, our "offhand" comments, and the way we carry our body in space, communicating something about who we are in relation to others and to a social hierarchy.

The Social Unconscious as Systemic Associations

For Fanon (1952/2008) the social unconscious is made up of associations in language. In a multiyear experiment he conducted with 500 participants (all white), he inserted the word "*Negro*" in a series of association tests, evoking automatic associations with the words "biology," "penis," "savage," "animal," and "sin," associations whose proportions went up when a white conferedate conducted the experiment—participants felt an unconscious "reticence" responding in the presence of a Black man (p. 128). Behind these associations is an image or schema of Black people in the collective unconscious of colonial, European society (p. 130). In contrast with Jung's mysticism, for Fanon the collective unconscious is a series of associations which "pass through" the individual's speech and behavior, a "drama… enacted every day" (p. 112). The purpose of this enactment is "*collective catharsis*. In every society… [there must be] an outlet through which the forces accumulated in the form of aggression can be released" (p. 112, emphasis original). We are in territory familiar to Freud, who conceived of society as providing compensations for the suffering it produces.

Fanon (1952/2008) points to political economy—the distribution of wealth, goods, and resources—alongside media and culture as structures that *communicate* who is valued and who deserves to live and thrive. All media (e.g., film, the news, the internet) convey a tacit language "behind the text," defining its heroes and villains, the conquerors and the conquered, what is and is not allowed to be imagined (p. 113). Media and the structure of inequality frames what one "sees" day in and day out, forming scripts drawing on our senses to turn "lived experience" into the final culprit. Not the *essential* culprit, mind you. The individual psyche is not the ringleader, though it is implicated in the social unconscious (Kabasakalian-McKay & Mark, 2022).

A personal example, speaking as someone who grew up in a colony, is illustrative. Growing up in Puerto Rico in the 1980s and 1990s, race and colorism were often unspoken and unbroachable. The reigning ideology was that all Puerto Ricans descend from a "harmonious mixture" of Spaniard, indigenous Taino, and African people—hence, there is "no racism" in Puerto Rico (see Rodríguez-Silva, 2012). Yet, as the white son of an ambiguously "Brown" Puerto Rican man and a white Cuban woman, my eyes, hair, and skin told a different story. I remember my classmates touching my hair, saying "I want to have *pelo bueno* [good hair] like you," or adults making comments about how I was born "*tan lindo, tan clarito* [so pretty, so light]!" alongside the evening news depicting "criminals" from "*caserios* [housing projects]" coded as Black and Brown. Although race and color were never named, the *lived experience* of these stimuli betrayed an unspoken language of hierarchy—who is "at the top," "bottom," ambiguously "in between," who deserves care and who does *not*, even as we are all sinking in the same colony.

The Political Economic and Psychic Function of Anti-Blackness

Fanon (1952/2008) sees anti-Blackness not primarily as a problem of inter-personal privilege, but the result of "a colonialist, capitalist society that is only accidentally white" (p. 157). Although whiteness is central to racial capitalism, as we will see it is not necessary for it to be "white" in order to be anti-Black. In line with our thesis of racism, cisheterosexism, and classism as compromise formations or *jouissance*, Fanon discusses how "the white colonial is motivated only by his desire *to put an end to a feeling of unsatisfaction, on the level of... overcompensation*" (p. 62, emphasis added). Fanon cites Sartre to underscore the compensatory function of anti-Blackness and anti-Semitism: "the rich for the most part exploit this passion," propagating it among the working class who, by treating Jews and Black people as inferior "affirm at the same time that I belong to the elite" (cited in p. 64). Hence, "the displacement of the white proletariat's aggression on to the black proletariat is fundamentally a result of the economic structure" (p. 64). The colony maintains itself through the fantasy that white and non-Black people will be protected from "sinking any lower" in the hierarchy (cited in p. 65).

Fanon's (1952/2008) thinking straddles two perspectives. On the one hand, he takes up the psychoanalytic theory of racist *jouissance* to examine how white, conditionally white (e.g., Jewish people), and non-white people of color participate in anti-Blackness to maintain capitalism. On the other, he critiques treating colonialism as distinct from other forms of racism, recognizing that "forms of exploitation resemble one another" (p. 65). As someone who fought the Nazis, Fanon feels a kinship with Jews facing anti-Semitic violence, and as a psychiatrist who witnessed colonialism in Africa, he also feels deep solidarity with Arabs, choosing to fight in the Algerian revolution (p. 67). As a healer and revolutionary, he called on us to be "concerned, be we white, black or yellow; and each time freedom is under siege, no matter where, I will engage myself completely" (cited in Duncan-Andrade & Morrell, 2008, p. 41).

Fanon does not argue that all oppressions are "the same," but that they are *linked* as part of racial capitalism, connecting anti-Blackness to other forms of racism and oppression. At the same time, he draws a distinction in how anti-Blackness functions to provide a compensation to other non-white people for their suffering, even as it tightens the chains of oppression around their neck. What Fanon dissects in *Black Skin, White Masks* was succinctly captured by one of my students—"crabs in a barrel." His point is not to blame the crabs for behavior symptomatic of being trapped in a barrel, but to dismantle the barrel that produces this behavior as such.

Nonbeing and Black Existence

At the beginning of the text, Fanon (1952/2008) writes of a "zone of nonbeing, an extraordinarily sterile and arid region, an utterly naked declivity where an authentic upheaval can be born" (p. 2). The "zone of nonbeing" is simultaneously a "downward slope" (declivity) into the bottom, yet one from which "an authentic upheaval," a transformative possibility, can emerge. As a therapist, Fanon was aware that living involves pain, sometimes even living through hell. But if we reckon with that pain, even when we touch the possibility of death, we emerge on the other side discovering a world of possibility. Working through the zone is to be "uprooted" from our habitual ways of being in the world, "the dissolution of the truths that he has worked out for himself one after another," and "to give up projecting onto the world an antinomy [i.e., conflict] that coexists with him" (p. 2). Overcoming our conflicts involves "a process of transcendence... haunted by the problems of love and understanding" (p. 2).

Fanon's zone of nonbeing resembles Spanish poet Garcia Lorca's (1981) encounter with the duende. Lorca distinguishes between different sources of inspiration in art, such as "the angel," "the muse," and "the duende." The angel provides guidance, the muse a stroke of insight. "The true struggle," he writes, "is with the duende" (p. 4). The duende has "neither map nor discipline. We only know it... rejects all the sweet geometry we understand, that it shatters styles" (p. 4). Duende undoes what makes us feel safe, appearing whenever death draws near "to shake those branches we all carry, that do not bring, can never bring, consolation" (p. 7). Duende shakes up those substitutive "branches" and introduces a wound, and it is "in trying to heal that wound that never heals, [that] lies the strangeness, the inventiveness of a man's work" (p. 7). It renders our masks before the world, while making it "easier to love, to understand, and be certain of being loved, and being understood" (p. 7). Risk opens the possibility of love and poetry.

The central problem for Fanon (1952/2008) is not the zone of nonbeing per se, but *avoiding* the encounter with the zone. And specifically, how non-Black people defer the encounter by projecting their anxieties onto Black people, preventing them from "being able to accomplish this descent into a real hell" (p. 2) from which transformative, creative potentials might emerge. Black people are emplaced into the orbit of the zone, "fixed" to it by an anti-Black society, but when they are able to cross its threshold, Fanon argues, they lay claim to an irruptive, transformative potential. To be clear, these are not "intrapsychic" issues existing in isolation, but the symptoms of an anti-Black, colonial capitalist system.

Fanon (1952/2008) arrived at this conclusion through a kind of self-analysis *à la* Freud, which he describes in a chapter translated as "The fact of Blackness" (the original French title was "The lived experience of being Black"). He reflects on the times he was called derogatory names, deprived of humanity before the white gaze, made into "an object in the midst of other objects" (p. 82). He makes a distinction between "ontology," the structure of who is defined as a human being, and "existence" as one's lived experience in the world. At the sociopolitical level, an "ontological fantasy" is that unconscious collection of associations, schemas, and stories society tells about who is human, who are "us" and "them." One might *experience* oneself as a living being, but if a society's ontological fantasy defines one as *not* a person, then it is as if one does not exist. Hence Fanon writes, "The black man has no ontological resistance in the eyes of the white man" (p. 83).

In his encounter with the white gaze, Fanon (1952/2008) describes the experience of embodiment, how the self emerges out of one's corporeal schema, the "implicit knowledge" of how to move one's body "in the middle of a spatial and temporal world," (p. 83). When he hears a racial slur escape the lips of a white world, he feels a burden on his body, his movements slowing to a crawl. He starts to dissociate, "the corporeal schema crumbled, its place taken by a racial epidermal schema" (p. 84). He was no longer "just a man," but a *Black* man, a racialized body *emplaced* below others, a sudden fall triggering "Nausea... I discovered my blackness" (p. 84; 85). "I shouted a greeting to the world and the world slashed away my joy," Fanon writes, "I was told to stay within bounds, to go back where I belonged" (p. 86).

Fanon tries to fight back with reason to disprove racist stereotypes, but finds it a feeble weapon against something which is fundamentally irrational, *psychotic*. He turns to Black history for proof that he comes from a civilized people and is not a "primitive," but this does not resolve the assault on his humanity. It dawns on Fanon that he "was repeating a cycle" (p. 99) in which "[every] hand was a losing hand for me" (p. 101). He turns to Marxism, but this too is a disappointment when white Marxists argue that Black people would "overcome" their Blackness in pursuit of the "universal" revolution, as if his Blackness was a footnote to a broader (whiter) cause. Although that does not deter his socialist politics, he feels robbed by a white world that denies his humanity outside of a rigid notion of Black identity. He falls victim to "a feeling of nonexistence" (p. 106), reminded of a crippled veteran's reprise to his brother, "Resign yourself to your color the way I got used to my stump; we're both victims" (p. 107).

At first, Fanon (1952/2008) defends against the zone as an ontological amputation:

I am a master and I am advised to adopt the humility of the cripple. Yesterday, awakening to the world, I saw the sky turn upon itself utterly and wholly. I wanted to rise, but the disemboweled silence fell back upon me, its wings paralyzed. Without responsibility, straddling Nothingness and Infinity, I began to weep. (p. 108)

Searching everywhere for an answer to this destitution, he tries to resist by overcompensating with a chauvinistic sense of superiority, but this too fails him. Suddenly something else emerges from the zone. He surrenders to this space between the "Nothingness" of death and the "Infinity" of life beyond death. He begins to weep, and from those tears something shifts.

Anti-Blackness as Traumatic "Scene"

What Fanon (1952/2008) explores in his self-analysis, using poetic language, is the relationship between Black people's lived experience (existence) and a society whose unconscious "frames" them as equivalent to the "not human" (ontology). He accounts for the different *neurotic positions* he took in relation to that ontological fantasy as a way of avoiding wrestling with his pain. Drawing on his own experience, Fanon psychoanalyzes the intersection between existence and ontology for Black and non-Black subjects, critiquing and reinventing psychoanalytic theory. In a chapter entitled "The Negro and Psychopathology," he explores not just the impact of anti-Blackness on Black people's mental health, but also the function anti-Blackness fulfills for the mental health and sense of being of *non-Black* people.

Fanon (1952/2008) reviews how psychoanalysis understands the individual's behavior in the context of the family, with the analyst uncovering in neurosis "a repetition, a duplication of conflicts that owe their origin to the essence of the family constellation" (p. 109). In the European context, the family is itself a repetition of the state: "As the child emerges from the shadow of his parents, he finds himself once more among the same laws, the same principles, the same values" (p. 109). The social world is presumed to be an "average, expectable environment" that provides most of what the individual needs. Hence, conflicts, neurosis, and mental illness arise essentially from tensions in the family. Put crudely, a "normal" family would equip the child to succeed in a "normal" world. Hence, the problem lies within the "abnormal" family.

Fanon (1952/2008) argues this schema is problematic in general, but especially so for Black people: "A normal Negro child, having grown up within a normal family, will become abnormal on the slightest contact with the white world" (p. 111). As we saw in the previous chapter, Fanon was perfectly aware that family conflict and childhood trauma were a source of psychopathology, and he was no less cognizant that people could be resilient. But the *essential* problem is not within the family, but the family in social context. Under ideal circumstances, a child may receive all the love they need to thrive, yet in society face a language that states: "Your life does not matter." Put concretely, a child's secure attachment may not necessarily protect them from systemic violence. Interestingly, Fanon here cites Freud's introductory lectures at Clark University:"symptoms were determined by 'scenes' of which they were the mnemic residues," meaning, symptoms are the imprints of these scenes (cited in p. 111).

Fanon reiterates Freud's theory that trauma leads to painful affects being "expelled" from consciousness, relieving suffering in the short term yet returning as a symptom serving as its "surrogate, its *Ersatz* [substitute]" (p. 111). Fanon extrapolates that repeated exposure to racialized violence constitutes a trauma, following the same processes of avoidance, coping, and symptom formation. However, while being victimized by racialized violence is a sufficient cause, it is not necessary for the trauma to be experienced personally.

We should remember a fascinating theory of Freud's (1918/1955), based on his work with a patient he called the "Wolf Man"—coincidentally, a paper Fanon had his residents read and discuss (Cherki, 2006). In brief, Freud deduces from the Wolf Man's dreams, associations, and fantasies the existence of a "primal scene," in which he saw his parents having sex as a child, with his father "behind" his mother. Confronted with this traumatic scene, the child misinterpreted passionate sex as an act of violence. The child is overwhelmed, rapidly shifting between identifying with the father as the "perpetrator," the mother as the "victim," or losing themselves as the "bystander" to this act. Freud is ambivalent as to whether this fantasy reflects an actual memory (possible given the cramped living conditions of the era), or a fantasy the child developed to address some other conflict. Turning back to Fanon (1952/2008), he draws on Freud's thinking to theorize about a scene that is repeated over and over again. It may be experienced directly, but it need not be. It is a scene, a "racial drama… played out in the open" (p. 116), in culture, social structure, and yes, lived experience.

Every time an act of racial, gender, sexual, and class violence is reported in the news and social media; every time rent is due; every time you are followed in a store; every time a right-wing demagogue opens their mouth; every time a liberal politician is complicitly silent; every time you walk into a space and nobody looks like or dresses like you; all these and other moments instantiate "a constellation of postulates, a series of propositions that slowly and subtly… work their way into one's mind and shape one's view of the world of the group to which one belongs" (Fanon, 1952/2008, p. 118). They constitute society's ontological fantasy—the *scene* of anti-Black, anti-Asian, anti-Latinx, anti-Semitic, anti-Trans, anti-poor hate. But instead of passion misinterpreted as violence (as in the Wolf Man), the subject witnesses the *actuality* of violence suffused with passion—with *jouissance*—time and again.

For the Black or non-Black person witnessing the "scene" of anti-Blackness, similar dynamics of identification to Freud's primal scene are enacted. But instead of father, mother, child, it is the scene of violence upon the Black subject, before which one "chooses" to identify with either victim, perpetrator, or the role of the bystander or witness. The scene threatens a compromise in the Black subject's psychic integrity, orienting them toward "The Other (in the guise of the white man), for The Other alone can give him worth" (Fanon, 1952/2008, p. 119).

Like Ferenczi, if your choices are between the victim and the perpetrator, you are likely to identify with the latter as a matter of survival. It is in their response to the scene of anti-Blackness that the Black subject may experience trauma over and above their immediate experience. But Fanon theorizes beyond the Black individual's response to the scene—he formulates the function of the scene for all other *non-Black* subjects. In the scene, "The Negro is a phobogenic object, a stimulus to anxiety" (p. 117). The non-Black person of color or immigrant who witnesses the scene faces a dilemma—identify with Black people as the victims of whiteness, identify with perpetrating whiteness, or an "in between" space as a bystander. The possibility of violence against non-Black people is also present, but so too the invitation to become "junior partners" to white supremacy, with anti-Blackness as labor and enjoyment (Wilderson, 2010).

The Pleasures of Anti-Blackness in Psyche and Society

Anti-Blackness is an ambivalent structure of fear and hatred alongside desire. Fanon (1952/2008) argues that in deciphering "all the tricks the ego uses in order to defend itself… its denials must in no case be taken literally" (p. 120). The anxiety aroused by Blackness guards against sexual desires, desires for power, the want to access some "hidden" pleasure to achieve an embodied wholeness, a compensation covering over a feeling of inferiority and lack (p. 122). Anti-Blackness, what Fanon calls "negrophobia," is related to the sense of the body in space, as the Black body "impedes the closing of the postural schema of the white man" (p. 124). He suggests the mirror stage explains the white subject's imaginary aggression toward the Black body: "the real Other for the white man is and will continue to be the black man. And conversely" (fn. 25, p. 124). Through identification, white people project desires and fantasies reflective of "Freud's life instinct," then behave "as if the Negro really had them" (p. 127).

Fanon draws a distinction here between the fantasized "threat" posed by Black people, and that posed by Jews, other people of color and immigrants. The latter are perceived as transgressing some threshold, taking "our" jobs, moving into "our" neighborhoods. But in anti-Blackness the threat is against life itself—the Black body is subjected to death to extract *life*. In a sense, all racism depends on the structure of *jouissance*, but Fanon draws attention to how anti-Blackness provides a particular form of *jouissance* for white and non-Black subjects.

The interruption of bodily coherence by the Black body "frustrates" the white psyche, leading to prohibitions, violence, and restrictions to frustrate the Black person—deriving pleasure from causing pain. Fanon (1952/2008) is aware he is engaging a psychoanalytic literature of anti-Semitism and anti-Blackness, citing Marie Bonaparte discussion of Fenichel's theorizing on how racism allows one to project "all his own more or less unconscious bad instincts... and sees himself in shining purity" by framing the racial other as a "devil" (cited in p. 141, fn. 47). Fanon is "remixing" this theory in ways that advance psychoanalytic critiques of racial capitalism, as well as psychoanalytic theory and practice itself.

Fanon (1952/2008) agrees with Jung that at the heart of European civilization is an archetype, "an expression of the bad instincts, of the darkness inherent in every ego," which is then projected onto Black people (p. 144). He differs from Jung in that the collective unconscious is not a genetically inherited fact, but "the sum of prejudices, myths, collective attitudes of a given group" (p. 145). For that reason, within much of our global capitalist system, "The archetype of the lowest values is represented by the Negro" (p. 146). "How else is one to explain," Fanon poses, "that the unconscious representing the base and inferior traits is colored black?" (p. 146). To the extent the unconscious is a topography of what is allowed into consciousness or condemned to the depths, "it is always a matter of descending or climbing" (p. 146). We create a hierarchy of feelings and thoughts as well as people, within and without.

There is a peculiar parallel between a societal hierarchy which promotes "[climbing] up toward whiteness and light" and avoiding "falling down" into

206 D. J. Gaztambide

its cavernous depths, and the structure of an unconscious equating what is "good" with "light" and what is "bad" with "darkness" (Fanon, 1952/ 2008, p. 147). Where the two collide, the unconscious mirrors the structure of the surrounding society. Fanon remarks, for example, how in some of his treatments, "Whenever the individual plunges down, one finds the Negro, whether concretely or symbolically" (fn 27, p. 127). Basic psychological defenses such as splitting become co-opted to serve racist ends: "Moral consciousness implies a kind of scission, a fracture of consciousness into a bright part and an opposing black part" (p. 150). To achieve a sense of coherence, all that is "bad" and "dark" must be disowned. In the case of Black people's experience, anti-Blackness makes it so that "[the] Negro is forever in combat with his own image" (p. 150).

It is important to underscore that this is not a description of "the white psyche," as Fanon is outlining the *imposition* of an ontological fantasy (e.g., definition of who is human) upon the world, including the global south. One should not be surprised that Black people and other people of color internalize this fantasy. As a result of political economic structures, people of color, Black people included, "[partake] of the same collective unconscious as the European" (p. 147). Internalized racism is not the result of a personal failure, but of socioeconomic conditions.

The *Jouissance* of Anti-Blackness for Other Colonized People

As mentioned earlier, Fanon (1952/2008) feels a deep solidarity with other oppressed people. In a later piece, he (1956/1988) traced how the idea of "primitivism" functioned as bedrock pseudo-science normalizing oppression, cataloging its various forms, "the 'emotional instability of the Negro,' the 'subcritical integration of the Arab,' the 'quasi-generic culpability of the Jew'" (p. 32). Yet despite this shared history of oppression, being a member of an oppressed community does not automatically incline one to solidarity. On the contrary, oppression may incline one to *not* join with one's neighbor but figure out how to climb above them. In North Africa Fanon came to understand a "pecking order" in the colony, with whites at the top, Black people at the bottom, and Jews and Arabs struggling in the middle, all mediated by performances meant to create distance between themselves and the "primitive" Black subject.

The colony maintains its stability precisely through this game of "king of the hill" weaponizing the suffering of Arabs, Jews, and poor whites. Fanon (1956/1988) writes:

> The Arab is told: "If you are poor, it is because the Jew has bled you and taken everything from you." The Jew is told: "You are not of the same class as the Arab because you are really white…" The Negro is told: "You are the best soldiers in the French Empire; the Arabs think they are better than you, but they are wrong." But that is not true; the Negro is told nothing because no one has anything to tell him, the Senegalese trooper is a trooper, the-good-soldier-under-command… (pp. 76–77)

Fanon reveals the *jouissance* offered on tap. The suffering of the Arab is directed toward Jews as the "true culprit." The persecuted Jew is reassured they are not like the Arab—they are white (whiteness expands and retracts as needed by capital). The Black person is "told nothing" because their suffering is the foundation of the compensation offered to others in the colony.

The hijacking of *jouissance* as a divide-and-conquer strategy does not end there. The "Negro is told nothing" *unless* they join the army and become an instrument of colonial capitalist power. Fanon (1952/2008) noticed how the French military sent Black soldiers to put down insurrections, "'men of color' who nullified the liberation efforts of other 'men of color,'" (p. 77). Black against Arab, Arab against Jew, Jew made "white" yet expunged from that category for being a Jew—a war of "all against all" maintaining the colony and its promise of "moving up," the anxiety to "keep one's place" and not "fall" to the bottom, the desperation to escape the bottom as such. Instead of the distribution of wealth, the colony provides a substitute, "the racial distribution of guilt" (p. 77). All have, in some way, become implicated in the system's poison. There is no prioritized subjectivity, no standpoint immune to its ministrations, no intersection of identity that has not heard the call of racial capitalism—not all the same, but all implicated.

Freud on Fanon's Couch: The *Jouissance* of Anti-Blackness for Psychoanalysis

Fanon's (1952/2008) analysis of anti-Blackness helps us understand psychoanalysis as a theory developed by a predominantly Jewish people surviving an anti-Semitic world. Drawing on Sartre's meditations on anti-Semitism, Fanon discusses how some Jews internalize anti-Semitic stereotypes and fear confirming them in their behavior, becoming "overdetermined from the inside" (cited in p. 87). Although Ashkenazi Jews can pass for white,[1] their culture and language risk revealing their Jewishness—they *look* white, but *not quite* (p. 87). Fanon is cognizant that Jews and other non-Black people experience brutal violence, but he underscores a distinction with his suffering as a Black man: "I am overdetermined from without. I am the slave not of the 'idea' that others have of me but of my own appearance" (p. 87).

For the Jew, the non-Black person of color, and the immigrant to be subjected to violence, there is usually some real or imagined transgression that "can be rationalized on a basic level" (Fanon, 1952/2008, p. 123). That is to say, it is a form of *contingent* violence, with an "*if, then*" structure (Wilderson, 2010). The immigrant is "stealing our jobs," Jews are "taking over the government," Arabs "want to institute Sharia law." This creates its inverse, a fantasy of what one "can do" to avoid violence—"*If* I change my hair, bleach my skin, change my clothes, speak the right way, *then* I will escape discrimination." These fantasies facilitate "passing," either literally (passing as white), or by assimilating to white culture.

This process can be conscious or unconscious. To give a concrete example, when I was an impoverished graduate student I had to contend with weird looks in restaurants, being followed in stores, and having "unfriendly" encounters with the police. Once I graduated and became "a doctor," complete with a hospital badge and some money, I decided to get better clothes. Suddenly—without being aware of it—the weird looks stopped, I was asked if I needed help instead of followed, and police encounters decreased in frequency. *Before* I had a degree, I was a "spic." *After* I had money, coupled with my skin as a white Puerto Rican, I became "span" (evoking the detergent, "clean"). I "moved up" economically and racially without being aware. But if I "get out of line" and "be where I'm not supposed to," the cops are only a phone call away.

While anti-Blackness includes such fantasies of contingency, its essence is fundamentally *non-contingent*, meaning that no transgression is necessary for the Black subject to be victimized—no "*if*" is necessary. What this means for Fanon (1952/2008) is that while the poor white, the Arab, and the Jew may turn on one another, *all* are able to turn against the African for self-definition, bodily coherence, and substitutive *jouissance*. Anti-Black violence becomes ritualized to ratify one's aliveness, *even if* one is exploited, brutalized, and subjected to violence as well—one cannibalizes the other's pain to ease one's own.

---

[1] Fanon speaks exclusively of white and white-passing Jews, as opposed to other members of the Jewish Diaspora.

Fanon's (1952/2008) critique is *not* an attempt to play "oppression Olympics." He issues this critique as a Jewish prophet calling the people back to righteousness, solidarity, and restitution. Stressing an insight Otto Fenichel recognized, Fanon writes "[The Jew] and I… have one point in common. Both of us stand for Evil. The black man more so, for the good reason that he is black" (p. 139). Speaking to the suffering of the Jew, he traces how internalized anti-Semitism is related to internalized anti-Blackness. Echoing the meditations on race of the early Jewish analysts, Fanon recalled the words of a professor from the Antilles, "Whenever you hear anyone abuse the Jews, pay attention, *because he is talking about you*" (p. 92, emphasis added). Fanon recognized a deeper truth, "an anti-Semite is inevitably anti-Negro" (p. 92).

In an anti-Semitic environment, a Jewish person may learn that they must "hide" their Jewishness to survive, and sometimes internalize "the validity of the Aryan system… Evil is Jewish. Everything Jewish is ugly. Let us no longer be Jews. I am no longer a Jew. Down with the Jews" (Fanon, 1952/2008, p. 140). Fanon recalls a Jewish patient who was being attacked by gentiles in an inpatient unit. A non-Jewish woman came to their defense, which resulted in the Jewish patient turning on *her*, "hurling every possible anti-Semitic calumny at her and demanding that that Jewess be got rid of" (p. 141). Fanon observes that anti-Semitism can be followed by anti-Blackness, noting how the violence the Black person is subjected to "places him beside the Jew" (p. 133) in the zone of nonbeing. However, by engaging in anti-Semitism or engaging in anti-Blackness, the Jew (the non-Black person of color, the immigrant) is able to "move up and out" from the zone. "*Wherever he goes*," Fanon makes the contrast explicit, "*the Negro remains a Negro*" (p. 133, emphasis original).

Fanon (1952/2008) gives the example of the Jewish physician Michel Salomon. In words that could apply to Freud, he writes, "He is a Jew, he has a 'millennial experience of anti-Semitism,' and yet he is a racist" (p. 156). Despite being victims of anti-Semitic violence, anti-Blackness provided Freud and Solomon with an "escape hatch" into whiteness. Solomon was no less infatuated with the "primitivity," "sensuality," and "prodigious vitality" of the Black man (p. 156).

What of Freud? What *jouissance* did anti-Blackness offer him? Freud (1913/1955) not only traded in stereotypes of global south peoples as "primitive," but if we return to his 1915 text, "The Unconscious," we catch a glimpse of his racial ontology. In between the unconscious as repressed "bottom" and the conscious allowed to "pass" into awareness, he identifies the *preconscious* as a liminal space that often "breaks into" consciousness, but is "incapable of becoming conscious… [t]heir *origin* is what decides their fate" (p. 191, emphasis added).

Discussing the origin of these "unconscious derivatives," Freud (1915) writes,

> We [must; lit. "*muß*"] compare them with individuals of mixed race [*Mischlingen*] who, taken all round, resemble white men, but who betray their coloured descent by some striking feature or other, and on that account are excluded from society and enjoy none of the privileges of white people. (p. 191)

The phrasing in the original ("One must [*muß*] compare them") stresses the theme of racial mixing, which is muted in the English translation. Further on Freud remarks that the unconscious "may be compared with an aboriginal population in the mind… something analogous to instinct in animals" (p. 195).

Here another German nuance is critical, as when Freud speaks of "derivatives of the unconscious," the word "derivatives" is *Abkömmlinge* in German, which means "descendant" in a genealogical sense. This is the same word Freud (1913/1955) uses in *Totem and Taboo* to refer to "present day savages" (*Abkömmlinge und Vertreter*), the descendants of "prehistory man."[2] Freud writes this almost "in passing," but the linguistic connection is clear—whiteness is associated with consciousness, "mixed race" with the preconscious, and Blackness with the *unconscious* (cf. Brickman, 2017). Freud's psychic racial hierarchy with Blackness at the bottom and the anxious position of "mixed-race" people—as Jews were framed in the anti-Semitism of his time (Gilman, 1993a, 1993b)—is key to understanding his theorizing on racism *and* his own racism.

One of the most provocative examples of Freud's relationship to race is his compulsive repetition of a racist "joke." Whenever Freud waited for an American patient, he looked at the clock and said "twelve o'clock and no negro" (his sessions started at 12). This was based on a newspaper cartoon in which a lion yawns looking up at the clock, "twelve o'clock and no negro." Claudia Tate (1996), in an almost Fanonian reading, points out Freud's identification with each of the positions evoked in the joke. By analogizing the devouring "lion" with the therapist, and the "negro" with the patient, Freud evoked a bipolar identification with the perpetrating "lion" and the victimized "negro" (Harper, 2012), his own position haunted by the turn-of-century anti-Semitic trope that Jews are "actually African" (Gilman, 1993).

---

[2] I am grateful to my New School colleague, Tara Menon, for bringing these linguistic connections in the original German to my attention (Menon, personal communication, November 3, 2021).

As a persecuted Jew surviving between emancipation and Shoah, Freud used this joke to cope with his anxieties in the face of a devouring anti-Semitism, a salve for his pain that allowed him ascension into whiteness. Through the performance of his joke, Freud enacts the "scene" of anti-Blackness to identify with a perpetrating, devouring "lion." In words Fanon might have used, Tate (1996) wrote that Freud erased "the Semitic black-ness presumed by Aryans... [being] absorbed into the category of whiteness" (p. 57). Freud gave us a psychoanalytic critique of racial capitalism, while enacting the very phenomena that theory seeks to explain.

Ferenczi on Fanon's Couch: Beyond a Two-Person Psychology

We can also read Fanon (1952/2008) as issuing a critique to Ferenczi. Although his words are directed at Alfred Adler, I apply his critique to relational-interpersonal thinking as well. Fanon evokes Lacan's mirror stage to explore the colonizer's wish to dominate the other and extract recognition from them, "I try to read admiration in the eyes of the other, and if, unluckily, those eyes show me an unpleasant reflection, I find that mirror flawed" (p. 164). If the other denies me recognition and challenges me "with his wish to have value (his fiction), I simply banish him without a trial. He ceases to exist" (p. 164). An intersubjective struggle for recognition ensues in which one's narcissism and value are at stake.

The colony, as a racial capitalist modality, breeds narcissism and competition: "one finds the man on top, the court that surrounds him, the in-betweens (who are waiting for something better), and the losers" (Fanon, 1952/2008, p. 165). The endgame of existing in such a hierarchy is survival, whether escaping one's place or protecting it. But the source of this conflict is not exclusively personal or even interpersonal. Insofar as an individual or relational perspective narrowly "embraces two terms"—a dyadic struggle between self and other abstracted from the social context—Fanon argues that this risks consigning the patient to ultimately "resign yourself to remaining in the place that has been assigned to you" (p. 168). Echoing Lacan, Fanon asks us to think of "a third term: Its governing fiction is not personal but social" (p. 168). The social third is a fiction or fantasy about "who" belongs "where" in the social, cultural, and political world.

This third term—the sociopolitical—complicates relational thinking. Similar to Benjamin (2017), Fanon (1952/2008) reads Hegel's meditation on intersubjectivity as suggesting that ruptures in our capacity to see the other as a separate and autonomous center of agency can lead to a vicious cycle of do'er and done-to. The way out of this cycle, in Fanon's reading, "is to restore to the other, through mediation and recognition, his human reality... The other has to perform the same operation" (p. 169). To this Fanon adds a caveat, in that mutual recognition across lines of difference is fraught because self and other are *not* on equal ground. Citing Hegel, Fanon notes that one can be recognized *without* confrontation: "The individual, who has not staked his life, may, no doubt, be recognized as a *person*, but he has not attained the truth of this recognition as an independent self-consciousness" (cited in p. 170, emphasis original). Writing about abolition, Fanon writes that one day the "White Master, *without conflict*," meaning, without an encounter with the other, "*recognized* the Negro slave. But the former slave wants to *make himself recognized*" (p. 169, emphasis original).

Writing in the context of French white liberalism, Fanon argues freed Black people were "recognized" within the coordinates of white charity as a person yet subject to white desire, without the confrontation that would ratify Black people as agentic subjects *outside* of white subjectivity. Fanon critiques how liberal white politics offer paternalistic recognition in exchange for being recognized as the "liberator" who out of the goodness of their heart "decided to promote the machine-animal-men to the supreme rank of *men*" (p. 171, emphasis original). If we read Fanon's later paper, "Racism and culture" (Fanon, 1956/1988), the context for his position comes into relief. He talked about how a minority culture becomes "closed, fixed in the colonial status... a mummification" (p. 34) before colonial institutions and policies. The colony engages in a performative "respect for the tradition, the cultural specificities, the personality of the subjugated people" (p. 34), but behind this respect for the other's culture is "the most utter contempt... the most elaborate sadism" (p. 34). The performative affirmation of difference does not see the other as a separate, autonomous being, betraying "a determination to objectify, to confine, to imprison, to harden" (p. 34). The other's difference is exotified to reinscribe colonial power, as if liberal recognition makes up for continued military and economic oppression.

Recognition by the colonizer is poisoned as this takes place in a fundamental context of inequality, with the racialized subject having no choice but to question whether they are truly considered a separate, authentic being. Hence, Fanon (1952/2008) argues that the colonized must engage in the work of "uncovering resistance, opposition, challenge" (p. 173). Just as the therapist must scrutinize their countertransference, the colonized subject *uncovers the resistance of the colonizer*. Under conditions of inequality, mutual recognition will be fraught, even "impossible." But by asserting their radical otherness, their "alterity. Alterity of rupture, of conflict, of battle," an aperture is created for the "possibility of the impossible" (p. 173).

Fanon (1952/2008) sees two ways out of this impasse. Either he obsesses over how to earn recognition or attempts to prove his value as a separate being, conceding this needs to be proven to begin with. Like his forensic patients, he exercises his "first right":

> In order to terminate this neurotic situation, in which I am compelled to choose an unhealthy, conflictual solution, fed on fantasies, hostile, inhuman in short, I have only one solution: to rise above this absurd drama that others have staged round me, to *reject* the two terms that are equally unacceptable, and, through one human being, to reach out for the universal. (p. 153, emphasis added)

Fanon expresses a therapeutic outburst to break out of the impasse he is emplaced in (cf. Aron, 2003). Preceding Lacan's theorizing on the "no," Fanon argues that while human beings are a "*Yes* to life. *Yes* to love. *Yes* to generosity," they are also a *no*, "*No* to scorn of man. *No* to degradation of man. *No* to exploitation of man. *No* to the butchery of what is most human in man: freedom" (p. 173, emphasis original). Given how the colonizer negates the colonized as a separate center of subjectivity, he speaks of a negation of this negation, a shattering refusal. The purpose of this refusal is to leave the colonizer "*bewildered*. The end of race prejudice begins with *a sudden incomprehension*" (Fanon, 1956/1988, p. 44, emphasis added). This *no* shakes up the colonizer's mappings of self and other in a way that demands not only recognition, but a reckoning. As Swartz (2018) put it, a "counter-recognition" that rejects the terms of engagement.

Relational Psychoanalysis from a Decolonial Lens: Yes and No

Putting this pointedly with regard to Ferenczi, anti-Blackness in his treatments with Severn and Sigray facilitated the fantasy that their treatments were just about "two people in a room," struggling to recognize the role of race in their struggles, eclipsing the recognition of a "third term"—the sociopolitical world enacted through their speech (see Chapter 3). Like Ferenczi, Fanon thought the process of rupture and repair was interpersonally important, but at the same time argued that something beyond the intersubjective relation is necessary. If, as Ferenczi once stated, love is what allows reality to come into view, then Fanon challenges us to see love as an act of reckoning not only with the other's otherness, but with that broader reality. While relationally informed therapists create a space where patient and therapist can explore their interpersonal dynamic in a spirit of mutuality, Paulo Freire (1973), inspired by Fanon's work, would argue that while we may begin with this kind of "relational work," we cannot remain there. For Freire, intersubjectivity is a "loving encounter of people, who, *mediated by the world, 'proclaim' that world*. They transform the world and in transforming it, humanize it for all people" (1973, p. 115, emphasis added). It is not only the relationship that is explored, but the social third that contextualizes—naming it so we can *transform* it.

Fanon's discourse on recognition and decoloniality suggests that the colonized, in seeking to establish their humanity, intervenes on the other with a spontaneous, surprising "No!" that rejects their colonial associations, and opens up the possibility of reflecting on our wider world. Freire (1972) is again instructive when he writes that it is "in the response of the oppressed to the violence of their oppressors that a gesture of love may be found" (p. 41). "Consciously or unconsciously," he writes, "the act of rebellion by the oppressed… can initiate love" (p. 42). If we recall Fanon's papers on the forensic examinee's refusal of his authority, and through him, their refusal of the colony, alongside his description of the cure as a "shock with reality" (see Chapter 5), then the patient's act of refusal toward the therapist provides a shock that establishes them as a separate, real other. If the therapist is vulnerable and radically open to this "no," an opportunity is created to not only rework their relationship but inaugurate a new social link that brings the broader world into view (cf. Hart, 2022; Knoblauch, 2020). Put schematically, one role of the intersubjective third as theorized in relational thinking might be for it to create a space in which the social third can be reflected on (cf. Altman, 2000). What is needed is not only recognition, but a reckoning.

Although beyond the scope of this book, there are developmental implications of this theorizing as well. Although Fanon believed attachment and familial dynamics are important, they are not the only factor in psychic life. To the extent we conceive of development in relational "two-person" terms, this must be conceptualized within a wider social third—a sociocultural network—that can scaffold, support, and hold this dyad or impede, intrude upon, and destroy it. We turn now to how early attachment disruption and a toxic social third interact.

"A Movement of Love": Object Relations and Attachment Amidst Racial Hierarchy

Fanon (1952/2008) is somewhat of a romantic, writing "authentic love… entails the mobilization of psychic drives basically freed of unconscious conflicts" (p. 28). To free ourselves to love is to allow ourselves to be driven not by external forces, but by our desire to act on behalf of what is valued. In this section, I draw on Fanon's psychoanalysis of René Maran's autobiographical novel to explore how inequality "trickles down" into the intimacy of our relationships, and end with examples of Fanon conducting treatment amidst revolution.

Like Freud and Ferenczi before him, Fanon (1952/2008) conceptualized the drives as a series of "movements," as being in "motion toward the world":

> a movement of aggression, which leads to enslavement or to conquest; a movement of love, a gift of self, the ultimate stage of what by common accord is called ethical orientation. Every consciousness seems to have the capacity to demonstrate these two components, simultaneously or alternatively. (p. 28)

Love is a "frustration" that entails holding our aggression and the willingness to give freely of oneself—vulnerability always includes a measure of anxiety. It requires that one expunge one's feelings of inferiority as this can defend against real intimacy. In his case studies, Fanon critiques the facsimile of love that is pursued in the interest of power and position.

Citing Anna Freud's work, Fanon (1952/2008) explores how defenses function to avoid pain, allowing withdrawal "from one field of activity [to be] compensated for by excellence in another," but if the ego and its defenses become rigid, it remains "obsessionally fixated to a method of flight, such withdrawal is punished by impaired development" (cited in p. 35). Fanon was struck by how colonizer and colonized become *fixated* to rigid forms of existence, with widening inequality leading both to "behave in accordance with a neurotic orientation" (pp. 42–43). Those struggling to stay afloat at the bottom, those fighting to keep from "falling further down" in the middle, and those reaching for even greater heights at the top *all* become neurotic, with the compensatory *jouissance* developed to subsist in each of these "rungs" serving to numb their pain. Drawing on Alfred Adler, Fanon situates the childhood development of neurosis within a social context, understanding one's lived experience and response (existence) to structures of being (ontology). He illustrates this via the work of Antillean novelist René Maran.

Fanon (1952/2008) examines Maran's novel *Un homme pareil aux autres* (*A man like any other*), through which the author uses the character Jean Veneuse as a "self-insert." In the novel, Veneuse was born a Martiniquan orphan abandoned by his mother and sent to a French boarding school where he made friends, but when they went back to their families during the summer, he remained alone. The young Veneuse was shy and ill at ease, a sensitive but studious boy enthralled by literature. Despite his shyness, he was well regarded by his friends and schoolmates, who referred to him as a "dreamer." Yet there is an edge to those relationships keeping Veneuse on alert. His friends remark that he seems withdrawn and sad but that he is a good kid, "the kind of Negro that a lot of white guys ought to be like" (cited in p. 47). He is the "good Negro," the unspoken implication being that Veneuse is "exceptional," whereas other Black people are not. His invisibility and hypervisibility, coupled with the daily sting of microaggressions, stayed with Veneuse throughout his life (see also Franklin, 2004).

In childhood, Venuse is exposed to bits and pieces of the "scene" of anti-Blackness, a language about the structure of the world and his place in it. He starts to develop a way of surviving that world, what Fanon (1952/2008) diagnoses as a neurotic position in relation to "the scene." As an adult he leaves Martinique and goes to Africa to serve in the army, after which he moves to France to become a civil servant. He "moves up" from the poverty and neglect of his childhood, yet "the scene" continues to affect his romantic relationships. When a woman flirts with him he demurs. "Courage is a fine thing," he tells her, "you're going to get yourself talked about… A Negro? Shameful—it's *beneath* contempt. Associating with anybody of that race is just utterly disgracing yourself" (cited in p. 47, emphasis added). Alongside this defensive distancing from his Blackness, he seeks to prove himself equal in the eyes of white men using his intelligence, class position, and cultural knowledge. "But let us not be misled," Fanon interjects, "Jean Veneuse is the man who has to be convinced. It is in the roots of his soul… that the doubt persists" (p. 47). His defenses orbit around the fear of his own abjection.

At one point, Veneuse falls in love with Andrée Marielle, a French white woman, whose sends him a letter confessing her love. This sends him into a panic. He hoped his intellect, his consumption of high culture, and his loyalty to France would free him to love as he wished, yet he fears "the white race would not accept him as one of its own and the black virtually repudiated him" (Fanon, 1952/2008, p. 48). Veneuse feels like he needs "authorization. It is essential that some white man say to him, 'Take my sister'" (p. 49). He writes to a white friend for advice, who "reassures" him he has nothing to worry about. He should go to her! Besides, "You have nothing in common with real Negroes. You are not black, you are 'extremely brown'" (p. 50). Veneuse is basically "a European," and anyone who sees him as Black "is mistaken, because you merely look like one" (p. 50). Veneuse cannot accept this. Deep down he feels this "extension" of humanity, this imaginary lightening of his skin, is a fraud. His white friend's "recognition" reinforces the association at the heart of his pain, that he *cannot* be loved as a Black man, only as a "Brown" man. He feels trapped between a desire for lighter skin and a white woman's love to validate his humanity, and the dread in the back of his mind that his Blackness places him on the other side of a gap that love cannot reach. After months of flirtation Veneuse meets Marielle anew, but instead of confessing his love he dances around the issue, taking refuge in silence.

Despite having all white friends, keeping his distance from other Black people, thinking in French, having French religion, being a European, etc., Veneuse "falls back down" into the zone of nonbeing where the scene plays out. The problem from Fanon's (1952/2008) point of view is that Veneuse continues defending against truly inhabiting and "descending" into this zone, from which "an authentic upheaval" can burst forth.

Fanon (1952/2008) cites Germaine Guex's *La névrose d'abandon* (*The abandonment neurosis*) to analyze Veneuse's conflict, identifying a tripartite structure of anguish due to feeling abandoned, anger and spite at every successive abandonment, and the devalued self that emerges from it. Fanon notes how a person who has suffered repeated abandonment inhibits their desire to connect, defending themselves against intimacy through resentment and aggression—often ending relationships abruptly. While this protects them from further abandonment, it reinforces the feeling that they are unlovable, feeling helpless that they will "never find love." They expect others to change while disavowing their role in the relationship's dissolution. With this theory of abandonment in mind, Fanon pays exquisite attention to the *words* Veneuse uses to tell his story. He notes Veneuse's hunger for love, "He did not like to be *abandoned*. When school vacations came, all the other boys went home; alone—*note that word alone*—he remained in the big empty white school" (p. 54, emphasis original). By paying attention to Venuese's words, Fanon drew out the associations constituting his struggles.

Fanon's (1952/2008) synthesis of Veneuse's difficulties has the air of an analytic interpretation. He identifies

Two processes. I do not want to be loved. Why not? Because once, very long ago, I attempted an object relation and I was *abandoned*. I have never forgiven my mother. Because I was abandoned, I will make someone else suffer, and desertion by me will be the direct expression of my need for revenge. I will go to Africa [to serve in the army]: I do not wish to be loved and I will flee from love-objects. (p. 55, emphasis original)

Time and again, Veneuse puts up a wall against abandonment at the cost of love, even as deep down he is hungering for someone to *disprove* his fears. What renders this more complex is precisely how the "third term"—the social context—textures his parental abandonment by equating abandonment with Blackness and love with whiteness. Veneuse "looks for appeasement, for permission in the white man's eyes. For him there is 'The Other'" (p. 55). He looks for recognition from the white gaze, hoping it will be "willing to give."

The problem with Veneuse's wish to be loved lies in its extremity. No matter how much love he receives, he "is insatiable." Singular proclamations of love are insufficient, "Before he forms an objective relation, he exacts repeated proofs from his partner. The essence of his attitude is 'not to love in order to avoid being abandoned'" (Fanon, 1952/2008, p. 55). He demands reassurance: "Tell me, Andrée darling... in spite of my color, would you agree to marry me if I asked you?" (cited in p. 56). Veneuse's cultural and professional pursuits offer additional attempts at compensation for his low self-esteem, yet no matter how high he climbs, this does not undo the worthlessness he feels within a white world. Stated more positively, within Veneuse's anxious demands for reassurance is a *wish* to no longer need them.

If Fanon (1952/2008) were to work clinically with Veneuse, he would focus on helping him "become aware of the potentials they have forbidden themselves," interrupt his destructive pattern of behavior, and empower him to "*stand up to the world*" (p. 57, emphasis original), to issue a "no" to its demands. Fanon rejects a purely situational or societal account for Veneuse's difficulties as much as a constitutional or individualistic account. Rather, his decolonial psychoanalytic account places Veneuse's struggles in context while underscoring how he seeks "to corroborate his *externalizing* neurosis" (p. 59). Veneuse's neurosis reflects his individual internalization of racist discourses *defensively* to protect against abandonment.

The problem Fanon (1952/2008) has with Maran's narrative in *Un homme pareil aux autres* is that it elevates one man's neurotic reaction to the scene of anti-Blackness to the status of an inborn, constitutive, almost "organic" difficulty in interracial relationships. He cites Lacan's dissertation again to argue against a reductive, pseudo-biological perspective on race, opting for a sociogenic perspective that integrates the personal and political. For Fanon, neurosis is the formation within the ego "of conflictual clusters arising *in part* out of the environment and *in part* out of the purely personal way in which that individual reacts to these influences" (p. 60, emphasis added). Thus, Veneuse's conflict is not a personal failing, an interpersonal dynamic, or reducible to "society." As Lacan might say, it involves a "knotting" of each of these dimensions.

Fanon does not see the answer to racism as a Sisyphean effort against a racist world. His approach can be compared to that of contemporary dialectical behavior therapy practitioners when they say "You didn't *cause* racism, but you have to deal with it anyway" (Pierson et al., 2022). At the same time our struggles are an imprint, a *symptom* of a structural dynamic. Psychotherapy is inherently limited in that it addresses the symptomatic expression of the essential causes, which are political, economic, and socio-cultural in nature. Citing Claude Nordey, Fanon (1952/2008) writes, given the system, "is it not understandable that [the Black man] will try to elevate himself to the white man's level? To elevate himself in the range of colors to which he attributes a kind of hierarchy?" Perhaps, but Fanon argues there is another solution than trying to "win" at racial capitalism, "It implies a restructuring of the world" (p. 60).

Mental Health Amidst Revolution and War

Years later Fanon committed himself to exactly such a restructuring, working as a gun runner and soldier for the Front de Libération Nationale (FLN) while providing psychiatric care to victims of French repression and FLN soldiers. He treated a number of cases during this time, published in his posthumous *The Wretched of the Earth* (1963). Although read as a political text, the chapter entitled "Colonial War and Mental Disorders" reveals his clinical thinking during revolutionary conflict. In this discussion, I draw on some of the cases he provides. Fanon remarks on how colonialism is a "fertile purveyor for psychiatric hospitals" (p. 249) due to the rampant inequality tearing Algeria apart. Returning to the questions that animated his "second" dissertation, he writes, "colonialism forces the people it dominates to ask themselves the question constantly: 'In reality, who am I?'" (p. 250). He traces the suffering of his patients—Algerian revolutionaries, French citizens, or military police—back to the violence of the colony. We may each inhabit different rungs, but different rungs in the same burning building.

Love Beyond Duty and Patriarchy: The Case of "B"

The first case Fanon reports is of a married, 26-year-old revolutionary named "B" seen at the FLN's health service for insomnia and chronic headaches, a taxi driver who transported revolutionary soldiers to and from their military targets. In one instance, a number of FLN commandos were routed, leaving him no choice but to abandon his car. Days later he found himself unable to get home, and was ordered to deploy for several months as part of a squad, unable to contact his wife and two-year-old daughter. B learned that his town was ransacked by the police, and two years later received a message from his wife asking him to forget about her, "for she had been dishonored and he ought not to think of taking up their life together again" (Fanon, 1963, p. 255). B was flooded with anxiety, begging his commander to let him to visit his wife. The commander denied his request, but arranged for another FLN member to contact her. Two weeks later B learned the police had discovered rifle magazines in his taxi and had gone to his house, where they arrested his wife and interrogated, beat, and raped her for over a week, with the soldiers telling her, "If ever you see your filthy husband again don't forget to tell him what we did to you." It was after being released that she had sent B the letter "confessing" she had been dishonored.

He was shocked by the news, yet threw himself into the war to forget about his wife's violation. But the war would not comply with his defenses. For months he heard story after story of Algerian women being raped or tortured, often talking to the husbands while "his personal misfortunes and his dignity as an injured husband remained in the background" (p. 256).

In 1958, when B returned from a mission outside Algeria his peers noticed he was not altogether "there," referring him to Fanon (1963). At first, B was amicable and well related, yet he exhibited "a mobile face: perhaps a bit too mobile. Smiles slightly exaggerated; surface well-being" (p. 256). B claimed he was "feeling better," so if Fanon could give him some vitamins, he would be on his way. Suddenly he experienced a panic attack, leading Fanon to admit him to hospital. The following day the façade melted away, the "screen of optimism" gone, revealing "a thoughtful, depressed man, suffering from loss of appetite, who kept to his bed" (p. 256). Fanon noticed that in sessions, B avoided any news related to politics or the revolution. Over the course of several days, Fanon helped B feel safe enough to explore his difficulties, leading to their reconstructing the events underlying his symptoms. It turned out that during his mission abroad B cheated on his wife, but was unable to "perform."

Thinking this was due to being undernourished, B tried again two weeks later and was again unsuccessful. He talked about it with a friend who recommended vitamins, which resulted in "another attempt, another failure." But there was more: "a few seconds before the [sexual] act, he had an irresistible impulse to tear up a photo of his little girl" (Fanon, 1963, p. 256). Fanon wondered if there was a "symbolic liaison" at play here suggesting unconscious incestuous wishes, but held fast to meeting the patient where they are, leading to a dream in later sessions. In the dream, B saw a little cat that was quickly rotting, followed by a foul smell. A few sessions later, B spontaneously shared, "That girl," referring to his daughter, "has something rotten about her." Following this disclosure B became increasingly anxious and his insomnia worsened, leading Fanon to wonder how seeing his daughter as "rotten" and cheating on his wife fulfilled a function for B which nonetheless deepened his suffering.

It was then that B spoke about his wife in a dysregulated manner, laughing while uttering "She's tasted the French." Fanon (1963) saw through his defensive use of crass, sexist humor and led him to talk more about his wife. Throughout B's "confession," Fanon gently interpreted his story, helping him with "[the] weaving of events to form a pattern" (p. 257). B disclosed for the first time that he thought about his wife before every attempt to have an affair. He had married her although he had feelings for his cousin, whose parents arranged a marriage with another man. B accepted the first wife his parents selected for him, and although she was "nice... I didn't love her" (p. 257). He would say to himself "You're young yet; wait a bit and when you've found the right girl, you'll get a divorce and you'll make a happy marriage" (p. 257).

B was distant from his wife, and once the war began he allowed this distance to deepen, often coming home after missions to eat and sleep without saying a word. When he heard about her assault he was enraged but then said to himself with the same detachment, "she wasn't killed. She can start her life over again" (Fanon, 1963, p. 257). It was weeks later when it hit him—she was raped because they were looking for *him*. She could have told them his name or that of any FLN soldier to end the torture, which could have led to the collapse of the rebel forces. B realized his wife was a woman "who was ready to put up with everything rather than sell her husband. And the husband in question, it was me" (p. 258). B's wife saved him and the FLN, but it was because of him that she had been "dishonored." Instead of blaming him for her trauma, she told him to move on and forget about her.

B was conflicted as to whether he should abandon his wife as he had wished for so long. He was shaken, however, when he witnessed men drying their wives' tears after they had been raped before their eyes. "I must admit," he told Fanon (1963) "that at the beginning I couldn't understand their attitude" (p. 258). The men's devotion made him consider returning to his wife, but he did not know what to do if he saw her. Fanon listened to B's ambivalence, misogyny, and anxiety patiently, doing nothing more than inviting him to continue to speak. His demeanor and acceptance of B's shame as an Algerian man allowed him space to put into words the anxieties animating the dream of the "rotten daughter." Often, when looking at his daughter's photo, "I used to think that she too was dishonored, like as if everything that had to do with my wife was rotten" (p. 258). B continued associating to his fears— if she had been physically tortured he "wouldn't have minded." "But that *thing*," he expressed, "how can you forget a thing like that? And why did she have to tell me about it all?" (p. 258). Suddenly noticing Fanon's presence, B asks if he thought his "sexual failing" was due to his worries. Fanon knew the answer, but also knew B did as well. Fanon replied succinctly: "It is not impossible" (p. 258).

B sat up in his hospital bed. "What would you do if all this had happened to you?" Fanon (1963) replied honestly, aware of his identification with B, "I don't know." B pressed further, "Would you take back your wife?" Fanon thought about it, then answered with the same honesty, "I think I would." B felt like he finally *saw* Fanon: "Ah, *there you are*, you see. You're not quite sure…" (p. 258, emphasis added). He saw Fanon's humanity, ambivalence, and limitations as a human being, a man who could be conflicted as he was. B put his head in his hands, a silent sob released between the two of them. After a few seconds he stood up and left the room.

From that point B was able to listen to political discussions and news surrounding the war, and his headaches, lack of appetite, and insomnia improved. After two weeks he was discharged and returned to active service. Before he left the unit he said to Fanon (1963), "When independence comes, I'll take my wife back. If it doesn't work out between us, I'll come and see you in Algiers" (p. 259). By making space for B to explore the impact of patriarchy on his desire, how he distanced himself from his wife, and how his wife's love shattered his perception of her, Fanon helped him get a critical distance from a discourse which framed his wife and daughter as "dishonored" and "rotten" by sexual assault. B's dreams and speech revealed the influence of patriarchal norms in the context of anti-colonial war, alongside his renewed love and respect toward his wife. Her loyalty to him and the FLN, alongside Fanon's openness, provided a surprise that challenged his preconceptions. Fanon was also open to showing B a man who could be vulnerable, unsure, but willing to be open to his wife despite restrictive cultural norms out of love.

The Pleasures of Torture: The Case of "R"

Another case Fanon (1963) shares is that of a 30-year-old French detective, "R," who self-referred to his outpatient service. In their first session R reported "things weren't working out" with his wife and three children. Fanon noticed this was a vague statement, encouraging him to go on. R talked about his stress, smoking five packs of cigarettes a day, losing his appetite, and experiencing frequent nightmares. Suddenly R turns to Fanon and casually asks, "Can you give me an explanation for this, doctor: as soon as someone goes against me I want to hit him" (p. 267). R *hated* being contradicted, lashing out in what he called "fits of madness." "Even outside my job,"—Fanon wondered, did these "fits" start at work?—"I feel I want to settle the fellows who get in my way, even for nothing at all" (p. 267). R gives the example of going to buy a newspaper. Because the man tending the kiosk is a friend, he "cuts the line" to get the day's paper. But another man on the line shoots him a dirty look, saying, "Wait your turn." R feels the urge to beat him up, saying to himself, "*If I had you for a few hours* my fine fellow you wouldn't look so clever afterwards." Fanon was aware of what French police did when left "for a few hours" with Black and Arab people. A possibility forms in his mind.

R is startled by any subtle noise, evoking that same impulse to lash out. He explodes at home, beating his wife and children, including a two-year-old, "with unaccustomed savagery" (Fanon, 1963, p. 268). R became terrified of his impulses after one rage episode in particular. His wife had criticized him for hitting the children so much, "My word, anyone'd think you were going mad." R attacked her and tied her to a chair while saying to himself, "I'll teach her once and for all that I'm master in this house." It was his children crying at the top of their lungs that got him to stop. He realized he was torturing his family, untied his wife, and the next day decided to seek help. Despite the horror Fanon was hearing, he kept himself open to a man that, despite his violence, was deeply suffering. He inquired, had things always been this way? R replied he was not like that *before*—he rarely punished his children and never fought with his wife. These rages started recently, "since the troubles." *The troubles*? Fanon invited R to say more, "The fact is… nowadays we have to work like troopers" (p. 268). The French government denied there was war in Algeria, calling it a "crime wave." R was cynical, "But there is a war going on in Algeria, and when they wake up to it it'll be too late. The thing that kills me most is the torture" (p. 268). The proverbial cat comes out of the bag.

"You don't know what that is, do you?" R asks Fanon (1963). As an FLN operative and therapist to torturers and their victims, Fanon knows full well what torture is but does not respond, allowing R to speak. R describes in detail how he tortures people for up to ten hours. Fanon intervenes, "What happens to you when you are torturing?" "You may not realize, but it's very tiring…" R describes it clinically—he takes turns with other officers, but struggles with when to let others "have a go" so he can rest, worrying he will "lose" at the "game" of torture. Each officer thinks he is *just about* to get information from the victim, "and takes good care not to let the bird go to the next chap after he's softened him up nicely, when of course the other chap would get the honor and glory of it" (p. 268).

R is *unable* to let go—the next punch, the next burn, the next threat to their loved ones… *jouissance* is just around the corner. Sometimes the victim is let go, sometimes they're not. Out of desperation, R offers money out of his own pocket to get them to talk. He regales Fanon with the "art" of torture and the pain and pleasure it brings him, "It's a question of personal success. You see, you're competing with the others. In the end your fists are ruined" (p. 269). He speaks about it with a sense of thrill and excitement. The true torture, R, explains, is giving the victim hope. You bind their life to yours, so they come to depend on you. Hope loosens lips. I summarize the details here for the reader, but it is important to note that Fanon reports *the entire* description of R's torture methods. One gets the sense Fanon himself might have felt *tortured* by R. "*But*," R's speech changes direction, "the thing that worries me most is this affair with my wife. It's certain that there's something wrong with me. You've got to cure me, doctor" (p. 269).

Fanon (1963) recommended sick leave, but R's superiors refused. Fanon tried to treat him while he was "working full time," but came to regret this (p. 269). It became clear R "knew perfectly well that his disorders were directly caused by the… interrogations… even though he tried to throw the responsibility totally upon 'present troubles'" (p. 269). R could not imagine *not* torturing people, as he would have to resign. Despite the crisis in *jouissance* that brought him to Fanon, "he asked me without beating about the bush to help him to go on torturing Algerian patriots without any prickings of conscience, without any behavior problems, and with complete equanimity" (pp. 269–270). The treatment did not "work out." Despite the costs, the *jouissance* offered by oppression is "too good" for some, and they are not willing to give it up even if this would bring peace to them and their family. It is also possible Fanon was aware his countertransference as a Black man and FLN supporter would not have permitted him to treat R. Not without reason.

The Costs of Police Work: The Case of "A"

An interesting comparison case is Fanon's (1963) treatment of "A," a 28-year-old, married, French policeman, referred by his superiors due to depression and behavior problems. Fanon and A established a strong rapport in their first session, in which he spoke openly about his troubles. He had good relationships with his wife but reported that at night he "heard screams which prevented him from sleeping" (pp. 264–265). He closed all the windows, stuck cotton into his ears, turned on the television, or put on music to drown out this "nocturnal uproar," to no avail. Compared to R, who was more dissociated from his experience, A was more reflective. He disclosed that months earlier he was transferred to a special anti-FLN unit, surveying shops and cafes where revolutionary activity was suspected, before being assigned to "special interrogations" at the police station. At first, A minimized the brutality of these encounters, saying the interrogations never occurred without some "knocking about."

Fanon (1963) kept his composure. A continued, explaining that if his victims had "a bit of consideration" they would "speak out without forcing us to spend hours tearing information word by word out of them" (p. 265). As his questions often received an "I don't know" from prisoners, he tortured them relentlessly (p. 265). "But they scream too much," he remarked, stating that at first this made him laugh—perhaps out of enjoyment *and* horror— but over time he "was a bit shaken." A becomes attuned to the *type* of screams his victims had. They are afraid of being killed, but A doesn't want to kill anyone. He just wants information—something, *anything*, so he can end the violence. In Fanon's presence, A notices the contradiction in his own words. He does not want to hurt anyone, but he is engaging in *torture*. A's participation in the colony came at a cost—"Now… I hear their screams even when I'm at home" (p. 266).

Horrified by his participation in oppression as a cop, A declares to Fanon (1963), "Doctor, I'm fed up with this job. And if you manage to cure me, I'll ask to be transferred to France. If they refuse, I'll resign" (p. 267). Sensing A's motivation for change, Fanon prescribed sick leave and—since A refused admission to the hospital's day program—treated him in his private practice. Before one of their sessions, Fanon received a call from the hospital. A had arrived at Fanon's home office early and his wife asked him to wait for Fanon to arrive. Having time to kill, A went for a walk in the hospital grounds.

As Fanon (1963) was going to his home office he bumped into A, who was leaning against a tree having a panic attack. After making sure he did not need to be hospitalized, Fanon drove him back to his home office. "Once he was lying on the sofa," Fanon writes, "he told me he had met one of my patients in the hospital who had been questioned in the police barracks" (p. 266). Fanon learned that A had tortured this patient with his own hands. Facing the humanity of someone he had brutalized shocked him, inducing a panic. Fanon treated A and administered a sedative to calm his anxiety, and after the session ran back to the hospital where the FLN soldier was being treated. The staff had not noticed anything out of the ordinary, but the patient had disappeared. Fanon searched the premises until he found him in the bathroom trying to commit suicide. They were able to save the soldier, who had "recognized the policeman and thought that he had come to look for him" (pp. 266–267).

Fanon maintained confidentiality for *both* patients, but it took a long time for the revolutionary to feel safe again in the unit. He continued seeing A in his private practice, who after several sessions made a "definite improvement," and secured a transfer to France to end his role as a torturer. In comparison to R, A became conscious of how his violence was traumatizing his victims *and* traumatizing him—leading him to overcome the colony's *jouissance*.

The Alienation of Privilege: The Case of a Young French Woman

The last case I will review is Fanon's (1963) treatment of a 21-year-old French woman, a college student who consulted him due to anxiety inter-fering with her studies and her relationships, experiencing profuse sweats, chest constrictions, headaches, and frequent nail biting. What stood out to Fanon, however, was her "over-easy" demeanor and a rapid, pressured speech betraying "a severe anxiety… underlying the facile approach" (p. 276). In describing recent events, the young woman lightheartedly mentioned the death of her father, which attracted Fanon's attention. He picked up on her chatty, nonchalant mention of his death as a defense: "we quickly directed our investigations toward her relations with her father" (p. 276). By inviting her to talk more about her father, Fanon noticed the young woman's rationalizing defenses alongside her "uneasiness and the nature and origin of her conflict" (p. 276). She described her father as a high-ranking official in charge of a large rural municipality. "As soon as the troubles started,"—Fanon noticed a motif among his white French patients, referring to the outbreak of war as "the troubles,"—"[my father] threw himself into the Algerian manhunt with frenzied rage" (p. 277).

Her father was consumed with hunting down Algerian rebels and stopped eating and sleeping, enraptured by "a state of *excitement* over putting down the rebellion" (Fanon, 1963, p. 277, emphasis added). She was terrified of her father's *jouissance*, and decided not to see him any more. When Fanon inquired further, she disclosed that "every time I went home I spent entire nights awake, for screams used to rise up to my room from down below… Algerians were being tortured so as to obtain information" (p. 277).

She was terrified at the monster her father had become. How could he hear these screams yet continue abusing other human beings? The few times he came to visit her, "I wasn't able to look him in the face without being terribly frightened and embarrassed" (Fanon, 1963, pp. 277–278). Fanon helps the young woman work through her anxious, upbeat demeanor to process her terror and shame. She had lived most of her life in their village and knew all the families living there, and although she had played with Algerian boys her age since childhood, now her father was ripping apart their families and community. She felt tremendous anxiety and shame walking down the street, feeling the hatred of Black and Arab Algerians toward her as the white daughter of a white torturer. "In my heart I knew that those Algerians were right," she reflected, "If I were an Algerian girl, I'd be in the [the revolutionary army]" (p. 277).

One day, she received word her father had been ambushed by the FLN and was dying from his injuries. When she went to his funeral she was disgusted with the French officials in attendance who were weeping over her father whose "high moral qualities conquered the native population" (Fanon, 1963, p. 277). In her sessions she tapped into her rage toward her father and the elites who enabled his behavior. She saw them as hypocrites who knew well her father ran interrogations across the entire region. Reflecting with Fanon on the French government's offer of an allowance, she refused it, "I don't want their money. It is the price of the blood spilt by my father. I don't want any of it. I am going to work" (p. 277).

Beneath her gregarious façade lay a multitude of conflicts—between her and her father, their family and the community, the French army and the Algerian people. She was privileged and "owed" care by the state, but receiving these funds meant staining her hands with the blood of her neighbors. Making room for her anger and shame allowed her to acknowledge her privilege within the colony, and enter into solidarity with the Algerian people. She took an ethical stance, rejecting colonial patriarchal care for the dignity of her own work.

A "Total Liberation": Fanon's Decolonial Legacy

In reflecting on these cases Fanon (1963) reprises how racial capitalism distorts the humanity of all involved—*differently* depending on our social position and privilege, but in an interconnected fashion. He borrows a metaphor from veterinarians who remind us of the "'peck order' which has been observed in farmyards," with food the object of "relentless competition" (p. 308). "Certain birds, the strongest," Fanon writes, "gobble up all the grains while others who are less aggressive grow visibly thinner. *Every colony tends to turn into a huge farmyard, where the only law is that of the knife*" (p. 308, emphasis added).

Across his cases, Fanon is sensitive to how his patients are perceived and perceive themselves in the "pecking order" of the colony, "rungs" that need to be reproduced to divide everyone to the benefit of the wealthy. From Freud to Fanon, we can say that society offers different compensations that maintain our attachment to the social order. These privileges provide obvious material and psychological benefits, but at the same time exert a cost. White workers may be exploited, but racism offers a substitutive satisfaction that accentuates their identification with the white elite, along with the promise that *some day*, they can be wealthy as well. Workers of color and a growing ethnic-minority middle class may seek upward mobility even if this alienates them. Non-Black people of color may "vamp" on anti-Blackness as a way of maintaining their precarious "in-between" position, despite the threat of white racism.

Fanon's analysis reveals a logic of change that is as much clinical as it is political. In each of his cases, the attachment to a position of power is both a source of privilege and of suffering exerting real costs. What is at stake is a willingness to—as Freud might say—*renounce* the pleasures of privilege and positionality to overcome its costs. Du Bois bears repeating, to renounce repression in favor of liberty. René Maran would have to renounce his desire to be "accepted" by the white gaze, freeing his desire to find love and connection. B had to renounce his patriarchal beliefs to make room for intimacy with his wife. A had to renounce his position as a police officer to rediscover his humanity and that of the people he tortured. The young woman had to renounce her privilege as part of the French colony to find true solidarity and meaning in her own labor. R, by contrast, did not renounce the pleasure of the colony—as Gherovici (2022) quips, despite the suffering it causes, "It hurts so good" (p. 277). Too good.

For Fanon no one is immune from colonial logic, and he was clearly critical of the Arab and Black middle classes who sought to "move up" within the colony and leave their communities struggling at the bottom. He was also aware that the white working class has not consistently heeded the call for solidarity. At the political level, his work calls on us to renounce our attachment to positions of power in exchange for solidarity, working through differences in race, class, gender, and sexuality through a shared, insurgent universality that demands material, structural changes for all and leaves no one at the mercy of "the bottom" (Táíwò, 2022). What is needed is a "total liberation," of psyche and society (Fanon, 1963, p. 310). Thus, Fanon (1963) concludes, "For Europe, for ourselves, and for humanity, comrades, we must turn over a new leaf, we must work out new concepts, and try to set afoot a new man" (p. 316).

Reflection Questions

- In increasingly hierarchical societies, inequality can instill a desire to "move up," to compete with others for position, and to pull others down. How do you notice this vertical push and pull in your own life and practice? How may it reflect an attempt to survive unequal conditions at an individual level?
- Fanon offered a rethinking of recognition outside the immediate self–other relation that accounts for the social context, and in which change is initiated not by the self's (or the therapist's) attempt at recognition, but by the other's *refusal* of recognition and its very framing. In what ways have you experienced someone—patient or otherwise—reject your attempts at empathy, acknowledgment, or recognition? Is this shocking? How might it offer a different perspective outside your own?
- Interpersonal relationships, culture, and society all contribute to how Fanon thinks of the etiology of psychopathology. At the same time, he also rejects a purely sociological explanation that erases our role as agentic beings. How do you think about the relationship between the individual, relational, and societal in mental health? Do you find yourself privileging one dimension over another? What might be gained by emphasizing each of those aspects?

Further Reading

Fanon's Work and Legacy
- Arnall, G. (2019). *Subterranean Fanon: An underground theory of radical change.* Columbia University Press.
- Gordon, L. R. (2015). *What Fanon said: A philosophical introduction to his life and thought.* Fordham University Press.
- Marriott, D. (2018). *Whither Fanon.* Stanford University Press.

References

Altman, N. (2000). Black and white thinking: A psychoanalyst reconsiders race. *Psychoanalytic Dialogues, 10*(4), 589–605.

Aron, L. (2003). Clinical outbursts and theoretical breakthroughs: A unifying theme in the work of Stephen A. Mitchell. *Psychoanalytic Dialogues, 13*(2), 259–273.

Benjamin, J. (2017). *Beyond doer and done to: Recognition theory, intersubjectivity and the third.* Taylor & Francis.

Brickman, C. (2017). *Race in psychoanalysis: Aboriginal populations in the mind.* Routledge.

Cherki, A. (2006). *Frantz Fanon: A portrait.* Cornell University Press.

Duncan-Andrade, J. M. R., & Morrell, E. (2008). *The art of critical pedagogy: Possibilities for moving from theory to practice in urban schools* (Vol. 285). Peter Lang.

Fanon, F. (1952/2008). *Black Skin, white masks.* Pluto Press.

Fanon, F. (1963). *The wretched of the earth* (R. Philcox, Trans). Grove Press.

Fanon, F. (1988). *Toward the African revolution: Political essays.* Grove Press.

Freire, P. (1972). *Pedagogy of the oppressed.* Continuum.

Fanon, F. (1973). *Education for critical consciousness.* The Seabury Press.

Freud, S. (1913/1955). Totem and taboo: Some points of agreement between the mental lives of savages and neurotics (1913 [1912–13]). In *The standard edition of the complete psychological works of Sigmund Freud, volume XIII (1913–1914): Totem and taboo and other works* (pp. VII–162).

Freud, S. (1915). The unconscious. In *The standard edition of the complete psychological works of Sigmund Freud Volume XIV (1914–1916): On the history of the psychoanalytic movement, papers on metapsychology, and other works* (pp. 159–215).

Freud, S. (1918/1955). From the history of an infantile neurosis. In *The standard edition of the complete psychological works of Sigmund Freud, volume XVII (1917–1919): An infantile neurosis and other works* (pp. 1–124).

Gherovici, P. (2022). Hate up to my couch: psychoanalysis, community, poverty and the role of hatred. *Psychoanalysis and History, 24*(3), 269–290.

Gibson, N. C. (2020). Fanon and Marx revisited. *Journal of the British Society for Phenomenology, 51*(4), 320–336.

Gilman, S. L. (1993a). *The case of Sigmund Freud: Medicine and identity at the fin de siecle.* The Johns Hopkins University Press.

Gilman, S. L. (1993b). *Freud, race, and gender.* Princeton University Press.

Harper, E. (2012). *Homelessness and violence: Freud, Fanon and Foucault and the shadow of the Afrikan sex worker* [Unpublished doctoral dissertation]. Retrieved April 20, 2023, from www.Academia.edu

Hart, A. (2022). From multicultural competence to radical openness: A psychoanalytic engagement of otherness. In B. J. Stoute & M. Slevin (Eds.), *The trauma of racism* (pp. 244–250). Taylor & Francis.

Kabasakalian-McKay, R., & Mark, D. (Eds.). (2022). *Inhabiting implication in racial oppression and in relational psychoanalysis.* Taylor & Francis.

Knoblauch, S. H. (2020). Fanon's vision of embodied racism for psychoanalytic theory and practice. *Psychoanalytic Dialogues, 30,* 299–316.

Lorca, F. G. (1981). *Theory and play of the Duende: And, Imagination, inspiration, evasion.* Kanathos.

Pierson, A. M., Arunagiri, V., & Bond, D. M. (2022). "You didn't cause racism, and you have to solve it anyways": Antiracist adaptations to dialectical behavior therapy for white therapists. *Cognitive and Behavioral Practice, 29*(4), 796–815.

Rodríguez-Silva, I. (2012). *Silencing race: Disentangling blackness, colonialism, and national identities in Puerto Rico.* Springer.

Sue, D. W. (2010). *Microaggressions in everyday life: Race, gender, and sexual orientation.* Wiley.

Swartz, S. (2018). Counter-recognition in decolonial struggle. *Psychoanalytic Dialogues, 28*(5), 520–527.

Táíwò, O. O. (2022). *Elite capture: How the powerful took over identity politics (and everything else).* Haymarket Books.

Tate, C. (1996). Freud and his "negro": Psychoanalysis as ally and enemy of African Americans. *Journal for the Psychoanalysis of Culture and Society, 1,* 53–62.

Wilderson III, F. B. (2010). *Red, white & black: Cinema and the structure of US antagonisms.* Duke University Press.

7

Integrating Decolonial Psychoanalytic Theory and Empirical Research: Clinical Implications and Case Illustrations

Having worked our way through our "mobius strip" from Freud to Fanon, I now synthesize the previous chapters through the lens of contemporary research to underscore the centrality of two interconnected psychological systems—one focused on affiliation, closeness, and attachment, the other focused on status, hierarchy, and power. The implication of these systems in speech and the body's orientation in space opens up new vistas for intervening on the relational and the social in clinical practice. Lastly, I return to the case discussed at the beginning of this book, alongside others from previously published excerpts (Gaztambide, 2022), to illustrate the model in practice. With this research, I follow Fanon's (2018) insight drawn from the science of his day: "The neurological point of view converges with the psychoanalytic point of view" (p. 521).

The Linguistic-Embodied Unconscious: The Psyche as a System of Associations

The brain evolved to (a) regulate affective arousal, and (b) maneuver the body in space (Barrett et al., 2022). The brain regions implicated in sensorimotor functioning—our perception of the body in physical space—evolved a network of connections giving rise to language and the navigation of *social* space. Hence, the navigation of a symbolic universe, our relationships and society, is dependent on our maneuvering the body in physical space. For example, embodied cognition research shows how speech is embedded

D. J. Gaztambide, *Decolonizing Psychoanalytic Technique*, https://doi.org/10.1007/978-3-031-48476-6_7

in bodily and spatial metaphors (Bargh, 2022), supporting psychoanalytic insights. Paul Wachtel (1967) observed that

> the movements and positions of the body communicate a great deal about what a person is like and how he is feeling. Everyday phrases like 'keep your chin up,' 'down in the mouth', or 'walking on air' reflect the degree to which we all assess others' moods by bodily cues… (p. 97)

Similarly, when we "feel warmly" toward someone our body temperature rises (Williams & Bargh, 2008a), and when we feel excluded—"given the cold shoulder"—we feel colder (Zhong & Leonardelli, 2008). In turn, holding something physically warm engages the same brain regions as when engaging in fun activities with loved ones (Inagaki & Eisenberger, 2013). When we feel betrayed, this activates the same regions as when holding something cold (Inagaki et al., 2016). Think of when you betray a friend in a board game and they respond, "that's *cold*, man!".

Somatic metaphors are also complemented by spatial ones (Williams & Bargh, 2008b). When a lover shares something intimate and you reply "I feel closer to you," this is not a figure of speech—your body responds *as if* you are physically closer, often in an act of intimacy like a hug. Similarly, we feel "put down" by our boss, "beaten down" in life, "over the moon" after winning an award, or "lower than dirt" when we fail. Such language, one "horizontal" and focused on closeness, the other "vertical" and implying where we stand in a hierarchy, are part of everyday speech communicating "where we are" in the world—often unconsciously.

The fact that unconscious processes shape our behavior is well established, and they may well do so through somatic channels (Bargh, 2022; Weinberger & Stoycheva, 2019). Thinking is never purely conscious, but part of a series of "embodied decisions," carried out in coordination with the environment (Barret et al., 2022 p. 5). Recently I was writing on a train with a cup of coffee by my side. I blinked and suddenly found my body bent over my seat, my hands clasping my coffee *just* before it hit the ground. I had no awareness of the cup falling yet found myself exclaiming "Oh shit," as I contorted my body to save my coffee. The calculations involved in curving my torso, which hand to "strike out," etc., happened in milliseconds. And thank goodness. If I had had to *think* about these steps, I would have made a mess. This was a series of unconscious, bodily *if, then* contingencies shifting dynamically with each millisecond.

Budson et al. (2022) review how at a timescale of 500 milliseconds (half a second) or less, consciousness does not flow in a linear fashion, with awareness of an event taking place *after* it has transpired. Consciousness is *too slow* to guide our behavior, whether playing an instrument or negotiating our relationships. There is an afterwardness to consciousness, as our "slow mind" struggles to catch up to our "fast mind"—a process of *remembering* what has already transpired. My consciousness of grabbing my fallen cup was in fact me *remembering* that my body initiated this behavior, with consciousness "replaying" the event in half-second intervals. Budson et al. (2022) reference Daniel Kahneman's distinction between a fast, intuitive, automatic, stereotypic, and unconscious "System 1" and a slow, rational, effortful, conscious "System 2," noting the latter helps us reflect and provide feedback to unconscious systems, "an additional layer of information that our unconscious brain can use (or not) to make decisions and act accordingly" (p. 9), such as helping it *slow down*. Inverting Freud's take on the psyche, *it is the unconscious that perceives and reacts to the world in real time*, and only later "cues in" consciousness for feedback.

In talking about primary process, we must remember its role in associations. Fanon et al. (2018) spoke of neurons as a "large number of bundles of associations; there is no point of the brain that is not linked to all the others" (p. 520). Research shows the hippocampus—implicated in language, memory, and spatial-social navigation—is "an associative device," synchronizing neurons into salient networks (Hill & Dahlitz, 2021, p. 60). For example, a study showing participants a picture of Jennifer Aniston led a specific neuron to "light up," coordinating other cells implicated in the visual recognition of her face, and others in the recall of her name—"associating" name to face. Neurons may be the vehicle for psychological associations.

Think of a single string on a guitar. If you "string" it on its own, it just produces noise. If you place your fingers in a certain way on the neck of the guitar and string a series of chords in rhythm, suddenly you produce *music*. Neurons work in a similar way, coming together to produce the phenomenal experience of memory, language, and song. Decolonial psychoanalytic technique is how we use the resonance of our words—and the "words" implied in our behavior—to evoke neuronal "strings" implicated in the patient's relational and sociocultural world. When you "pluck" on a certain string, other connections in the network resonate.

Earlier I mentioned how one function of the brain is to regulate the level of excitation in the body, and alluded to the "calculations" the brain makes in navigating the world. As Rabeyron and Massicotte (2020) write, the brain "evolved in order to simulate its environment and diminish the effects of surprise thanks to a Bayesian model" (p. 8). Named after mathematician Thomas Bayes, "Bayesian" refers to our tendency toward prediction and sense-making, binding, and organizing sensory information about the world. We create and prune associations to the extent they minimize the effect of surprise in the form of (a) information that does not comform to our models of reality, and/or (b) sudden, overwhelming affect.

Holmes and Nolte (2019) draw on neuroscientist Karl Friston's work on the "free energy principle" to explain how the brain, as an "inference engine," pursues the path of least possible surprise by minimizing the difference between our predictions of the world and our sensory perceptions of it. We bind chaotic energies into a predictive, contingent model of the world (e.g., "*If* I protect myself, *then* I won't be hurt again). Friston describes the brain as "a literally *fantastic* organ… a purveyor of fantasies, hypotheses, [and] models" (Painting Onions Podcast, 2022, emphasis added). In exchanging reality for fantasy, however, "freedom is sacrificed for the sake of a degree of security" (Holmes & Nolte, 2019, p. 7). We cling to a sense of self and world that is rigidly bound, unable to "update" or actualize our experience with new information, through what Fanon et al. (2018) called the "benevolent and realistic (*actualisant* [lit. "updating"])" help of the other (p. 442). Hence, Holmes and Nolte (2019) argue that a "degree of negative capability, or creative not-knowing… for exploration and innovation" plays a role in therapeutic change (p. 7). Such "creative not-knowing" makes room for play and spontaneity, reintroducing the element of surprise through a managed unbinding of the "ego" (cf. Saketopoulou, 2023). Per Fanon (2018), opening up to "relearn" and "rediscover the meaning of freedom" (p. 332).

The unconscious runs a series of associative processes, calculations, and "streams" in parallel without contradiction, rendering it *normatively arational* as a matter of course (Weinberger & Stoycheva, 2019). Conflict is normative instead of inherently pathological, insofar as the operations of the brain depend on compromise. Pathology, then, is a matter of function, of how well our compromises *work* in a given context—relational, cultural, and social. Given that associations change with experience, learning can be understood as the forming of new connections, shifting "the nature and strength of associative connections in the brain/mind" (p. 305). Such learning is often unconscious, but "the old learning would not be replaced by the new. Rather, they would exist side by side" (p. 315). For example, a patient with chronic fears of abandonment would not fully "extinguish" those fears in therapy, but give them new meaning in a new associative context, e.g., "I am afraid of being abandoned, *but* I know that I am loved." A refrain from the literature is that the brain works through addition, *not* subtraction—think of Suzanne Hommel's treatment with Lacan in Chapter 4.

Wish, Defense, and *Jouissance*: A Neurobiological Account

Research by Howard Shevrin and colleagues (reviewed in Bazan, 2017), shows that activation ("priming") of threatening stimuli outside of awareness triggers defense mechanisms, especially when an unconscious wish is associated with anxiety. A person may wish to engage with others, but if this wish is associated with the fear that others will be rejecting, they may withdraw from social situations so the wish cannot be fulfilled *or* frustrated (p. 1450). Research on "reward devaluation" shows we not only fear a negative outcome, but also avoid *positive, rewarding* outcomes because at some point they became *associated* with negative outcomes (Winer & Salem, 2016). This is why for some patients, chaotic relationships may be experienced as soothing, whereas consistent love is destabilizing and threatening. We come to fear our need for love.

Defenses allow a compromise between our wishes and fears to secure our needs in the least threatening manner, constructive bindings that later in life begin to fail. Like the concept of compromise formation, *jouissance* helps explain how symptoms fulfill a function despite their costs. Bazan and Detandt (2013) define *jouissance* as "*the (benefit gained from) the motor tension underlying the action which was (once) adequate in bringing relief to the drive*" (p. 2, emphasis original). When effective, it drives our "readiness" to act to fulfill a need. When dysregulated, it results in a need for repetition, even if this leads to costly consequences. Bazan and Detandt (2013) point to what neuroscientist Jaak Panksepp calls the "SEEKING" system, which closely parallels Freud's drive theory (Shevrin, 2003; Solms & Panksepp, 2012; see Chapter 2).

When the SEEKING system is activated, dopamine is released to "mark" the sequence of behaviors that led to pleasure (i.e., was rewarding). However, when activation accompanies a behavior that was once, perhaps by chance, "marked" as effective but is currently destructive, these circuits fire *in anticipation* of reward, even if the consequence is disastrous. Such behaviors "relentlessly... push for their repetition," resulting in patterns that are no longer pleasurable and even damaging (e.g., addiction), driven by an underlying (non)logic "continuously balancing between reward and anxiety... a constant push to act and to repeat" (Bazan & Detandt, 2013, p. 11). What happens when we compulsively repeat not just patterns of relationship, but patterns of domination within a brutal, hierarchical system? How do the relational and societal intersect?

The Psyche Is Linguistically Organized Around Attachment and Status: Horizontal and Vertical Axes of Human Experience

Consider some of the motivations "wired" into the brain. While motives can be conscious, they often operate unconsciously (Kihlstrom, 2019). Two over-arching goals identified by the research are (a) our desire for affiliation and intimacy, and (b) our desire for belonging and status (Weinberger & Stoy-cheva, 2019, p. 189). These motivational systems have cross-cultural validity (Jones et al., 2021), with growing consensus that social cognition operates along two intersecting dimensions—a "horizontal" axis organized around warmth and closeness, and a "vertical" axis organized around competition, aggression, and status (Abele et al., 2021). We "map" our world in terms of others' closeness to us on a horizontal plane, and in relation to where we perceive our body on a vertical hierarchy—an unconscious process impli-cating the hippocampus (Zhang, Chen et al., 2022). By drawing on networks implicated in our "map" of the physical world, the hippocampus generates a three-dimensional map of our social world.

These findings support the insights of psychoanalytic thinkers including Fanon, Pinderhughes (see Chapter 1), and Moss (2006). Moss (2006) writes about how we "map" our object relations onto these vertical/horizotal axes:

> The vertical axis reads difference hierarchically. This hierarchy is anchored by idealized types on one end, degraded types on the other. Objects are lined up according to their distance from the idealized and the degraded… The object map's horizontal axis measures distance… One object, then, might be located at a point that marks it as both intimate and degraded; another, say, as distant and idealized. (p. 278)

Relatedly, as income inequality increases, so do "ambivalent stereotypes," where objects are simultaneously "warm" but of lower status, or "cold" but more deserving (Durante et al., 2017). Put psychoanalytically, the splitting of "good" and "bad," deserving and undeserving, is rampant in more unequal societies.

These two motivational systems—affiliation/warmth/connection and status/aggression/assertiveness—can become incongruent or "split" among implicit and explicit systems. Someone may pursue a conscious motivation to "move up" socially, yet feel dissatisfied due to unfulfilled unconscious desires for connection. Or someone may pursue an explicit goal to maintain relation-ships at the cost of their boundaries, finding that at the end of the day their needs are not met. Not surprisingly, conflict between different motivations (connection or power) and motivational systems (conscious and unconscious) is implicated in poorer mental health (Schultheiss, 2021). Given the hippocampus' role in socio-spatial navigation and language (Levinson, 2023), this suggests that our mappings of the self in relational and political contexts are deeply involved in our capacity for language, and find expression through speech as such.

Research on language from cognitive-behavioral therapy (CBT) researchers provides an important piece of this puzzle. "Relational frame theory," or RFT, emerged from research on "derived knowing," our ability to abstract or "derive" associations from the environment without their needing to be taught or explicitly *known* (Barnes-Holmes et al., 2020; Villatte et al., 2015). Relational frames define the nature of an association, including coordination (A *is like* B), opposition (A is the *opposite* of B), space and time (*when and where* something is located), and their place on a hierarchy (a billion is more than a million). We learn these frames organically within our linguistic communities, relating objects in ways that can be arbitrary and symbolic, i.e., non-logical (Barnes-Holmes et al., 2018).

Remember the case we discussed in Chapter 1 of a student struggling with OCD. I must come clean to the reader—this was a case treated in CBT informed by RFT (Villette et al., 2015, p. 26). It just so happened that this research gave CBT a "psychoanalytic" flavor. Remember how that patient coped with their contamination fears by avoiding physical contact with water. Regardless, water "kept popping up in his relational network" through the letters "H_2O" in their chemistry textbook (p. 26). The symbolic association between H_2O and water evoked an aversive response *as if* reading the letters *was like* being physically contaminated.

RFT has a theory of the "self" and its embeddedness in language, involving three contextual relations: the relational *I–You*, the spatial *Here–There*, and the temporal *Now–Then* (Barnes-Holmes et al., 2020). These frames orient us in relation to others and the world. For example, at the start of a date one person may be sitting in a restaurant booth (here), while their date sits across from them (there). As the night goes on and closeness builds, their date *moves* to sit next to them on the booth—"there" becomes "here." In terms of status, a patient might say "I feel I'm not where I *should be* at my job." This implies a hierarchical sense of location, communicating "I am *here*, in this lower position when I should be *there*, in a higher one."

Our associations between self, other, and place form within linguistic communities that tacitly communicate which associations are allowed, and which are punished or remain unformulated (think of Lacan's Symbolic Order). "Thus," Barnes-Holmes et al. (2018) write, "the more readily emitted pattern of responding is indicative of the natural contingencies operating in the wider verbal community" (p. 166). These "natural contingencies" can be understood in Fanonian terms—our social unconscious framing who is "above" or "below," who is and is not "kin." RFT also discusses conscious and unconscious processes in terms of "extended and elaborated relational responses" (secondary process or System 2) and "brief and immediate relational responses" (primary process or System 1), which is relevant for the following example.

Based on their research on implicit bias, Barnes-Holmes et al. (2018) write about how white people in segregated neighborhoods, exposed to images of Black people as violent and dangerous, etc., are likely to express anti-Black bias if presented with pictures of Black males carrying guns below the time threshold for conscious awareness (half a second). However, without the time constraint such bias appears absent "based on additional relational responding, such as *It is wrong to discriminate on the basis of race* and *I am not a racist*" (p. 167, emphasis original). RFT supports what psychoanalysis has long maintained, that we "behave in two qualitatively different and potentially conflicting ways" (Hughes & Barnes-Holmes, 2016, p. 49).

Our history of interactions with the world gives rise to automatic, rapid, implicit responses that emerge without awareness. These responses, however, are not reducible to the individual, "There is no person or individual… as such, contained within the field; in a sense the person is a constantly changing or actualizing field of verbal interactants" (Barnes-Holmes et al., 2020, p. 621). In imagining the human subject as textured by language, and a linguistic unconscious that is transindividual, we find psychoanalysis and CBT on the verge of convergence, insofar as "therapy is… a complex and dynamical field of verbal interactants" (p. 621). Instead of a one-, two-, or three-person psychology, perhaps we can talk about a *no-person* psychology.

We often think of a "person" as a self-contained organism with its own "internal" thoughts and feelings separate from the environment. My quip about a "no-person" psychology gestures at how human beings are *very* porous, not self-contained, and have thoughts and feelings that "slip" or "flow through" them that are not strictly "theirs." Our embeddedness in culture, language, and the body leads entire worlds to speak through us.

For example, in the US terms such as "honey" are commonly used with intimate others. Ren et al. (2015) found that priming participants by feeding them candy led to appraisals of a potential partner as sweet and attractive, triggering an unconscious, somatic association between the taste of sweetness and seeing another as "sweet." In another study in Israel, Gilead et al. (2015)

found that participants who ate a candy evaluated another person as disin-genuous, given that in Israeli culture being "sweet" is interpreted as being "phony" (e.g., "saccharine"). Hence, cultural-linguistic practices can inform preverbal, somatic processes. While the body gives rise to language, cultural associations in language frame the experience of embodiment. Put differ-ently, the brain does not rigidly distinguish between "verbal speech" that is spoken and "body language" that is enacted—the verbal and embodied are both vehicles for language.

Another example of how social structures, language, and the unconscious interact is through implicit bias, often understood as individual, automatic associations about different groups, such as "white = competent" or "Black = dangerous" (Banaji & Greenwald, 2013). While at the *individual* level implicit bias is not strongly associated with behavior or stable over time, at the *systemic* level of institutions, cities, states, etc., it is stable and predictive of inequality—leading to gender, racial, and economic disparities in health, wealth, and opportunity (Ayala-López et al., 2020; Payne & Hannay, 2021). Some researchers argue for a shift from individual minds to—per Fanon— associations constituted within socio-structural contexts.

For example, the aggregate level of bias in universities is a function of structural—not individual—factors such as faculty diversity, the presence of Confederate monuments, and low social mobility (Vuletich & Payne, 2019). Another study showed that US states with a higher prevalence of slavery in 1860 had higher pro-white bias, mediated by contemporary structural factors such as racial wealth inequality, segregation, and economic mobility (Payne et al., 2019). Unconscious bias, then, is a psychological *symptom* of structural forces.

Payne et al. (2017) proposed the "bias of crowds" model to explain how the *accessibility* of an association in the environment makes it more likely to be retrieved when a social category (e.g., Black, immigrant, female, queer) is activated. "[When] we use one concept," they write, "other related concepts… become more likely to be accessed… spontaneously and invol-untarily" (p. 235). For example, when we read the words "bed," "rest," and "dream" we are more likely to "fill in" a prompt such as "sle__." Paralleling Lacan, implicit bias is "a social phenomenon that *passes through* individual minds, rather than residing in them" (p. 236, emphasis added). In that sense, implicit biases are "extrapersonal associations" (p. 239).

The inequality of our world presents us with a "theater play" whose set pieces are designed to feel real. The brain—and by extension the uncon-scious—is thoroughly empirical, making sense of the world that is "there," without awareness of its social construction. From this reality we derive associations around certain groups. Payne and Hannay (2021) write:

> The frequency with which a word occurs in the language, for example, determines how easily retrieved that word is. The frequency with which two words co-occur determines how likely one associate is to come to mind when the other is presented. That is why… in US culture, Islamic cues terrorism more than terrarium… associations based on statistical regularities will be systematically biased, so long as it operates in an environment that is characterized by pre-existing stereotypes and inequalities. (p. 929)

Structural forces create environments that foment biased associations, with the psyche forming "real-time inferences based on regularities in the environment" (p. 931). That is not to say these biases are *true*, only that when the wealthy, white, and male create a society in their image this structures our social unconscious. This does not mean biases cannot be resisted, or that we are not accountable for them. Rather, we recognize what Fanon (1956/1988) teaches us: "The habit of considering racism as a mental quirk, as a psychological flaw, must be abandoned" (p. 38).

Our language and embodiment exist within a broader network of values and associations, with policy structuring the world we relate to according to the needs of the powerful. For example, using data from 160 countries, Goudarzi et al. (2022) showed how neoliberal policy has shaped individual beliefs around equity and redistribution over the past 40 years. "Fairness beliefs at the micro level," they write, "are thus shaped by those beliefs' macro-level instantiations" (p. 1431). Looking at this study, a colleague of mine wondered why structures shape beliefs but not the other way around. I quipped that beliefs *do* shape structures—the beliefs, fears, and fantasies of the powerful. Power and wealth decide whose fantasies shape reality, and what associations become the very air we breathe.

The Relational and SocioPolitical in Psychotherapy: Intersecting Dimensions

Attachment and relationships form part of the "horizontal" dimension of social cognition, and research confirms that the efficacy of psychoanalytic treatment involves negotiating closeness and distance between patient and therapist (Egozi et al., 2021). In this section I integrate relationality with the role of status, culture, and identity in the therapeutic encounter, starting with the role of attachment and the negotiation of interpersonal needs, followed by the negotiation of cultural values, identity, and power in treatment.

In a classic contribution, the Boston Change Process Study Group (2010) introduced the concept of "implicit relational knowing," a tacit, unarticulated, unconscious way of being with others. Central to their theorizing are "moments of meeting," where ruptures and their repair open up those habitual ways of relating for reconsideration. These moments

> are unfamiliar, *unexpected* in their exact form and timing, unsettling or weird. They are often confusing as to what is happening or what to do. These moments are pregnant with an unknown future that can feel like an impasse or an opportunity... accompanied by expectancy or anxiety because the necessity of choice is pressing, yet there is no immediately available prior plan of action or explanation. (p. 16, emphasis added)

"Moments of meeting" are unknown territory, an experiment with new ways of relating where the therapist's action—paralleling Ferenczi with Lacan—"must be novel and fashioned to meet the singularity of the moment" (p. 19). Such novel interactions create new modes of implicit relational knowing. Here the authors recognize that embodiment and language share "the same root origins in common body experience" (p. 174), concurring with Weinberger and Stoycheva (2019) that any new "insight" *must become unconscious to effect change.* We cannot have an "aha!" moment in our heads. It must become embedded in our bones.

Such theorizing on "implicit relational knowledge" converges with the research above on how the unconscious perceives reality prior to consciousness being brought to bear. This implies psychotherapy intervenes primarily at the level of procedural knowledge—our implicit, habitual ways of being. In line with our discussion of the "safe surprise," research suggests that effective therapists initially behave in ways that are "complementary" to the patient's attachment style, but once trust is established they "gently challenge the patient by responding 'out of style' to their attachment defenses... [shifting] their ways of responding over time in accord with the patients' needs either for safety or exploration" (Slade & Holmes, 2019, p. 154). Talia et al. (2020) argue that what facilitates this is the therapist's not-knowing stance, their "ability to keep their minds open and allow a space for their patients to reflect on their own" (p. 203). They relate this to an insight of the poet Keats, the skill of "*negative capacity*... capable of being in uncertainties, Mysteries, doubts, without any irritable reaching after fact and reason" (cited in p. 203). Attempting to change implicit knowledge requires an openness to experimentation and surprise.

This process is not necessarily "led" by the therapist, however. Research from the perspective of control-mastery theory (CMT, Rodomonti et al., 2021) underscores the patient's active role. We scan the environment for signs of safety, informed by the beliefs we developed to survive, but with an unconscious sense these beliefs are self-limiting. We are highly motivated to *discomfirm* our unconscious beliefs, and have a somewhat articulated though unconscious plan for doing so (p. 143). Patients work to change their unconscious fantasies through "transference tests," enacting relational conditions with the potential to *disrupt and disprove* them. These include "trial actions," experimental behaviors to gage the level of safety in treatment. For example, a patient who struggles with self-assertion asks for a change in session time. If the therapist welcomes the patient's self-assertion, this "passes" the test. The patient tests the relationship by (a) observing if the therapist treats them as a hurtful other from the past, and/or (b) behaving *as* that other toward the therapist—the patient may behave in a domineering way to test if the therapist submits to them or asserts their boundaries. The patient either behaves in a new way, and/or tries to evoke a new response from the therapist—a welcome surprise.

Patients also "coach" the therapist through indirect clues as to what will help them grow in accordance with their plan (Rodomonti et al., 2021). They are enacting the relational conditions that "keep things the same" in hopes of changing them, with research suggesting that formulating what the patient's unconscious plan might be leads to better outcomes (Gazzillo et al., 2019). Another example of such case formulation is the core conflictual relationship theme (CCRT), which conceptualizes the patient's unconscious wish, the feared response of the other, and the response of the self to defend against that fear (Luborsky & Crits-Christoph, 1998). Understanding the patient's fantasized response of the other clarifies what therapeutic responses might be helpful (Grenyer & Marceau, 2022). If the patient's expectation of others is that they will be dismissive, then the therapist's curiosity and interest is salubriously "counter-script." To be clear, the purpose of such formulations is *not* to develop a rigid "formula" for how to contradict the patient's schemas, but to get us *thinking* about what their plan *might* be, balanced with respect and humility toward their fundamental opacity, an openness to being surprised.

The unexpected disruption of our unconscious expectations of others and the world is intimately related to corrective emotional experiences, whether with the therapist or others in life. A landmark review of research across theoretical orientations (Hill et al., 2012) describes corrective experiences as the "new or unexpected thoughts, emotions, sensations, behaviors, or feelings about one's self that result from the client encountering an event that is different from (and thus disconfirming of) his or her frame of reference" (p. 356).

Corrective experiences do not need to be "dramatic," and are often a series of "little surprises" that accrue over time, especially "when the therapist takes a risk to do something unusual, bold, *or perhaps even benevolently shocking*" (Hill et al., 2012, p. 359, emphasis added). This "benevolent shock" could be a provocative reframe of the patient's struggles, or a self-disclosure that challenges their view of the therapist and others. Interestingly, this research implies that corrective experiences can also disconfirm cultural schemas (e.g., around gender, see p. 356). At the same time, corrective experiences take place in a social context, "family structure, cultural traditions, and economic considerations… [can] impede the full realization of CEs (e.g., significant others might actively oppose the change or tacitly sabotage it)" (p. 361). For example, cultural and familial values, discrimination, etc., may conflict with the lessons learned in therapy.

Angus and Constantino (2017) review a series of international, cross-cultural, multisite studies on corrective experiences showing that the therapist's flexibility and responsiveness impacts the patient's sense of feeling valued, with selective self-disclosures by therapists facilitating trust and engagement. The studies draw attention to the therapist's reflections, guided questioning, and *challenging* of the patient's negative expectations while providing a new, alternate perspective on their struggles. As a result of these experiences, patients were able to engage in "greater self-disclosure in interpersonal relationships as well as… engage in new, more productive behaviors (e.g., being appropriately assertive, diplomatic, participatory)" (p. 193).

Without question, relationality is central to psychotherapy, but Fanon shows us it cannot be *the only* axis of our work. While the role of attachment in mental health and psychotherapy process is well established (e.g., Levy et al., 2018), another body of research documents the impact of social status (Gilboa-Schechtman et al., 2020; Kim et al., 2021; Wetherall et al., 2019), with major reviews and studies finding a relationship between economic, racial, and gender inequality and mental health (Wilkinson & Pickett, 2020; Williams & Etkins, 2021; Yu, 2018). We become ill not only because we fear losing a beloved object, but also because we fear losing status and being defined as "lesser than," struggling between our need to "get along" and the urge to "get ahead," to belong, and have value (Gilboa-Schechtman et al., 2020, p. 107).

Therapeutic alliance research has similarly expanded to include the role of the institutional, systemic, and sociocultural context of therapy, what is called the "systemic alliance" (Quirk et al., 2018). Firth et al. (2019) found that "the effectiveness of therapy is not restricted to the therapist-patient interaction, and that the broader sociodemographic, socioeconomic, and geographic context… substantially contribute to patient outcome" (p. 23). For example, racial disparities in psychotherapy outcome are greater in predominantly white universities (Owen et al., 2021). Further, when the patient's social networks are misaligned with or opposed to the therapeutic work, addressing the alliance regularly protects against its erosion (Slone & Owen, 2015). For example, if the patient's family or culture disapprove of psychotherapy—or the patient's newly established boundaries—broaching and exploring those concerns, and ruptures that result from them, helps repair and maintain the alliance. As Slone and Owen (2015) assert, "the alliance is a far-reaching concept that extends beyond the walls of the office" (p. 283).

Actively bringing up culture and identity—as relevant to the patient— has a positive effect on psychotherapy outcomes (Day-Vines et al., 2018). Broaching is critical given the tendency by clinicians to *not respond*, invalidate, or be hostile to the patient's cultural material, including allusions to similarity and difference in the therapeutic relationship (Lee & Horvath, 2014), including allusions to cultural enactments (see Lee et al., 2018). At the same time, taking the initiative must be balanced with closely following the patient's speech (Lee et al., 2021), between initiating discussions *and* following their lead to prevent stereotyping (Chang & Yoon, 2011; Lee et al., 2019).

Davis et al. (2018) review the evidence in support of cultural humility. Informed by therapeutic relationship research, cultural humility is a "not-knowing" stance that is "other oriented" or "open to the other," in relation to those "aspects of cultural identity that are most important to the client" (cited in p. 91). It includes the recognition of one's limitations and knowledge, rejecting a sense of superiority toward the patient, reflecting upon and expanding one's level of comfort around discussing race, class, gender, and sexuality, and attending to "cultural opportunities" to broach and express curiosity toward culture- or identity-salient themes.

Reflecting on his own experience in therapy, clinician and researcher Jesse Owen remembered his therapist commenting that sometimes people draw on faith as a form of coping, and wondered if this was true for him (ICCE, 2020). Owen said it was not, but appreciated that his therapist broached the subject *without* assuming it was one way or the other. His therapist's willingness to ask, in a tentative and inviting way, fostered trust and safety.

Davis et al. (2018) found support for two dimensions through which cultural humility improves outcomes—"social bonds" and "social oil." "Social bonds" refers to how cultural humility regulates the level of "affinity…

that causes one to... prioritize the needs of the relationship" (p. 92). Communicating openness toward the patient's culture(s) *enhances* attachment. Conversely, microaggressions or cultural ruptures strain the alliance, and here cultural humility is a "social oil" that "buffers relationships from the deterioration that typically occurs due to traits or qualities that tend to erode relationships (e.g., competitiveness or relational power)" (p. 93). That is not to excuse when therapists (or patients) commit microaggressions, only that when reflected on and processed this protects the relationship "from 'heating up' too much when there is a potential for conflict to erupt and intensify" (p. 93). By staying open, inviting the patient's experience, and taking responsibility, the therapist facilitates a repair.

An updated research review (Zhang, Watkins et al., 2022) further supports how cultural humility enhances the alliance, reduces drop-out, improves outcomes, and lowers the frequency and impact of microaggressions (i.e., they are repaired). Some studies find the cultural humility–outcome relationship is mediated by a stronger therapeutic alliance, unconditional positive regard, and empathy, suggesting that addressing difference from a not-knowing stance facilitates "common factors" in the therapeutic relationship. Other studies reviewed suggest the salience of patients' identities—the extent to which they are central to them—moderate the impact of cultural humility. A separate study of cultural humility in psychodynamic therapy found that tailoring the *level* of attention to sociocultural issues to their *salience* for the patient enhances the alliance and outcomes (Dixon et al., 2022). Practicing a "not-knowing" stance in psychodynamic therapy was also found to foster the patient's own humility, working through reactive feelings of superiority or self-protective inferiority (Jankowski et al., 2021).

Processing cultural themes from a not-knowing stance opens patient and therapist to new ways of relating to one another and their social realities. Meta-analyses of culturally adapted psychotherapy—treatments tailored to the patient's sociocultural context—speak to this, evidencing superior outcomes over unadapted psychotherapy (Benish et al., 2011; Hall et al., 2016; Soto et al., 2018). Benish et al. (2011) found that the sole moderator of the superiority of cultural adaptation was the "adaptation of the illness myth," the explicit and implicit story a person has about their symptoms, their sociocultural consequences, and what cultural resources will help them heal (remember CMT on how the patient has an unconscious sense of what will help them). This makes psychotherapy a cultural system "that uses language to... reconstruct the client's interpretations of the world" (cited in p. 281), a *process* of negotiation rather than creating a static image of what different groups "need."

The illness myth can be evoked by inviting patients to express their beliefs about their struggles or exploring them over the course of treatment. Conveying respect establishes trust, and opens up the possibility of cocreating a new illness myth through the transaction with the therapist, between the patient and others, and between the patient and their intersecting identities. As Benish et al. (2011) put it, they "construct and reconstruct the illness explanation in a culturally congruent manner that is more adaptive, more empowering to the client, and more amenable to intervention than the client's previous understanding" (p. 287). Cultural attunement does not mean uncritically accepting the patient's myth, only that we invite it and communicate respect regardless of our agreement. This respect generates the trust necessary to explore those values more openly, and ask questions about the patient and therapist's cultural assumptions that challenge and reformulate them in more freeing ways.

Addressing culture is not a binary "on/off" switch, just as cultural issues are not "relevant" or "irrelevant," but require a fluid, evolving adaptation to the patient over time. Identity may take precedence at first, then as safety is established other issues come to the fore. Conversely, culture may be "irrelevant" initially, yet emerge as a central issue later on. If we reframe neutrality and unconditional regard not as "objectivity" but humility, not as "understanding" but openness to opacity, not as being "fixed" to one position (abstinence *or* empathy, culture is "relevant" or "irrelevant") but inhabiting and moving between a plurality of positions, then a psychodynamic stance—or *dance*—equips us to respond flexibly to the patient before us. If so, one mechanism through which psychoanalytic treatment leads to change is by modeling this fluidity, openness, and a tolerance for opacity.

Some may worry this metaphor of movement leads to "vertigo," as anxious clinicians "move around" in spurious activity, but this misunderstands the psychodynamic stance. A mind in motion must be willing to *move* from a position of activity to one of receptiveness without intervening verbally. Sometimes, we must learn to dance with the melodic stillness of therapeutic silence. That too is a "beat" in the song that requires attending to its rhythms, as research shows there are productive and obstructive forms of silence in psychotherapy (Levitt & Morrill, 2023).

Jesse Owen offers that cultural humility "is a *relational* framework" (ICCE, 2020, emphasis added), which brings up a fascinating parallel between the "not-knowing" of cultural humility and the "negative capacity" of Talia et al.'s (2020) relational research. If we read the research on attachment, culture, and status in psychotherapy through the lens of research on affiliation and status, then it stands to reason that we should attend to *both* from a not-knowing stance, attuning to what needs and desires are immanent in speech at a given moment. Put differently, attending to sociocultural matters is not a "distraction" from relationality, but its most elaborated form. Being mindful, open, and actively engaging of race, gender, sexuality, and class *builds* the therapeutic relationship and fosters a more secure attachment—communicating the patient is not just liked but valued and respected.

While there is empathy in the sense of "understanding" ("imaginary" empathy), there is a higher level of empathy that depends on *not-understanding*. If we look at the research, the highest levels of reflective functioning or mentalizing are *not* for thinking one "knows" the other's mind, but for recognizing the limitations of knowing before the opacity of the other (Fonagy et al., 1998). This opacity generates a plurality of meanings, perspectives, and possibilities the therapist remains open to and tries to evoke with the resonance of speech—I know-not the other's mind, but I desire to know without foreclosing possibilities ("symbolic" empathy). Among these possibilities, *something else* emerges from this opacity that ruptures meaning as such, is shocking, overwhelming, surprising, contrasting with how therapist and patient experience the world ("Real" empathy). "Real" empathy is precisely this willingness to tally with trauma, as Saketopoulou (2023) writes, to be "traumatophilic" as opposed to "traumatophobic." These three dimensions of "empathy," as understood here, must work in tandem, at different points in treatment and at different levels, in order for the therapeutic process to unfold.

If we are driven by unconscious processes concerned with the body's position in space, then we are "oriented" toward social positions just as much as we are oriented toward relationships. And if this orientation toward our relational and sociocultural worlds is expressed in speech—verbal and embodied—then psychoanalytically we have a tried-and-true tool for evoking those fantasies as they emerge in an organic and fluid way—*free association*.

Free Association as the Royal Road to the Social Unconscious

By free association, I am referring both to the formal invitation to "say what comes to mind," and the fact the psyche is *always* "free associating." The unconscious does not need to be "told" to associate, it does so as a matter of course. When we listen to the patient's speech with a not-knowing stance, we reflect back striking, curious, conflicted words or phrases in order to evoke other associations in their psychic network, in the process cultivating a space for surprise, "something," Scarfone (2018) writes, "for which free association seems tailor made" (p. 473).

Critical to this is what Freud called the *Einfall*, "the incidental thought, the unexpected and apparently unrelated idea; one that seems to come out of nowhere" (Scarfone, 2018, p. 473). Free association goes "against the grain" of the pleasure principle in that it challenges our avoidance to speak the unspeakable, though requiring a therapeutic relationship "secure enough… for surprise to be tolerated" (p. 473). Psychoanalytic treatment operates "as the clinically motivated reactivation—at low intensity—of ancient traumas; a somewhat controlled reopening of old wounds" (p. 474). This involves tolerating a repeated encounter that transgresses our schemas of the world, resulting in "a void of representations with its ensuing anxiety" (p. 475)—what Fanon called the zone of nonbeing—rendering the possibility of what Scarfone (2018) calls "a newly gained psychic mobility" that makes one "capable to play with—and enjoy—a newly found capacity to bind/unbind, a greater freedom to think" (p. 476).

Marriott (2018) explores Fanon in a similar manner, arguing that the revolutionary moment is "not synchronized… untimely" (p. 3). Its arrival is a force that erases just as it creates, "anti-colonialism can… signify also a blank slate" (p. 4). The refusal Fanon described suggests the revolutionary act is "necessarily self-interrupting, as irrevocably ruptured and discontinuous… a temporality diametrically opposed to that of narrative… [resisting any] schema that would reduce it to a final meaning" (p. 29). It disrupts meaning and the rush to impose it anew, offering an unbound space of renewed possibility. Via Marriott, a Fanonian interpretation of free association repositions it as a tool for evoking "a point of interruption as well as the gateway to a difficult, most urgent encounter" (p. 366).

Arnall (2019) extends this analysis of Fanon by recognizing two streams in his work, between conceptualizing change "as a sudden bursting into action that voids everything in a whirlwind of explosive energy… [versus] a dialectical overcoming of the current state of things that translationally reorganizes existing fragments into a qualitatively new configuration" (p. 61). Without necessarily resolving this tension in Fanon's work, clinically it speaks to the role of a disruptive, spontaneous emergence that unbinds our habitual ways of being *alongside* our tendency to bind, reflect, organize, and make meaning of our experience. Sometimes, if change is to be possible, out of clinical necessity the former must dismantle the latter.

Earlier we mentioned how conflict between different desires (relatedness or status) and motivational systems (conscious and unconscious) leads to worse mental health outcomes. Conversely, what is called the "referential process" facilitates congruence between these desires (Schultheiss & Strasser, 2012). The referential process is our ability to a) translate non-verbal bodily experience into verbal representations through labeling or "naming," and b) transform verbal representations into non-verbal experience through imagery and imagination (Bucci, 2021). Imagine someone who says "I liked the actor in that movie," versus "I was really touched by how the actor conveyed so much emotion in his face. When he found out the villain was his father, I felt his shock like a punch in the gut." The latter is more vibrant, moving back and forth between somatic experience and verbal expression ("feeling touched," "a punch in the gut").

Free association foments neural connectivity between verbal and non-verbal systems, and thus greater referential activity (Novac & Blinder, 2021). Negri et al. (2022) compared participants narrating life stories face to face versus when the interviewer sat out of view, with the latter evidencing *higher* referential activity—there's something to be said for the couch after all. A recent review of free association research showed how it can evoke a person's associative networks, including biases related to race, gender, sexuality, and class (Richie et al., 2022). Research also validates Fanon's study on free association, revealing how free association can evoke classist, sexist and racist schemas in an emergent way (Diniz et al., 2020; File et al., 2019; Kanyicska Belán & Popper, 2023; Techio et al., 2019). Free association, then, integrates verbal and non-verbal systems, allowing the body's positionality in space to be articulated, including how we are oriented interpersonally and in our social world. It facilitates greater flexibility and psychic freedom while symbolizing—Freire might say, concientizing—our world.

"The deployment of free association," Rabeyron and Massicotte (2020) write, "[allows] for a necessary relaxation of the psyche, thereby reviving processes of symbolization" (p. 9). The therapeutic alliance provides a containing space "for an increase in free energy allowing the subject to safely make prediction errors and confront surprise effects" (p. 11). Holmes and Nolte (2019) advocate for a therapeutic disruption that yields a "structured complexity… to increase the repertoire of [the patient's] models of themselves and their environment" (p. 10). This broadens the patient and therapist's capacity for "risk-taking and 'negative capability' [e.g. a not-knowing stance] needed for psychic change" (p. 10). Free association helps us unbind and rework our ways of being, facilitating the "simulation of future possibilities" (Novac, 2022, p. 2).

By giving us permission to dream possibilities and a different world, free association has potential as a decolonial praxis (Beshara, 2022), tapping into diverse streams of creativity and connection, bringing them into dialogue so the body can "speak" and the mind can "hear." From speech a new synergy emerges, a new song that expands older ensembles. Novac (2022) cites Jill Gentile's reflections on free association and democracy:

> The ironic definitional "rule" of free association was that *there was no rule to follow and no one's rule*. If free association was to prevail, the patient had to bypass conventional rules of conventional censorship, ceding herself to the impetus yet also imperial authority to desirous voice, her unconscious desire. (cited in p. 7, emphasis added)

Free association taps into energies, imaginings, and forms of play that reconfigure how we are in the world, allowing us to imagine—and enact—a different society, a different arrangement which demands current structures be torn down so new ones can come into being.

Integrating the Relational and Political in Psychoanalysis

To engage with the horizontality of affiliation and the verticality of hierarchy requires us to shift how we *hear* free association, dynamically "switching types of mentalization" (Liotti & Gilbert, 2011, p. 14). Mentalizing attachment may mean reflecting on relational needs for care and comfort, but mentalizing social rank may imply reflecting on our power, social position, cultural values, and need to be respected and valued. We must complement our listening for verbal and non-verbal markers of closeness and intimacy (or lack thereof) with listening for the verbal and non-verbal markers of hierarchy, positionality, and status. And then, inverting Lacan, use the semantic resonance of our remarks to "play on the symbols of power" that slip through the patient's speech and behavior, and be open to our patients doing the same to *us*.

Attending to how the patient's speech and behavior unconsciously communicates something about their position in society, cultural values, and fantasies breaks us out of the theoretical and technical impasse discussed in Chapter 1—do we "bring up" identity or wait for the patient to do so? The social is always already *there* in the consulting room, and the consulting room is always already *there* within the social, immanent in the words we use to communicate about our world. By punctuating or reflecting back signifiers and symbols of verticality, hierarchy, and power in speech, we evoke associative networks that draw out the verticality of the social alongside the horizontality of the relational.

Seeing and Not-Seeing Race: The Case of "Berto"

Here I return to the case of "Berto," mentioned in the beginning of this book. Berto was a young adult, Spanish-speaking, Afro-Latinx, working-class cis-gender man presenting to treatment with severe anxiety and depression, substance use and self-harm. At the start of treatment Berto was unemployed, living in a one-bedroom apartment with his mother, and had recently dropped out of college. He struggled with intense, on-again-off-again romantic relationships, conflict at various jobs, and ongoing conflict with his mother which belied his substance use to cope with anger and distress. Over the initial assessment, I engaged Berto in collaboratively developing a treatment plan around safety and vocational/educational rehabilitation (see Yeomans et al., 2015), including a plan for managing his self-harm between sessions and attending a weekly Narcotics Anonymous meeting alongside individual therapy. We also agreed he would attend an educational support program to return to college.

During our first session Berto alluded to his immigration experience as a child and his mother's comments putting him "down" around his dark skin or "bad hair." These allusions led me to wonder how race may play out in our therapeutic relationship. I expressed appreciation for his wanting to work with me as a Latinx Spanish speaker, though I wondered what it would be like for him to work with me as a white Puerto Rican man. Laughing, Berto reassured me that race is not a factor in his life. At first, I conveyed appreciation and respect for Berto's position while also noting to myself that *he* was the one who brought up the topic of race. Was he, perhaps, conflicted about the role of race in his life? If so, what purpose did this conflict serve? Was this a test to see if race was a subject that could be explored between us?

In our first year of treatment, we focused on conflicts between Berto and his mother, in dating, with peers at his college prep program, and co-workers at part-time jobs. Whenever he felt I did not take enough of his "side" in an argument he became angry with me, resulting in ruptures we processed together. Often, I became aware of times in which in bringing a different perspective I strayed from his experience and made him feel abandoned. Though owning this behavior helped repair our relationship, at other times I felt him use these moments to assert power in our relationship, and stood my ground even as I verbally empathized with how difficult it can be to hear a different perspective. Through this dance, Berto learned that a difference in perspective did not spell doom for a relationship, which generalized to other relationships across vocational, familial, and intimate domains, helping reduce his self-harm and substance use. Berto was surprised by my willingness to reflect on my behavior, and my openness to say "*No*, I disagree, actually." Both created space for Berto to negotiate his needs in more fulfilling ways.

Although we engaged in meaningful work over that first year, I noticed over time that he periodically brought up the subject of race, only to dismiss it. My attempts to broach the topic were unsuccessful, leaving me wondering if Berto was testing whether I would approach the topic of race or withdraw from it. Since trying to broach the subject made him withdraw further, I shifted my stance to one informed by Lacanian approaches to the patient's speech, filtered through a Fanonian lens. I thought if I inhabited a "not-knowing" stance in which I did not presume Berto's meaning but allowed him to relate to his own words, something might shift.

This came to a head at the beginning of our second year of treatment. Berto was exploring an argument with his mother around his moving out now that he had stable employment—a conversation from which his mother recoiled. While he harbored a lot of anger toward her, in this session he tapped into his ambivalence, the fact that he loved her deeply despite her limitations. Berto then said the following (I provide the original Spanish and its translation):

(Spanish)	(English)
"Yo... *mi amo*—perdon, perdon quiero decir...yo *amo a mi* mama."	"I... *my master*—sorry, sorry I mean... I *love my* mom"

Both Berto and I were caught off guard, surprised by the "Fanonian slip" that came through his lips, and all the implications that came alive in the room.

The word *amo* in Spanish has an ambivalent meaning depending on context and dialect. The Afro-Cuban poet Nancy Morejón, for example, deploys and subverts this signifying chain in her poem "*Amo a mi amo*" ("I love my master"), tracing the experience of an enslaved woman working through her subjugation to her master, ultimately killing him. Cuban scholar Miller (2005) comments on this tension between *amo/*"(I) love" as a first-person active verb expressing love for another, and *amo/*"master" as the masculine noun signifying the "owner" of a person. According to Miller, Morejón's poem "*Amo a mi amo*" "produces significant semantic dissonance, because it is difficult for contemporary readers to assimilate 'love' or the action of loving with the unequal relationship between slave and master" (p. 7). Perhaps Berto's unconscious was writing us a poem? Perhaps slips are the very poetry of the unconscious, reverberating with diverse meanings, pointing toward a scene we are always already embedded in. To be clear, I did not know what this meant at the time. I just reflected back this word as a question.

Me: *Amo*? [Love/master?]
   Berto: Yeah, I think about the memories we had back in [*my home country*], raising me in grandfather's *hacienda*.

Hacienda—another word just as evocative but no less fraught. Depending, again, on dialect and culture, *hacienda* could simply mean a big house in the countryside, or a farm. But it can also mean plantation. I felt my mind rushing with associations carrying the weight of 500 years. I reflected this word back as well.

Me: *Hacienda*? [big house/farm/plantation]
   Berto: Oh, it was this *big hacienda*…

He went on to paint an idyllic, rustic picture of life back in his home country with his mother and grandfather, raising chickens, milking cows, and riding horses. Enthralled by his description, I was struck by an obvious fact. Berto was describing a massive estate, implying a level of wealth he and his mother did not currently enjoy. Also lurking in the background was the history of slavery, colonialism, and capitalism in Latin America, their associations rushing through my mind like a hurricane. I limited myself to a simple question.

Me: I see, what social class was your family?
   Berto: Well… *they* were middle class, very class conscious. Like it often felt like *I* had to do everything right…

He started describing his grandfather's brutal punishment whenever he "stepped out of line" of class expectations, not dressing in an "appropriate" way or not showing a respectful enough demeanor. He showed no awareness that earlier in treatment he had denied any experience of physical abuse, and related these beatings, implements of punishment, and episodes with a very flat affect. At one point he repeated the phrase "I had to do everything right"/ "*Todo tenia que ser a la perfeccion.*" I repeated the implied contingency— "If you didn't"/"*Porque si no…*" to which he replied, "Then you're of lower class"/"*Entonces eres de clase baja.*"
   Berto became quiet, with silence between us for a few beats. Finally, he continued, "I guess that's why grandpa didn't approve of dad, who was— *no Negro pero oscurito* [Not *Black*, but a *little dark*]—more than mom."

This was the first time Berto brought up race, not as something happening "out there," but as a force within own life. Suddenly I became aware that although I knew what Berto looked like—he was a dark-skinned man—and now learned that his father was darker than his mom, I still was not clear where he "sat" between them. It was almost like he implied some hierarchical space or continuum organized around skin color. His statement that his father was *no Negro pero oscurito*, "Not *Black*, but a *little dark*" was also curious. In many Spanish dialects, the diminutive form of a word can mean its opposite. For example, if I say "*Voy ahora*," "I'm coming now," it usually means I will be there soon. But if I say "*Voy ahorita*," "I'm coming now-ish," I am definitely arriving three hours late (or not going to show up at all!). Berto's use of the diminutive form—"A *little* dark"—softened the description of his father as "Black" even as it evoked the opposite, the image of a dark-skinned man like himself.

"And *where* were you?"/"*Y donde estabas tu?*" I asked Berto, implicitly asking where he "placed" himself between his mother and father. Berto began to weep, sobbing in a way I had not seen before. We sat with his sorrow for a while, and finally I asked Berto what came up for him. He realized this was the first time he had connected his grandfather's emotional and physical abuse to his Blackness, and how his resemblance to his father—also an Afro-Latinx man—played into this. It allowed us to have a conversation about race, colorism, class, and love, and how these played into his family dynamics. His maternal grandmother was a Brown woman of indigenous descent, whereas his grandfather was Creole and white. As in many Latin American countries, the demand to *mejorar la raza* or "improve the race" simultaneously called for interracial relationships while demanding lighter and white-looking offspring, with "whitening" tied directly to upward mobility. Or as Fanon (1963) put it, "you are rich because you are white, you are white because you are rich" (p. 40).

Love, money, and contempt textured Berto's family intergenerationally. While his mother also suffered his grandfather's wrath as someone who was Brown and seen as "lesser than," the two joined in their contempt for Berto's father. Berto's mother felt the same mixture of contempt and love for him, feelings intimately tied to their family's *downward* mobility, as they were losing economic and political prominence in their country, triggering anxieties in Berto's extended family around their social standing. His grandfather's fortunes took a turn for the worse, but the scapegoat was already at hand—the "polluting" of their family line through Berto's father had "sunk" their position. Berto's parents broke up shortly thereafter, and he found himself growing up without his father. Many sessions afterward were spent mourning this loss and its embeddedness in a world of race, class, gender, and sexuality. In the process, there was further improvement in Berto's functioning, leading in turn to a rapprochement with his mother, allowing both to mourn the losses they experienced not only relationally, but societally.

How did we accomplish this from a technical point of view? By repeating back key words and phrases fraught with ambivalent meanings (*amo, hacienda*, etc.), the sonic quality of these words resonated with other words, meanings, and experiences in Berto's wider associative network. As already mentioned, broaching race directly led to greater avoidance and minimizing of the subject on Berto's part, deepening an enactment in which race was both raised and dismissed, and which attempting to address with relational processing only further entrenched. However, in discussing his feelings of love and hate toward his mom, Berto was tapping into unconscious associations between love and whiteness and hate and anti-Blackness cultivated in his childhood, especially through his grandfather's emotional and physical abuse, and the relationship between Berto's skin color and his resemblance to his father.

These fraught associations sought expression through Berto's "Fanonian slip," with *amo* referencing his love toward his mother and the ways in which he felt dominated by her and his grandfather's wrath. Repeating back this word indirectly stimulated other associations in the network—between his Blackness and his father's, how this positioned them as objects of derision, his deep yearning to receive his mother's love, the sense of loss at growing up without his father. Reflecting back these words and phrases strengthened the salience of these associations, leading them to irrupt into Berto's consciousness in a surprising manner that disrupted his mappings of self and other.

These interventions also opened space for us to address how race textured our transference–countertransference relation. His choosing me as a therapist belied a desire to talk about race, and the fantasy that working with a white Puerto Rican would prevent its expression. In simultaneously raising and disavowing race, he was enacting an act of provocation and resistance to me as a "stand-in" for his Creole grandfather. He wished for me to welcome and even pursue his interest in discussing race, my curiosity and broaching of the subject repeatedly communicating my sincere interest in engaging it with him. At the same time, the visibility of race for him and his father made him a target of physical and emotional violence from which he needed to protect himself by performing a certain dismissiveness towards it. In dismissing race as a factor in his life, he was both identifying with the white colonial perpetrator, while also hoping for its disruption. The use of punctuation put him in a situation in which he had to reckon with parts of himself that sought expression.

A Case of "Falling": Maurice

"Maurice," (pseudonym) was a young adult white cisheterosexual male entrepreneur who sought psychotherapy for anxiety and difficulty managing his anger at work and in relationships. He presented to treatment following a series of failed romantic relationships, alongside conflict at work that made him worried about losing his job. We contracted for treatment, which included individual therapy as well as attending an anger management group between sessions. Mindful that my practice was predominantly young adult working- and middle-class people of color—my website showed this very prominently—I wondered about Maurice's interest in seeking treatment with me as a Puerto Rican man, so I asked him. He replied that he was "very liberal," and had friends of "every color, race, and creed," thus our differences would not "be an issue." Although I understood what he was saying, I felt a twinge in my gut. He seemed eager to do the work, with some insight into how his competitiveness at work and in relationships was driving his troubles. I wondered, however, if he saw me as a "safer" therapist of color given my phenotype, hair, and complexion, *legible* as white.

In treatment, Maurice explored his difficulties in his romantic relationships with women, noting that he often pursued very career-driven partners with whom he would then feel insecure and "lesser than" financially. No matter their attempts to reassure him that he "was enough," he became increasingly competitive with his girlfriends, trying to "one-up" them until they became exhausted and ended the relationship. This very much related to stress and disappointment in his job and industry, where he often felt he "wasn't where I *should* be." I was struck by the verticality of this language, reflecting back "where you *should* be?" This prompted him to vent about how he always felt "passed over" in promotions, which would often go to "the wrong people." "The wrong people?" I reflected back. "Yeah," he continued, "you know, people who don't deserve it. *Those* kind of people." I bristled, which Maurice likely picked up on. Before I could explore this further he quickly changed topics back to his dating life. In that abrupt shift, a grammar of *who* he had in mind as undeserving lay unspoken.

A few weeks after this exchange Maurice came in for our appointment in the wake of the "Unite the Right" neo-fascist, white supremacist rally in Charlottesville, Virginia. The rally had been on both of our minds. "Did you hear about this?!" he said, agitated, "It's these left extremists that are the problem!" He went on a tirade endorsing Trump's remark that there were "fine people on both sides," while expressing fear of "antifa" and Black Lives Matter protests. The response by leftists to the fascist rally reminded him of the Occupy Wall Street protests occupying Zuccotti Park by the financial district in New York City where he worked. I listened to Maurice with anger, anxiety, and disbelief in equal measure. Was he truly afraid of the Occupy Wall Street protests? Was he, a "liberal" white man, siding with neo-Nazis to provoke me?

Suddenly, Maurice related a dream from the previous night. He described it like a scene out of a George Romero zombie film, where the "wretched of the earth" (my words) broke into the high-rise building he lived in (in the dream). He ran frantically up each floor with the "hoard" flooding up after him. Once he reached the rooftop, the floor collapsed and he "fell down into the darkness." I was equal parts angry and bemused listening to Maurice's dream. How do I even begin exploring this? It was only when he made the passing comment "Well, I don't know how *you* feel about this, but…" that I picked up on his allusion to our relationship. "You might be worried about my reaction to this dream," I reflected. "I feel like…" he began, "I worry deep down you *hate me* as a white guy with money." "That I hate you… as a white man with money?" "And wanna, like, bring me down." Struck by his bluntness, I searched myself to make sure I answered honestly. Without question I was anxious and angry at the possibility that he was a Trump supporter and an overt racist, though before this session I cannot say I felt hatred toward him. Though I was aware of his privilege, my role was trying to build a relationship that best "served his needs." It was this association that caught my attention. Not "meet," "understand," "care," or "help him meet" his needs. "*Serve*"—the word hung in my mind.

It was almost as if I saw my role, unconsciously, as that of "serving" him as a wealthy white man. Was this a reflection of the power and privilege he held relative to me in this society, a tacit sign of submission? Was I more comfortable with a transactional relationship, an emotional distance to buttress my own vulnerability? I started to become aware of how power and care became confused in our relationship, our differences across class and ethnicity interlocking with my caretaking role in a way that prevented true intimacy. But Maurice was not quite operating like a dominant figure—he was *afraid* I looked down on him and wanted to "take him down a peg." Seeing him not only as someone inhabiting a structural position (white, male, wealthy, etc.), but as someone who was afraid thawed my anger and anxiety. I reflected, "I wonder if you also fear I'm not open to your anxiety of losing your place."

Maurice was struck by my question. After a pause, he let out a nervous laugh, almost shaking a bit. "I don't... I don't know why," he started to say, "that's making me so emotional." "What's coming up right now?" I asked. Maurice's face was pained, vulnerable in a way I had not seen before. He started to talk about his childhood growing up in a working-class Irish-Italian neighborhood, perpetually put down by his father for never getting the highest grades or—as an adult—the top-paying jobs. Whenever Maurice "fell short," his father derided him, saying he was not "raised to be a welfare queen." His father was himself the son of Irish immigrants who faced working-class exploitation and ethnic marginalization from the American Dream. Yet as the racial politics of the United States shifted with anti-Blackness as its fulcrum, so too his family's values shifted. For Maurice, pursuing the American Dream meant distancing himself from Blackness as a stand-in for what his father and American society deemed unwanted, undeserving, and alien, even if at the same time he was never quite "white" enough to earn his father's love. Whiteness—symbolically associated with power and wealth—was a performance he experienced himself as always falling short from. From Latin to "North" America, Fanon's words continue to ring true. To be white is to be rich, to be rich is to be white—unless you fall short of its dizzying heights. The "blank check" of whiteness can sometimes bounce.

As Maurice filled in this aspect of his childhood, I shared with him my complex feelings around his vulnerabilities and our relationship as a cross-cultural dyad. In exploring the subtle exchanges of our relationship—my feelings of being in "servitude" to him as a Puerto Rican man, his feeling that he needed to control others to earn their love—we realized that to him I was simultaneously an undeserving racial other "clawing" at him from the bottom, and at the same time the white father who shamed and ridiculed him for never quite reaching "the top." The combination of my racial ambiguity as a white Puerto Rican allowed him to position me in his social unconscious as either a "lesser than" racial other to be beaten back "down," or a vicious father who "lorded over him" as someone who was *just* about to fall all the way down to the bottom, the relational and political blending and blurring as part of his social cognitive "gestalt." As we explored these dynamics, Maurice became more self-aware in his relationships and his competitive feelings and insecurities with women diminished, allowing him to form more meaningful and intimate relationships. Over time, as we reflected on our relationship alongside his political beliefs, Maurice became more aware of the pain and confusion that fueled his attraction to regressive ideologies, leading to a shift in his politics and how he saw the world.

A Case of Being Stuck in the "Middle": Rafa

"Rafa" (pseudonym) was a young adult Latinx woman who sought treatment due to work-related stress, anxiety, and immigration trauma. She worked in a non-profit organization which, although committed to progressive causes, was experiencing intense conflict between the (predominantly white) "old guard," and newer (and more diverse) hires such as herself. This included a very intense, public argument with one of her white supervisors, who ridiculed and attacked her in front of their colleagues during a staff meeting. Although a Human Resources complaint was initiated by her and her colleagues, she experienced the process as more akin to a police investigation in which she felt like "the criminal," "interrogated" time and again about the incident in a way that felt like attempts to undermine her. The experience triggered older traumas related to her immigration experience coming into the United States. After surviving violence and persecution coming into this country, Rafa underwent a grueling asylum process which involved successive meetings with mental health practitioners, lawyers, and government officials. With the help of extended family, Rafa was able to procure a visa and later US citizenship. Yet the experience cast its shadow over her life, with recurrent fears of immigration officials sending her and her family back into a context of recurrent political strife.

In inviting her to explore the sociocultural determinants of her presenting problem—racial conflict at work, the influence of previous immigration trauma—I also invited Rafa to tell me more about her values. Alongside her nationality, Rafa described herself as a "Brown and proud" Latina committed to racial justice and immigration reform. I wondered to myself about her experience of race before coming to the States, alongside how she navigated the white space of her organization. As I was reflecting internally on this, she remarked on how much she appreciated "finding a *Brown* therapist who can understand my culture." I blinked for a moment, taking in her words. On the one hand I understood what she was saying—she felt comfortable with me as a Latino therapist. At the same time, was her including me within the category "Brown" a form of reassurance, an erasure of our difference? I did not question it at the time, though something about it stood out to me. Session after session we processed her experience of the tensions at work, and how these evoked aspects of her immigration trauma.

In a later session, Rafa discussed her anger at witnessing a group of police officers accosting a young Black boy in her neighborhood, leading to a broader discussion of recent and ongoing incidents of police murder of Black men and women. In discussing this topic, I noticed Rafa become increasingly anxious. When I drew attention to her affect, she disclosed that she was experiencing flashbacks of police violence she had witnessed in her home country. We slowed down and used a combination of reflection, tracking the anxiety in her body, and distress reduction skills to help her regulate the emotions coursing through her body. As she came to feel more grounded, Rafa began associating to how she engaged in solidarity with Black people by serving as a mentor to teenage Black girls at her church, supporting them in pursuing a career in different human services fields. Yet in discussing this she seemed to become *more* anxious. I noticed anxiety rising within myself in turn, along with a sense of confusion and disorientation. "I don't mean to interrupt you," I intervened, "but I'm wondering if we can slow down a bit—I'm noticing some… kind of tension in the air, do you relate to that at all?" Rafa seemed to not quite register my question—or perhaps she did—switching the topic back to work again for the first time in the session, talking about an ongoing conflict with her co-worker Patty.

Patty, one of the few Black women in their organization, had told Rafa about her frustration with her and other Latine colleagues who were silent when their white supervisors would single out Black co-workers and especially Black women. I was struck by the parallels with Rafa's own situation, as much by her co-worker's experience of *her* passivity. Rafa described how she became defensive, retorting that "we're in this together" as people of color. Then why, Patty asked, had Rafa not stood up for her when she was picked on by their white supervisors? "What was it like hearing Patty's question?" I asked. "Some people just want to get ahead, you know?" she replied. "Get *ahead*?" I reflected back, which prompted Rafa to elaborate on how we people of color need to stick together and not "tear each other down," but that some people can be "ungrateful" when receiving support, often using it as a stepping stone to "try to get ahead." This language, implying that Patty was somehow trying to "get ahead" of Rafa, kept being repeated in her speech. Something about it, again, made me anxious. When this motif emerged again later in the session ("*Some people* just want to *get ahead*"), I reflected back a present yet unspoken phrase—"Get ahead of *you*." Rafa paused for a moment, then offered a nervous smile, "You probably think I'm a horrible person."

I was surprised by this response. "… a horrible person?" I queried. Rafa began to articulate how she wanted to be an ally and improve working conditions for people "below me… so long as they didn't *pass* me." This singular word, "pass," along with the spatial metaphor of those "below me," evoked a series of associations in me. Who was "passing" her from below? Was there, perhaps, something she was also "passing" into? I punctuated the word with a question, "pass?" This opened up a conversation about her fear of being "passed by" Black people at her job, alongside the emergence of a subtle desire to "pass into" a different position at her job that would simultaneously bring a higher income, as well as place her alongside her white co-workers and supervisors—a fantasized "passing into" whiteness and middle-class status. Although her Brown skin had made her a target of racism and discrimination, her being lighter also emerged as a source of privilege, which she had been tacitly aware of.

As we explored her anti-Blackness and fantasies regarding her positionality, I could feel her deep shame—the way she averted her eyes, her body "shrinking in" on itself, the depth in her voice—becoming aware I did not address her fear that I thought she was "a horrible person." Why had I missed that? I got in touch with my own anxiety around colorism in Puerto Rico, how it textured my relationships yet was rendered silent by the discourse of *mestizaje*. Was I positioning myself as an "ally" to Patty to avoid my own shame around my "Latino whiteness?" To elide how skin color was silent within my own family? I shared the following:

> I'm mindful that we're focusing on you, and how ashamed you feel despite your experience of racism. It puts it squarely on you, you're the "horrible person," as if I'm somehow "pure." I know that growing up in Puerto Rico, I was privileged as a white Puerto Rican, even as it put down Puerto Ricans who were darker skin and Black…

Before I could finish speaking, this disclosure hit on something for Rafa, who began sobbing uncontrollably. I was taken aback, as I could not understand what moved her so. She described for the first time that she had not witnessed violence in her home country only as a victim. She disclosed that white, lighter-skin, and Brown members of her family *perpetrated* violence against her Black family members as part of the ruling party's military police. This recontextualized Rafa's anxieties around race and positionality, allowing us to explore her experience as both victim and bystander, a victim of racism and someone who also benefited due to her lighter skin.

My owning and disclosing my own history of white and colorist privilege in Puerto Rico opened space for Rafa to explore her own racism and privilege alongside the ways in which she was also subject to racism and political violence. In processing how power, privilege, and positionality impacted her ability to be present in solidarity with her Black co-workers, she was able to make a repair to Patty and engage in more effective interactions with their organization, leading to a robust union renegotiation to address labor conditions alongside more effective grievance and diversity policies. This also allowed unspoken aspects of our relationship to be named. We became aware that in declaring herself as "Brown and proud," she wished that I also identify as "Brown" as a Latino man. This would effectively erase any differences in color and phenotype between us, and make my whiteness explicit as a source of love and hate.

A Case of Seeing and Being Seen at the Bottom: Jessie

"Jessie" (pseudonym) smiled in a way that aimed to put others—including me—at ease, even as it left me wondering what she was really thinking and feeling at times. She was a young adult cisheterosexual Black woman of African American descent working in the tech sector, an affable and charming person whom friends described as a "jokester." She sought treatment after a recent breakup with a Black man she similarly described as a "joker" (I noticed the ambivalently toned nature of her adjective). While they connected over shared interests and culture, there was an underlying sense that he did not take her feelings seriously, dismissing them with an off-handed joke as if they were not real or legitimate. I observed the "storytelling" quality of how she told her story, as if she was building up to a punchline, though it was marred with heartbreak. As she explained how the relationship "fizzled out in a funny way," ending without any communication or closure, I said "I appreciate you breaking this down for me. It does seem kinda funny how things turned out, *and yet*, I imagine how painful it was to not have your feelings taken seriously." Her smile wavered for a moment. "Yeah," she laughed to bring the mask back up, "I feel like I need to learn how to take *myself* more seriously."

Early on in our work, as protests against police brutality filled the streets of New York, we talked about her feelings toward the demonstrations, often inviting her to explore her experience of race in our work together. Jessie laughed. "As a Black woman, I know racism is real," she once said, "but I don't really think about race *like that*." "Like… *what*?" I queried. "It's not really a thing I experience often, or with people, y'know?" I was struck by the language—racism is *not really* something she experiences *often*, or *with people*. Is it something she *really* experiences *sometimes*, *with* people? I made a mental note, following up by reflecting "Race may not really come up here between us." I tried to stay within her experience, while implying, paradoxically, that perhaps it *may* come up here, between us. Jessie made a dismissive gesture with her hand, "Oh, I know you're a light-skin brother with a caramel center!" I chuckled at her describing me this way—it was funny—though felt like making me laugh was a misdirection. The laughter and humor served a function to reduce tension and conflict—but at what cost? I did not want to assume her experience so I did not pursue it further at the time, even as I wondered if laughter signaled a rupture, a naming and avoidance of race on both our parts.

As treatment progressed, we became aware of Jessie's ever-present fear that if others "got too close," they would see all her flaws and leave her. Between others in life and the two of us, we explored how her humor was a tool to devalue herself and keep others at a distance. If others cannot get too close, they cannot abandon her—the cost of this compromise being real intimacy. In a different session, Jessie explored an incident with a white co-worker at her job, stating "I think he was a *little bit* racist" in passing. "A little bit?" I invited her to expand further. "Well, you know," she said with a laugh, "Black people always make things about race!" In line with our discussions about her use of humor, I reflected, "I'm mindful that here again, between us, is a joke. What would it be like if we valued what you're saying?" "No, no, I hear you," Jessie replied with a deep sigh. She started talking about how her colleagues at work, especially white co-workers, seemed to not "see" her, jesting "How can I be invisible when I got these jokes?".

The juxtaposition of Jessie's dilemma was striking. She could be outgoing, the "life of the party" who drew others in, reflecting an underlying wish to be loved and accepted. At the same time her humor kept others from getting *too* close, as closeness triggered fears of abandonment. "I wonder if joking," I interpreted, "lets the world know you exist in a way it can accept you—by disappearing." "It feels weird to be ignored," she replied, "as if I just didn't matter." Her quotidian smile disappeared in a way I had not seen before. I felt my face contorting with hers, noticing her throat tightening, her body folding, hands to face, chest heaving without tears, her body convulsing. I leaned toward her, clasping my hands, just accompanying her in this moment. After some silence, Jessie looked up, "Does seeing me like this scare you?" I am not quite sure what about her question impacted me. I thought about the questions surrounding my body growing up. What do people *see* when they see me? Someone white? Non-white? "Brown?" What was *I*? *Where* was I? I felt the colony on my skin, my Puerto Ricanness a moving target. "Is it possible," I asked, "you want me to *see and not see* you?" "I don't know," Jessie replied, "I want you to see me, but not... see me? Like I want you to see through me." "Through you?" "I wish my skin was transparent." We explored how Jessie wished I see "through" her, bypassing her existence as a Black woman, and how being seen was welcoming yet carried a dangerous vulnerability. She also saw me and my whiteness more clearly.

Jessie took another deep breath as a memory came to mind. She remembered being in class in middle school, one of the few Black children at her school. She raised her hand with excitement, waiting for the teacher to call on her to answer a question, yet she was ignored. Jessie was confused, so she raised her hand ever higher, almost jumping in her seat until the teacher called on a white student next to her. Later that afternoon, she told her mother about the incident. Her mother held her close, reassuring her that "the world can't handle a smart, beautiful girl like you." Jessie's mother spoke with her father, and the two decided to bring this to the school's principal. The following week, her family met with the principal and her teacher after school while she sat in the hallway. Her friends noticed her sitting outside the principal's office and worried that she was in trouble. Jessie became afraid, overwhelmed with anxiety. She felt a gap open between herself and her predominantly non-Black peers. She bridged the gap with a joke.

"Ugh," she rolled her eyes, "the parentals are worried I flunked math or whatever." One joke led to another, her anxiety dissipated in the company of her friends. "You made them feel safe," I told Jessie. "I didn't want them to *know*," she replied. "Know…?" "That I was there because I'm Black." Jessie had grown up in the aftermath of Trayvon Martin's murder by George Zimmerman, a white Latino who appointed himself judge, jury, and executioner on behalf of white supremacy. Her being one of the few Black kids in her middle school made her both invisible and hyper-visible, especially in the aftermath of Zimmerman's acquittal. Her joking and stressing sameness between us as people of color was how she held at bay associations that periodically came to mind between my ethnicity, gender, and my *race*. As we explored this in our relationship and elsewhere in her life, Jessie realized that even when hiding herself she was always in a fundamental sense unsafe. "The world can't handle me," she said, "but I can't even handle myself." "Handle yourself?" Tears welled up in her eyes, "Why can't I love me how my parents love me?" "You came to believe that if you make me and others feel safe," I reflected, "*then* maybe the world will love you." "Even when it doesn't," she replied.

As we deepened this exploration, Jessie began to acknowledge her anger in the face of the world, "Why do I feel so angry when I had so much love?" "Love doesn't make sense in a world that hates you," I reflected. Staying close to Jessie's experience of feeling hated as a Black woman meant tolerating and inviting other feelings that at first did not "make sense." Although her parents were loving and responsive, she began to tap into feelings of anger toward them for not being able to protect her from an anti-Black world. At the same time, we also explored anger toward me as a white Latino man privileged by that world. While the social unconscious can be expressed through ruptures, it does not depend on them for its ever-present immanence. Put concretely, I do not need to do *anything*, consciously or unconsciously, to be structurally privileged by my gender identity, the color of my skin, or my class position. Jessie and I were processing not only her feelings about my interpersonal behavior per se, but her feelings around the structural position I inhabit. More precisely, her feelings around a rupture that preceded us, emplacing our bodies in different positions of status and privilege. Enactment is sufficient, but not necessary to be implicated in systems of oppression.

Inviting these feelings helped Jessie mourn the fantasy her parents could fully protect her from the world, while facilitating her reconnecting with the strength and resilience offered by their love. Our ability to make space for her feelings—around race, love, power, and closeness—increased Jessie's ability to "take [herself] seriously" and practice greater assertiveness in her professional and personal lives. In her dating life, Jessie began setting limits with a new partner, stating incisively that her feelings were "not a joke." To her surprise, expressing herself so valiantly with someone she yearned to be close to "drew the best" out of him, an act of power and vulnerability that deepened their relationship. At work, this also manifested itself in her being a presence that was respected, and not afraid to set limits. Our work was nearing its close.

We processed these gains at the end of our therapeutic relationship, as we processed the relationship itself. As we neared the end of the session, Jessie asked a question that caught me off guard—"How would you feel if I was shot by the police?" This was no joke. It provoked me, but it also did not feel like a provocation, more like she was working something out. I took a deep breath, "I'd be devastated. I can't fathom losing you like that and be powerless to stop it." Jessie nodded, "I was always afraid of people truly seeing me. Would they leave me? See me as lesser than?" "Feeling seen felt dangerous," I replied. "I wonder if my parents also felt that powerlessness, that same danger," she continued, "doing what they could to protect me even though they couldn't. But you do it anyway. That's love."

Reflection Questions

- One finding from this review is that the unconscious "perceives" external reality first, and later cues in consciousness to provide secondary feedback. How can understanding this relationship between conscious and unconscious inform our clinical practice? What would it mean to consider that for our patients (and ourselves) it is unconscious schemas, fears, and anxieties that "read the world" first, before any capacity for reflection can be brought to bear? How might it change our practice to consider that when we speak, it is the patient's unconscious that listens first?

- A recurring theme across this book is the tension between establishing safe enough conditions for change and evoking a therapeutically disruptive "surprise" that shakes up how patient and therapist relate to each other and the world. How do you think about this balance between "meeting the patient where they are" and engaging in a process of change? Between regulating emotional intensity versus heightening it? What are your fears and concerns about this process? How do you know when your patients (or you) are ready for change?
- One technical recommendation of this chapter is to shift how we listen to patients moment to moment, tracking themes, key words or phrases related to attachment alongside themes related to status and identity. And then, reflect them back to stimulate the patient's associative network, allowing thoughts and feelings around these concerns—especially status and identity—to emerge organically for exploration and discussion. What would it be like to listen to patients (and people in general) with this framework in mind? To practice repeating those words and phrases back, and seeing what emerges? What might be some challenges of practicing this way?

Further Reading

The Evidence Base for Psychoanalytic Theory and Ideas
- Cieri, F., Carhart-Harris, R. L., Mathys, C., Turnbull, O., & Solms, M. (2023). Frontiers in psychodynamic neuroscience. *Frontiers in Human Neuroscience, 17,* 1170480.
- Weinberger, J., & Stoycheva, V. (2019). *The unconscious: Theory, research, and clinical implications.* Guilford Publications.

The Evidence Base for Psychoanalytic Treatment
- Leichsenring, F., Abbass, A., Heim, N., Keefe, J. R., Kisely, S., Luyten, P., Rabung, S., & Steinert, C. (2023). The status of psychodynamic psychotherapy as an empirically supported treatment for common mental disorders—An umbrella review based on updated criteria. *World Psychiatry, 22*(2), 286–304.
- Leuzinger-Bohleber, M., Solms, M., & Arnold, S. E. (Eds.). (2020). *Outcome research and the future of psychoanalysis: Clinicians and researchers in dialogue.* Routledge.

The Evidence Base for Cultural Competence/Humility
- Anders, C., & Kivlighan, D. M., III. (2023). Identity salience: An intersectional approach to understanding multicultural processes and outcomes in psychotherapy. *Journal of Counseling Psychology, 70,* 477–485.
- Asnaani, A. (2023). *A cultural humility and social justice approach to psychotherapy: Seven applied guidelines for evidence-based practice.* Oxford University Press.

References

Abele, A. E., Ellemers, N., Fiske, S. T., Koch, A., & Yzerbyt, V. (2021). Navigating the social world: Toward an integrated framework for evaluating self, individuals, and groups. *Psychological Review, 128*(2), 290–314.

Angus, L., & Constantino, M. J. (2017). Client accounts of corrective experiences in psychotherapy: Implications for clinical practice. *Journal of Clinical Psychology, 73*(2), 192–195.

Arnall, G. (2019). *Subterranean Fanon: An underground theory of radical change.* Columbia University Press.

Ayala-López, S., & Beeghly, E. (2020). Explaining injustice: Structural analysis, bias, and individuals. In E. Beeghly & A. Madva (Eds.), *An introduction to implicit bias* (pp. 211–232). Routledge.

Banaji, M. R., & Greenwald, A. G. (2013). *Blindspot: Hidden biases of good people.* Bantam.

Bargh, J. A. (2022). The cognitive unconscious in everyday life. In A. Reber & R. Allen (Eds.), *The cognitive unconscious: The first half century* (pp. 89–114). Oxford University Press.

Barnes-Holmes, D., Barnes-Holmes, Y., & McEnteggart, C. (2020). Updating RFT (more field than frame) and its implications for process-based therapy. *The Psychological Record, 70*(4), 605–624.

Barnes-Holmes, D., Finn, M., McEnteggart, C., & Barnes-Holmes, Y. (2018). Derived stimulus relations and their role in a behavior-analytic account of human language and cognition. *Perspectives on Behavior Science, 41*(1), 155–173.

Barrett, L., Henzi, S. P., & Barton, R. A. (2022). Experts in action: Why we need an embodied social brain hypothesis. *Philosophical Transactions of the Royal Society B, 377*(1844), 20200533.

Bazan, A. (2017). Alpha synchronization as a brain model for unconscious defense: An overview of the work of Howard Shevrin and his team. *The International Journal of Psychoanalysis, 98*(5), 1443–1473.

Bazan, A., & Detandt, S. (2013). On the physiology of jouissance: Interpreting the mesolimbic dopaminergic reward functions from a psychoanalytic perspective. *Frontiers in Human Neuroscience, 7*(709), 1–13.

Benish, S. G., Quintana, S., & Wampold, B. E. (2011). Culturally adapted psychotherapy and the legitimacy of myth: A direct-comparison meta-analysis. *Journal of Counseling Psychology, 58*(3), 279–289.

Beshara, R. (2022). A liberation psychoanalytic account of racism. *Awry: Journal of Critical Psychology, 3*(1), 77–94.

Boston Change Process Study Group. (2010). *Change in psychotherapy: A unifying paradigm.* W. W. Norton & Company.

Bucci, W. (2021). Overview of the referential process: The operation of language within and between people. *Journal of Psycholinguistic Research, 50*(1), 3–15.

Budson, A. E., Richman, K. A., & Kensinger, E. A. (2022). Consciousness as a memory system. *Cognitive and Behavioral Neurology, 35*(4), 263–297.

Chang, D. F., & Yoon, P. (2011). Ethnic minority clients' perceptions of the significance of race in cross-racial therapy relationships. *Psychotherapy Research, 21*(5), 567–582.

Davis, D. E., DeBlaere, C., Owen, J., Hook, J. N., Rivera, D. P., Choe, E., Van Tongeren, D. R., Worthington, E. L., Jr., & Placeres, V. (2018). The multicultural orientation framework: A narrative review. *Psychotherapy, 55*(1), 89–100.

Day-Vines, N. L., Booker Ammah, B., Steen, S., & Arnold, K. M. (2018). Getting comfortable with discomfort: Preparing counselor trainees to broach racial, ethnic, and cultural factors with clients during counseling. *International Journal for the Advancement of Counselling, 40*(2), 89–104.

Diniz, E., Castro, P., Bousfield, A., & Figueira, S. (2020). Classism and dehumanization in chronic pain: A qualitative study of nurses' inferences about women of different socio-economic status. *British Journal of Health Psychology, 25*(1), 152–170.

Dixon, K. M., Kivlighan, D. M., Jr., Hill, C. E., & Gelso, C. J. (2022). Cultural humility, working alliance, and Outcome Rating Scale in psychodynamic psychotherapy: Between-therapist, within-therapist, and within-client effects. *Journal of Counseling Psychology, 69*(3), 276–286.

Durante, F., Fiske, S. T., Gelfand, M. J., Crippa, F., Suttora, C., Stillwell, A., & Teymoori, A. (2017). Ambivalent stereotypes link to peace, conflict, and inequality across 38 nations. *Proceedings of the National Academy of Sciences, 114*(4), 669–674.

Egozi, S., Tishby, O., & Wiseman, H. (2021). Changes in clients and therapists experiences of therapeutic distance during psychodynamic therapy. *Journal of Clinical Psychology, 77*(4), 910–926.

Fanon, F. (1963). *The wretched of the earth* (R. Philcox, Trans). Grove Press.

Fanon, F. (1988). *Toward the African revolution: Political essays*. Grove Press.

Fanon, F. (2018). *Alienation and freedom*. Bloomsbury Publishing.

File, B., Keczer, Z., Vancsó, A., Bőthe, B., Tóth-Király, I., Hunyadi, M., Ujhelyi, A., Ulbert, I., Goth, J., & Orosz, G. (2019). Emergence of polarized opinions from free association networks. *Behavior Research Methods, 51*(1), 280–294.

Firth, N., Saxon, D., Stiles, W. B., & Barkham, M. (2019). Therapist and clinic effects in psychotherapy: A three-level model of outcome variability. *Journal of Consulting and Clinical Psychology, 87*(4), 345–356.

Fonagy, P., Target, M., Steele, H., & Steele, M. (1998). *Reflective Functioning Scale (RF) [Database record]*. APA PsycTests.

Gaztambide, D. (2022). Love in a time of anti-blackness: social rank, attachment, and race in psychotherapy. *Attachment & Human Development, 24*(3), 353–365.

Gazzillo, F., Genova, F., Fedeli, F., Curtis, J. T., Silberschatz, G., Bush, M., & Dazzi, N. (2019). Patients' unconscious testing activity in psychotherapy: A theoretical and empirical overview. *Psychoanalytic Psychology, 36*(2), 173–183.

Gilboa-Schechtman, E., Keshet, H., Peschard, V., & Azoulay, R. (2020). Self and identity in social anxiety disorder. *Journal of Personality, 88*(1), 106–121.

Gilead, M., Gal, O., Polak, M., & Cholow, Y. (2015). The role of nature and nurture in conceptual metaphors: The case of gustatory priming. *Social Psychology, 46*(3), 167–173.

Goudarzi, S., Badaan, V., & Knowles, E. D. (2022). Neoliberalism and the ideological construction of equity beliefs. *Perspectives on Psychological Science, 17*(5), 1431–1451.

Grenyer, B. F., & Marceau, E. M. (2022). Helping patients master core conflictual relationship themes in psychotherapy. *Journal of Clinical Psychology, 78*(3), 386–395.

Hall, G. C. N., Ibaraki, A. Y., Huang, E. R., Marti, C. N., & Stice, E. (2016). A meta-analysis of cultural adaptations of psychological interventions. *Behavior Therapy, 47*(6), 993–1014.

Hill, C. E., Castonguay, L. G., Farber, B. A., Knox, S., Stiles, W. B., Anderson, T., Angus, L. E., Barber, J. P., Beck, G., Bohart, A. C., Caspar, F., Constantino, M. J., Elliott, R., Friedlander, M., Goldfried, M. R., Greenberg, L. S., Grosse Holtforth, M., Hayes, A. M., Hayes, J. A., ... Sharpless, B. A. (2012). Corrective experiences in psychotherapy: Definitions, processes, consequences, and research directions. In L. G. Castonguay & C. E. Hill (Eds.), *Transformation in psychotherapy: Corrective experiences across cognitive behavioral, humanistic, and psychodynamic approaches* (pp. 355–370). American Psychological Association.

Hill, R., & Dahlitz, M. (2021). *The practitioner's guide to the science of psychotherapy.* W. W. Norton & Company.

Holmes, J., & Nolte, T. (2019). "Surprise" and the Bayesian brain: Implications for psychotherapy theory and practice. *Frontiers in Psychology, 10*, 592.

Hughes, S., & Barnes-Holmes, D. (2016). Relational frame theory: Implications for the study of human language and cognition. In S. Hayes, D. Barnes-Holmes, R. Zettle, & T. Biglan (Eds.), *Handbook of contextual behavioral science* (pp. 129–178). Wiley-Blackwell.

Kanyicska, D., & Popper, M. (2023). Different minority groups elicit different safety, economic, power, and symbolic threats. *Human Affairs, 33*(1), 51–66.

International Center for Clinical Excellence (ICCE). (2020, August 5). Improving cultural responsiveness in psychotherapy: An interview with Dr Jesse Owen [Video]. YouTube. https://www.youtube.com/watch?v=IqplgWGFCZc

Inagaki, T. K., & Eisenberger, N. I. (2013). Shared neural mechanisms underlying social warmth and physical warmth. *Psychological Science, 24*, 2272–2280.

Inagaki, T. K., Irwin, M. R., Moieni, M., Jevtic, I., & Eisenberger, N. I. (2016). A pilot study examining physical and social warmth: Higher (non-febrile) oral temperature is associated with greater feelings of social connection. *PLoS-One, 11*, e0160865.

Jankowski, P. J., Captari, L. E., & Sandage, S. J. (2021). Exploring virtue ethics in psychodynamic psychotherapy: Latent changes in humility, affect regulation, symptoms and well-being. *Counselling and Psychotherapy Research, 21*(4), 983–991.

Jones, B. C., DeBruine, L. M., Flake, J. K., Liuzza, M. T., Antfolk, J., Arinze, N. C., & Sirota, M. (2021). To which world regions does the valence–dominance model of social perception apply? *Nature Human Behaviour, 5*(1), 159–169.

Kihlstrom, J. F. (2019). The motivational unconscious. *Social and Personality Psychology Compass, 13*(5), e12466.

Kim, J. J., Gerrish, R., Gilbert, P., & Kirby, J. N. (2021). Stressed, depressed, and rank obsessed: Individual differences in compassion and neuroticism predispose towards rank-based depressive symptomatology. *Psychology and Psychotherapy: Theory, Research and Practice, 94*, 188–211.

Lee, E., Greenblatt, A., & Hu, R. (2021). A knowledge synthesis of cross-cultural psychotherapy research: A critical review. *Journal of Cross-Cultural Psychology*, 1–22.

Lee, E., & Horvath, A. (2014). How a therapist responds to cultural versus noncultural dialog in cross-cultural clinical practice. *Journal of Social Work Practice, 28*(2), 193–217.

Lee, E., Johnstone, M., & Herschman, J. (2019). Negotiating therapy goals and tasks in cross-cultural psychotherapy. *Journal of Social Work Practice, 33*(4), 447–462.

Lee, E., Tsang, A. K. T., Bogo, M., Johnstone, M., & Herschman, J. (2018). Enactments of racial microaggression in everyday therapeutic encounters. *Smith College Studies in Social Work, 88*(3), 211–236.

Levinson, S. C. (2023). Gesture, spatial cognition and the evolution of language. *Philosophical Transactions of the Royal Society B, 378*(1875), 20210481.

Levitt, H. M., & Morrill, Z. (2023). Silences in psychotherapy: An integrative meta-analytic research review. *Psychotherapy, 60*(3), 320–341.

Levy, K. N., Kivity, Y., Johnson, B. N., & Gooch, C. V. (2018). Adult attachment as a predictor and moderator of psychotherapy outcome: A meta-analysis. *Journal of Clinical Psychology, 74*(11), 1996–2013.

Liotti, G., & Gilbert, P. (2011). Mentalizing, motivation, and social mentalities: Theoretical considerations and implications for psychotherapy. *Psychology and Psychotherapy: Theory, Research and Practice, 84*(1), 9–25.

Luborsky, L., & Crits-Christoph, P. (1998). *Understanding transference: The core conflictual relationship theme method*. American Psychological Association.

Marriott, D. (2018). *Whither Fanon*. Stanford University Press.

Miller, M. (2005). Slavery, Cimarronaje, and poetic refuge in Nancy Morejon. *Afro-Hispanic Review*, 103–125.

Moss, D. B. (2006). Mapping racism. *The Psychoanalytic Quarterly, 75*(1), 271–294.

Negri, A., Bianchi, F., Milesi, S., & Scirocco, D. M. (2022). The chair and the couch: A comparison between the two settings based on a linguistic analysis. In *Therapist responsiveness: Challenges and opportunities* (pp. 159–160).

Novac, A. (2022). Free association, synchrony, and neural networks as evolutionary exponents in psychoanalysis. In P. Azzone (Ed.) *The wounds of our mother psychoanalysis-new models for a psychoanalysis in crisis*. IntechOpen.

Novac, A., & Blinder, B. J. (2021). Free association in psychoanalysis and its links to neuroscience contributions. *Neuropsychoanalysis, 23*(2), 55–81.

Owen, J., Coleman, J., Drinane, J. M., Tao, K., Imel, Z., Wampold, B., & Kopta, M. (2021). Psychotherapy racial/ethnic disparities in treatment outcomes: The role of university racial/ethnic composition. *Journal of Counseling Psychology, 68*(4), 418–424.

Painting Onions Podcast. (2022, January 29). Karl Friston on the free energy principle, psychology, and psychotherapy [Video]. YouTube. https://www.youtube.com/watch?v=9DZ7-De22Mg

Payne, B. K., & Hannay, J. W. (2021). Implicit bias reflects systemic racism. *Trends in Cognitive Sciences, 25*(11), 927–936.

Payne, B. K., Vuletich, H. A., & Brown-Iannuzzi, J. L. (2019). Historical roots of implicit bias in slavery. *Proceedings of the National Academy of Sciences, 116*(24), 11693–11698.

Payne, B. K., Vuletich, H. A., & Lundberg, K. B. (2017). The bias of crowds: How implicit bias bridges personal and systemic prejudice. *Psychological Inquiry, 28*(4), 233–248.

Quirk, K., Smith, A., & Owen, J. (2018). In here and out there: Systemic alliance and intersession processes in psychotherapy. *Professional Psychology: Research and Practice, 49*(1), 31–38.

Rabeyron, T., & Massicotte, C. (2020). Entropy, free energy, and symbolization: Free association at the intersection of psychoanalysis and neuroscience. *Frontiers in Psychology, 11*(366), 1–15.

Ren, D., Tan, K., Arriaga, X. B., & Chan, K. Q. (2015). Sweet love: The effects of sweet taste experience on romantic perceptions. *Journal of Social and Personal Relationships, 32*(7), 905–921.

Richie, R., Aka, A., & Bhatia, S. (2022). Free association in a neural network. *Psychological Review*, advance online publication.

Rodomonti, M., Fiorenza, E., Gazzillo, F., & Dazzi, N. (2021). Progress in psychotherapy: The perspective of control-mastery theory. *Psychodynamic Psychiatry, 49*, 131–159.

Saketopoulou, A. (2023). *Sexuality beyond consent: Risk, race*. NYU Press.

Scarfone, D. (2018). Free association, surprise, trauma, and transference. *Psychoanalytic Inquiry, 38*(6), 468–477.

Schultheiss, O. C. (2021). Motives and goals, or: The joys and meanings of life. In J. Rauthmann (Ed.), *The handbook of personality dynamics and processes* (pp. 295–322). Academic Press.

Schultheiss, O. C., & Strasser, A. (2012). Referential processing and competence as determinants of congruence between implicit and explicit motives. In S. Vazire & T. D. Wilson (Eds.), *Handbook of self-knowledge* (pp. 39–62). Guilford Press.

Shevrin, H. (2003). The psychoanalytic theory of drive in the light of recent neuroscience findings and theories. *1st Annual C. Philip Wilson M. D. Memorial Lecture*.

Slade, A., & Holmes, J. (2019). Attachment and psychotherapy. *Current Opinion in Psychology, 25*, 152–156.

Slone, N. C., & Owen, J. (2015). Therapist alliance activity, therapist comfort, and systemic alliance on individual psychotherapy outcome. *Journal of Psychotherapy Integration, 25*(4), 275–288.

Solms, M., & Panksepp, J. (2012). The "Id" knows more than the "Ego" admits: Neuropsychoanalytic and primal consciousness perspectives on the interface between affective and cognitive neuroscience. *Brain Sciences, 2*(2), 147–175.

Soto, A., Smith, T. B., Griner, D., Rodríguez, M. D., & Bernal, G. (2018). Cultural adaptations and multicultural competence: Two meta-analytic reviews. *Journal of Clinical Psychology, 74*, 1907–1923.

Talia, A., Muzi, L., Lingiardi, V., & Taubner, S. (2020). How to be a secure base: Therapists' attachment representations and their link to attunement in psychotherapy. *Attachment & Human Development, 22*(2), 189–206.

Techio, E. M., Lima Leite, E., Pimentel da Silva, R., & Rosas Torres, A. R. (2019). Stereotypic content and the discourse about racial prejudice in Bahia. *Avances En Psicología Latinoamericana, 37*(1), 179–194.

Villatte, M., Villatte, J. L., & Hayes, S. C. (2015). *Mastering the clinical conversation: Language as intervention*. Guilford Publications.

Vuletich, H. A., & Payne, B. K. (2019). Stability and change in implicit bias. *Psychological Science, 30*(6), 854–862.

Wachtel, P. L. (1967). An approach to the study of body language in psychotherapy. *Psychotherapy: Theory, Research & Practice, 4*(3), 97–100.

Weinberger, J., & Stoycheva, V. (2019). *The unconscious: Theory, research, and clinical implications*. Guilford Publications.

Wetherall, K., Robb, K. A., & O'Connor, R. C. (2019). Social rank theory of depression: A systematic review of self-perceptions of social rank and their relationship with depressive symptoms and suicide risk. *Journal of Affective Disorders, 246*, 300–319.

Williams, D. R., & Etkins, O. S. (2021). Racism and mental health. *World Psychiatry, 20*(2), 194.

Williams, L. E., & Bargh, J. A. (2008a). Experiencing physical warmth promotes interpersonal warmth. *Science, 322*(5901), 606–607.

Williams, L. E., & Bargh, J. A. (2008b). Keeping one's distance: The influence of spatial distance cues on affect and evaluation. *Psychological Science, 19*(3), 302–308.

Wilkinson, R., & Pickett, K. (2020). *The inner level: How more equal societies reduce stress, restore sanity and improve everyone's well-being*. Penguin Books.

Winer, E. S., & Salem, T. (2016). Reward devaluation: Dot-probe meta-analytic evidence of avoidance of positive information in depressed persons. *Psychological Bulletin, 142*(1), 18–78.

Yeomans, F., Clarkin, J. F., & Kernberg, O. F. (2015). *Transference-focused psychotherapy for borderline personality disorder: A clinical guide*. American Psychiatric Publishers.

Yu, S. (2018). Uncovering the hidden impacts of inequality on mental health: A global study. *Translational Psychiatry, 8*(1), 1–10.

Zhang, H., Watkins, C. E., Jr., Hook, J. N., Hodge, A. S., Davis, C. W., Norton, J., Wilcox, M. M., Davis, D. E., Deblaere, C., & Owen, J. (2022). Cultural humility in psychotherapy and clinical supervision: A research review. *Counselling and Psychotherapy Research, 22*(3), 548–557.

Zhang, L., Chen, P., Schafer, M., Zheng, S., Chen, L., Wang, S., Liang, Q., Qi, Q., Zhang, Y., & Huang, R. (2022). A specific brain network for a social map in the human brain. *Scientific Reports, 12*(1), 1–16.

Zhong, C. B., & Leonardelli, G. J. (2008). Cold and lonely: Does social exclusion literally feel cold? *Psychological Science, 19*(9), 838–842.

8

Conclusion: A Psychotherapy for All—Building a World Worth Living In

The current work reveals a psychoanalysis at odds with itself. The early psychoanalytic movement developed a revolutionary theory of mind and a clinical treatment *dissociated* from a theory of race, class, and culture, leaving us with a series of "broken circuits." On the one hand, Freud theorized about race, class, culture, and identity as a marginalized Jewish man. Indeed, Freud (1925) believed that psychoanalysis required a "readiness to accept a situation of solitary opposition... with which no one is more familiar than a Jew" (p. 222). The predominantly Jewish identity of the early analytic movement and their leftist politics in the context of social democracy fomented a progressive ethos, advocating for civil rights, socialized medicine, and a "psychotherapy for the people" (Danto, 2005). On the other hand, Freud (1900) also identified as a patriarchal *conquistador*, and there is no lack of racism, sexism, and queerphobia in his life and work (Aron & Starr, 2013). How do we account for *both* realities, a psychoanalysis for liberation *and* a psychoanalysis for the status quo?

Reckoning with Our Legacy: A Fanonian Account of Psychoanalysis

The rise in anti-Semitic, anti-left sentiment across Europe and the US decimated the leftist psychoanalytic movement (Danto, 2005). For analysts like Otto Fenichel who tried to maintain a progressive psychoanalysis, McCarthyism and anti-Semitism made such politics life-threatening, leading

D. J. Gaztambide, *Decolonizing Psychoanalytic Technique*, https://doi.org/10.1007/978-3-031-48476-6_8

many like him to repress their politics. Similarly with Sandor Ferenczi. Despite his prescient insights on how psychoanalysis reveals society in the individual, he was terrified by the rise of fascism, withdrawing from politics into the intimacies of the consulting room, retreating from the political to find refuge in the relational. And then there is Freud, who in failing to apply his theories to *himself* left psychoanalysis with a massive blind spot.

Fanon (1952/2008) offers us a framework for understanding this split. Borrowing from the theory of racism-as-compensation which the early analysts developed in parallel to Du Bois, Fanon argued that racial hierarchy protects capitalism through divide-and-conquer strategies that offer pleasures maintaining our attachment to the system. Fanon helps us understand Freud as someone who suffered oppression yet desired to enter the category of the colonizer through racist performances facilitating the fantasy that he could achieve a "higher" social position, even as his world burned all around him. By putting Freud on Fanon's couch, we develop a nuanced picture of the origins of psychoanalysis, understanding Freud as a fraught, complex ancestor capable of potent insights on oppression while no less vulnerable to enacting oppressive dynamics himself.

The problem is not that psychoanalysis "neglects" the sociocultural, but that Freud and the early analysts *did* address oppression and identity but turned away from them because of their own trauma (Aron & Starr, 2013). Rather than rejecting or eulogizing Freud, I argue we learn from what is useful in his work, and as an example of the pitfalls we should avoid. While I have felt tempted to "replace" him with Fanon, this well-intentioned move risks whitewashing our history. *We must wrestle with our history* instead of covering over those parts we do not like, and this should include teaching and reading Freud as the illustration *par excellence* of Fanon's theory of colonialism— how the oppressed can become the oppressor within racial capitalism. We should learn from Freud's mistakes and become his heirs without being his descendants.

From Ghosts to Ancestors, Descendants to Heirs

In asserting Fanon as Freud's most disputatious *heir*, I play with a distinction borrowed from Richard T. Ford by way of Antonio Viego (2007). Viego cites Ford:

It may be that the price of providing our descendants with a world free of social stigma and oppression of identities such as race, a world we could be proud to call more just, is that they would not share our identities, *that they would be our heirs but not our descendants.* (cited in location 1540–1542, emphasis added)

It may be that the "price" of a decolonial psychoanalysis is that we not share Freud, Ferenczi, and Lacan's identities as analysts, but that like Fanon we be their heirs but not their descendants. As I alluded to in Chapter 1, while the decolonial perspective includes our broader ancestry within a mobius strip, we can insert a "cut" between Freud and Fanon, producing *two* interconnected strips joined by this common cause called "psychoanalysis." Freud may not have been able to imagine me in all my complexity, but I imagine *his* complexity despite his limitations to break an intergenerational curse, letting my ancestors speak without their having the final say. The "final say" is ours.

We should *not* be Fanon's descendants either. Put colloquially, *all* of our "faves" are problematic, and we should resist elevating any one ancestor to an idealized position. Fanon was no less likely to reproduce oppressive discourses, such as sexism. There is a tacit way his work assumes the universal subject, even the colonized, as presumptively male and masculine (Bergner, 1995). Further, there is a way the colonial drama in his writings is primarily one of white men (and women) in relation to Black men, minimizing the role of Black women's experience. This is not to read Fanon as a wholesale sexist, however. As Yokum (2022) cautions, "Engaging with Fanon… means properly acknowledging his 'failures' without overreacting and senselessly declaring him to be antifeminist" (p. 15). We reckon with Fanon at his best and worst, and as with each of the theorists in this book, feel free to "pick and choose" what is helpful and do away with what is not. This book should be treated similarly.

Central Findings: Decolonial Psychoanalytic Theory and Technique

What I have attempted to do is return to the foundations of our field to handle some "unfinished business," the fundamental dissociation between psychoanalysis' theory of mind, clinical technique, and the critical-decolonial theory that emerged from it. As a preamble to the political implications of this book, it bears reviewing its theoretical and clinical conclusions.

Decolonial Psychoanalytic Theory: The Psyche in the World

What is decolonial psychoanalytic *theory*? We live in a world of profound inequality along lines of race, class, gender, and sexuality—racial capitalism and its twin snake, cisheteropatriarchy. This world maintains itself through the machinations of the wealthiest who weaponize racism (particularly anti-Blackness), among other "isms" to divide and conquer, turning us against each other in a sociopolitical game of "king of the hill," or "crabs in a barrel." These tools of political distraction enrapture us in supporting politicians who promise to "deal" with "those people," even as they enact neoliberal policies that entrench our suffering.

Inequality renders us more sensitive to our place in the "pecking order," making us struggle with trust, connection, and love. In response to the question "Why do I suffer?" the system offers the same reprise, "It is the other who has stolen your joy, jobs, and pleasure" (cf. George & Hook, 2021). In crafting the world according to their dreams, desires, and fantasy, the wealthy succeed in creating a series of political and economic structures, policies, and ideologies that become "ingrained" into reality as such. Politics, policy, law, economics, and culture convey a tacit, implicit "language" around who is deserving and who is not, who is above or below, who is and is not deserving of love. This may be explicit, or more insidiously, *implicit*, letting our psyches do the rest of the work through processes of internalization and derivation.

The unconscious is organized around two primary goals, navigating the body in space, and regulating the level of bodily excitation to minimize the likelihood of surprise. To navigate space means moving about in physical, literal space, as well as symbolic, *social* space across two axes—a horizontal axis of closeness and distance, affinity, relationality and attachment, and a vertical axis of "higher" and "lower," deservingness, positionality, and status. These modes of navigation correlate to two fundamental needs, wishes, or desires: (a) the drive to connect and prevent the loss of relationship, and (b) the drive to achieve and maintain status, while preventing its loss. In navigating these spaces and desires, we strive to pursue pleasure (what meets these goals) and avoid pain (what frustrates these goals). The psyche is a fundamentally associative organism, in that the parts of the brain implicated in navigating the physical and social world are also implicated in language. Because of the circularity of these circuits, when we speak we are always communicating something about our body's orientation in space—literal and symbolic, intimate and sociopolitical. Put more precisely, *these spaces speak through us.*

The unconscious operates according to a primarily non-logical, associative system, *always* making connections, building relationships between experiences, stimuli, thoughts, feelings, and behaviors according to what will help us pursue pleasure and avoid pain. The unconscious "perceives" the world around us first, with our conscious mind "catching up" about a split second later. In the interim, most of our cognitive operations, perceptions, and emotional reactions have already taken place, with consciousness registering them after the fact, if at all. Our unconscious capacity for non-logical associations lies at the heart of creativity, lateral thinking, art, and spirituality. But also, our capacity for falling ill and recovering.

Over the lifespan we encounter moments we could not have predicted, loss and trauma that "surprise" us, overwhelming our capacity to regulate ourselves. In trying to survive, we stumble upon a surprising solution, as if by chance. Our psyche becomes organized around this strategy, establishing a set of "*if*, *then*" contingencies, an unconscious fantasy or schema such as "*if* I feel vulnerable, *then* I will be made fun of, *therefore* I should put myself down first before others can." This works for a time. Eventually, the benefits we derive from this strategy accrue a series of costs. To address those costs and drawbacks we (again) depend on our "tried and true" strategies. After a certain point, pleasure and pain, gain and cost, become blurred, confused, stuck in vicious cycles that thwart our capacity for real pleasure. This dialectic between homeostasis and change lies at the heart of what we call "symptoms."

As we cling to those defenses that help and hinder, our psyches begin deriving an unconscious plan to break out of this cycle, some tacit sense of what will help us heal. We move throughout life with both tendencies, a desire to maintain the homogeneity of our unconscious scripts (they are safe and known) and an enduring hope that those scripts can be disproven, "testing" our environment for signs it is safe enough to let them go, allowing space for a "blank slate" upon which a new story can be written. We test our world in hopes of stirring up something or someone to disrupt our "gut" sense of how the world works—to rediscover what it means to be free, to be loved, to have value as a human being. The circuitry of our *jouissance*, our compromise formations, our defenses play out in different ways depending on what motivational system is implicated, whether affiliation or status. This helps us understand how we negotiate difficulties in relationships, as well as the complex ideologies, "isms," and fears that capture our political imagination, our cultural values, our "place" in society.

This dialectic of pleasure and pain is central to what I call the intersectionality of suffering. It is not an equivalence between the suffering of the oppressor and oppressed, or even the relatively privileged. It is a recognition that in an unequal society suffering is interconnected—different and distinct, though related by systemic forces. It implies that our very identities can be hijacked as tools of oppression, providing compensations attaching us to the system. At the individual level, change becomes possible when we are open to reimagining those identities in a more flexible way through the recognition that "The cost of liberty is less than the price of repression" (Du Bois, 1909, p. 25).

That said, is decolonial psychoanalytic theory a one-, two-, or three-person psychology? Is it more "sociocultural," interpersonal, or intrapsychic? Is it more relational-interpersonal, Lacanian, or Freudian? My jest about a "no-person" psychology gestures to a point that RFT (ironically, a CBT theory) helps clarify. *All* psychoanalysis is "relational psychoanalysis," whether its focus has been on intrapsychic associations or interpersonal transactions. The decolonial approach stipulates that associations are by definition *relationships*, whether between thoughts and feelings, between people, cultural values and group identities, and so on.

This means the unconscious is a transindividual, collective system for organizing relationships in this broader sense, especially on a gradient of "closer–distant," "above–below." Before we are born and develop our own "intrapsychic" associations, we are preceded by and embedded in associations sanctioned by our respective cultures and societies, our families across generations, our intimate relationships, and then ultimately ourselves. Associations-as-relationships are simultaneously "internal," "interpersonal," and "societal"—they are the basic building blocks of the psychoanalytic enterprise, both as theory and as practice.

Decolonial Psychoanalytic Technique: A Safe (Enough) Surprise

What treatment follows from this theory? Decolonial psychoanalytic technique begins from two foundations, the primacy of the therapeutic relationship and the fundamental rule of free association—to say what comes to mind without censorship. It is not necessary for the "fundamental rule" to be formally instituted, as the patient's mind (and our own) will unconsciously associate material unprompted. Whether the rule is introduced or merely implied, the clinician does their best to "join" with the patient's orientation toward the world, relationally, culturally, and politically. It cannot be stressed enough that this does not mean endorsing or agreeing with their relational or sociocultural frame but communicating—explicitly or tacitly—that the patient's views are respected as a valid way of construing the world.

From this stance, the therapist listens to the patient's speech as closely and intimately as possible, attending to the language of (a) closeness, distance, and intimacy, and (b) "higher," "lower," and positionality in tandem. Sometimes, the focus is squarely relational and interpersonal, while at others it is social, cultural, and political—often it is both. The therapist tracks the symbols of power and relatedness in the patient's speech, and selects key moments to reflect back those words, phrases, and symbols to stimulate and evoke their broader associative networks, i.e., to elaborate their speech. This may take the form of a question, an empathic reflection, an interpretation, but just as well the simple act of reflecting back, remixing, punctuating the patient's own words and phrases. In the process, the therapist hears core schemas of self and other, tacit and explicit cultural values, and schemas of self and other in terms of identities, group categories, and socioeconomic positions.

The therapeutic goal is to encourage the patient to speak and act despite the inclination to avoid, to experiment with actualizing their unconscious plan for change both (a) with the therapist, and (b) in daily life, especially with others outside of treatment, pursuing opportunities for experiencing a safe (enough) surprise that challenges their fantasies of self and world. This can occur through the therapist's open, non-judgmental stance, but often takes place through a process of rupture and repair, an enactment in which they initially act in ways predicted by the patient's expectations of others, and takes ownership of their impact. This safe enough surprise—call it a corrective experience, a shock, or an encounter with the Real—creates opportunities for rewriting the patient's scripts in ways that are more empowering and freeing.

Alongside therapeutic responsiveness is the patient's speech. By reflecting back, remixing, or punctuating evocative aspects of speech, the therapist offers the patient an opportunity to relate to their words—and the world implied in those words—in a new way. This includes tacit assumptions about their relational world, as well as unconscious biases on a social, cultural, and political register. Helping the patient re-experience these scripts in a new— surprising—way, renders them more open to a new perspective. Often, what is mutative is the therapist bearing witness to the patient coming to terms with different "voices" and self-states in a new way. This is analogous to Paulo Freire's notion of "reading" the word to read the world.

Whether through repeating back evocative words or phrases in speech, engaging in rupture and repair, challenging unspoken assumptions, or simply being an open presence, all of these provide opportunities for shifting the conversation from the "interpersonal" realm of the patient-therapist relationship into the broader "social" realm of culture and politics. When is it helpful to shift "modes of mentalization?" This is a matter of following the patient's speech, attuning to the dimension of social cognition that is active at a given moment. As we saw in Chapter 7, attending to the relational dance between patient and therapist is salubrious in reconfiguring core attachment schemas. But attending to the implied sociocultural dance between them, and tacit cultural themes in general, also helps us explore basic assumptions we hold about our identities, cultural backgrounds, and social world. Knowing when to attend to the relational and sociocultural by tracking speech allows us to move organically and effortlessly between intervening on each domain and where they interact. The dialog *between* patient and therapist can also facilitate a dialog about the world the two share beyond the dyad.

This study also offers a link between how we conceptualize symptoms and how we conceptualize identity. Symptoms serve a purpose, a function, a compensation to help us maintain connection and prevent loss of status, allowing us to examine identity and positionality in terms of their benefits and costs. Clinical exploration of identity, whether marginalized or privileged, would involve considering their function societally and psychologically. From a position of respect for the patient's cultural frame, can we explore the possibility of greater flexibility or reconsideration of the contours of that frame? The same is true of exploring the therapist's countertransference and intersecting identities. How does the therapist's understanding of their positionality serve and hinder them, especially in relation to the patient? This formulation of identity and positionality connects therapeutic mechanisms of change with changes in sociocultural understandings of self and other. Put briefly, in exploring the contours of our and our patients' identities, we create opportunities for surprise to challenge those contours, a kind of "corrective cultural experience."

Our review of psychoanalysis' technical history from a decolonial lens gives us another aperture for expanding the scope of technique today, emphasizing intervening through the therapeutic relationship but also *outside* of it. Freud, Ferenczi, and Fanon, for example, experimented with techniques that are prototypes of CBT, such as exposure, behavioral activation, and homework. Lacan's practice of punctuating sessions necessarily brought the patient face to face with the world evoked in their speech. At the same time, they understood the *limitations* of these techniques in the absence of a strong alliance. That caveat notwithstanding, the history of psychoanalytic technique opens the door for psychotherapy integration (Norcross & Goldfriend, 2005). Fanon availed himself of such interventions as well, bringing together behavioral and family systems therapies in his practice. A decolonial psychoanalytic treatment, then, opens the door to an array of techniques that serve an analytic function.

If, as research shows, treatments from different theoretical orientations have similar or equivalent outcomes, then we must shift from specific "brands" of treatment to processes of change (Westra, 2023). How is it that exploring the therapeutic relationship (psychodynamic), behavioral experiments outside the session (CBT), or "chair work" (humanistic-experiential)—where patients alternate between self-states by moving between two chairs—all work? How can both "talk" and "behavior" therapy (broadly defined) lead to change? The research in Chapter 7 gives us a clue. If the parts of the brain involved in language and sensorimotor navigation are highly associated and reciprocal, then at a fundamental level when we "approach" difficult experiences through talk or behaviorally (by moving in space) we are targeting different circuits within the same neurocognitive system. Different schools of therapy are grabbing different "parts" of the proverbial elephant—and *all* of them make it "move."

I can talk to one of my cisgender male patients, verbalizing the part of them that feels they must be "tough," alongside the part of them that wishes they could just be held. My colleague Amanda Garcia Torres, a "chairwork" therapist, may ask a similar patient to "place" the part that needs to be tough in one chair, and speak to it from the self that wants to be cared for in another chair. Later, he physically gets up and moves to the other chair, and allows the "tough guy" to get a hug (he hugs himself) (see Kellogg & Garcia Torres, 2021). The clinical question becomes what to do when these systems—linguistic and sensorimotor—are dissociated from each other. Getting off the couch and engaging in behavioral interventions may be necessary, just as when a homework fails it may be necessary to *talk it out*. Not just in terms of what did not work, but what the homework failing might reflect about the therapeutic alliance.

My colleagues may bristle at including "behavioral" interventions within psychoanalytic technique. We should remember that neither Freud, Ferenczi, or Lacan would "make the cut" as a "good" Freudian, relational-interpersonal, or Lacanian practitioner today—and that's a *good* thing. We uncovered example after example of these theorists doing things decidedly "off-script" for these schools today—Freud self-disclosed, Ferenczi was confrontational and assigned homework, Lacan could be "relational," Fanon minimized transference work yet was willing to "give" as befit the patient—often with a salubrious impact on their treatments. I was regularly *surprised* by the available archive, especially with Freud and Lacan. Reading how they all did something "extra" beyond what they or their followers described as the "core ingredients" of treatment reminded me of an anecdote by existential-humanistic therapist Irvin Yalom (1980).

Yalom (1980) tells the story of a cooking class he took with an Armenian matriarch and her assistant. Since they did not speak the same language, he and the other students learned by watching her cook—what ingredients she used, in what order, etc. They tried to replicate her recipes, but always fell short of her delicious dishes. What gave her cooking that "special touch?" One day, Yalom paid especially close attention as the teacher carefully prepared a dish with an aura of gravitas and depth, then handed it to her assistant to put in the oven. Without breaking stride, the assistant threw in one after another assortment of spices and condiments. "I am convinced," Yalom writes, "that those surreptitious 'throw-ins' made all the difference."

Psychoanalytic treatment—all therapy truly—is more than a series of theories and techniques, or a set recipe to be followed assiduously. Freud, Ferenczi, Lacan—even Fanon—all described what they saw as the essence of psychoanalytic treatment, yet they all had various "throw-ins," interventions that did not exactly "fit the model" but were mutative. Just as there is no single decolonial approach, this book does not reproduce a singular way of working but models a diversity of interventions among the ancestors of major schools, offering beginning and seasoned clinicians *permission* to discover and rediscover their own "throw-ins."

For example, I was once working with an elderly Spanish-speaking Puerto Rican woman with a history of trauma who had recently migrated to the United States after the death of her husband. Over the course of a session she became very anxious about a conflict with one of her sisters. Noting her distress was making it difficult for her to talk through it, I was moved—whether due to my countertransference toward her as an *abuela* or a *tia* (auntie), or just as an elder from back home—to offer her that we "take a turn about the room." I stood, offered my arm, and we walked in my office, talking about the books and pictures on my wall until she felt regulated.

When we sat down, she suddenly began shaking with emotion. Not knowing what was happening, I asked what was "coming up" for her. She shared that when she was a young woman her family would take her and her sister to dances in San Juan (they were from *el campo*, the countryside). Hoping to be asked to dance or "take a turn about the room" by a handsome *caballero*, she always wound up on the sidelines while her sister—lighter skinned, "good haired," favored—received all the attention. This spontaneous act in the context of a transference-countertransference relation between a darker-skinned and a white Puerto Rican evoked a somatic experience that brought associations into awareness, an enactment bringing to the fore her desire to be valued, allowing us to talk about how colorism came up in her family, between her and her sister, and between us. My supervisor at the time frowned on this as "not analytic." Imagine my reaction when I discovered Freud too could get up and move with his patients.

While the decolonial psychoanalytic frame comprises tools from diverse traditions, one may still have a specific "home base." I, for example, will continue being "relational-interpersonal," although Lacan and Fanon's thinking on language has forever changed how I practice. I still engage in an interpersonal approach that stresses the role of rupture and repair, and thinking about the mind in terms of multiple, rapidly oscillating, self-other states relationally and culturally. The decolonial perspective is not a "brand" among other brands of therapy, but more of a waystation, a "home with many rooms," in which different practitioners committed to social justice can break bread, build community, and drink fine coffee together.

The social and cultural world does not *need* to be "brought up" or "brought in"—*they are always already there* if we attune our ears to the words our patients speak and their bodies imply. If we pick up on the language of verticality ("above," "below," "falling," symbols of positionality, etc.) along-side our quotidian attention to the language of horizontality and closeness, we have ever-present opportunities for broaching identity and culture from a culturally humble position as a matter of course—we reflect back choice words, bring up what is tacitly said, invite the patient to comment on how their issues *may* be related to identity and culture, while letting them set the terms of what these mean to them. The stance I advocate for is decidedly not "neutral." I argue for active *psychoanalytic* listening where we punctuate, reflect back, and underscore key words and phrases that signify either/both relatedness and positionality, while allowing room for diverse kinds of clinical activity. For example, sometimes you just have to "call a spade a spade."

I will never forget a video I watched in Nancy Boyd-Franklin's diversity class as a doctoral student at Rutgers University. In it Harry Aponte, a family therapist, was working with a Black family, a mother and her middle-school son who had been repeatedly disciplined in school in ways that seemed extreme and unfair. Aponte wondered aloud, *why* might this be happening to him specifically? Mother and son looked at each other for a moment, then looked at Aponte—"We don't know." He inquired again, what *could* be the reason he is singled out? After a few rounds of "beating around the bush," Aponte finally broached the subject—could it be because of racism? The family almost gave a sigh of relief. They seemed to have avoided naming race, worried they might offend Aponte—a white Puerto Rican man. From there the treatment moved forward, supporting this family with navigating the role of racism in their lives.

From Therapeutic to Political Action: Off the Couch and to the Streets

Although my focus has been clinical, the theory and technique elucidated in this book moves us—like a mobius strip—from the "inside" of the consulting room to the "outside" of politics. We should remember Freud's (1927) words, "a civilization which leaves so large a number of its participants unsatisfied and drives them into revolt neither has nor deserves the prospect of a lasting existence" (p. 12). Fanon (1956/2018) echoed those words, "A society that forces its members into desperate solutions is a non-viable society, a society that needs replacing" (p. 435). As hc (1952/2008) teaches us, for the clinician there is a "need for combined action on the individual and on the group." "As a psychoanalyst," he writes, "I should help my patient to become *conscious* of his unconscious… but also to act in the direction of a change in the social structure" (p. 74, emphasis original). While the patient engaging in political action is not ruled out in a decolonial perspective, I want to read this charge as applying to *clinicians*. To the extent we seek to relieve suffering, we must address its social determinants as well.

This is not to denigrate the importance of clinical work, only recognize its limitations. Let me offer an analogy through the "parable of the Starfish," penned by American anthropologist Loren Eiseley (1979). The contemporary version goes something like this:

> A man was walking on the beach when he saw a little girl picking up and throwing starfish into the ocean. He asks, "What are you doing?" She replied, "I'm throwing them back into the ocean. If I don't, they will die." The man looked around, noticing the beach filled with starfish. *She could never save them all*, he thought. He laughed and said to her, "Don't you realize there's hundreds upon hundreds of starfish? Your throwing them back won't matter." The little girl threw another starfish into the sea, "It mattered to *that one*."

While this version emphasizes the value of individual action, Eiseley's (1979) original has a different message. After reflecting on our relationship to nature and the universe, the man returns to the child and helps them throw starfish back into the ocean. "Only then I allowed myself to think," he reflects, "[the child] is not alone any longer. After us, there will be *others*" (p. 181, emphasis added). The original version is not about the solitary effort of the individual, but about how when we come together in recognition of our interconnectedness, we create change.

I want to imagine a sequel to this story. The little girl, moved by the experience of being helped to save the starfish, starts asking *why* so many wound up on the beach. In adulthood she becomes a marine biologist whose research concludes starfish are at risk due to global warming. *Why* is global warming accelerating? She digs deeper, discovering that pollution by major corporations is the immediate culprit. *How* are they able to get away with this? She discovers these corporations fund politicians running on a platform of racial fear to impose draconian legislation corroding civil rights for people of color, immigrants, women, and LGBTQ people, enact tax breaks for the wealthy, *and* destroy environmental protections. The starfish are a symptom of political arrangements made possible by how racism and other isms divide us at the whims of the wealthy. Connecting the dots, she realizes protecting the environment means confronting racism and capitalism's cannibalism of our planet (Prakash & Girgenti, 2020).

What I envision is for us to "connect the dots" between the symptoms we witness "in the room" and our broader world. I could be the most effective heart surgeon drawing on the latest techniques for "repairing" a broken heart, but if I never raise the question of what conditions belie the cacophony of broken hearts showing up in my practice, I will be bereft in understanding the underlying, "distal" causes of what ails us. To borrow from Rudolf Virchow, "Politics is nothing else but medicine on a large scale" (cited in George & Whitehouse, 2021, p. 130).

There Is No Anti-Racism Without Anti-Capitalism

Liberation and decolonization were not abstract concepts for Fanon (1957/2018). He envisioned liberation through "popular assemblies, the equitable distribution of wealth, the respect of freedoms and the elimination of all structures of oppression" (p. 548). The question Fanon (1963) thought critical to our survival was nothing less than the "redistribution of wealth. Humanity must reply to this question, or be shaken to pieces by it" (p. 98). He is quite clear on the destructive effects of racial capitalism. Fanon spoke candidly about socialism as a system centered on the people, "[making] impossible that caricature of society where all economic and political power is held in the hands of a few who regard the nation as a whole with scorn and contempt" (p. 99). This is also not a domestic matter but an international one. The Euro-American world was built "with the gold and raw materials of the colonial countries: Latin America, China, and Africa… Europe is literally the creation of the Third World" (p. 102). Hence, a decolonial clinician must account for the domestic and global face of racial capitalism.

Let's get very concrete. The history of racism in the United States—and much of the world—is the history of how "the free" yet exploited are compensated for that exploitation through the creation of a collective "bottom," and how racial division props up the power of predominantly white, male, and cisheterosexual elites. Its power is not monolithic, however, challenged time and again by multiracial coalitions seeking change. These same coalitions and resistance movements, however, have been broken time and again, either through sheer violence or the seductions of racial capitalism's symbolic wages. How does this typically work?

Lopez (2019) breaks down the blueprint behind the production of whiteness and racial fear, inspired by Du Bois' insights. He describes the "dog whistle politics" used by politicians—coded appeals to unconscious racial bias with the plausible deniability of not being seen as overtly about race. A crude example might be a politician declaring "We want better schools for our children, which is why we need to make sure their seat doesn't go to someone else. We need to put America—and Americans—first, get government out of our schools, and give parents back choice over their kids' education." Although not overtly about race, such a message unconsciously primes a sense of "us" ("our children") versus a "them" ("someone else's").

The "them" are coded as taking *our* children's place, leading to "worse" schools. The addition of "put America—and Americans—first" similarly primes unconscious, racialized notions of who is and is not a citizen. The statement "get government out of our schools" and "give parents back choice" does another piece of ideological work emphasizing choice in the "free market." Such messages have three implicit components: (1) do not trust dangerous, underserving others (people of color, immigrants, feminists, LGBTQ people); (2) do not trust government and collective action as the solution to our problems; and (3) trust the market. This last point reflects the idea that we cannot come together to address our problems, depending only on our own effort as individual agents. That we are, in essence, alone before the world.

In electoral politics, these messages of fear split the populace while empowering politicians into office who eviscerate civil rights, and enact policies that enrich the wealthy and destroy the environment (Lopez, 2019; Prakash & Girgenti, 2020). These policies and how they increase racial and economic inequality translate directly—"trickle down" as it were—into the issues we bear witness to in the consulting room. Income inequality leads to higher rates of mental illness (Sami & Jeter, 2021), while making adverse childhood experiences more prevalent across the economic spectrum (Halfon et al.,

2017). Income inequality also predicts the likelihood of bullying and competitiveness among children in school (Elgar et al., 2019). Social comparison, competitiveness, and getting the measure of one another becomes rampant, leading us to engage in risky behavior in the pursuit of pleasure to "live it up" like those higher on the food chain (Hannay et al., 2021; Schmidt et al., 2019).

Racism as a tool of class warfare worsens not only economic inequality, but patriarchy as well, leading to ever more rigid gender norms and social pressures toxic to both cis men and women—not in the same way, but as we have argued, in a related fashion (cf. Danylova & Kats, 2019). Similarly, mental and medical health outcomes for whites worsen with the increasing wealth inequality enabled by racism (Blacksher & Valles, 2021), and income inequality is directly implicated in the persistence of racial disparities (Manduca, 2018). The intersectionality of suffering emerges here not only as a clinical principle but as a tool of political analysis, helping us see how behind the façade of the "wages" of whiteness, patriarchy, and classism is suffering that—while *not* the same—links us and our destinies together.

How do such macro-level forces affect outcomes at the micro level of our daily lives and relationships? When income inequality increases, our capacity to trust one another becomes impaired, becoming fixated on our position in the social hierarchy, our capacity to relate giving way to our need to exert control for a higher position (Wilkinson & Pickett, 2017). Relationships fray, competition soars, and the world burns ever hotter as we reshuffle seats on the Titanic, fighting to ensure *we* are not below deck but sailing "first class," literally or symbolically. My point here is not to overwhelm clinicians, only outline the scope of the problem. If ecology, economy, and culture wars around gender and sexuality worsen due to racism being weaponized by the wealthy and powerful, then what is the solution? Politically speaking, it is to curtail the power of the wealthy at every turn through sound policy if not outright revolution.

All for One and One for All: Policies for a Different World

My recommendations for policy include "universal" and "population-specific" policies, such as reparations for descendants of slavery. I follow Táíwò's (2022) approach to this discussion, in that reparations are part of a program "to not only repair the harms of the past, but build a new world for the future" (p. 3). Addressing social injustice related to race, class, gender, and sexuality includes addressing past and ongoing harm, as well as "thinking more broadly about how to remake the world system" (p. 1). For example, redistributive tax policy raises incomes across the board while exerting a larger effect for Black households (Hardy et al., 2022). Raising the minimum wage improves mental health outcomes (Kuroki, 2021), reduces suicide rates (Kaufman et al., 2020), and lowers rates of child maltreatment (Schneider et al., 2021), while also closing racial disparities in health and wealth (Derenoncourt & Montialoux, 2021; Williams & Cooper, 2019). Direct cash payouts, such as stimulus checks over the course of COVID-19, reliably lowered rates of anxiety and depression (Chu & Teng, 2022). Economic and redistributive policy *matters* for mental health.

Universal childcare also has a positive effect for all families but especially poor families of color (Herbst, 2017). The Affordable Care Act reduced economic and racial health disparities (Buettgens et al., 2021), with universal healthcare offering the possibility of further reductions in disparities (Siddiqi et al., 2016). Historically, racism is a central reason why the United States lacks universal healthcare—efforts to marginalize Black workers from the New Deal ensured healthcare was tied to employment and regional restrictions (Interlandi, 2019). Today, racism impacts support for universal healthcare overall (Shen & LaBouff, 2016), echoing Metzl's (2019) finding on how racial fear fuels a self-destructive thought process akin to "If people of color get healthcare, then I don't want it."

We must take care of each other from the cradle to the grave. Universal baby bonds—publicly funded trust accounts set up at birth (see Hamilton & Darity Jr, 2010)—reduce the racial wealth gap while improving the economic conditions of all young adults, in part by reducing the concentration of wealth among the wealthiest (Zewde, 2020). In the case of France, expanding social security eligibility also has positive effects on mental health (Simpson et al., 2021). While I cannot possibly cover all potential universal policies, examples show how they improve the lives of all of us—white and non-white—while narrowing racial disparities. At the same time, I also believe population-specific policies along the lines of race, gender, and sexuality will make us all safer and healthier and curtail elite power. I also cannot cover all the possible population-specific policies we could consider, so here I focus on one race-conscious policy—reparations for descendants of slavery in the United States as an economic and *public health* policy (Bassett & Galea, 2020).

As Fanon (1963) recognized, writing about reparations in the aftermath of abolition and decolonization, this is the result of a "a double realization: the realization by the colonized peoples that *it is their due*, and the realization by the capitalist powers that in fact *they must pay*" (p. 103, emphasis original). Reparations would have concrete effects, closing the wealth *and* longevity gaps between Black and white people (Himmelstein et al., 2022) with a "bottom-up" improvement in well-being for African Americans leading to gains for white people and other people of color (Bowser & Austin, 2021). We are indelibly interconnected.

My argument includes the matter of moral redress but goes beyond it. The issue at hand is not merely repair, but the creation of a more just world. As Táíwò (2022) writes, "the point of justice is not to eliminate something—whether it be natural or social difference or the brute effects of luck—but to create instead a community where we all stand on terms of equality with one another" (p. 100). In a landmark contribution outlining the principles of a "public psychology," Neville et al. (2021) advocate for a "social justice orientation stance to improving society and the lives of people through an antioppression lens, *including anticapitalism*" (p. 1263, emphasis added). An anti-capitalist politics without question centers labor and a multiracial working-class coalition. Labor unions are here paramount.

Given that close interpersonal contact across identity improves cross-cultural competence and inter-group relations (Meleady et al., 2021), labor unions provide a unique space for fostering multiracial solidarity (McGhee, 2021). In this regard union participation has been shown to reduce racial resentment and increase support for policies that specifically benefit African Americans (Frymer & Grumbach, 2021). As bastions of political education, union organization provides opportunities for folks across lines of race, gender, and sexuality to come together and practice an ethics of communion that renders the intersectionality of suffering a lived experience that brings us together to fight for one another, and ultimately ourselves.

Racism and the Ultrawealthy: The Culprit Was Racial Capitalism All Along

What this combination of universal and population-specific policies aims to do is aptly captured by White (2021) in the title of their article on reparations—"*shake up American capitalism*" (emphasis original). More bluntly, to limit the power of the wealthy to transfer their wealth into political power, with our mental health and well-being on the line. Freeman (2021) documents in painstaking detail how the ultrawealthy use their money and influence to bankroll politicians into office and lobby to ensure their interests are represented in education, criminal justice, immigration law, and the economy. The results can be seen in every area of our lives—underfunded schools, militarized police and a surveillance state, inhumane immigration policies, tax cuts for the rich, environmental decay, voter suppression, and so on. Each malady reveals the hyper-wealthy as "racism profiteers" pushing for policies that reap massive profit (p. 302).

Racial capitalism transforms "collective action problems" into individualized solutions (Eichner, 2019). We all prefer a different system than what we currently have, but without joint action we are left with the "choices" fed to us as individuals in order to survive, even if these lead to a worse outcome for society as a whole. For example, over half of voters support Medicare for All in the United States, and seven in ten support a public option (Galvin, 2021). When racial fearmongering associating public goods with "undeserving" people of color (Metzl, 2019) comes together with the fear of losing employer-provided healthcare, we get a situation in which people would rather *not* get stuck at certain jobs but do so out of necessity, while the fear that extending healthcare will also benefit people of color reduces support for such policies. Conversely, a sense of shared destiny and conviction that such policies benefit everyone increases support for universal healthcare (e.g., Maldonado et al., 2019).

As Freeman (2021) outlines, strategic racism as a divide-and-conquer strategy is lucrative for the ultrawealthy: "If they can pit white people against people of color, middle-class people against low-income and working-class people, African Americans against Latinx people, and so on, then our collective power becomes diffuse" (p. 313). We become so fraught, distraught, distracted, and obsessed with where we are in the pecking order, whether around race or class, gender or sexuality, that we are not able to consolidate our collective power. "Ultimately," Freeman writes, "we become far less than the sum of our parts" (p. 313). Conversely, we stand to tap into tremendous power when we acknowledge our interdependence—what I call the intersectionality of suffering. Seeing my well-being, happiness, and flourishing as connected to yours creates new possibilities for solidarity and transformation.

Coming Together Across Difference: The Solidarity Dividend

It is recognizing how racism and other isms *cost* all of us while drawing on the power of the "sum of us" that lies at the heart of Heather McGhee's (2021) work, and her collaborations with Lopez (2019) and communications specialist and poll researcher Shenker-Osorio (2020). McGhee draws attention to the history of "drained pool politics" in the United States, where whites in the first half of the century preferred to drain, cement, and close public pools instead of integrating them with Black people, leading whites themselves to no longer have public pools in different districts. White people misled by racism profiteers vote to destroy and limit public goods instead of sharing them, a "zero-sum" logic of racial hierarchy (we might add other hierarchies as well)—if things get better for Black people and other people of color, it *must* be at the expense of white people. If people of color "move up," if racial gaps are closed, then white people are "falling down."

As we have seen throughout this book, racial capitalism instills such a zero-sum logic in our fantasies around hierarchy—"splitting" by another name. It turns collective action problems into "individual" problems we feel deep shame for, or turns them into problems caused by the "other" who steals our pleasure, happiness, and well-being. We get stuck in those systems, ideologies, and ways of coping even as they deepen our collective misery. What McGhee (2021) calls the "solidarity dividend" offers part of the answer to this dilemma. The solidarity dividend is the benefit of rejecting scapegoating around race, gender, sexuality, and class, redirecting blame toward the powerful, and coming together to solve our problems (p. 256).

McGhee (2021) offers the example of Bridget, a white woman and mother of three who worked in the fast-food industry for over ten years. When she was approached by another worker about joining "Stand Up KC," an organization fighting to increase the minimum wage in Kansas City, she was skeptical. She did not believe her life would ever change, and certainly did not think others would vote to give a fast-food worker like her 15 dollars an hour, but went to the meeting anyway. During the meeting, a Latinx woman stood up and shared her story of how she was raising her three children in a two-bedroom apartment with bad plumbing, feeling trapped in a life she did not believe would get better either.

Bridget was moved by her story: "I was really able to see myself in her. And at that point, I decided that the only way we was gonna fix it was if all of us came together" (p. 134). Bridget shared how before joining this movement, "I had been fed this whole line of 'These immigrant workers are coming over here and stealing our jobs…not paying taxes, committing crimes, and causing problems.'… us against them" (p. 134). She realized that "it's not a matter of me coming up and them staying down. It's the matter of, in order for me to come up, they have to come up, too—because we have to come up together. Because honestly, as long as we're divided, we're conquered" (p. 134). They were able to get the city council to raise local wages to $13, a success that provoked the Republican state legislature to pass a law forbidding municipalities from raising wages above the state's $7.70.

The fight for a livable wage, universal healthcare, reparations, and other universal and specific policies is happening across the United States and internationally. In the United States, these struggles reveal a core set of lessons time and again: "workers of color suffer the most acute economic injustices, but most of the people harmed… are white" (McGhee, 2021, p. 135). Cross-racial solidarity gives us the strength to fight for a labor movement which sees common cause in the struggle for racial, gender, and sexual orientation equality. Lopez (2019), one of McGhee's collaborators, summarizes the results of their field research on what messaging seems most effective at fostering this solidarity. He distinguishes between the racial fear message, the economic populist message prioritizing economic injustice while being colorblind, and the racial justice frame centering addressing racial oppression against people of color. Their research demonstrates that color-blind economic populism struggles against racial fear messaging, whereas racial justice messages inadvertently reinforce the right-wing's logic of racial competition.

To put it in McGhee's (2021) terms, zero-sum racial justice narratives that call on white people to "give up" their privilege risks providing a mirror image to the right-wing's message that betterment for people of color *must* mean worsening conditions for white people—if one must come up, the other must come down. Further, Lopez (2019) found that racial justice messaging had a depressogenic effect not only on whites, but on people of color, as such messages stress a fundamental divide reinforcing pessimism about the possibility of solidarity. Colorblind economic messaging was less effective as their silence on race cedes ground for the right to monopolize conversations on race with racial fear. Lopez criticizes how some on the left avoid addressing race in political messaging, and advocates for the need to talk about racism *differently*—not as an almost ontological conflict between white people and people of color, but as a weapon of the ruling class to divide and rule.

The "race-class" message, following Du Bois's insights, was field tested against these messages and found to be effective at mobilizing white people and people of color toward more progressive agendas (Lopez, 2019). This style of messaging includes three components: call out greedy elites sowing division; call for solidarity across racial lines; and demand a government and economy that works for all, Black, white, and Brown (p. 174). This messaging was most effective for persuadable voters, white voters writ large but especially voters of color. Drawing on Derrick Bell's theory of interest convergence, Lopez theorized that "People of color seem to have more confidence in cross-racial solidarity when they understand why whites have their own clear stake to join in coalition" (p. 190). For white people and people of color, the race-class frame facilitates the very realization we have spoken about clinically and politically through Du Bois (1909): "The cost of liberty is less than the price of repression" (p. 25). True liberty and freedom lead to *gains* over and above the gratifications of whiteness, patriarchy, and capitalism.

This is not a matter of costs and benefits on a spreadsheet, especially at an unconscious level where there is no hard and fast line between morality, self-interest, or cultural values, as these blend with our sense of what will help us and our loved ones. Lopez (2019) writes,

> The blending of morality and self-interest also means, though, that as people see how something helps them, they become much more open to moral demands pushing in the same direction… Persuadables more fully open themselves to embracing anti-racist values once they see that their and their children's well-being will flow from cross-racial solidarity. (p. 193)

When real alternatives to racism and racial demagoguery are available and demonstrated to aid people in their survival, it renders the zero-sum logic that supports it unnecessary, fostering a centering of anti-racist values organically.

Lopez, McGhee, Shenker-Osorio and activists such as Alicia Garza, Linda Sarsour, and Cesar Torres hold a tacit psychological theory conversant with psychoanalytic thinking—most people, and especially the persuadable, are *conflicted* and of more than one mind on different social and economic issues, values and beliefs which are often *dissociated* from one another (Giridharadas, 2022). Think, for a moment, of your *abuelas*, uncles, aunties, cousins, and friends who may both hold "progressive" *and* "regressive" views on different topics simultaneously. All of us, including people of color, women, LGBT, and poor people are complex and have contradictory beliefs. And whoever tilts us to *one* side of the equation, *wins*.

Lopez (2019) gives the example of a training he led at a conference for union leaders. He felt apprehension at the room full of white people before him, wondering whether they would listen to the Latino professor talk about race. He starts by asking if the union leaders thought they had a "racism problem" in their union. Some respond there is racism in their union, while others laugh saying "but it's not a problem." Hoping to provoke Lopez, another union leader raises the question of why they can't "say the n-word?".

He (2019) initially tries to answer their question with a question—how would others respond to their union brother? This, however, goes nowhere amidst side talk and nervous laughter. Others repeat the challenging question and make the implicit explicit. How come *they* get to call each other that, and we whites can't say the word? He notices the body language across the room as arms cross, people lean back in their chairs, chests rise: "The room seems to be letting me know they're not going to lie down for another mini-sermon on their racism" (p. xi). Lopez changes tactics. He acknowledges that people should be treated the same, but that society can put us in different positions, so that actions can carry different meanings. Referring to the civil rights successes of the 1960s that drove the n-word out of public discourse, he underscores how its use today is a reminder of the racial violence in our history—and present.

Lopez (2019) pivots here: "This is not just a moral issue... At stake is the future of their union" (p. xii). He starts to connect how dog whistle politics calling for "law and order" in the late 1960s provoked racial division to gain support from white working- and middle-class families, while simultaneously cutting taxes for the rich, slashing social spending, increasing corporate power, surging police violence against communities of color, and greater hostility toward unions. Lopez asks these union leaders why, despite the harms of these policies, white working families vote for these politicians? The answer: they have been convinced to fear people of color. He closes the morning talk by asking them if they see a future for their children in the union, to which they respond they do not. "Isn't it true," Lopez asks, "that racism against people of color is the biggest threat your own families face?" (p. xiv).

After their lunch break, the union leaders return to the training asking Lopez more about unconscious bias, strategic racism, and how to effectively build strength across race. By avoiding a more confrontational, sermonizing stance, Lopez created a space where these union leaders could arrive at a more anti-racist stance as something intrinsically related to their goals and values, building on the efforts of other union leaders who had also been advocating for greater attention to the destructive role of racism in the labor movement. Put differently, the value of anti-racism had to be experienced as more salient and meaningful than the costs and relative value of rationalizing racism in their unions. This points to not only an analytic lens and form of political messaging, but a mode of dialog and relationality that facilitates change.

Deep Canvassing: Dialogue Between the Clinical and Political

In university settings, randomized trials have found that inter-group dialogue (IGD), a dialogical intervention to facilitate exploration around identity, power differences, and shared values inspired by Paulo Freire's work, reliably promotes change in biased attitudes, preparedness for social action, and greater solidarity across race, gender, sexuality, and class (Frantell et al., 2019). The core processes that make these dialogues effective include a combination of training group members in active listening skills, facilitating emotional expression, and addressing conflict in session, and developing a politicized identity connected to systems of power and privilege. What is unique about this intervention is that whereas most college courses around diversity are primarily didactic in nature, in IGD participants focus on building relationships, trust, and active listening and conflict resolution skills *before* discussions of power and privilege occur (Gurin et al., 2013). Differences in identity and power can take place alongside naming common values that build motivation for addressing systems of inequality directly.

While this kind of dialogue may work in university settings, what about the "real world" of politics and grassroots organizing? In a novel study, Broockman and Kalla (2016) conducted a randomized trial comparing traditional door-to-door canvassing—often didactic and focused on providing information to voters—with "deep canvassing," based on the work of David Fleischer, an LGBT activist promoting marriage equality in California (Demetrious, 2022).

While the psychological literature frames prejudices as deeply ingrained and difficult to change, Broockman and Kalla (2016) demonstrated that canvassers engaging in "deep," ten-minute dialogues evoking voters' values, concerns, and fears around equality for trans people, conveying *empathy* for these beliefs, and only then sharing narratives that *challenged* those fears while connecting over shared values successfully reduced transphobia. In line with this book's framework, they argue that while unconscious System 1 (primary) processing is related to implicit bias and prejudice, active, effortful System 2 (secondary) processing of bias through dialog was more likely to change attitudes (p. 220).

How is it that initially expressing empathy for voters' transphobic beliefs and then sharing narratives led to change? In follow-up trials examining mechanisms of change, Kalla and Broockman (2020) found that canvassers engaging voters in a non-judgmental exchange of narratives had a durable impact on transphobic and anti-immigrant attitudes, overcoming the *resistance* to persuasion evoked by these topics. They define deep canvassing as an attempt to persuade voters "by providing to or eliciting from them narratives about relevant personal experiences while non-judgmentally listening to the views they express" (p. 2).

Kalla and Broockman (2020) draw on the psychological literature on persuasion and active listening to explain how when people's political views are challenged there is often an ambivalent reaction—a desire to acknowledge the merits of alternate positions, and resistance to changing their views and "being in the wrong," which threatens their sense of self. They contrast deep canvassing with persuasion drawing on moral condemnation and shaming, which may backfire and entrench others in their positions. Providing evidence for this point, their studies showed that removing the non-judgmental component erased the effects of the intervention. Deep canvassing works by drawing on storytelling, providing affirmation (though not necessarily agreement) while reducing the threat to the voter's sense of self. To paraphrase the insights of Chapter 7, feeling *heard* helps us *hear*, whether in the consulting room or at voters' doorsteps.

Across their studies, Kalla and Broockman (2020) found that when canvassers created a non-judgmental interpersonal context, this provided a "safe space" for voters to acknowledge different points of view. They write, "no viewpoint should be less threatening to the self than one's own; and so such conversations may even encourage individuals to explicitly acknowledge the merits of alternative viewpoints, promoting so-called 'self-persuasion'" (p. 7). Change in schemas can be evoked *from the inside* in the context of an accepting relationship. This was especially the case when canvassers conveyed curiosity in voters' views and experiences, and avoided negative judgments even when they made biased or prejudiced remarks (p. 10). During these exchanges, canvassers raised questions to prompt voters to come to their own conclusions, with the goal of "self-generating and explicitly stating aloud implications of the narratives that ran contrary to their previously stated exclusionary attitudes" (p. 10).

This research invites us to engage in a delicate balancing act. Creating a culture in which one should expect condemnation for bias needs to be balanced with conditions in which individuals "do not feel threatened by discussing their attitudes and experiences with those who wish to persuade them" (Kalla & Broockman, 2020, p. 33). We are not talking about "coddling" the privileged. On the contrary, this research underscores the importance of *building community and solidarity* so it becomes obvious certain beliefs are destructive not only to the marginalized, but to the relatively privileged as well. In a recent series of experiments, Kalla and Broockman (2023) examined to what extent the canvasser sharing personal experiences was as important as *eliciting* the voter's own experiences and values for generating change, finding that evoking and exploring the voter's perspectives and narratives by themselves reduced bias. Lastly, it should be noted this is not theoretical research in a lab—deep canvassing has played a meaningful role in electoral politics (Kalla & Broockman, 2022).

"Depth" Canvassing: A Case Example

What does this look like in practice? In an evocative lecture, Fleischer (TEDx Talks, 2017) shares a video of deep canvassing in action through the work of a queer activist named Virginia, engaging an older Latino man apprehensive about legislation to protect trans people using the bathroom that conforms to their identity. Through their conversation, Virginia learned he was a care-taker for his wife who had multiple disabilities and whom he loved deeply, showing them a picture. When the topic turned to trans people, however, he expressed apprehension around trans women using the women's restroom. Virginia remained non-judgmental, expressing curiosity about "where that comes from." The voter states that his South American culture informs his values, as "in South America, we don't like [f-word]." The canvasser explores whether this applies to gay people or trans people specifically. The voter responds, "Be whatever God made you… not cut yourself out to be some-thing else." As they continue the conversation, Virginia discloses, "So for me… I'm gay, so you said [f-word]…" Virginia's disclosure of their sexual orientation has an impact on him. He stretches out his arms as if offering a hug, recognizing he insulted them, "Oh *you're* gay? Oooooh…" he says with *surprise*. In the context of the warmth they developed, he was suddenly challenged by an experience he did not expect.

This older Latino gentleman suddenly becomes *curious* about Virginia, "Tell me, tell me what makes you… I'm just trying to study the person. I'm asking—if you are, you are, God Bless you—what made you take that deci-sion? Because you have a woman's body!" Virginia laughs but remains open, "For me, it wasn't really a decision, this is just who I am. How I feel is I love who I love… my gender doesn't necessarily conform to how I'm seen, I don't identify as a woman, actually." Virginia asks if he ever met anyone who was gay or trans. "Never, I never liked it!" he replies. Virginia offers a gentle confrontation, "So, we don't usually use [f-word], just gay or trans-gender." You can see the gentleman feels mortified not because Virginia is scolding him, but because he realized he hurt someone he just built rapport with. Virginia offers him reassurance, "I can tell that when you say it, you're not meaning it with like, negative or bad feelings." The man underscores he did not mean to offend them.

Virginia goes deeper, "One of the things… why I know it's not really a choice for me is I am *madly in love* with this person named Lourdes"— the gentleman smiles, emphasizing the name in Spanish, "*Lourdes!*" Virginia offers that since he showed them a picture of his wife, they share a picture of Lourdes. "I'm head over heels," they continue, "I can't even begin to tell you how I want to spend the rest of my life with this person." Virginia reflected that when the gentleman speaks of his wife, "there is a lot of love in your tone too." "Oh," he replies, "one thing about love is… fifty-eight years married and now I have to take care of her, but *really* take care of her." "How does that make you feel?" Virginia asks. He replies, "I feel like God gave me the love to love a disabled person. And care about her." "That resonates a lot with me," they reflect back, "I know that I will take care of Lourdes for the rest of my life…" "Or maybe," the gentleman interjects, "*she* will take care of you." "We'll take care of each other!" they say.

Virginia pivots to connect their shared values around love and caretaking with pro-trans legislation. "For me these laws and including transgender people are about that," they share, "about how we treat one another, they may not stop who goes into the bathroom or not…" "No," he replies, "because what I say is that a woman that says 'I'm a man' and would come to urinate next to me, I would move away." Virginia picks up on the affect underneath the action, "Is that, your moving away, is there anything else you can picture happening?" He thinks for a moment, "There is only… the feeling that one of us doesn't belong there because that's what you are, I am what I am, two different feelings… that's the way I was growing up." "Does it scare you?" He scoffs, "Scare? No." She reframes, "I think that what you're talking about there is a comfort level thing, it's not scary…" "There you go!" he responds emphatically. Acknowledging a part of himself may feel anxious or scared might be too vulnerable based on cultural values around *machismo*. Virginia adeptly reframes it in words that help him feel seen and heard.

At the end of their conversation, the gentleman expresses his appreciation for Virginia's openness: "I tell you the truth, this is the first time—and I thank you—that I could ask questions like this and be responded with elegance…" "That's why we're out here!" Virginia replies. "Listen," he says with humility in his voice, "probably… I was mistaken." Virginia validates him, "the thing about the comfort is… [a] fear of the unknown… what Lourdes faces is a big reason why I'm out here today, knowing that my partner, like your wife, right, when the people we love are dealing with something that impacts them daily…" The gentleman finishes their sentence, "It impacts you too." Although this book has centered race, culture, and class, many of its principles also apply to gender and sexuality—as this example illustrates, justice for trans people is eminently a matter of justice for all (Faye, 2022).

All You Need Is…

The beauty of this example notwithstanding, a few caveats bear mentioning. Just because this approach is effective does not mean marginalized people now "owe" this level of empathy to people with privilege. It only means that to the extent our goal is to evoke change, this will be more effective when we engage people in a non-judgmental, open, and empathic manner. As Fanon underscores, meeting people with humility creates conditions which thaw defenses—people are more open, reflective, and capable of considering alternate viewpoints. It was in this context that Virginia offered this voter what Fanon et al. (2018) called a "simple confrontation" (p. 502). This man was offered a surprise that challenged his preconceptions while drawing on shared values—specifically, love. A link was made between his care for his wife, Virginia's care for their partner, and ultimately, how we need to take care of each other and those we love.

That the approach to politics reviewed here reflects an ethic of relationality is no accident, as its flows from the theory and technique of this book. In the clinical setting, the same applies insofar as we engage our patients in a process of change by first "joining" with them, and over time helping them "shift" perspective in a novel way. The intersectionality of suffering offers us not only a way of thinking about suffering across difference in clinical work, but a way of thinking about politics and the political that encourages decolonial practice beyond the clinical encounter. The clinical and political themselves form part of a mobius strip in decolonial psychoanalysis, the "inside" becoming "outside" and vice versa. Across both domains a basic principle applies—whether love is kind or love is tough the answer is, and always will be, love.

A Coda to a Credo: Finding Home

Contemporary psychoanalysis is at a crossroads—if not civil war—between those clamoring for the return of a "neutral" clinical practice, and those calling for a socially and politically engaged psychoanalysis (Conroy, 2023). To the extent we ever shared a collective "credo"—a set of beliefs that inform how we listen and engage in the psychoanalytic process (Salberg, 2022)—that credo is now broken. But out of that rupture exists the possibility of something new. A plurality of credos, a home with many rooms.

As the Holmes Commission Report on Racial Equality (2023) recently stated, for those "willing to read, think, learn, and revise, the psychoanalytic cannon is perpetually expanding, as the branches of the psychoanalytic family tree continue to sprout and grow" (p. 195). The report calls for greater attention to race and culture as part of our field's growth, "rather than as an obligatory add-on forced on 'traditional' psychoanalysis" (p. 195). While I am clearly on one side of this debate, I exercise my "right of refusal" toward the terms of the debate itself. It is not just the branches that continue to "sprout and grow." It is also our understanding of psychoanalysis' very roots and routes (see Hall, 1997) that continue to expand, be elaborated on, and rediscovered, returning like our discipline's collective underside.

To the extent clinical and political neutrality are *illusions* that do not reflect the practice of Freud and the first psychoanalysts, and to the extent questions of race, class, gender, sexuality, and coloniality have *always* been a part of psychoanalytic history going back not only to Vienna, but to Latinx, Black, Asian, and indigenous clinicians across Latin America, Africa, Asia and the Pacific, then those who claim to defend "tradition" are actually ardent revisionists, and those calling for a sociopolitical consciousness are in fact returning to a tradition that is very old, worthy of being conserved, and whose canon has only begun to be explored. Or written.

This book was a labor of love, a project of "recovering historical memory," rescuing those aspects of psychoanalysis that served yesterday and today for liberation on the couch, and off the couch and in the streets (cf. Martín-Baró, 1994). If a credo is a set of values, beliefs, and *drives* to do psychoanalytic work, then this book is my credo—much like liberation theologians call for a "preferential option for the oppressed" (Cone, 1997; Gutierrez, 2023), psychoanalysis bends our ear with a "preferential option for the repressed," listening for what is excluded, marginalized, unspoken, and unheard. Which is to say, to make an option for all of us.

When I was a child, I was told psychoanalysis had a home for me, a haven for understanding suffering in our world. When I became an adult, I was told there was no place for me, leaving me without a home, an ancestry, a tradition. Through friends, mentors, and research I discovered Juliano Moreira, Ramon Fernandez Marina, Heisaku Kosawa, Bingham Dai, Solomon Carter Fuller, and Girindrasekhar Bose, finding and refinding a home that was always there with a place for all of us—rediscovering Freud through Fanon, and Fanon through Freud.

And *that* was a welcome surprise.

Reflection Questions

- Across this book we have explored how the founders of major schools—Freud, Ferenczi, Lacan, and Fanon—were more flexible in their clinical practice than is often talked about. How do our theories or schools of thought sometimes constrict our ideas of what is "allowed" in psychotherapy? How does this limit our ability to explore what works for us and our patients? How might envisioning a different image of these founders' practice make more room for experimentation and improvisation in psychotherapy?

- One political recommendation of this book is the enactment of social democratic policies to (a) reinvest resources back into the public good and (b) curtail the power of elites who exploit racism, sexism, and classism to enrich themselves. What is your reaction to this program? What would it mean to trace problems at the "micro" level of interpersonal relationships to social and economic conditions? How can clinicians and policy makers collaborate not just to fund treatment, but to create a political economic environment in which mental health treatment is less egregiously needed—in which we thrive?

- Like a mobius strip, this book moved from the "inside" of the clinical encounter to the "outside" of activism and organizing. What is it like to see core clinical skills of empathy, building relationship, and confrontation being translated into the world of political organizing? Do these skills translate or not? What obstacles or possibilities might you imagine? How do we balance the fervor and energy involved in pushing for social change with the need to persuade and build a larger coalition?

Further Reading

Solidarity and Politics
- Dabiri, E. (2021). *What White people can do next: From allyship to coalition.* Penguin UK.
- Giridharadas, A. (2022). *The persuaders: At the front lines of the fight for hearts, minds, and democracy.* Knopf.
- McGhee, H. (2021). *The sum of us: What racism costs everyone and how we can prosper together.* One World/Ballantine.

References

Aron, L., & Starr, K. (2013). *A psychotherapy for the people*. Routledge.

Bassett, M. T., & Galea, S. (2020). Reparations as a public health priority— A strategy for ending black–white health disparities. *New England Journal of Medicine, 383*(22), 2101–2103.

Bergner, G. (1995). Who is that masked woman? Or, the role of gender in Fanon's Black Skin, White Masks. *PMLA, 110*(1), 75–88.

Blacksher, E., & Valles, S. A. (2021). White privilege, white poverty: Reckoning with class and race in America. *Hastings Center Report, 51*, S51–S57.

Bowser, B. P., & Austin, D. W. (2021). Summary: Racism's impact on White Americans in the age of Trump. In D. W. Austin & B. P. Bowser (Eds.), *The impact of racism on White Americans in the age of Trump* (pp. 235–252). Palgrave Macmillan.

Broockman, D., & Kalla, J. (2016). Durably reducing transphobia: A field experiment on door-to-door canvassing. *Science, 352*(6282), 220–224.

Buettgens, M., Blavin, F., & Pan, C. (2021). The Affordable Care Act reduced income inequality in the US: Study examines the ACA and income inequality. *Health Affairs, 40*(1), 121–129.

Chu, L., & Teng, L. (2022). Does stimulus check payment improve people's mental health in the COVID-19 pandemic? Evidence from US household pulse survey. *The Journal of Mental Health Policy and Economics, 25*(4), 133–142

Cone, J. H. (1997). *God of the oppressed*. Orbis Books.

Conroy, J. O. (2023, June 16). Inside the war tearing psychoanalysis apart: "The most hatred I've ever witnessed." *The Guardian*. https://www.theguardian.com/education/2023/jun/16/george-washington-university-professor-antisemitism-palestine-dc

Danto, E. A. (2005). *Freud's free clinics: Psychoanalysis and Social Justice, 1918–1938*. Columbia University Press.

Danylova, T. V., & Kats, L. A. (2019). "All animals are equal, but some animals are more equal than others": The negative impact of gender inequality on the global economy and public health. *Anthropological Measurements of Philosophical Research, 15*, 101–110.

Demetrious, K. (2022). Deep canvassing: Persuasion, ethics, democracy and activist public relations. *Public Relations Inquiry, 11*(3), 361–377.

Derenoncourt, E., & Montialoux, C. (2021). Minimum wages and racial inequality. *The Quarterly Journal of Economics, 136*(1), 169–228.

Du Bois, W. E. B. (1909, March). Evolution of the race problem. In *Proceedings of the national Negro conference* (pp. 142–158). National Negro Conference, New York.

Eichner, M. (2019). *The free-market family*. Oxford University Press.

Eiseley, L. C. (1979). *The star thrower*. Houghton Mifflin Harcourt.

Elgar, F. J., Gariepy, G., Dirks, M., Walsh, S. D., Molcho, M., Cosma, A., Malinowska-Cieslik, M., Donnelly, P. D., & Craig, W. (2019). Association of early-life exposure to income inequality with bullying in adolescence in 40 countries. *JAMA Pediatrics, 173*(7), e191181–e191181.

Fanon, F. (1952/2008). *Black skin, white masks.* Pluto Press.

Fanon, F. (1963). *The wretched of the earth* (R. Philcox, Trans.). Grove Press.

Fanon, F. (2018). *Alienation and freedom.* Bloomsbury Publishing.

Faye, S. (2022). *The transgender issue: Trans justice is justice for all.* Verso Books.

Frantell, K. A., Miles, J. R., & Ruwe, A. M. (2019). Intergroup dialogue: A review of recent empirical research and its implications for research and practice. *Small Group Research, 50*(5), 654–695.

Freeman, J. (2021). *Rich thanks to racism: How the ultra-wealthy profit from racial injustice.* Cornell University Press.

Freud, S. (1900). Letter from Freud to Fliess, February 1, 1900. In *The complete letters of Sigmund Freud to Wilhelm Fliess, 1887–1904* (pp. 397–398).

Freud, S. (1925). An autobiographical study. In J. Strachey (Ed.), *The standard edition of the complete psychological works of Sigmund Freud, volume XX (1925–1926): An autobiographical study, inhibitions, symptoms, and anxiety, the question of lay analysis and other works, 1–292* (pp. 1–74). Hogarth Press.

Freud, S. (1927). The future of an illusion. In J. Strachey (Ed.), *The standard edition of the complete psychological works of Sigmund Freud, volume XXI (1927–1931): The future of an illusion, civilization and its discontents, and other works* (pp. 1–56). Hogarth Press.

Frymer, P., & Grumbach, J. M. (2021). Labor unions and white racial politics. *American Journal of Political Science, 65*(1), 225–240.

Galvin, G. (2021). *About 7 in 10 voters favor a public health insurance option. Medicare for all remains polarizing.* Morning Consult. Retrieved May 6, 2023, from https://morningconsult.com/2021/03/24/medicare-for-all-public-option-polling/#:~:text=55%25%20of%20voters%20support%20Medicare,Democrats%20and%2056%25%20of%20Republicans

George, D. R., & Whitehouse, P. J. (2021). *American dementia: Brain health in an unhealthy society.* JHU Press.

George, S., & Hook, D. (Eds.). (2021). *Lacan and race: Racism, identity, and psychoanalytic theory.* Routledge.

Giridharadas, A. (2022). *The persuaders: At the front lines of the fight for hearts, minds, and democracy.* Knopf.

Gurin, P., Nagda, B. R. A., & Zúñiga, X. (2013). *Dialogue across difference: Practice, theory, and research on intergroup dialogue.* Russell Sage Foundation.

Gutierrez, G. (2023). *A theology of liberation: History, politics.* Orbis Books.

Halfon, N., Larson, K., Son, J., Lu, M., & Bethell, C. (2017). Income inequality and the differential effect of adverse childhood experiences in US children. *Academic Pediatrics, 17*(7), S70–S78.

Hall, S. (1997). Culture and power. Radical Philosophy , 86(27), 24–41.

Hamilton, D., & Darity, W., Jr. (2010). Can 'baby bonds' eliminate the racial wealth gap in putative post-racial America? *The Review of Black Political Economy, 37*(3–4), 207–216.

Hannay, J. W., Payne, B. K., & Brown-Iannuzzi, J. (2021). Economic inequality and the pursuit of pleasure. *Social Psychological and Personality Science, 12*(7), 1254–1263.

Hardy, B., Hokayem, C., & Ziliak, J. P. (2022). Income inequality, race, and the EITC. *National Tax Journal, 75*(1), 149–167.

Herbst, C. M. (2017). Universal child care, maternal employment, and children's long-run outcomes: Evidence from the US Lanham Act of 1940. *Journal of Labor Economics, 35*, 519–564.

Himmelstein, K. E., Lawrence, J. A., Jahn, J. L., Ceasar, J. N., Morse, M., Bassett, M. T., Wispelwey, B. P., Darity, W. A., Jr., & Venkataramani, A. S. (2022). Association between racial wealth inequities and racial disparities in longevity among US adults and role of reparations payments, 1992 to 2018. *JAMA Network Open, 5*(11), e2240519–e2240519.

Holmes, D. R., Hart, A., Powell, D. R., & Stoute, B. J. (2023, June 19). *The Holmes Commission report on racial equality in American Psychoanalysis.* American Psychoanalytic Association. Retrieved August 30, 2023, from https://apsa.org/wp-content/uploads/2023/06/Holmes-Commission-Final-Report-2023-Report-rv6-19-23.pdf?ver

Interlandi, J. (2019). Why doesn't the United States have universal health care? The answer has everything to do with race. *New York Times, 1619*.

Kalla, J. L., & Broockman, D. E. (2020). Reducing exclusionary attitudes through interpersonal conversation: Evidence from three field experiments. *American Political Science Review, 114*(2), 410–425.

Kalla, J. L., & Broockman, D. E. (2022). Voter outreach campaigns can reduce affective polarization among implementing political activists: Evidence from inside three campaigns. *American Political Science Review, 116*(4), 1516–1522.

Kalla, J. L., & Broockman, D. E. (2023). Which narrative strategies durably reduce prejudice? Evidence from field and survey experiments supporting the efficacy of perspective-getting. *American Journal of Political Science, 67*(1), 185–204.

Kaufman, J. A., Salas-Hernández, L. K., Komro, K. A., & Livingston, M. D. (2020). Effects of increased minimum wages by unemployment rate on suicide in the USA. *Journal of Epidemiol Community Health, 74*(3), 219–224.

Kellogg, S., & Garcia Torres, A. (2021). Toward a chairwork psychotherapy: Using the four dialogues for healing and transformation. *Practice Innovations, 6*(3), 171–180.

Kuroki, M. (2021). State minimum wage and mental health in the United States: 2011–2019. *SSM-Mental Health, 1*, 100040.

Lopez, I. H. (2019). *Merge left.* The New Press.

Maldonado, L., Olivos, F., Castillo, J. C., Atria, J., & Azar, A. (2019). Risk exposure, humanitarianism and willingness to pay for universal healthcare: A cross-national analysis of 28 countries. *Social Justice Research, 32*, 349–383.

Manduca, R. (2018). Income inequality and the persistence of racial economic disparities. *Sociological Science, 5*, 182–205.

Martín-Baró, I. (1994). *Writings for a liberation psychology*. Harvard University Press.

McGhee, H. (2021). *The sum of us: What racism costs everyone and how we can prosper together*. One World/Ballantine.

Meleady, R., Seger, C. R., & Vermue, M. (2021). Evidence of a dynamic association between intergroup contact and intercultural competence. *Group Processes & Intergroup Relations, 24*(8), 1427–1447.

Metzl, J. M. (2019). *Dying of whiteness: How the politics of racial resentment is killing America's heartland*. Hachette UK.

Neville, H. A., Ruedas-Gracia, N., Lee, B. A., Ogunfemi, N., Maghsoodi, A. H., Mosley, D. V., LaFromboise, T. D., & Fine, M. (2021). The public psychology for liberation training model: A call to transform the discipline. *American Psychologist, 76*(8), 1248–1265.

Norcross, J. C., & Goldfried, M. R. (Eds.). (2005). *Handbook of psychotherapy integration*. Oxford University Press.

Prakash, V., & Girgenti, G. (2020). *Winning the green new deal: Why we must, how we can*. Simon and Schuster.

Salberg, J. (Ed.). (2022). *Psychoanalytic credos: Personal and professional journeys of psychoanalysts*. Routledge.

Sami, W. Y., & Jeter, C. (2021). The political economy and inequality's impact on mental health. *Journal of Mental Health Counseling, 43*(3), 212–227.

Schmidt, U., Neyse, L., & Aleknonyte, M. (2019). Income inequality and risk taking: The impact of social comparison information. *Theory and Decision, 87*(3), 283–297.

Schneider, W., Bullinger, L. R., & Raissian, K. M. (2021). How does the minimum wage affect child maltreatment and parenting behaviors? An analysis of the mechanisms. *Review of Economics of the Household*, 1–36.

Shen, M. J., & LaBouff, J. P. (2016). More than political ideology: Subtle racial prejudice as a predictor of opposition to universal health care among US citizens. *Journal of Social and Political Psychology, 4*(2), 493–520.

Shenker-Osorio, A. (2020). Vote is a verb: Applying lessons from social science to GOTV. In C. Derber, S. Moodliar, & M. Nelson (Eds.), *Turnout!* (pp. 79–83). Routledge.

Shim, R. S., & Compton, M. T. (2018). Addressing the social determinants of mental health: If not now, when? If not us, who?. *Psychiatric Services, 69*(8), 844–846.

Siddiqi, A. A., Wang, S., Quinn, K., Nguyen, Q. C., & Christy, A. D. (2016). Racial disparities in access to care under conditions of universal coverage. *American Journal of Preventive Medicine, 50*(2), 220–225.

Simpson, J., Albani, V., Bell, Z., Bambra, C., & Brown, H. (2021). Effects of social security policy reforms on mental health and inequalities: A systematic review of observational studies in high-income countries. *Social Science & Medicine, 272*, 113717.

Táíwò, O. O. (2022). *Reconsidering reparations*. Oxford University Press.

TEDx Talks. (2017, January 25). *How we can reduce prejudice with a conversation | David Fleischer | TEDxMidAtlantic* [Video]. YouTube. https://www.youtube.com/watch?v=xN6O5LTaGyg

Viego, A. (2007). *Dead subjects: Toward a politics of loss in Latino studies*. Duke University Press.

Westra, H. A. (2023). The implications of the Dodo bird verdict for training in psychotherapy: Prioritizing process observation. *Psychotherapy Research, 33*(4), 527–529.

White, A. (2021, May 25). *Reparations would shake up American capitalism—And that's a good thing*. Open Democracy. https://www.opendemocracy.net/en/oureconomy/reparations-would-shake-up-american-capitalism-and-thats-a-good-thing/

Wilkinson, R. G., & Pickett, K. (2017). The enemy between us: The psychological and social costs of inequality. *European Journal of Social Psychology, 47*(1), 11–24.

Williams, D. R., & Cooper, L. A. (2019). Reducing racial inequities in health: Using what we already know to take action. *International Journal of Environmental Research and Public Health, 16*(4), 606.

Yalom, I. D. (1980). *Existential psychotherapy*. Hachette UK.

Yokum, N. (2022). A call for psycho-affective change: Fanon, feminism, and white negrophobic femininity. *Philosophy & Social Criticism*. https://doi.org/10.1177/01914537221103897

Zewde, N. (2020). Universal baby bonds reduce black-white wealth inequality, progressively raise net worth of all young adults. *The Review of Black Political Economy, 47*(1), 3–19.

Index

nonbeing, zone of 200
non-Black people of color 111
   anti-Blackness 202, 204, 228
   jouissance and 205
   violence against 204, 208
non-viable society 288
Nordey, Claude 219
North African Syndrome 174
not-knowing stance 246, 254–255
   creative 236
   free association and 251
   in psychodynamic therapy 247
   Lacanian position of 151
   of Ferenczi and Rank 94
   of therapist 243
Novac, A. 252

O

Oberndorf, Clarence 69
   about race and therapeutic
      relationship 72
   align with Freud's interpretation
      of race 73
   double consciousness 72
   intergenerational transmission of
      contradictions 71
   psychoanalysis practice with
      Freud 69–71
   sensitivity to psychoanalysis' turn
      73
Oberndorf, Joseph 69
object. *See* object relations
object relations 45–46
   amidst racial hierarchy 215,
      217–218
   Lacan's critique of 124, 128
   theory 171–172
oppression 206
   clinicians' implication in systems
      of 174–176
   jouissance of 129–130
Orientalism 23
other-oriented stance 152

outpatient clinics 9
over-I. *See* super-ego (*über ich*)
Owen, Jesse 246

P

pain 44. *See also* jouissance
   avoidance of 46–47
   human suffering 21
   pleasure and 85–86, 281
   psychoanalytic treatment 52
pan-European identity 23
panic attacks 45, 187, 220, 225
Panksepp, Jaak 237
paranoid-schizoid positions theory
   112
Partie Populaire d'Algerie (PPA) 139
patriarchy 29, 137, 291
   connection with slavery and war
      22
   love beyond duty and 220–222
   suffering of cisheterosexual men
      and women 28
Payne, B.K. 241, 242
people of color. *See* Black people;
   racism
   confidence in cross-racial
      solidarity 296
   inequality 26–27
permissiveness 173
phenomenon of agitation 173
phobias
   negrophobia 204
   psychoanalytic treatment 90
   queerphobia 277
   talking cure technique for 66
   xenophobia 147
phonemes 123
pleasure in pain. *See jouissance*
pleasure principle 44, 46, 86, 91,
   102, 250
population specific policies 291–293
PPA. *See Partie Populaire d'Algerie*
preconscious process 44, 209

Made in the USA
Thornton, CO
01/22/25 20:41:05

96196f8d-f141-44e2-86f3-574e310754c6R01